Battling
Dragons

Battling Dragons

Issues and Controversy in Children's Literature

Edited by
Susan Lehr

HEINEMANN
Portsmouth, NH

Heinemann
A division of Reed Elsevier Inc.
361 Hanover Street
Portsmouth, NH 03801–3912

Offices and agents throughout the world

Every effort has been made to contact the copyright holders for permission to reprint borrowed material where necessary. We regret any oversights that may have occurred and would be happy to rectify them in future printings of this work.

Acknowledgments for borrowed material can be found on p. 288.

Library of Congress Cataloging-in-Publication Data
Battling dragons: issues and controversy in children's literature/
edited by Susan Lehr.
p. cm.
Includes bibliographical references.
Partial Contents: Pt. 1. Books under fire: issues of censorship in children's literature — pt. 2. The changing world of girls and boys: exploring family values and children's roles — pt. 3. Themes of freedom and oppression: new grit in historical and realistic books — pt. 4. Heroes for children: battling good and evil — pt. 5. Living in the real world of children's books.
ISBN 0-435-08828-9
I. Lehr, Susan S.   II. Title: Issues and controversy in children's literature.
PN1009.A1B36   1995
809'.89282—dc20   94-31973
                                                                        CIP

Editor: Carolyn Coman
Production: Vicki Kasabian
Book design: Jenny Jensen Greenleaf
Cover illustration: Leslie Evans
Cover design: Catherine Hawkes
Printed in the United States of America on acid-free paper
99 98 97 96 95   EB   1 2 3 4 5 6

Dedicated to Hans

Contents

Acknowledgments

I wish to thank Sharon Scavone and John Milne and their lively students at Geyser Elementary School in Saratoga Springs, New York. During my sabbatical they welcomed me as a teacher, learner, and researcher. Special thanks to Skidmore College for the Collaborative Research Grant that supported that research; Michael Marx in the Writing Center, who always has the last word on commas; my research assistant, Rebecca Woolbert, who is steadfast, energetic, and tireless; Christie Bull, an extraordinary secretary; Carolyn Coman, a warm and wonderful editor. A special thank you to the woman who read so many stories to me as a child and fostered a love of books, my mother, Dorothy Maris Stewart.

Introduction

Several years ago before the walls in Eastern Europe collapsed, a Russian student visited my children's-literature class when I happened to be sharing *Once There Was a Tree* by Russian author Natalia Romanova and Russian illustrator Gennady Spirin. During class this nineteen-year-old woman began to cry. She later shared that she was upset to see this book in my hands, when it was not available in her own country. Although the book was originally published in Russian in 1983 as *Chei eto pen?*, this student said that books like it were not available to her in stores. This year a Chinese student wrote in her children's-literature journal that in her elementary school in China there were only a few textbooks in her class, which students had to share. She was truly amazed at the thousands of richly written and illustrated books that are available to children in the United States.

Children's literature is a luxury, a vital luxury, that educators have come to know and use in the classroom. That children can connect with children through story whether it's fiction or nonfiction, is a truly amazing phenomenon that occurs in classrooms in countries where the sharing of print is a basic human right.

When I first met Ahmed, Sami, Dara, Vithy, and Naledi in books written by Judith Gilliland, Minfong Ho, Allan Ballie, and Beverley Naidoo, I was overwhelmed with the isolation experienced by many children in this twentieth-century world. These fictitious children, representing real children that the authors have known in their lives, knew more about freedom, oppression, bombs, concentration camps, and refugee camps than any of the children I've ever known. They embodied a set of experiences that were far removed from the daily routines of children in the schools in which I have worked. In these stories children faced diverse and dangerous obstacles. That we hear their voices and experience small bits of their lives is a tribute to the many authors who have decided to record their stories. These gutsy authors have brought the stories of children from many parts of the world—places like Vietnam, Iran, Cambodia, Cairo, Lebanon, South Africa—together with readers in countries like the United States, Great Britain, New Zealand, Canada, and Australia, touching their readers deeply. I have shared these strongly written stories with thousands of teachers, college students, and children and have watched them cheer.

Imagine living without these stories. Take the scenario a step further. Imagine heaping these stories onto bonfires and watching them burn. Authors of fiction like Nat Hentoff have written books about book burnings. *Fahrenheit 451* looks into a future where books are enemies of the people and as such are systematically burned. Over the past twenty years there have been real book burnings that have destroyed objectionable titles found in public libraries, school libraries, and classrooms. One must ask to whom are these books objectionable. That books are seen as enemies is documented by authors like Beverley Naidoo, whose book about apartheid was not allowed into South Africa, and organizations like the American Library Association (ALA), which reports that censorship is on the rise with about four hundred cases reported annually. In support of textbook censorship Mel Gabler says:

> If you're talking about censorship it's the traditional values which have been cen-sored. Schools are indoctrinating children against their home-taught values, 'cause our textbooks continually indoctrinate the students that the solution for problems is more government control. And let me clearly identify to begin with, textbooks largely determine how a nation votes, what it becomes, and where it goes. Your textbooks across the nation are selected by a tiny percentage of the educators and since children become what they are taught the philosophy selected by this tiny percentage will become the philosophy taught to our children. (*Books Under Fire*, 1982)

In *Battling Dragons* the voices, perspectives, and experiences of authors and educators from all over the world come together to form a collage of ideas and images about well-written children's books. These dynamic writers offer their views of children's literature on topics ranging from censorship, violence, raw images in picture books, depictions of the black family in the past twenty years, the myth of emancipated women, political correctness in writing for children, creating ethical heroes for children, the realities of selling books to the public, and teacher and librarian views toward using these controversial books in public schools.

A growing number of authors are writing about the diverse and often frightening experiences of children around the world through realistic fiction and fantasy. One can find stories about children escaping from the Khmer Rouge as in Allan Baillie's *Little Brother* or Minfong Ho's *The Clay Marble*, from Iranian soldiers as in Elizabeth Laird's *Kiss the Dust*, and from the secret police of Vietnam as in Gloria Whelan's *Goodbye Vietnam*. In reading these books children can experience life in a refugee camp along the Thai border and in a warehouse in Hong Kong. Children can feel the bite of prejudice in an imaginary world where one is born into slavery as in Sherryl Jordan's *Winter of Fire*. Children can read a picture book that shows an American child living in an airport as in *Fly Away Home* by Eve Bunting, or a novel about a child who not only has lost his home, but also has become separated from his parents in New York City for a long period of time and is forced to live on the streets and sleep in a cardboard box as in *Monkey Island* by Paula Fox. The stories about these children are often horrifying and told in a matter-of-fact manner. The violence and neglect that many children experience on a daily basis have become a permanent part of children's literature. They are vivid echoes of adult books like Jonathon Kozol's *Savage Inequalities* and *Rachel and Her Children* and Alex Kotlowitz's *There Are No Children Here*. These stories link children with other children through literature. Some offer new interpretations of history through fiction; others explore social issues in fantasy; still others deal with harsh themes of injustice in picture book formats. The books provide real and often disturbing views of life, challenging readers to think about issues from which some would rather shelter children. Through a wide variety of genres—including nonfiction, historical fiction, realistic fiction, fantasy, biography, folktales, poetry, and picture books—the authors and illustrators offer threads of hope, even as they expose readers to the realities of women's con-stricted cultural roles, sexual identity, apartheid, the civil war in Lebanon, and prejudice against African Americans.

Not surprisingly, the diverse voices and stories of these authors and illustrators are often the targets of censors. Some censors are politically motivated as in the case of the censorship of South African writer Beverley Naidoo, whereas others are motivated by a sense of morality and the charge to determine what is appropriate for all children. A third group of censors is concerned with the racial makeup of authors. This concern is connected to issues of authenticity and a wariness related to exposing children to stereotypes. All three groups of censors, to some extent, would like to monitor and control which books children can read rather than having it remain a matter of individual choice.

Voices of Authors

The seven authors writing essays in this book could all be considered controversial writers. I suspect they would welcome that label because it suggests they are tackling themes and issues of substance. Judith Gilliland writes about her motivation for writing gritty contemporary picture books about children around the world, ranging from an eight-year-old boy who sells butagaz (cooking gas) in Cairo to a young boy who lives in a basement in Lebanon during the civil war. Gilliland lived in the Middle East for a long period of time and recalls lying on the floor of her apartment as the civil war erupted. Her depiction of Sami, a child who spends much of his time hiding in a basement with his family, is based on her own experiences. Some would argue that her voice is not authentic, since she is an outsider looking in. I would challenge that view with the thought that Sami's voice is heard because of Gilliland's unique position.

Consider the violence that many children experience on a daily basis. Brian Jacques is often accused of writing books that are too violent for children. For the first time readers hear the powerful story of his own childhood in Liverpool. One could ask if art is imitating life or simply offering slices of reality? Jacques' vision of good battling evil leaves little question for whom children cheer. His autobiographical sketch is hardly unique, because many children grow up in poverty and under harsh conditions. As Jacques writes, he didn't perceive himself as poor because he was surrounded by other families just like his. His protagonists are small and simple field animals who outwit evil invaders. The power of right is on their side throughout the skirmishes and battles. These creatures like nothing better than a good feast. They are not fighters by nature, but fight they do when their homes and families are threatened. Jacques offers a rare glimpse into his own origins and early battles.

Freedom can be an odyssey for the oppressors as well. When one grows up with assumptions about society's structure and the role of groups within that structure, one can inherit prejudicial attitudes. Beverley Naidoo takes the reader on a journey into apartheid and censorship, having experienced apartheid as a privileged white child in South Africa. Her version of reality is not placid, and her brief depiction of the white madam in *Journey to Jo'burg* is one of the most chilling scenes in books for children. Readers react harshly against this character's deeply ingrained prejudices as shown in Chapter 9, where I report on a study with fourth-grade children. Naidoo and I did not know each other before beginning this book. We have since exchanged letters in relation to her powerful themes and the equally powerful responses of children to books like *Journey to Jo'burg*. Books like these have a strong impact on the thinking of children, and I will explore this in Chapter 9, my chapter on response to literature.

Allan Baillie, an Australian who worked in the Cambodian refugee camps, and Minfong Ho, a native of Burma who also worked in the camps, both write about children who survived the forced labor camps and slaughter of the Khmer Rouge in Cambodia in the 1970s and 1980s. One character immigrated to Australia and one returned with her family to her Cambodian village to plant seeds and start all over again. Why do these authors write of these horrors for children? In these two essays Ho and Baillie talk about their experiences in Thailand and show how the stories of the children they met had to be told.

Offering children fresh visions of heroes is a vital function of children's literature. Mem Fox cautions that women still are shortchanged in books and that their roles are still passive. Princess Furball was a refreshing female Cinderella in a sea of passive females in folklore. Ironically Charlotte Huck's vision of Furball got sidetracked by hundreds of livid animal-rights activists who were appalled at the slaughter of one thousand animals in this traditional folktale. Charlotte Huck writes about her spunky heroine in *Princess Furball* while trying to process the angry letters received from animal-rights activists appalled at the coat worn by Furball. Is folklore to be reinterpreted in order to pacify current wisdom? This introduces the broader issues related to historical perspectives, authenticity, and not perpetuating old prejudices and injustices, which Joel Taxel tackles in his chapter on political correctness.

Other fictitious heroes have faced prejudice and limited roles for women. Grace Chetwin's heroes live in fantasy worlds, yet they experience harsh situations like Baillie's Vithy and Ho's Dara. Their worlds are filled with violence, and they live in societies that support oppression. These fictitious characters must escape or strive to change the status quo. Fantasy mirrors society and tackles the hard questions in imaginary worlds.

Books reflect personal odysseys in which authors offer their stories and personal secrets. As readers we crawl into the authors' minds and connect for a brief bit of time. We listen to their voices, experience their lives, see through their eyes—literally crawl under the skin of another living being. When created with passion, these stories become a permanent part of us. They are to be treasured. In this book twenty-one writers offer their views of children's literature. These are not placid voices. They offer candid insights into a wide range of provocative topics. I hope you will take issue with them.

PART ONE

Books Under Fire:
Issues of Censorship in
Children's Literature

Books are targets. The authors in this book are some of the more obvious targets, but in my experience with teachers, parents, and students I have found that all books have the potential for being controversial. In a large city in Ohio a veteran second-grade teacher shared how one parent reacted after she read "Hansel and Gretel" in the classroom. His angry letter suggested that she had no right to share a book like that with his child. This man went on to share that he was a Vietnam veteran and that the folktale in question was violent and abhorrent to him as a parent. A first-year teacher, a former student of mine teaching fifth graders on Long Island, shared how C. S. Lewis' *The Lion, the Witch and the Wardrobe* stirred a controversy in her school that went to the principal and the school board. As a first-year teacher she was vulnerable to attack. The parent had never read the book; she had simply sampled a portion and found it satanic. Quite an irony for a book shared in Christian settings.

There is no question that books evoke strong and emotional responses from readers. In Part 1 of this book, Beverley Naidoo, a professor and author from South Africa who now resides in England, relates how censorship blocked her book *Journey to Jo'burg* from entry into South Africa. Naidoo also writes about her motivations for authoring *Journey* and shows how prejudice is passed on to children using her own childhood as a poignant example. Her childhood experiences underscore the need for many literary perspectives in the classroom.

Issues of conflict cannot be avoided in writing realistic books for children. Even the safest of books for young children like *Dr. Desoto* by William Steig, *Alexander and the Wind-Up Mouse* by Leo Lionni, or *Chrysanthemum* by Kevin Henkes have underlying themes of prejudice and violence. Whether a mouse is about to be eaten by a fox, beaten by a broom, or mocked by peers, one cannot escape conflict in books for children. I chose these three titles to illustrate that conflict and pain reside

1

in books that we consider safe, mundane, or even harmless. Characters with whom children identify experience life in all of its pains and glories. Even *Rosie's Walk* by Pat Hutchins is fraught with danger!

Carl Tomlinson explores the balance between writing books that explore issues realistically and use violence appropriately. As Sharon Scavone and John Milne point out in their chapter in Part 5, children play and watch violent games on TV and in some respects have been desensitized to violence. These two teachers go on to argue that well-written books help children understand and experience the results of violent acts. Among other titles Tomlinson takes a close look at versions of "Little Red Riding Hood" that contain troubling visual depictions of a familiar folktale in which two characters are eaten by a wolf. In the happy versions of this tale the wolf is cut open so that the main characters can escape death by ingestion. The versions Tomlinson discusses are dark, shadowy, and suggestive. Are there acceptable depictions of ingesting characters?

Barbara Kiefer takes a look at the broad spectrum of picture books for children that deal with a wide range of social issues. The books hit hard and deliberately and there are many of them being published. Who are they for? How can they be used? How do illustrators use art to influence mood, manipulate readers, soften difficult topics? Picture books for children target topics related to illiteracy, displaced persons, nursing homes, dropping the A-bomb, the homeless, concentration camps, civil war, the destruction of the rain forest, the slaughter of animals in a zoo, prejudice, to name just a few. Is this a new phenomena in children's literature? Are these books even appropriate for children? Does a book like *Let the Celebrations Begin* by Julie Vivas, in which bald and emaciated concentration camp victims are shown in soft pastels, belong on the shelves of children? What are the author and illustrator trying to achieve, and are they successful? One could argue that the topic and depictions as described above are nothing more than grotesque. Kiefer analyzes the use of art in these books as a vehicle for exploring social issues.

Amy McClure opens the dialogue with a broad view of censorship. Citing a range of topics and books under fire, McClure suggests that censorship has diverse targets and originates from both conservative and liberal coalitions. She offers strategies for dealing with censorship. Her figures of reported incidences are frightening, but not surprising. Many incidents go unreported. Examples of censored books include hundreds of books that teachers share with children.

As literature continues to be read in the elementary classroom these issues will remain at the forefront of controversy. As Norma Gabler says in the 1982 video entitled *Books Under Fire*, "I do not feel that a library book is a library book if it is assigned to your or my child for classroom material. In other words, if he is told that he has to read a certain book and do a report on it, it's no longer a library book. It becomes a part of the curriculum."

ONE

Censorship of Children's Books

—

Amy McClure

Once upon a time and far away children's books were perceived as simple things, concerned with naughty little rabbits, perplexed toy bears, and fairy princesses. Today they're often viewed as a pernicious enemy with the ability to corrupt impressionable minds and destroy our country. Those who hold this opinion seek then to remove these terrible influences from classrooms and libraries.

It is true that children's books have changed. Although some still deal with topics like who is going steady, if best friends can survive a fight, or whether the princess (female) will be rescued by her prince (male), today's books also talk about formerly taboo topics like drugs, sex, homosexuality, and death. And they often use realistic language, including nonstandard English and expletives. Coincidentally, our society has become more conservative. Many people believe that our country is experiencing a "collapse of values." They blame it on what's been taught in schools— and feel powerless to control or reverse these changes. And can we blame them? We have led parents, our former students, to believe that books contain great truths and that masterpieces are such because of their power to influence our lives. Why should it now be surprising that parents, discovering curse words, sex, and so on in books, believe those elements are just as influential as the ideas we advocated in *Silas Marner* and *Julius Caesar*? Those who believe it's futile to fight Washington view local schools and libraries as accessible targets. Therefore, they vent their frustrations on these institutions, using censorship as the weapon.

What censors seem to have in common is the desire to protect children from influences they perceive as evil or harmful. This perception arises from their own biases: liberals don't want children to be exposed to racist or sexist stereotypes; conservatives generally fear books that feature characters questioning God or parents. Those who cherish the ideals of the First Amendment and intellectual freedom are increasingly concerned. They fear that if children don't encounter ideas that are disquieting or different from what they've always believed, they will not grow into thoughtful adults, able to function in a society full of contradictions and contrasting

3

viewpoints. Yet, as responsible educators and librarians, we cannot smugly sit back and assume it is always censorship when someone raises concerns about a book and that it is "responsible selection policies" when educators make decisions about which books to use. Censorship is not a problem of good versus evil but "your" perception of good versus "my" perception of good.

So, the central questions we must ask are: Do adults have the right and responsibility to protect children from what we believe is harmful to them? Or do children have the right to read anything they need in order to attain intellectual maturity? And where do we draw the line? Are controversial topics permissible in a classic? Or is a good classic a story that does not include "questionable" topics?

This chapter will explore the complex issue of children's book censorship. I will (1) describe what is being censored, (2) identify some of the most common censors, (3) discuss the differences between censorship and selection, (4) offer some suggestions for handling challenges when they occur, and (5) make some final comments to set the issue within the broad perspective of intellectual freedom and the First Amendment.

Would You Let Your Child Read This Book: Types of Books Censored

Would you let young children read *Julie of the Wolves? National Geographic Magazine? Caddie Woodlawn?* How about *The Bible* or the dictionary? Be careful—every one of these books has been censored. A wide variety of books has come under attack from realistic fiction to folklore to poetry. This section will describe some of the most common categories of objections. Representative books will be listed in each category to illustrate specific objections. Those listed will be confined mainly to books for preadolescents but readers should be aware that censorship of books for older children is just as pervasive.

Issues of Satanism, Witchcraft, and Anti-Christian Themes

The most frequent rationale for challenges cited in recent reports (People for the American Way 1991, 1992)* was that the materials were "anti-Christian," "Satanic," or advocated anti-Christian sentiments. Alvin Schwartz's popular folktale collections *Scary Stories to Tell in the Dark* (1981) and *More Scary Stories to Tell in the Dark* (1984) are currently the most frequently challenged materials for elementary children and have been censored for this reason. Objectors state the stories "advocate cannibalism, brutality, the religious practice of witchcraft, and violence" (54). The illustrations have been said to "contain a high degree of occult/Satanic symbolism" (49) and an emphasis on death over life. Objectors often cite a specific story in which a child gobbles up her teacher as particularly offensive. It should be noted

---

*All references to censorship incidents are drawn from these reports, unless otherwise indicated.

that these books are extremely popular with young children, having won several state children's choice awards. They were also selected for the International Reading Association's Children's Choice List. Other books to which similar objections for references to witches and witchcraft are made include Merriam's *Halloween ABC* (1987) ("heightens awareness of the macabre and piques children's curiosity about the occult"), Kimmel's Caldecott Honor awardee *Hershel and the Hanukkah Goblins* (1985) ("contains illustrations with Satanic resemblances"), Dahl's *Witches* (1985), O'Connor's *Lulu and the Witch Baby* (1986), and Snyder's *The Witches of Worm* (1972) as well as traditional folklore like "Hansel and Gretel." Kellogg's *Best Friends* (1986) was also challenged for explicit pictures of demon faces, evil spirits, serpents, ghosts, and a skull as was Base's *Animalia* (1986) for his drawings of dragons and unicorns, which are allegedly satanic. References to Santa Claus are also considered satanic because the letters in his first name can be arranged to spell Satan. Rylant's Newbery awardee *Missing May* (1992) was cited for its references to spirits and ghosts.

Even the classics are not immune to these attacks. Susan Cooper's Newbery Medal book *The Dark Is Rising* (1973) has been accused of teaching Satanism and cultism. The overall mystical theme of Madeleine L'Engle's *A Wrinkle in Time* (1962) has raised concerns that children reading the book would "interpret reality mystically and strive to enhance their spirituality through the use of occult practice" (65). Additional complaints state that much of the book is based on Hindu and Buddhist religions, biblical facts are misrepresented, and occult indoctrination prevails. The fact that the book associates Jesus with other great historical figures is the final straw for some. C. S. Lewis' *The Lion, the Witch and the Wardrobe* (1950) has also been challenged for being anti-Christian and pagan. These objections are particularly curious when one considers that L'Engle has a strong Christian background and Lewis was a noted British theologian.

Interestingly, attacks from the opposite side have also been made. Wicca, an organization of witches tried to get "Hansel and Gretel" removed because it allegedly teaches that it's allowable to burn witches and steal their property. The organization also protested the use of the *Impressions* reading series because it included stories they perceived as portraying witches inaccurately.

Other objections in this category relate more directly to fundamentalist Christian religious beliefs. For example, Paterson's *Bridge to Terabithia* (1977) was accused of providing students with "contempt for the church through negative religious images and references in the book" (36) (mainly for an allegedly "comic and cruel portrayal" of a preacher). Also cited were forty instances where the word *Lord* was used as a curse word and two of the word *hell*. Objections further complained that "the book teaches that children are innately good, whereas God's word teaches us that we are all sinners and that the only way to God and heaven is through faith in Jesus Christ" (153). Paterson's *The Great Gilly Hopkins* (1978) faced similar problems for allegedly derogatory remarks about God and religion, in particular Gilly's reference in a letter to her mother that people who pray and read from the Bible are "religious fanatics." Objectors to L'Engle's *Many Waters* (1986) disliked the book because it was so closely intertwined with the Bible. As one person stated, "It would appear [to be] a resource and guide to an inexperienced reader of the Bible, leading some to think it was a viable interpretation of the Bible" (95). Concern rose over Conrad's *Stonewords* (1990) as exemplifying morbid "New Age" theology and not promoting Christian family values.

Even books that present traditional religious figures in a realistic way have been viewed unfavorably. For example, Spier's *Noah's Ark* (1977) realistically shows a frustrated Noah, as well as piles of manure and the fate of those animals left behind. Censors of the book believe that young children should not be exposed to such a realistic portrayal of a religious figure. Others contend this objection is unwarranted, contending the book addresses questions children naturally ask like where the animals went to the bathroom and what happened to the animals who didn't get on the ark.

Do these charges have any validity? Are students lured into satanic activities by the books they read? Advocates of these materials contend that some of the most popular and memorable stories, those that help us explore the taproots of our existence as humans, are drawn from fantasy and folklore and these stories tend to be more comforting than scary.

In *The Child and the Book: A Psychological and Literary Exploration*, British psychologist Nicholas Tucker (1981) states that occasionally a child may respond negatively to a book, but such a situation can best be modified by discussion afterwards rather than censorship before (in Booth 1992, 34).

Yet, when members of satanic cults are arrested, they often have books on witchcraft in their possession. And children do question God and the teachings of the Bible. Does this mean we should keep books with enduring literary value that help children learn to cope with a complex, confusing world away from them if these controversial issues are included?

Damn That Book: Objectionable Language

Another common basis for complaints in recent surveys is the inclusion of obscene language in books. For example, an outcry developed over *The Upstairs Room* (Reiss 1972), a novel dealing with the hardships engendered by Hitler's extermination of the Jews, because it contained fourteen swear words (mostly *damn* and one *bastard*). Some object to Paterson's funny irreverent Gilly in *The Great Gilly Hopkins* who says words like *Christ, Hell, Good God*, and *Crap*. The language of Jess in Paterson's *Bridge to Terabithia* is similarly criticized. Many of Judy Blume's books come under attack for this reason. Other books challenged on the basis of obscenity include Rockwell's *How to Eat Fried Worms* (1973) (uses the word *bastard*), Hermes' *Kevin Corbett Eats Flies* (1986) (for using the terms *barrell-butt* and *mosquito-ass* and the line, "It happens all the time. Grown-ups have sex too you know."), Roald Dahl's *Revolting Rhymes* (1986) (using the word *slut*), Richard Peck's *A Day No Pigs Would Die* (1976) (for use of swear words and a boy getting hurt in his "privates"), and several dictionaries (which define "dirty" words like *faggot* and *bed*). *My Friend Flicka*

Mary O'Haras (1941) (for referring to a female dog as a "bitch" and using *damn*) has been another target. Vivien Alcock's *Ghostly Companions: A Feast of Chilling Tales* (1984) was attacked for its allegedly obscene description of a ship's figurehead as having "breasts as big as watermelons, that seemed ready to burst out of her sea-green dress" (59).

Books that describe bathroom habits are also considered obscene. *My Special Best Words* (Steptoe 1974) shows a child sitting on the toilet, and Sendak's *Some Swell Pup* (1976) pictures a dog urinating. Munsch's *I Have to Go* (1989) uses the word *pee*. All have had objections filed against them.

Supporters of censorship on the basis of obscene language and content argue that children should be protected from exposure to this. They contend that if teachers and librarians use curse words as they read aloud and if such books are readily available, children will feel as if the use of such words is condoned by the school and community. Their opponents point only to the many examples of obscenity children encounter on playgrounds, bathroom walls, television, and even in their own families. (In one interesting court case, a woman protesting obscenity in books listened as her husband testified about the profane language she used at home.)

Katherine Paterson (1989) eloquently defended her Gilly's language when a child questioned her as to why Gilly had to use obscenities.

> "Well," [Paterson replied,] "a child who lies, steals, fights, bullies, and ferociously acts out her racial prejudices is not usually a child who says 'fiddlesticks' when frustrated."
>
> "But," [the child] said, "if you put it in a book, you might think it's okay of us kids to talk like that."
>
> "Then, of course," [Paterson] countered, "you would also think it's okay to lie, steal, fight, bully emotionally disturbed children, and make ugly racist remarks."
>
> The child recoiled in shock. "Oh, no," she said, "of course not." (5–6)

In reply to a child who had complained about the obscene language in her book, *Winning* (1977), Robin Brancato stated:

> When I employ "bad language" as you call it . . . it is not because I think these are needed to sell books or hold the reader's interest, but because sex and body functions and the names for them, both polite and impolite, are parts of life, and I am interested in portraying life as it really is. If I fudge on details by creating an angry football player who says, "Oh, sugar!", who will trust me later, when I try to convey the important things that athletes think and feel? (in Klein 1983, 138)

The point is that just because a particular character uses obscene language doesn't mean the author advocates such words. Rather, it means the author felt that the language reflected the character and that person's way of interacting with the world.

So, who's right? Should children be allowed to read any words in books? Should potentially offensive words in library books be changed or blacked out to protect children? If we do this, which words should be considered offensive? Should teachers and librarians omit potentially troublesome words when reading aloud to children?

Intercourse to Homosexuality: Objections to Sexual Content

Sexual content is another common basis of complaints. Many object to children reading about subjects like menstruation, masturbation, young adolescents' developing sexual awareness, and premarital sex—all topics these books address.

Judy Blume's books are a favorite target particularly *Are You There God, It's Me, Margaret* (1970), *Deenie* (1973), and *Forever* (1975). The explicit sex scenes in *Forever* have particularly caused concerned parents to make comments like the following:

> It's not just sexually explicit. It's arousing to a teenager. You can't just get them aroused and leave them with no place to go. . . . This is the Bible belt and most people have high moral standards. (Udow 1992)

In Wisconsin, a principal banned *Forever* after casually thumbing through a copy in a cafeteria. In response, students, parents, librarians, and teachers organized to protest the action, creating "Judy Blume for Principal" and "Judy Blume for President" signs, which were posted all over the school.

Some challenges require creative leaps of imagination to make the sexual connection. For example, a Wisconsin parent objected to Dahl's *James and the Giant Peach* (1961) because a passage in which a female spider licks her lips "can be taken in two ways, but I [the censor] feel it's implied to be sexual" (17). George's *Julie of the Wolves* (1972) was removed from several Ohio school libraries because of an alleged "rape" scene (Julie's fiancé chases and captures her, then drags her to the ground at the end of a chapter).

Nudity is often considered obscene. As a result, Sendak's nude Mickey in *In the Night Kitchen* (1970) often has Magic Marker shorts drawn on him or the book is removed from the library. One parent in Florida stated she thought the book would encourage child molestation. "Children should be taught that private parts are private," she stated. *Where's Waldo?* Handford (1987) has been objected to because there's a picture on one page of a woman at the beach with her breast exposed (Quindlen 1993), while Silverstein's *A Light in the Attic* (1981a) was attacked for one illustration of a character with a bare bottom. *National Geographic* magazine and *Leonardo Drawings*, an art book compiled by the Whitney Museum, came under attack for nudity. Readers should note, however, that the Cat in the Hat is nude except for gloves, tie, and hat and Winnie the Pooh wears no pants. So beware! (Quindlen 1993).

Homosexuality seems to be a particularly touchy subject. Books for older children that deal with this topic like Holland's *The Man Without a Face* (1972) are routinely censored. Books for younger children like *Daddy's Roommate* (Willhoite 1990) and

Heather Has Two Mommies (Newman 1989) that feature gay and lesbian parents have also come under attack. Opponents of these two books in North Carolina accused the library of "taking the lead in promoting homosexuality" and took out newspaper advertisements asking, "Can prostitution, bestiality and incest be far behind?" (Udow 4). They also suggested that citizens vote down a library tax referendum in retaliation, clear evidence that censorship groups are becoming more political to add clout to their complaints.

Nonfictional sex education books are also often censored. *Show Me!* (McBride 1975), a particularly graphic photo essay, has long been a target. Kaufman's *How We Are Born, How We Grow* (1969) faced recent opposition for illustrations of male and female frontal nudity. Books like *My Puppy Is Born* (Cole 1991), which includes photographs of the actual birth, and several animal books that mention the word "mating," have been pulled off library shelves.

The censors of sexual content believe that children must be protected from knowledge of these topics, suggesting that early exposure will inevitably lead to experimentation and liberal attitudes about sex. They contend that authors of these books are not merely describing but advocating such behavior. Those who oppose this censorship assert that such protection may deny children the very information they need. These issues are significant and of natural interest to young preadolescents, and they will certainly learn about sex education. The question is, from whom: from peers, from MTV and movies, or from a book in conjunction with frank, honest discussion? Some think that healthy sexual attitudes are better formulated over a book than in the back seat of a car. Further, they contend that children will not pick up a book with content beyond their interest or stage of development, simply because it will be boring to them.

Yet, one wonders how much sexual content is acceptable—and where the line should be drawn. Should *Playboy* and *Hustler* magazines be part of library offerings? What makes *National Geographic* less objectionable than the *Sports Illustrated* swimsuit issue? Should a book or magazine's "literary quality" be the determining factor? How is this judged? (Some would assert that Judy Blume's books aren't particularly literary yet those people would probably not advocate their removal from classrooms or libraries.)

Racism and Sexism: Censorship From the Left

Censorship is not the exclusive domain of conservatives. Groups traditionally viewed as liberal and progressive have also censored books. Their motives are the same: protecting children from influences that may corrupt them; in this case, messages of stereotyping and humiliation. However, censors from the left are less likely to call for the removal of offensive books. Rather, they often try to sway the opinions of librarians and editors—those who purchase books and determine their content— to encourage them to support books that are politically correct, from their perspective.

Reactions to Zemach's *Jake and Honeybunch Go to Heaven* (1982) and Brown's

Shadow (1982), both Caldecott Medal winners, are typical. An article in the Interracial Council on Books for Children *Bulletin* denounced both books as "blatant affronts to African American sensibilities, assaults on cultural traditions and lifestyles of African Americans" (Banfield and Wilson 1983, 5). Both authors are accused of misrepresenting and misunderstanding the black experience. *Jake and Honeybunch* allegedly misrepresents the African American view of spiritual life. For example, the book shows barbecued ribs, chicken, and pies floating around heaven. These depictions are criticized because not only are they stereotypically associated with the black experience but because milk and honey are the only acceptable heavenly foods, according to experts in African American folklore. Heaven's inhabitants are shown wearing everyday clothes (standard for heavenly wear in African American culture is white with gold shoes, wings, and crown); a jazz/blues band plays in a heavenly nightclub (only choirs sing in heaven); and a train is what kills Jake, sending him to heaven (African American authors would never use a train to kill a character because trains are transports to glory as well as a symbol of freedom through the Underground Railroad) (Banfield and Wilson 1983).

Similar concerns were expressed about Brown's *Shadow*. This book allegedly violates the portrayal of primary African spiritual/religious symbols. For example, the depiction of several white disembodied masks and masklike faces are said to be grotesque and frightening. Objectors state that true African masks are specifically made not to look frightening and white is considered a spiritual rather than ghostly or frightening color. Additionally, the silhouetted figures all seem to be wearing grass "skirts," which are not standard dress for African people. Similarly, a number of thatched huts are shown. Again, objectors state that this does not reflect the rich variety of African architecture (Banfield and Wilson 1983).

Books that portray African Americans in a derogatory or submissive role or use offensive language like *nigger* are also attacked. From this perspective, Taylor's *The Cay* (1969) was condemned by the NAACP for its implication that "blacks are stupid, ugly and ignorant" and for "perpetuating white supremacy and self-fulfilling, self-hate among blacks." One objector was adamant in his concern: "We've had 400 years of rape, abuse, castration and destruction of the black race. Now we have Theodore Taylor capitalizing off that experience" (Bannerman, 42). *Little Black Sambo* (1899), Wilder's *Little House in the Big Woods* (1953), Paterson's *The Great Gilly Hopkins* (1978), and Fox's *The Slave Dancer* (1973) have also been attacked for passages and characters seen as derogatory to African Americans.

Twain's *The Adventures of Huckleberry Finn* is one of the most frequently attacked of all books for its depiction of the character Jim as a gullible, simple-minded, and superstitious figure and the book's frequent use of the word *nigger*. One black parent eloquently described her feelings of "extreme discomfort and pain" during her own reading of the book, which were renewed when her son faced the same situation (Allen 1984) and was asked to read the parts of Jim aloud to the class.

Opponents of those who censor on racist grounds claim that deleting books with these characteristics still is censorship. In an article explaining these arguments,

Burress (in Moore and Burress 1981) stated that "if librarians refuse to purchase a book or take a book off the shelf because they have decided the book is racist or sexist, that fulfills the standard definition of censorship" (16). Some experts see value in exposing children to racist attitudes. Proponents of *Huckleberry Finn*, for example, contend that it is a brilliant attempt to make a society look at its own prejudices and the socially destructive consequences of society. Taylor claims a similar purpose for *The Cay*. His black character, Timothy, is based on a real person. It would have been extremely unlikely for an East Indian black man to be literate or to talk in standard English, contends Taylor, and he denies any intention of racism in his character (Taylor 1993). Possibly the milieu of the time in which a book is set should be considered for its influence upon the book's perspective and content. There may be value in comparing attitudes espoused in books set in historical times with those held today.

Similar arguments could be used to confront those who object to books on the basis of sexist stereotyping. Books censored for this reason range from *Caddie Wood-lawn* (Brink 1973) (Caddie gives up being a tomboy) to *Pippi Longstocking* (Lindgren 1950) (the strong female character is the fantasy one), *The Giving Tree* (Silverstein 1964) (the self-sacrificing tree is referred to as "she") and even *Back to School with Betsy* (Haywood 1971) (two turn-of-the-century girls play outside wearing dresses). Maybe these books should be considered within their historical and cultural perspective as well. For example, one might ask what alternatives in lifestyle were available for young women on the Wisconsin frontier in the 1880s or what clothing choices girls had at the turn of the century. Must all these books be condemned because they accurately reflect their times?

So, then, if a book includes elements that may be interpreted as sexist, racist, or otherwise politically incorrect, should those books be censored? Is this actually censorship or the careful use of selection policies? Is there value in exposing children to situations of stereotyping? Should we evaluate literature on a single dimension? And should we allow special-interest groups of any sort to influence the book selection process?

Anti-American, Anti-Family Concerns

Some do not want children reading books that challenge parental and governmental authority. Modern realistic fiction novels by Norma Klein, Betty Miles, and Judy Blume that discuss divorce, extramarital living arrangements, maladjusted adults, and child abuse are particularly targeted. Thus, Blume's *Starring Sally J. Friedman As Herself* (1977) was attacked for wording that allegedly encourages the questioning of adults. *Blubber* (1974) was criticized for advocating "stealing, cheating and lying" with the main character "psychologically destroyed" by the end of the book. DeClements' *Sixth Grade Can Really Kill You* (1985) was attacked for "devaluing the character of the mother."

Other books challenged for this reason include such diverse titles as Paterson's

The Great Gilly Hopkins (1978) (endorses unwholesome values like stealing, smoking, drinking, and rebelling against authority), Browne's *Piggybook* (1986) (allegedly ridicules the traditional role of women in families), Silverstein's *Uncle Shelby's ABZ Book* (1981b) (encourages disobedience in children) and Viorst's *I'll Fix Anthony* (1969) (for promoting sibling rivalry). A parent in Missouri objected to Jean George's *Julie of the Wolves* (1972) because of what she called "socialist, communist, evolutionary and antifamily themes" (Krug 1972, 806). Parents in several states have requested removal of "The Three Bears" from schools because Goldilocks gets off scot-free after committing petty larceny and vandalism (Delfattora 1992). *Sylvester and the Magic Pebble* (Steig 1969) was censored in the 1960s for its portrayal of police as "pigs" (although every character is an animal, including the "donkey" hero). Even Santa Claus is considered a sacred figure not to be tampered with. Briggs' *Father Christmas* (1973), a book that shows Santa dressing, going to the bathroom, and complaining about his work load, has been attacked because some fear this realism would cause children to become cynical.

Proponents of books that explore these issues contend that real stories cannot always present perfect pictures of stereotyped families wrapped up with a moral or platitude. Authors must present the world honestly and realistically, they say, to help children understand that everyone has their faults as well as strengths. But are children influenced in their attitudes towards parents and authority when they read about less than perfect examples in books? To what extent are such attitudes influenced by books? And, as with other categories of objections, should we let a narrow issue determine the availability of books for children?

Additional Types of Censorship

Relatively few objections are made on the basis of violence. Evidently the fourteen *damns* in *The Upstairs Room* are considered more harmful than the traumatic incidents associated with war depicted in that book (Hearne 1982). Most concerns about violence focus on allegedly frightening story lines (Sendak's *Outside Over There* [1981] and Dahl's *The BFG* [1982]) or depiction of violent actions (Greene's *Elie Wiesel: Messenger From the Holocaust* [1987], Fitzhugh's *Bang Bang, You're Dead* [1969], and many traditional fairy tales like "Snow White" and "The Three Billy Goats Gruff"). One parent probably voiced the opinion of many when she stated, "Childhood is a very special period and should remain free of horrors and unnecessary stress" (89). Those who oppose censorship on the basis of violence contend that books don't go into detail like a Freddy Krueger movie. Evil is eventually punished— Cinderella's sisters have their eyes pecked out, a troll bully is bumped off his bridge, and Hitler's machine is defeated. Yet the stories don't go into the details of a battlefield or mutilation (Tunnell 1993).

Special-interest groups also often object to books that ostensibly attack their values. Health-food proponents advocate removal of all references to junk food and gum-chewing. Dahl's *James and the Giant Peach* (1961) was challenged in Wisconsin because it mentions wine, tobacco, and snuff. Hyman's version of "Little Red Riding Hood" was similarly challenged for its inclusion of wine in Riding Hood's basket. A parent in Indiana asked for the removal of Adoff's *The Cabbages Are Chasing the Rabbits* (1988) because the book might cause children to "think all hunters are bad, evil and hateful." In Oregon, Killingsworth's *Eli's Song* (1991), a book about a boy who threatens to jump out of a tree if loggers cut down a forest, was attacked for allegedly negative portrayal of loggers, the timber industry, and the state of Oregon. Seuss' *The Lorax* (1971) was also attacked for advocating ecological sensitivity.

Who Are the Censors? Diverse Voices

For the most part censors of materials used in schools are parents who are motivated by the desire to protect their children from the complexities and horrors of contemporary life: AIDS, drugs, pregnancy, violence, war. Parents also often don't understand the rationale behind new approaches to teaching literature and language arts; approaches that are often quite different from what they experienced in school. They don't know why their children are reading contemporary fiction and keeping personal journals rather than answering long lists of comprehension questions from a basal text or diagramming sentences. They become disturbed when they read passages out of context that contain four-letter words or depict parent-child conflicts. Combine these anxieties with the "Back to Basics" movement and one can see how parents become concerned—with censorship an outcome of this concern.

Unfortunately, what often happens is that parents seek to control more than their own child's education. They go beyond asking that their child not be exposed to a particular book and demand the removal of a book from the classroom or library, effectively denying all children access to the literature. The following represents the voice of such a parent:

> I'm frankly scared. Our children are exposed to so much these days on TV but also everywhere they look. When do they get to be children? Do I want them to know about AIDS, sex, drugs, before they're a teenager? Do I want them to hear a teacher read aloud dirty words? No, I don't. Isn't that advocating the use of this kind of language? When I hear them saying nasty words and being disobedient I wonder where it comes from. And I worry about where it will lead. But they're exposed to it all the time and I can't stop it whether I like it or not. So is it better for them to read about it in books than talk to me?
>
> My daughter is now reading *Anne of Green Gables*—to my delight. When I asked her why she picked that book she said, "I'm sick of reading about problems all the time. I want to read a happy book." I frankly can't blame her.

Increasingly it seems that parents' efforts to remove books are being guided by political action groups, particularly those with a conservative perspective. The motives of these groups are usually phrased in moral terms but are often actually political.

Even in cases where no group seems to be orchestrating the censorship attempt, similarities in target and rhetoric occur across the country, causing suspicion that a parent has been assisted by a group with experience in orchestrating these protests.

Some of the most influential groups are Jerry Falwell's Moral Majority, Phyllis Shlafly's Eagle Forum, Robert Simmonds' Citizens for Excellence in Education, and the Gablers' Educational Research Analysts Inc. Their concerns generally focus on the satanic, anti-American, antifamily issues, and particularly their belief that America is involved in a war between secular humanism and Christianity. They contend that schools are failing to teach love of God and country and instead are advocating evolution, situation ethics, sexual permissiveness, anti-biblical bias, one-world government, and death education. They do not want their children to hear others' ideas or to know that anyone considers non-Western ideas important.

Their tactics have become increasingly politicized. Not content to object quietly and directly to school authorities, they flood newspapers with carefully orchestrated letters. They illegally enter classrooms with tape recorders, then lift portions of the recordings out of context and use them against people. They threaten school personnel, make bomb threats, and start destructive rumors about personal lives. They tend to be extremist in their language and actions. Those who oppose them are labeled unpatriotic, anti-Christian, antifamily, pro-Satan and pro-Communist among other derogatory names. On one talk show, an objector to a book ripped it apart, stomped on it, then raked the fragments off the stage, explaining he was ridding the garden of weeds. "We're not running from this," he then stated, "we're warriors of God" (Booth 135). The following are two sample voices from this perspective. The first is from a concerned parent influenced by organization.

> Young children are very responsive and it's easy to impose on a child's eagerness to please. But I don't think it's appropriate for children to be taught to think for themselves because God makes all decisions and virtue consists of obedience to His will. I want my child to think: "Does the act I am considering conform to the Word of God and/or the commands of my parents?"
>
> What I'm most concerned about is that occult and anti-Christian themes get much more and better shelf space than Christian-based literature. There is no Bible in our school library. Bible-related stories are set apart on a high shelf. On the other hand, these books about witchcraft are right in front.
>
> I want my children to grow up sharing my values and those of my parents. You're trying to promote change through reading books—and I don't like it. We send our children to school to give them what we can't give them at home, but we don't want the school to change them from the way we made them. America has been so busy focusing on "rights" that we have lost our focus on "right" and "wrong." (in Delfattore 1992)

This is the Christian organization's voice:

> There are only *two* general world views. . . . One is God's view—the other is man's view. These two views produce two different people. The humanist or worldly

person is basically EGO or self-oriented. The Christ-ian person or follower of God is "other person" oriented.

Humanism says there is no God. Christianity says there is a living Creator God. Each of these two views . . . comprise their own world view. All belief systems fit into one of these two diametrically opposite camps. . . . (in Delfattore, 15)

It just may be that Hitler's burning of anti-Nazi books prior to World War II has made us have an unholy respect for anything printed in book form. Just because a book has been published does not mean that it has an external right to exist or to be read . . . some things must be kept and yes, some things must be burned. (in Booth, 55)

Organizations from the left have their own rhetoric. One, the Council on Interracial Books for Children (CIBC), lobbies school officials, librarians, and publishers to reconsider the use of books containing any material CIBC judges as biased against minorities or women, or advocates ageism, elitism, materialism, individualism, escapism, and conformism (in Moore and Burress 1981). The following is the voice of Robert Moore, a former director of CIBC's Racism/Sexism Resource Center for Educators, which provides a sense of the rationale for this perspective:

Objecting to race and sex bias is *not* censorship. Presenting alternative views to those predominating in establishment review media is not censorship. If the children's book establishment honors and recommends books like *Little Black Sambo, The Cay* and *Words By Heart* is it censorship to offer librarians and teachers additional viewpoints and broader perspectives to consider in making decisions? Or to recommend other books and present reasons for urging their adoption? . . . CIBC does *not* list books to be removed. . . . We encourage educators to consider various criteria on content before selecting books—criteria designed to raise consciousness of issues and concerns affecting the portrayal of various groups. . . . Diverting attention from the issues of racism and sexism in effect upholds the biased status quo. By claiming that objection to racist and sexist children's books and textbooks is censorship, they malign legitimate protest by women, Third World people and others. (Moore and Burress 1981, 14–15)

Minority parents also contend that negative stereotypes and language in books can be harmful to children. The following voice of an African American mother eloquently confirms this opinion:

I was first introduced to *Huck Finn* in 1957. I was thirteen and in the ninth grade of a large, middle-class, suburban, predominately white high school in Portland, Oregon. I was the only Black student in the class . . . as we began to read the story the dialect alone made me feel uneasy. And as we continued, I began to be apprehensive, to fear being ridiculed, or made fun of because of my color and only because of my color. . . . I would pray like the dickens that no one would use that awful word—the very word my parents had taught me was used only by people who were ignorant or of low moral character. And there it was, in print, that word, staring me in the face over and over again, throughout the entire book.

I need not tell you that I hated the book! Yet, while we read it, I pretended that it didn't bother me. I hid, from my teacher and classmates, the tension, discomfort and hurt I would feel every time. I heard that word or watched the class laugh at Jim and felt some white youngster's stare being directed my way as if to say, "Hey, it's you and your kind we're talking about in this book." (Allen 1984, 9)

This woman actively pursued removal of the book from the required curriculum in her son's school.

There is another more subtle group of censors—editors and publishers. When publishers ask authors to gloss over controversial issues, tone down language, or delete certain references to sex and human anatomy, they justify the changes on the basis that "book clubs would not like a scene," "it just doesn't seem to work," "librarians will have a fit" or "it won't sell" (Keresy 1984, 133–36). Anne Rinaldi, an author of historical fiction for young adults, tells of an editor's request to delete the word "Christmas" and references to the enemy troops drinking and smoking when she described George Washington's crossing of the Delaware on Christmas Eve (Weiss 1989). Norma Klein was asked to make the mother in her book divorced rather than never married and to leave out the scene in which the mother's boyfriend sleeps over (Klein 1983).

In other instances, the potentially controversial material has been left in the original book but it is then expurgated when used for a reading series or school book club. For example, Barbara Cohen was asked to delete portions of *Molly's Pilgrim*, including all mention of Jews, Sukkos, God, and the Bible, before the story could be included in a third-grade reader (Cohen 1986). Betty Miles was asked to delete the following passage from *All It Takes Is Practice* before Scholastic would purchase it for book clubs (the requested deletions are underlined).

> "Then Anne pulled me over to the side of the room.
> "Is Peter's mother really black?" she asked.
> I sort of tightened up. "Yeah," I said, "What of it?"
> "Nothing," Annie said, "It's interesting, that's all. <u>I just finished this book about a white boy who falls in love with a black girl, but in the end they break up. I wanted them to get married. I don't see why they shouldn't, if they really love each other.</u>"
> <u>"That's what I think," I said.</u>

Miles bowed to the request but Scholastic's editorial board later voted not to publish the book at all because they thought it was too radical (Klein 1983).

Now publishers are cautious about anti-Christian or satanic concerns. One editor reported that a major book club was interested in buying the rights to a set of miniature books called *The Little Box of Witches* (Greaves 1985) but decided against the sale because they were concerned the witch subject would offend their conservative members (West 1988).

Thus, an atmosphere of fear and self-censorship has evolved. A publisher's concern over controversy can cause the company to reject a manuscript or ask for numerous changes. Or authors may shy away from controversial topics, resulting in unimaginative plots and lack of material on topics like AIDS, which are of compelling interest to modern children. And some books are never considered for the widespread distribution afforded by book clubs or readers because they are too controversial. What's even more alarming is that books with textual changes are often published with no notation that they have been edited.

One can't blame the authors either. Integrity can come at a high price, in a field of low financial rewards. When faced with the prospect of changing some things in return for exposing your work to as many as half a million children, it is difficult to be noble. And authors are often ecstatic just to get published. As Norma Klein described her feelings upon receiving an acceptance letter for *Mom, the Wolf Man and Me* (1983):

> Changes? I would do anything. I would change men to women, birds to giraffes. I would have reset the book in the Congo, so delighted was I at the prospect of being a real honest-to-goodness novelist. (Klein 1983, 148)

Amid all this controversy it's no surprise that teachers and librarians do quite a bit of self-censoring, seemingly in an attempt to avoid controversy. As one librarian stated:

> My main observation is that teachers, librarians, media personnel and supervisors practice self censorship; let's do it to them before they do it to us seems to be the prevailing attitude. Most of the time, the people doing the censoring do it out of fear and misinformation. (in Donelson 1987, 210)

A California librarian put it the following way: "We haven't been censoring but we have been conservative" (Donelson 1987, 212).

Usually it's difficult to tell if censorship of this type has occurred. Teachers and librarians have a wide variety of books to pick from; if they want to avoid controversy they just don't select the controversial ones. When schools select authors for school visits, they avoid inviting those with potentially troublesome works. Sometimes librarians vehemently deny that what they do is censorship. For example, a leading censorship advocate looked through the card catalog in an elementary school library and noticed no Judy Blume books were listed. When asked why, the librarian replied,

"Our young women are much too sophisticated for Judy Blume." Is this censorship? There's really no way of knowing (O'Neal 1990, 772).

Censorship or Selection?

So is there a difference between censorship and selection? Censorship has been defined as the removal, suppression, or restricted circulation of literary, artistic, or educational images, ideas, and/or information on the grounds that they are morally or otherwise objectionable (National Council of Teachers of English 1982). From this perspective, then, virtually any attempt to keep children from reading certain books, no matter how well-intentioned, could be construed as censorship. But, what happens when librarians remove a book from a collection simply because it is rather boring and nobody is checking it out? If the central character is a female or a minority or elderly or a witch, will the librarian be accused of bias or censorship? The same questions might be raised when teachers select books to use in their classrooms: some are included, others are excluded. How do we decide when these choices constitute judicious selection and when it is censorship?

The National Council of Teachers of English (1982) has developed the following set of criteria to discriminate between censorship and selection:

Examples of Censorship

1. Exclude Specific Materials or Methods
   Example: Eliminate books with unhappy endings.

2. Are Essentially Negative
   Example: Review your classroom library and eliminate books that include stereotypes.

3. Intend to Control
   Example: Do not accept *policeman*. Insist that students say and write *police officer*.

4. Seek to Indoctrinate, to Limit Access to Ideas and Information
   Example: Drug abuse is a menace to students. Eliminate all books that portray drug abuse.

Examples of Professional Guidelines

1. Include Specific Materials or Methods
   Example: Include some books with unhappy endings to give a varied view of life.

2. Are Essentially Affirmative
   Example: Review your classroom library. If necessary, add books that portray groups in nonstereotypical ways.

3. Intend to Advise
   Example: Encourage such limiting alternatives for *policeman* as *police officer, officer of the law* or *law enforcer*.

4. Seek to Educate, to Increase Access to Ideas and Information
   Example: Include at appropriate grade levels books that will help students understand the personal and social consequences of drug abuse.

5. Look at Parts of a Work in Isolation to Each Other and to a Work
   Example: Remove this book. The language includes profanity.

5. See the Relationship of Parts as a Whole
   Example: Determine whether profanity is integral to portrayal of character and development of theme in the book.

Essentially the goal of censorship is to remove or eliminate particular materials whereas the goal of professional guidelines is to provide criteria for selection, using both standards for literary quality and knowledge of child development. Jalongo and Creany (1991) use the example of books on the AIDS topic to differentiate censorship and selection. The censor would want this issue ignored because the disease is usually transmitted through sexual contact. The selector would defend the rights of children to have access to AIDS information as long as it is accurate and developmentally appropriate.

This perspective does not assume that all books are equally appropriate for children of all ages, nor does it deny that children are influenced by what they read. Rather, it suggests that teachers and librarians must be professional in determining the criteria for book selection and use research to support those choices. This means we collect reviews from respected sources, guidelines for literary quality, and policy statements to back up our choices (Booth 1992). This also means we must recognize our biases and struggle against them to help ensure we are providing a balanced program that will help our students become not only readers, but also lovers of literature. We must be open to a wider definition of quality and accept differing points of view about how that term is defined and operationalized. Just because we disagree with a book's perspective (sexual, racist, satanic, and so on), does not mean we restrict the reading of it.

What to Do When the Censor Comes

Censorship is unpredictable. People are often surprised when someone in their community tries to remove a book. This lack of awareness sometimes then causes panicked responses: to avoid publicity, a book is often removed without discussion. But when one looks at demographic statistics of areas where censorship occurs, it is clear that book banning knows no boundaries. Therefore all teachers and librarians must be prepared to meet these challenges in an organized, constructive, professional manner so small incidents don't escalate into confrontations.

One of the most important things educators can do is keep current in the field of children's literature. If you know which books are considered the best—and why—you will be better equipped to defend them. Reviews from professional journals like *The Horn Book, Language Arts, The Reading Teacher, School Library Journal,* and others can help. Criteria developed by the American Library Association (1983), the Council on Interracial Books for Children (1979), the National Council of Teachers of English (1982), and the International Reading Association (1988) provide helpful guidelines for selecting books. Knowing children's books helps you respond knowledgeably to challenges and questions. You will also begin to identify those books you are willing to fight for.

Secondly, both teachers and school librarians need to communicate what they're doing with books. Some advocate keeping parents in the dark under the idea that "the less said, the better." However, experience seems to suggest that generally the more knowledge parents have, the more capable they are of making informed responses to what children read. If they understand a book's value and why it appeals to children, they are less likely to object to it. They also are apt to realize that children have unique, diverse responses to books and often focus on quite different elements of stories than adults might expect. For example, when a parent challenged the presence of Raynor's *Mr. and Mrs. Pig's Evening Out* (1976) in a Maryland school library, the librarian urged her to read the book aloud to her child. The parent, who had been concerned that her child would never trust babysitters again after reading the book, reported back that the child was not frightened at all by the book. Rather, he found it hilarious that the pig parents failed to notice the babysitter was a wolf (O'Neal 1990).

One way to educate parents is to have meetings where parents actually read and discuss books that will be used by children. One teacher organized an evening discussion about Judy Blume books (Swibold 1982). Parents and teachers read at least one Blume book, children wrote their own reactions to the books, which were shared with the group, and the adults discussed the books using questions like, "What is the value of reading Blume books? Why do they appeal to children? Do the characters seem real in these books?"

Children should also be adequately prepared for what they will encounter in their reading. If they are forewarned of four-letter words or an incident of child abuse, they may be less disturbed when these elements are encountered in the text. Young readers need also to be taught to make informed, critical judgments about the books they read. Thus, they should be given different versions of the same story of differing literary quality so they can begin to acquire a sense of good writing. They also need to be exposed to several books on the same topic. Children who read both Forbes' *Johnny Tremain* (1945) and the Colliers' *My Brother Sam Is Dead* (1974) are more likely to have a balanced perspective on war. Finally, children should learn that writers are people; they have prejudices, opinions, and often interesting insights. Much can be gained by reading their ideas—but they are not infallible, nor does what they write exemplify absolute "truth."

Despite one's best efforts to educate the public, challenges to books can still occur. Therefore, schools and librarians must be prepared. A written policy for selecting materials and filing complaints that includes the following elements should be developed:

1. A statement of the philosophy of materials selection such as is given in the Library Bill of Rights.
2. A statement that the governing body of the district is legally responsible for the selection of instructional materials.
3. A statement detailing the delegation of this responsibility to professional personnel.
4. Criteria for instructional materials selection in the school or district.
5. Procedures for implementing selection criteria.

Similarly, guidelines for handling complaints should be clear and describe explicitly the steps in the review process, the people responsible at each step, and appeal procedures. Materials should be viewed as "innocent until proven guilty" rather than whisked away until the matter is resolved. Ideally, guidelines should encourage the resolution of complaints at the most direct point—first the teacher or librarian, then the principal, and so on. The school board should be the last resort. Evidence suggests that requiring parents to talk directly to the person using the book often helps them see the professional as dedicated and caring with a good sense of the educational validity for using the book in question. This means that teachers must listen to parental concerns with respect, responding diplomatically and with an attitude of encouraging compromise. Confrontation or an attitude that "I know what's best for your child" will probably only lead to further problems. Mutual understanding may not always occur but efforts to this end should be the cornerstone of the complaint procedure.

Other suggested components of a complaint policy include the following:

1. Guidelines should require that formal, written complaints be filed to trigger the review process. Complainants should be encouraged to read the complete work and to address their concerns in relation to the context of the school's educational goals.
2. Guidelines should require that review committees have broad representation including parents, teachers, and school administrators. Some advocate including students in the group. Others contend this practice could lead to charges of poisoning children's minds (Booth 1992). The review committee should focus their evaluation on the educational merit and quality of the challenged material (People 1992).
3. Guidelines should state that the procedure is applicable to all individuals, including school personnel and board members (Davis 1979).
4. Guidelines should state that materials will not be removed during the review process.

Once guidelines are in place, they must of course be implemented and not circumvented.

Most importantly, schools must maintain communication and develop support networks within the community. Censors, in order to gain credibility, will often claim the entire community supports them. Parent Advisory Boards, local writers and journalists, and civil liberty organizations can publicly counter claims made by censors. Assistance and information on legal ruling, organizations behind challenges, how to resist, and so on can be obtained from state and national organizations like People For the American Way, National Coalition Against Censorship, American Library Association (ALA), National Council of Teachers of English (NCTE), and others.

Teachers can also develop rationales for any books read in common, explaining why they have decided to use various materials. While many things can go into a rationale, Donelson (1975, 24) suggests that a basic rationale should include the answers to at least five questions:

a. Why would a teacher consider using this book with a specific class?
b. What particular objectives, literary, psychological, or pedagogical, does the teacher have in mind in using this book?
c. How will the book be used to meet these objectives?
d. What problems of style, tone, or theme or possible grounds for censorship exist in the book, and how will the teacher plan to meet those problems?
e. Assuming that the objectives are met, how will the students of this specific class be different because of their reading of the book?

Teachers can share the burden of writing rationales by dividing the work, then pooling what they've written. One system in Ohio publishes the rationales for books as a curriculum guide given to all teachers (Burkert 1990). Local NCTE affiliates also often publish rationales and several books of them are available from NCTE and ALA.

As a corollary to rationales, teachers can keep files of students' written responses to books. Besides corroborating that writing is required, these responses can provide compelling evidence that students are not focusing on the prurient aspects of the books but on literary characteristics and personal meanings.

Some view the writing of rationales as a double-edged sword that can be used against teachers. A few organized censorship groups have actually picked apart rationales word by word so that teachers have to spend an inordinate amount of time carefully wording things or making sure rationales are available for every book that might conceivably be objected to. In some cases, teachers have been required to write rationales for every single book in their room, including those in their class libraries. It's easy to see how this would begin stifling teachers' use of literature.

Most importantly, each challenge must be treated with respect. Reasoned, thoughtful responses to situations can help diffuse an explosive situation. But educators should be prepared to have their statements taken out of context or misconstrued or even twisted to support the censor's message. Often, especially in the case of organized groups, emotionally laden language or subtle emotional pressure is used.

For example, officials in one Ohio school system were asked for names of teachers using objectionable materials so they could be the focus of prayers by a group identifying themselves as "Prayer Warriors for Children." Teachers must also be aware that rumors and gossip will often spread through the community about people's personal lives. Difficult as it may be, we must remain professional with children and adults and not stoop to retaliation.

One teacher, after going through a prolonged censorship battle, questions the use of any established procedures. In her opinion, a detailed complaint policy provides a blueprint for the legal removal of books. She recommends replacing formal bureaucratic procedures with the following policy:

> In the event that a citizen is unable to work out an acceptable alternative with the teacher and wishes to file a formal, written challenge to any material, the [school] system will provide a forum in which all parties will be heard. At the conclusion of the public hearing, each family will make its own decision. Mutually agreeable alternate selections and procedures are always available to any family. (Pipkin 1993, 37)

Although this perspective diverges from generally accepted wisdom on how to handle censorship incidents, it is certainly an opinion to consider.

Balancing the Rights of Parents, Educators, and Children

It is evident that censorship of young children's reading has been and continues to be pervasive. Is this appropriate? Do children have a fundamental legal right to intellectual freedom? Some would argue that they do; that the concept of children's rights was firmly established in the Tinker case of 1969. The majority opinion in this case stated the following:

> School officials do not possess absolute authority over their students. Students . . . are "persons" under our constitution. . . . In our system, students may not be regarded as closed circuit recipients of only that which the state chooses to communicate. They may not be confined to the expression of those sentiments that are officially approved. (Krug 1972, 809)

Some interpret this decision to mean that the horizons of children, be they six, twelve, or twenty, should not be limited. Rather, children should have access to whatever books they desire, in order to develop the understandings and skills needed to function in our society.

Others are not so sure. In a separate concurring opinion for this case, Justice Stewart expressed some doubts that many parents share. He said, "I cannot support the courts' uncritical assumption that . . . the First Amendment rights of children are co-extensive with those of adults."

It seems safe to assume that most adults don't believe a nine-year-old has unfettered First Amendment rights. Yet the exact extent of these rights have not been clearly determined. The use of ambiguous terms and lack of precise definitions leave the question still open to debate.

An even more fundamental issue must also be considered. *Should* children have the right to read whatever they wish? Or should they be protected from matters that adults deem morally or politically inappropriate? Most parents know that children cannot really be sheltered from knowledge of the world's evils and that we can't censor the world—although every parent has probably wished that this was sometimes possible. We must remember that the trend toward realism is not a recent phenomena; children's books have always reflected society's evils as well as its ideals. Early children's books were filled with threats of hell and punishment as well as promises of rewards for good behavior. In their own way, these books were just as shocking as the sex and obscenity that disturb parents today. Children know there is evil as well as good in the world. What we need to do is help them learn to cope with it.

Children need well-written books that tell them honestly about the world, giving them a chance to understand it. Even fantasy must be "grounded in reality"—with some connection to basic human truths—before children will accept it. Otherwise literature will seem hypocritical and irrelevant. Books that treat realistic subjects with skill, care, and imagination are probably preferable to a street-corner encounter. Also, children tend to read only that which they can relate to or understand. Few children continue to struggle through books that have no meaning for them. Conversely, if they understand the book they are probably ready to read it.

Further, it is impossible to determine how different children will react to a particular book. As P. L. Travers wrote,

> "Who is to know what child will be moved by what book and at what age? Who is to be the judge? Every child brings to reading a unique set of past experiences, perceptions, and prejudices, which influence individual response to a book. Thus there is no one final formula that will embody everyone's perception of what is appropriate or "true." (in Holland 1980, 207)

Isabelle Holland presents an interesting scenario when she suggests that all the "no-nos" be fed to a master computer, resulting in a book that will offend no one. Every bad character of any age, shape, sex, race, ethnic strain, and nationality would be matched by a good character of the same group. The result, she asserts, "would be a very dull story. And I wouldn't be surprised if the child, after attempting to digest this automated pap, would cease to be a reader and the whole problem would go away because reading would stop" (203). Good writers create a story that needs to be written. Any attempts to limit that need will most likely result in a book that is dishonest and superficial.

Yet we cannot deny the very real concerns of parents over the values they wish to instill in their own children. Many reasonable, intelligent adults believe some children are not ready at a particular age for the graphic sex of *Forever* or the alternative parental life-style portrayed in *Mom, the Wolf Man and Me*. It seems that those who wish to shield their children from works they consider unsuitable should have the right to do so—and this right should not be subsumed by other considerations, such as the expertise of professionals or the acknowledged merit of the book in question.

This valid parental concern forms the basis for one solution to the censorship problem: careful tailoring of books to students' needs, past experience, and stage of development. Teachers and librarians have a responsibility to provide books that they believe children are prepared to handle. Yet I also think it's important for parents to have the right to some say in the selection of materials for their own child. But these same parents have no right to make that decision for other children. Censorship should be a private decision. When it becomes a public issue, someone's rights will be abridged. While protecting the minority, we must still allow free choice for the majority.

There is a fine line between protection and control, however; protection without love and through fear can lead to overcontrol and the stifling of a developing mind. It's probably healthier for a child and parent to confront controversial issues together rather than to deny their existence. Yet I believe parents should have the right to decide what is appropriate for their own child.

Conclusion

Censorship does not achieve its goal. Surveys reveal that often censored books become bestsellers. Additionally, communities become polarized and teachers demoralized—greatly magnifying the situation beyond its initial importance.

However, an even greater moral issue is at stake. We cannot afford to stifle the development of critical thinking in our children. Our democratic society is based on the fundamental premise that citizens, by exercising their moral judgment, will recognize propaganda, poor logic, and bias. I don't think we are willing to sacrifice our heritage of this freedom in order to be "protected" against what others think is bad for us. Pressures toward conformity and protection are natural in times of rapid change. Yet suppression of ideas is even more dangerous. We need to keep open to opportunities for novel and creative solutions. In this way change comes through choice and critical analysis of options rather than fear.

As educators, we must be sure we're fulfilling our responsibilities: to provide children with high-quality literature that challenges them to explore different ideas and perspectives. We must also help them critically examine these ideas so they will be able to think for themselves and develop judgment, imagination, and a sense of responsibility. This will enable them to control their own minds and destinies.

Professional References

ADAMS, DENNIS. 1986. "Literature For Children: Avoiding Controversy and Intellectual Challenge." *Top of the News* (spring): 304–308.

ALLEN, MARGOT. 1984. "Huck Finn: Two Generations of Pain." *Interracial Books for Children Bulletin* 15(5).

AMERICAN LIBRARY ASSOCIATION. 1983. *Intellectual Freedom Manual.* 2d edition. Chicago: ALA.

BANFIELD, BERYLE, and GERALDINE WILSON. 1983. "The Black Experience Through White Eyes: The Same Old Story Once Again." *Interracial Books for Children Bulletin* 14(5).

BERKLEY, JUNE. 1979. "Teach the Parents Well: An Anti-Censorship Experiment In Adult Education." In *Dealing With Censorship*, edited by James E. Davis. Urbana, IL: National Council of Teachers of English.

BOOTH, DAVID. 1992. *Censorship Goes to School.* Ontario, Canada: Pembroke.

BURKETT, KAROLYN. 1990. "Insuring Your Students' Right to Read." *Issues in English* (October).

COHEN, BARBARA. 1986. "Censoring the Sources." *School Library Journal* (March).

COUNCIL ON INTERRACIAL BOOKS FOR CHILDREN. 1979. *Guidelines for Selecting Bias-Free Textbooks and Storybooks.* New York.

DAVIS, JAMES, ed. 1979. *Dealing With Censorship.* Urbana, IL: National Council of Teachers of English.

DELFATTORE, JOAN. 1992. *What Johnny Shouldn't Read: Book Censorship In America.* New Haven: Yale University Press.

DONELSON, KEN. 1975. "What to Do Before the Censor Arrives." *Today's Education* (January/February): 22–26.

———. 1987. "Six Statements/Questions From the Censors." *Phi Delta Kappan* (Nov): 208–14.

HEARNE, BETSY. 1982. "Sex, Violence, Obscenity, Tragedy, Scariness and Other Facts of Life In Children's Literature." *Learning* 10 (February).

HOLLAND, ISABELLE. 1980. "On Being A Children's Book Writer and Other Dangers, Part One." *The Hornbook Magazine* 56: 34–42.

INTERNATIONAL READING ASSOCIATION. 1988. "Resolution on Textbook and Reading Program Censorship." Newark, DE: International Reading Association.

JALONGO, MARY RENCK, and ANNE CREANY. 1991. "Censorship in Children's Literature: What Every Educator Should Know." *Childhood Education* 67(3): 143–48.

KERESY, GAYLE. 1984. "School Book Club Expurgation Practices." *Top of the News* 40 (winter): 131–38.

KLEIN, NORMA. 1983. "Some Thoughts on Censorship: An Author Symposium." *Top of the News* (winter): 137–55.

KRUG, JUDITH. 1972. "Intellectual Freedom and the Child." *English Journal* 61 (September): 805–13.

MAYERS, HENRY. 1982. "Censorship Loses to Honest Debate." *Columbus Dispatch*, September B3.

McCLURE, AMY. 1983. "Intellectual Freedom and the Young Child." *Children's Literature Association Quarterly* 8(3).

MOORE, ROBERT, and LEE BURRESS. 1981. "Bait/Rebait: Criticism vs. Censorship: The Criticizing of Racism and Sexism by the Council on Interracial Books for Children Is Not Censorship." *English Journal* 70: 14–19.

NATIONAL COUNCIL OF TEACHERS OF ENGLISH. 1982. Statement on Censorship and Professional Guidelines. Urbana, IL: National Council of Teachers of English.

O'NEAL, SHARON. 1990. "Leadership In the Language Arts: Controversial Books In the Classroom." *Language Arts* 67 (November): 771–79.

PATERSON, KATHERINE. 1989. "Tale of a Reluctant Dragon." *The New Advocate* 2(1): 1–8.

PEOPLE FOR THE AMERICAN WAY. 1991, 1992. *Attacks on the Freedom to Learn.* Report 1991–92; 1992–93. Washington, DC: People for the American Way.

PIPKIN, GLORIA. 1993. "Challenging the Conventional Wisdom of Censorship." *ALAN Review* 20(2): 35–37.

QUINDLEN, ANN. 1993. "The Breast Ban." *New York Times*, 7 April. Reprinted in *Censorship News* 48(2).

SIMMONDS, ROBERT. *Pro-Family Forum Newsletter.*

SWIBOLD, KAREN. 1982. "Bringing Adults to Children's Books: A Case Study." *The Reading Teacher* 35 (January): 460–64.

TAYLOR, THEODORE. 1993. Speech at National Council of Teachers of English Annual Convention, Pittsburgh, November.

TUCKER, NICHOLAS. 1981. *The Child and the Book: A Psychological and Literary Exploration.* Cambridge: Cambridge University Press.

TUNNELL, MICHAEL. 1993. "The Double-Edged Sword: Fantasy and Censorship." Speech presented at the 38th Annual Convention of the International Reading Association, San Antonio, Texas.

UDOW, ROZ. 1992. "Censorship News." *Newsletter of the National Coalition Against Censorship* 46(5).

WEISS, JERRY. 1989. "A Dangerous Subject: Censorship!" *The ALAN Review* 16(3): 59–61.

WEST, MARK. 1988. *Trust Your Children: Voices Against Censorship.* New York: Neal-Schuman.

Children's Literature

ADOFF, ARNOLD. 1985. *The Cabbages Are Chasing the Rabbits.* Illustrated by Janet Stevens. San Diego: Harcourt, Brace, Javonovich.

ALCOCK, VIVIEN. 1984. *Ghostly Companions: A Feast of Chilling Tales.* New York: Delacorte.

BANNERMAN, HELEN. 1899. *Little Black Sambo.* London: Grant Richards.

BASE, GRAEME. 1986. *Animalia.* New York: H. N. Abrams.

BLUME, JUDY. 1970. *Are You There, God, It's Me, Margaret.* New York: Bradbury.

———. 1973. *Deenie.* New York: Bradbury.

———. 1974. *Blubber.* New York: Bradbury.

————. 1975. *Forever.* New York: Bradbury.

————. 1977. *Starring Sally J. Friedman As Herself.* New York: Bradbury.

BRANCATO, ROBIN. 1977. *Winning.* New York: Knopf.

BRIGGS, RAYMOND. 1973. *Father Christmas.* New York: Coward, McCann, & Geohegan.

BRINK, CAROLYN. 1973. *Caddie Woodlawn.* Illustrated by Trina Schart Hyman. New York: Macmillan.

BROWN, MARCIA. 1982. *Shadow.* New York: Scribner's.

BROWNE, ANTHONY. 1986. *Piggybook.* New York: Knopf.

COHEN, BARBARA. 1983. *Molly's Pilgrim.* New York: Lothrop, Lee & Shepard.

COLE, JOANNA. 1991. *My Puppy Is Born.* New York: Morrow Junior Books.

COLLIER, JAMES, and CHRISTOPHER COLLIER. 1974. *My Brother Sam Is Dead.* New York: Four Winds.

CONRAD, PAM. 1990. *Stonewords.* New York: Harper & Row.

COOPER, SUSAN. 1973. *The Dark Is Rising.* New York: Macmillan.

DAHL, ROALD. 1961. *James and the Giant Peach: A Children's Story.* Illustrated by Nancy Ekholm Burkert. New York: Knopf.

————. 1982. *The BFG.* Illustrated by Quentin Blake. New York: Farrar, Straus & Giroux.

————. 1985. *Witches.* New York: Farrar, Straus & Giroux.

————. 1986. *Revolting Rhymes.* New York: Bantam.

DAVINCI, LEONARDO. 1980. *Leonardo Drawings.* New York: Dover Publications.

DECLEMENTS, BERTHA. 1985. *Sixth Grade Can Really Kill You.* New York: Viking Kestrel.

FITZHUGH, LOUISE. 1969. *Bang, Bang, You're Dead.* New York: Harper & Row.

FORBES, ELEANOR. 1945. *Johnny Tremain.* Illustrated by Lyn Ward. Boston: Houghton Mifflin.

FOX, PAULA. 1973. *The Slave Dancer: A Novel.* Illustrated by Eros Keith. New York: Bradbury.

GEORGE, JEAN. 1972. *Julie of the Wolves.* Illustrated by John Schoenherr. New York: Harper & Row.

GREAVES, MARGARET. 1985. *The Little Box of Witches.* New York: Olympic Marketing.

GREENE, BETTE. 1987. *Elie Wiesel: Messenger From the Holocaust.* Chicago: Children's Press.

HANDFORD, MARTIN. 1987. *Where's Waldo?* New York: Little Brown.

HAYWOOD, CAROLYN. 1971. *Back to School With Betsy.* San Diego: Harcourt, Brace, Jovanovich.

HERMES, PATRICIA. 1986. *Kevin Corbett Eats Flies.* San Diego: Harcourt, Brace.

HOLLAND, ISABELLE. 1972. *The Man Without A Face.* Philadelphia & New York: Lippincott.

KAUFMAN, JOE. 1969. *How We Are Born, How We Grow.* New York: Follett.

KELLOGG, STEVEN. 1986. *Best Friends.* New York: Dial.

KILLINGSWORTH, MONTE. 1991. *Eli's Song.* New York: Maxwell Macmillan.

KIMMEL, ERIC. 1985. *Hershel and the Hanukkah Goblins.* Illustrated by Trina Schart Hyman. New York: Holiday House.

KLEIN, NORMA. 1972. *Mom, The Wolf Man and Me*. New York: Pantheon.

L'ENGLE, MADELEINE. 1962. *A Wrinkle In Time*. New York: Farrar, Straus & Giroux.

———. 1986. *Many Waters*. New York: Farrar, Straus & Giroux.

LEWIS, C. S. 1950. *The Lion, the Witch and the Wardrobe*. New York: Macmillan.

LINDGREN, ASTRID. 1950. *Pippi Longstocking*. New York: Viking.

McBRIDE, WILL. 1975. *Show Me*. New York: St. Martin's Press.

MERRIAM, EVE. 1987. *Halloween ABC*. Illustrated by Lane Smith. New York: Macmillan.

MILES, BETTY. 1976. *All It Takes Is Practice*. New York: Knopf.

MUNSCH, ROBERT. 1989. *I Have to Go*. Toronto: Annick Press.

NEWMAN, LESLEA. 1989. *Heather Has Two Mommies*. Boston: Alyson Publications.

O'CONNOR, JANE. 1986. *Lulu and the Witch Baby*. New York: Harper & Row.

O'HARA, MARY. 1941. *My Friend Flicka*. New York: Lippincott.

PATERSON, KATHERINE. 1977. *Bridge to Terabithia*. Illustrated by Donna Diamond. New York: Crowell.

———. 1978. *The Great Gilly Hopkins*. New York: Crowell.

PECK, RICHARD. 1976. *A Day No Pigs Would Die*. New York: Knopf.

RAYMOR, MARY. 1976. *Mr. and Mrs. Pig's Evening Out*. New York: Atheneum.

REISS, JOHANNA. 1972. *The Upstairs Room*. New York: Crowell.

ROCKWELL, THOMAS. 1973. *How to Eat Fried Worms*. Illustrated by Emily McCully. New York: Watts.

RYLANT, CYNTHIA. 1992. *Missing May*. New York: Orchard.

SCHWARTZ, ALVIN. 1981. *Scary Stories to Tell in the Dark*. Illustrated by Stephen Gammell. New York: Lippincott.

———. 1984. *More Scary Stories to Tell in the Dark*. New York: Lippincott.

SENDAK, MAURICE. 1970. *In the Night Kitchen*. New York: Harper & Row.

———. 1976. *Some Swell Pup*. New York: Farrar, Straus & Giroux.

———. 1981. *Outside Over There*. New York: Harper & Row.

SEUSS, DR. 1971. *The Lorax*. New York: Random House.

SILVERSTEIN, SHEL. 1964. *The Giving Tree*. New York: Harper & Row.

———. 1981a. *A Light In the Attic*. New York: Harper & Row.

———. 1981b. *Uncle Shelby's ABZ Book*. New York: Simon & Schuster.

SNYDER, ZILPHA. 1972. *The Witches of Worm*. New York: Atheneum.

SPIER, PETER. 1977. *Noah's Ark*. New York: Doubleday.

STEIG, WILLIAM. 1969. *Sylvester and the Magic Pebble*. New York: Windmill Books.

STEPTOE, JOHN. 1974. *My Special Best Words*. New York: Viking.

TAYLOR, THEODORE. 1969. *The Cay*. Garden City, NY: Doubleday.

Twain, Mark. 1918. *The Adventures of Huckleberry Finn*. New York: Grosset & Dunlap.

Viorst, Judith. 1969. *I'll Fix Anthony*. New York: Harper & Row.

Wilder, Laura Ingalls. 1953. *Little House in the Big Woods*. Illustrated by Garth Williams. New York: Harper.

Willhoite, Michael. 1990. *Daddy's Roommate*. Boston: Alyson Publications.

Zemach, Margot. 1982. *Jake and Honeybunch Go to Heaven*. New York: Farrar, Straus & Giroux.

TWO

Undesirable Publication: A Journey to Jo'burg

BEVERLEY NAIDOO

In 1985 my sister-in-law on a farm in South Africa received a letter from The Controller of Customs and Excise. "Madam," it said,

> The above mentioned literature addressed to you ex UK has been ruled by the Directorate of Publications to be undesirable and importation is prohibited vide Section 113 (1)(f) of the Custom and Excise Act No. 91 of 1964. The books are therefore seized. . . .

The two books in the intercepted parcel were copies of *Journey to Jo'burg* (1988), newly published in England and inscribed to various nephews and nieces. I was not surprised at the banning, only at how swiftly they had identified my "undesirable" parcel. I have an image of uniformed men and women beside a conveyor belt eagle-eyeing all the parcels and letters being unloaded from every plane and boat that landed in South Africa. What made a parcel look suspicious? Did they have to memorize lists of "subversive" names? Who actually read all the material intercepted? And—what I should most like to know—what did they actually *do* with my copies of *Journey to Jo'burg*? Were they incinerated, shredded, or locked in a steel cabinet? Or was there in fact a proper library—complete with a discreet librarian cataloging and shelving the Banned Collection to be made available only to "special" people with "special" permits? For instance, the Special Branch Security Police searching out evidence of subversive thought . . . or well-placed politicians, wanting to check out the latest in pornography in order that they should know what needed to be stamped out. . . .

My mental scenario easily develops into high farce. And that was not difficult to find in apartheid South Africa. If you don't cry, you laugh. But let me present you with another scenario. This time from an almost all-white primary school in a green and pleasant English county. As part of my job at the time I used to visit the school regularly to help a few children with reading difficulties. One day I was approached by a teacher who had been very surprised to see my picture in a publisher's catalog. As I was an author, would I agree to talk to her class about writing? I said I would be happy to do so, but it would be a good idea if the children read something I had written before the session. I suggested *Journey to Jo'burg*. The following week she seemed somewhat embarrassed. She had given the book first of all to "Sir" (the head teacher!) to read, and he felt the children "might not understand your perspective." "You mean he doesn't want them to read about the lives of black South African children?" I asked. "Don't worry," the teacher replied, anxious to soothe over any controversy, "I told him you would talk to them only about the *process* of writing!" I had to inform her that I did not write somewhere in the clouds but down on earth, dealing with matters of the earth. I never did speak to her children.

So it is, in various forms, that adults act as gatekeepers to children's knowledge. When children in the United Kingdom ask me why *Journey to Jo'burg* was banned in South Africa, I usually throw the question back to them to unravel. Frequently they decide that the all-white government of the day would have been more concerned to prevent white children reading the book than black children. Black South African children already had knowledge of apartheid and oppression through their own experience, they argue. But white children would be kept as much as possible from knowing, and their parents and teachers wouldn't want them to start asking awkward questions.

I find it heartening that children can attribute so much power to a novel—the power to raise serious questions. Certainly it is that which keeps me writing, although my own research study *Through Whose Eyes? Exploring Racism: Reader, Text and Context* (1992) focuses on the socially- and culturally-framed filters that thirteen-year-old readers already carry around in their own heads, preventing them at times from seeing new perspectives that challenge their version of the world. Thus we become our own gatekeepers.

My motivation for writing *Journey to Jo'burg* was linked very closely, at a number of levels, to resistance to particular forms of censorship. In the early 1980s a librarian friend asked me to look at a newly published nonfiction book on South Africa for young people. Although I had been working in British schools for over a decade, it had never occurred to me to look at what was on the library shelves about South Africa. When I began to investigate, I was shocked. It was still the world's most overtly racist society, yet the books presented the same versions of sanitized reality I had been given as a white child growing up in South Africa in the 1950s. The focus was usually on the country's climate, its beaches, the gold, and, of course, the wonderful flora and fauna. There was complete censorship of the brutal, dehumanizing nature of apartheid and life for the majority of South Africans.

In my local Anti-Apartheid group, we widened our research and began a campaign to alert teachers and librarians to our findings. While many books sinned through omission, others sinned through commission, propagating openly racist views. Bernard Newman, author of the most widely stocked book at the time, *Let's*

Visit South Africa, described how "The Kung Bushmen have a tiny brain . . ." and how their language "sounds more like the chatter of baboons than the talk of men" (1974, 82–84) A reader might well have come away with an impression of apartheid as a benign system designed for the benefit of backward black people. When our campaign ended I wrote up the research in a book called *Censoring Reality: An Examination of Non-fiction Books on South Africa* (1985). I imagined a twelve-year-old student doing a project on South Africa and what she would find. Although the focus of the study was South Africa, the implications were much wider. If this was how South Africa was being presented to young people, what was the representation of other societies where racism was embedded in far more covert ways?

My audience for this study, however, was largely an adult one, and I had begun to want to communicate directly with young people themselves. The opportunity came through my participation in an organization in the United Kingdom concerned with supporting the families of political prisoners in South Africa and keeping people's consciences alive to what was happening there. I had joined the Education Committee of the British Defense and Aid Fund for Southern Africa in the early 1980s. As educationists we were extremely concerned about the misrepresentation of South Africa. We wanted to open up the reality of apartheid to young people in Britain and decided that it was important to reach the heart as a way of engaging the head. What was needed was a work of fiction. I still recall the meeting where the question was asked whether any of us knew a children's writer who might take on the theme of apartheid. I put up my hand. I didn't know any children's writers but would like to try to write such a story myself. Despite the group's initial surprise—I hadn't written anything before—I was given three months to come up with something!

There was a story I wanted to tell, one that explored my own past but from a very different childhood perspective. I felt intensely angry about the racist distortions of reality that were presented to me as a child. I was brought up with the usual conceptions most white South Africans had, completely taking for granted the services of our cook-cum-nanny whose own three children lived more than three hundred kilometers away, cared for by . . . I don't know. She cared for me as a second mother, and I grew up calling her Mary. Her first language was Tswana but to work for an English-speaking family you needed an easy English name. African names were censored out. Furthermore, while by African custom it would be extremely rude for a child to call an adult by his or her first name, I was white. The prerogative of the "Master" and "Madam" to call their servant by a first name passed down to the white child. Indeed, as that white child, I grew up using the even more debasing terminology by which any black adult was referred to—"boy" or "girl."

All this was done quite naturally, without any deliberate viciousness that I can recall on the part of white adults around me. The dehumanization and the racism— part and parcel of colonization with its premise of superiority—were completely normalized. But while I remained uncritical and unquestioning as a child, nevertheless certain images were deeply implanted in my consciousness during childhood— images that still retain the power to disturb. Perhaps the most seminal is of Mary receiving a telegram and collapsing in front of me. The telegram informed her that two of her three young daughters had died. It was diphtheria, something against which I, as a white child, had been vaccinated.

It was only years later that I began to realize the meaning of that scene. I must have continued to spout with the arrogance of white youth the customary rationalizations: the servants who worked for us were lucky because we gave them jobs, sent presents to their children at Christmas, and so on. Racism, with apartheid one of its most extreme manifestations, segregates our experience, mentally as well as physically. I now look back and see how language was an intrinsic part of shaping my ways of seeing as a child—a means of censoring my reality. So it is no accident that I chose to use words and writing as a means of challenging, and pitting my own imagination against, that segregation of experience caused by racism. It was the seminal memory of a mother collapsing at the sight of the telegram telling her of the death of her children—and my own personal connection to that terrible event— that was to lead to Journey to Jo'burg.

In telling the story I deliberately chose to place myself (and thereby my readers) in the position of the children I had not been—the children whose mother had been taken away from them by apartheid. In addition, however, I wanted to explore the spirit of resistance of young black South Africans, which had exploded in the uprising of the 1970s against Bantu Education and the system that was designed to keep them forever servants. The journey undertaken by my central characters, Naledi and Tiro, is more than a physical one. It is a psychological journey of growing awareness. The adults close to them in their village have attempted to protect them from full knowledge of the devastating harshness of apartheid. When their mother visits them, she does not talk of her life as a servant in the city. Yet in making their own journey to find their mother when their baby sister is ill, Naledi and Tiro begin to discover for themselves some of the pain.

In my sequel, Chain of Fire (1993), this process continues even more directly. The children are two years older when they are caught up in the events that follow the white government's decision to destroy their village as part of its policy of mass removals and "ethnic cleansing." Having opened up a brief glimpse of life under apartheid through the small window as it were of Journey to Jo'burg, I wanted to find a way of giving readers a deeper understanding of the corruption that comes with almost uncontrolled power. I knew that over four million people, mainly black South Africans, had had their homes bulldozed down and that they had been physically removed to so-called homelands. How can one possibly conceptualize events on this scale, so massive a crime against humanity? To understand it for myself I needed to write, to explore it through an individual's eyes.

I was unable to return freely to South Africa at the time but had access to hundreds of interviews with people who had suffered the experience. These had been published by the Surplus People Project whose researchers had traveled across the country in the early 1980s tracking down removal victims in order to record their stories firsthand. The interviews provided very detailed information—how many chickens, pigs, and goats someone had been forced to leave behind; how a family's prize crockery was randomly smashed by a soldier sweeping his gun across a shelf and forcing them out of their house; how the house built by a grandfather was systematically reduced to rubble . . . and so on and so on. Sometimes there were photographs showing the results of this legalized mass vandalism as well as photographs of barren resettlement camps.

Having absorbed myself for months in this buried material, I began to write. I found myself quickly drawn into the head of fifteen-year-old Naledi, forcing myself to imagine at each point what the experience would be like for her. All the events of the novel were drawn from the kind of events I had been reading about. There was no fabrication of the reality at that level, only the fabrication of the novelist's reworking of that reality into fiction.

But should we not protect young readers from exposure to brutality in human behavior? Should children not simply be allowed to enjoy themselves . . . to enjoy fantasy and fun as long as possible before having to face the harsher realities of the adult world? Underlying these questions is the belief in the right of the child to a childhood safe from fear and a recognition of the responsibility of adults to provide that protection. These are fundamental values to which I subscribe. However, the same questions also raise a number of issues.

First, while any sane person would wish for a world free from brutality, it seems to be a part of the human condition, and frequently the victims include children themselves. So when we talk about protecting young readers, which young people are we referring to? Are we perhaps already referring to an exclusive group who have the good fortune not to be directly exposed to the kind of brutality experienced by children under apartheid? I, however, would want to argue that as long as there are children whose basic entitlements as human beings are denied, then it is important that all children be encouraged to reflect on, and respond to, this reality.

My second point is that pain has many forms and it is simplistic to think that there are children existing in completely sanitized, pain-free environments. While the experience of children separated from their parents because of apartheid laws was particular to South Africa, there are many children across the world—including the United Kingdom and the United States—who experience painful separation from parents. It may be through divorce or death of a parent. Even to imagine being separated from a parent is enough to cause most children anxiety, hence perhaps the readiness to empathize with Naledi and Tiro. Literature offers a medium through which readers can explore what it is to be human—and this inevitably involves the experience of pain. Furthermore it offers a safe domain in which children can carry out that exploration.

Third, it is obviously important to consider the age of readers. Writing for seven-year-olds can be very different from writing for readers seven years older. I say "can be" because *Journey to Jo'burg* is accessible to young people across a wide age range. I receive letters from seven-year-olds as well as from fourteen-year-olds. While the complexity of response obviously varies, I believe the wide readership is because it is written in the simple but unpatronizing, ageless language of the storyteller, addressing "to whom it may concern." *Chain of Fire*, on the other hand, is much more clearly addressed to young people approaching, or in, their teens. Having got into Naledi's head, I was immediately drawn into a more complex representation of events. As a writer I am also very concerned about the perspective from which I set up the reader to view the story. The brutality of the police response to the resistance to the imminent removal is shown close up in *Chain of Fire*. Naledi is present at the murder of the community leader Saul Dikobe. In contrast, in *Journey to Jo'burg*, direct brutality is only briefly glimpsed, more often it is intimated through the stories the children hear.

The point I am making is that as a writer I select what I intend to show and how I show it. In common usage the word *censorship* has negative connotations while *selection* has positive ones. While arguing strongly that children's literature should acknowledge and explore areas of pain as well as of pleasure—in other words it should not censor the domain of human pain experienced by children—I would also argue strongly that this has to be done with considerable care. I would not adopt an anticensorship position of "anything goes," and I certainly want young people to be protected from gratuitous violence.

Racism, in any form, is gratuitous violence. It brutalizes quite wantonly and indiscriminately, while the whole process can seem absolutely normal. During the colonial era, there were three predominant ways in which black people were represented in books for children: as savage, comic buffoon, or faithful servant. Such images promoted and reinforced ideas of European superiority in a young generation, denying and violating the individuality of people enslaved, colonized, and oppressed. Oppression also rests on the oppressor's sensibilities being brutalized so that she or he does not acknowledge the equal humanity of the oppressed.

However, while librarians have a great responsibility in their selection of books to which young people of varying ages will have open access, educators also have a responsibility for developing critical awareness in young readers themselves. Children need to learn how to deconstruct racist imagery and to understand the processes by which people have been, and are, denied their humanity. A book like *Let's Visit South Africa*, for instance, which has no place on a library shelf, can be extremely useful in a classroom where children have been reading *Journey to Jo'burg*.

An educational environment in which young people are encouraged to develop this kind of critical awareness, and particularly to reflect on the influences on their own thinking and those around them, presupposes political freedom. While this freedom clearly did not exist in the English county school where "Sir" effectively banned *Journey to Jo'burg*, it also worries me when I find children reading the book in classrooms where the issues are kept firmly six thousand miles away in South Africa. It worries me when, during writer-in-school workshops, I find young people who express horror at apartheid while at the same time see nothing wrong with the racist jokes that are a regular part of the culture of their own playground.

What we need are educators who can create the space for young people to explore such contradictions—the kind of educators I never had as a child. Despite my identification with the oppression of Jewish people in Europe through my Jewish mother, and despite the different versions of Christianity I learned both at the Anglican Church that I attended with my father and in my Catholic school, I was never challenged to contrast the underlying values of fairness and "love thy neighbor" with the reality of our daily life. Today it is common to hear espoused the values of equality and justice. But as human beings we are often unperturbed by our own contradictions. What, for instance, are the implications of values such as equality and justice for the substrata of our own thinking and behavior in everyday affairs?

While many of the letters and other writing I receive from young people express strong feelings about the injustices experienced by Naledi and Tiro, every now and again I hear the voice of a young reader genuinely questioning herself and her own perceptions of the world around her. That's exciting. When eleven-year-old Asma wrote a long letter to me from London, her responses were spilling over with questions relating to the wider society:

> Why shouldn't young people learn what is really happening on Earth. I mean kids our age only learn about the good things, but we never learn the facts. The quicker we learn the facts and forget about fiction, the more intelligent and strong willing we shall become. That way we can make peace.

In replying to Asma, I explained my own understanding of fiction—that it need not only be "made up" and fantasy, but that it could also be an exploration of reality. Her letter, however, contained a more disturbing note of a young person discovering the curbs to her idealism and desire to be able to cross some cultural boundaries:

> I sometimes wonder why the world is like this. I just don't understand how people can be so cruel. Why do people think they're more superior than others? What can we do to change this? How did it start in the first place? I'm always searching through my brains to find the answers. Why does there have to be a different race, culture, religion. Why can't we just be "one" because we can if we try enough, but I guess that's much too much to ask for.

The disillusion implicit in this last statement by an eleven-year-old is surely a sad reflection on our adult society. I only hope that Asma continues her critical resilience.

I began this chapter with the story of an intercepted parcel, and I should complete that tale. In 1991, when I returned freely to South Africa for the first time after many years, I learned from a newspaper cutting that *Journey to Jo'burg* had been unbanned. I assume that *Censoring Reality* has also been unbanned by now. Authors don't get informed directly of such things. However, in 1993 on a return visit to Johannesburg I found myself attending a surreal event—the kind of unprecedented affair for which South Africa has gained a reputation, especially in these extraordinary years of transformation. It was a debate entitled "The Censors Meet the Censored." On the platform a number of formerly banned writers sat alongside the former Chief Censor, the man who in 1984 banned the film version of *Roots* on the grounds that it would be "prejudicial to the relations between black and white"! He was also responsible for the banning of my work. But by 1993 he had done a 180-degree turn and here he was arguing for the minimal amount of censorship required for a democratic and human-based society!

I never asked the question about whether there was actually a Banned Collection with a now redundant librarian. Questions about the future of a society attempting to unlock and unleash itself, with newly released fumbling feet and fingers grasping their way to a supposition called freedom, were far more pressing. Apartheid leaves behind it a terrible legacy, yet there are now fragile possibilities of some kind of peace. So many people have lost their lives in the struggle against apartheid, and so many are still struggling with the legacy. Yet Nelson Mandela has offered out his hand to his ex-jailers, and former archenemies have been forced to sit down and work together for the sake of a future. In these circumstances I believe as a children's writer there is a great responsibility both to be true to the present, which is inextricably linked to the past, and to provide oxygen for the future. As I now work on my next book, I am conscious that it will be for children in South Africa as well as for children in Britain, the United States, and elsewhere. This to me is my biggest challenge.

Professional References

NAIDOO, BEVERLEY. 1985. *Censoring Reality: An Examination of Non-fiction Books on South Africa.* London: British Defense and Aid Fund for Southern Africa/Inner London Education Authority.

———. 1992. *Through Whose Eyes? Exploring Racism: Reader, Text and Context.* Stoke-on-Trent: Trentham Books.

NEWMAN, BERNARD. 1974. *Let's Visit South Africa.* London: Burke Publishing Company.

SURPLUS PEOPLE PROJECT. 1983. *Forced Removals in South Africa.* Cape Town: Surplus People Project.

Children's Literature

NAIDOO, BEVERLEY. 1993. *Chain of Fire.* New York: Harper Trophy.

———. 1988. *Journey to Jo'burg.* New York: Harper Trophy.

THREE

Justifying Violence in Children's Literature

CARL TOMLINSON

Violence, like a thin but noticeable thread, runs through every inch of the fabric of children's literature. Children of ancient Greece heard horrific tales of gods such as Cronus, who sought to retain his place as lord of the universe by swallowing each of his newborn children and keeping them imprisoned in his stomach for ages. Abandonment, decapitations, disembowelings, serial murders, and poisonings were everyday fare in the folktales of the Middle Ages. Even in prudish Victorian times, barbaric torture and gore in literature were considered character-forming for young readers and were all the rage (Kearney 1986). *Struwwelpeter* (Hoffman 1845), one of the all-time best-sellers of German children's literature (Freeman 1977), shocked children into good behavior with such stories in verse as that of Conrad, whose thumbs were cut off because he sucked them, or of Paulina, who was burned to a pile of ash as a result of playing with matches. In modern times the thread of violence has become a fist-sized cable with the advent of the horror-cum-slasher genre and a new, electronic storyteller—television—which offers to the unsupervised child viewer a veritable smorgasbord of violence from soap operas to cartoons to newscasts to talk shows.

Regardless of the fact that violence in children's literature is nothing new, there are those who question its appropriateness, perhaps as a result of the recent and frightening escalation in the incidence of violent crimes committed by young people. Anita Silvey (1989), editor of *The Horn Book Magazine*, comments:

> There are some disturbing changes in the body of books being published for children. More and more frequently, we are seeing distressingly violent books; the subjects chosen for biography, like Peter the Great, seem to be people who have lived violent

I would like to thank my graduate assistant, Jenny Jacobs, for her assistance in preparing this manuscript.

lives; and even Nancy Drew has been repackaged in order to appeal to readers raised on "Miami Vice." If this trend were limited to mediocre books for children and young adults, it would not be quite as upsetting. But violence is also pervading the work of our best and our brightest creators. . . .

As reviewers who care about the content of children's and young adult books, we are appalled at this trend. Sometimes by being a reflection of the times, books become a part of the problem. (5)

In contrast, James Giblin (1972), noted children's book editor, has commented that "today very few subjects are inappropriate in and of themselves; it's all in how the author treats them" (65). "It goes without saying," he continues, "that we don't want or need manuals *for* violence in books for young people, but I think we could use more manuals for personal survival in violent situations" (66).

The Nature of Violence

Social philosophers argue that from the moment of our birth, our existence is polarized between Self and Other. A battle ensues for finite resources, such as our caregivers' time, attention, and love. The struggle soon expands to become one between Those Like Me and Those Like Them, as families, communities, cultures, and nations develop a collective intelligence (in Schostak's words, a "violent imagination"[33]) about justice and injustice, violation and nonviolation. Modern societies exist within a balanced framework of legitimate and illegitimate violence. For example, societies condone some measure of violence on the part of parents to punish, and thereby prevent, the violent or destructive acts of their children. Likewise, society accepts violence by police and armed forces that counteracts and keeps in check violence by criminals and invaders. In both examples the former is considered justifiable, legitimate violence; the latter, illegitimate, unjustifiable. According to Schostak (1986), "The violent imagination becomes a way in which people make sense of the world, identifying structures of justice and of injustice, freedom and slavery, creation and destruction, war and peace" (33–34). Violence is at the very bedrock of civilization.

In light of the foregoing, it follows that violence cannot be avoided in literature, even literature for children, for literature serves to explain the human condition. Regardless of the legitimate concerns of those like Silvey, it is unlikely that violence will cease to be an important element in children's literature. The issue is not whether violence has a place in children's literature, because history has shown that it has. The issue is whether violence in a children's book can be justified. The following examination of a variety of children's stories will demonstrate that some violence in children's books can be justified in terms of the deeper understanding it provides of past events and present conditions, just as institutional violence may be justified in terms of the worthy social and political goals it helps to achieve.

Violence in Traditional Literature

Folktales have plots that frequently hinge on violent acts, and today's illustrated versions make it possible for violence in the stories to be conveyed both visually and textually. Originally aimed at a wider, more mature audience than they are today, folktales often featured cruelty, brute force, and other anxiety-producing elements. Today, many of these stories have been rewritten to "soften" or omit the violence and to bring to the foreground the elements of magic, wish-making, and make-believe to render these tales suitable for very young audiences (Messner 1989). Perhaps, however, middle school and junior high school students would benefit from the earlier, more violent, versions of these timeless tales. Two recent and controversial renderings of "Little Red Riding Hood," one published by Creative Education (now, Creative Company) with illustrations by Sarah Moon, and one published by Doubleday with illustrations by Beni Montresor, are excellent examples. Both versions preserve the older, cautionary tone of this tale and omit the "softening" elements of a woodsy savior and a happy ending. Sarah Moon's chiaroscuric black-and-white photographs (see Figure 3–1) and her use of a long, black sedan as the wolf's conveyance bring this tale forward to our time and render the wolf-man symbolism much more transparent and, hence, more immediate. The concluding line, "Saying these words, this wicked wolf fell upon Little Red Riding Hood, and ate her all up" (34), and the final scene of a bed in terrible disarray show the awful consequences to children whose poor judgment or disobedience get them in serious trouble. Montresor shows the wolf actually stuffing Red Riding Hood, head first, into his mouth (see Figure 3–2), a violent image that brings this cautionary tale's lesson home much more forcefully than would the text alone. Montresor's final illustrations show Red Riding Hood suspended, trance-like, in the wolf's fire-red stomach (womb?), yet the silhouette of an approaching woodsman in the final illustration suggests that the errant child *may* be given another chance (a "rebirth"). Should she or should she not be given this chance? Montresor leaves the decision to the reader.

In "softened" versions of this tale Red Riding Hood's being eaten is never illustrated, and she is barely dispatched before she is saved by a handy woodsman with whom she celebrates her good fortune and the wolf's demise. The tale thus presented becomes no more than an amusing adventure story. Without its violent end, "Little Red Riding Hood" loses its point—strangers and dangerous places should be avoided—and its power as a cautionary tale. Especially in today's often predatory world, the original message in "Little Red Riding Hood" is relevant, and the violence in Moon's and Montresor's versions seems justified, when shared with children and young people who are old enough to be going out on their own.

Violence in Historical Fiction and Nonfiction

Human history is filled with violent episodes. We begin teaching history to our children in the fourth grade and acknowledge that one of the benefits of knowing

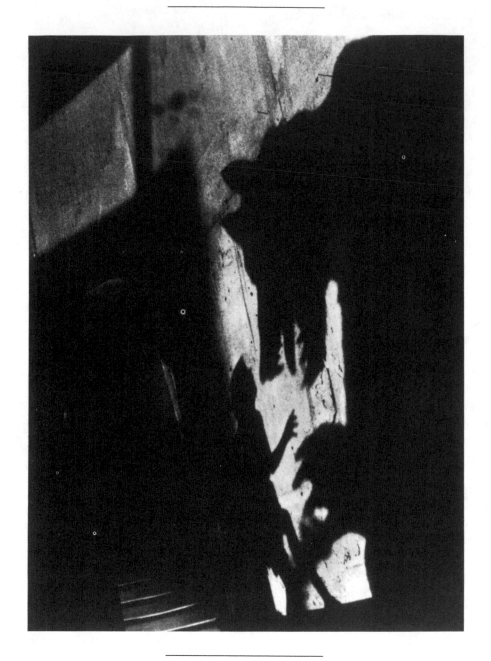

FIG. 3–1

Fig. 3–2

the truth about our past is that it will help prevent our making the same mistakes again. But is it enough to give children the facts alone? Consider, for example, the following passage from a typical middle school history textbook's treatment of the Holocaust.

> The Nazi government's aim was to wipe out all the Jewish people in the lands it conquered. The Germans built huge camps. They brought the Jewish people to these camps. The Jews were branded, tortured, and put to death in gas chambers and furnaces. At first, the treatment of the Jews seemed too horrible to be believed. Only later, when American and Russian soldiers entered these camps, did the world get to see the scenes of the Nazi crimes. When the war ended, the truth about the Nazi cruelties was made known. Six million defenseless and innocent Jews had been

43

killed by the Nazis. This killing of so many Jews has been called the *Holocaust*. (Schwartz and O'Connor 1981, 440–41)

What effect is this passage likely to have on seventh graders? Will the Holocaust, when presented in such dry, academic tones as a list of facts about a remote place and nameless people, become a lesson to remember? Compare that passage to the following segments from the Holocaust novel *Friedrich*, in which the narrator, a peaceful boy, is drawn into the hysteria of a mob and helps destroy a Jewish home.

> It was then that I caught myself shouting "one–two–three" and edging closer with each shout. All at once, I, too, was straining at the door and didn't know how I had gotten there. . . . Very slowly the door gave way. . . . I was pulled along with the throng. When I had a chance to look around me, the sounds of crashing and bumping came from all parts of the house. . . . All this was strangely exhilarating. . . . At first I just played with the hammer. . . . Gently I tapped a cracked pane of glass and it fell out of its frame. By now I was enjoying myself. I swung so hard against the third pane that its splinters fell in bursts to the floor.
>
> With my hammer I cut myself a path through the corridor, smashing aside whatever barred my way: legs of chairs, toppled wardrobes, chamber pots and glassware. I felt so strong! I could have sung I was so drunk with the desire to swing my hammer.
>
> All of a sudden I felt tired and disgusted. On the stairs, I found half a mirror. I looked in it. Then I ran home. (Richter 1970, 91–93)

The message in this disturbing and violent passage is that we are all susceptible to the influence of others, and we can all make dreadful mistakes. The passage, with its vivid images, its known character, its immediacy and intimacy, is far more likely to arouse an emotional response in young readers than the textbook passage. So, too, will the hellish visual images in Maruki's (1980) picture book account of the immediate aftermath of the atomic bombing in *Hiroshima No Pika* (see Figure 3–3) and the unflinching brutality in Spiegelman's (1973) illustrated Holocaust story, *Maus: A Survivor's Tale* (see Figure 3–4) objectify the cruelty of war and permit their messages to connect with readers. In *Hiroshima No Pika*, minutes after the bomb has turned the city into a cauldron, Mii and her mother make their way through the ruins, carrying Mii's badly burned father toward the river.

> There were crowds of people fleeing the fire. Mii saw children with their clothes burned away, lips and eyelids swollen. They were like ghosts, wandering about, crying in weak voices. Some people, all their strength gone, fell face down on the ground, and others fell on top of them. There were heaps of people everywhere. (14)

The piles of charred and writhing bodies in Maruki's roiling, grisly, green and red drawings is the true message about war: people, including innocent children, die or are wounded in great numbers. Likewise, Spiegelman's stark, surreal drawings leave

FIG. 3–3

little doubt that war is montrous and can bring forth the "monster" (that is, evil, capacity for violence) that resides in each of us. Unlike textbook accounts and television coverage of war, which most often focus on acts of aggression, well-written trade books focus on the results of aggression—the uprooted and ruined lives, the suffering from pain and sadness, and the waste of lives, energy, and resources. If the violence in these stories can convince young people that they must find peaceful ways to settle their differences, it is justified.

The history of the United States has its share of violent episodes. Particularly relevant are the many instances of oppression, often overtly violent, sometimes subtle, perpetrated on minorities in this country. These controversial episodes and the accompanying issue of racism have often been omitted from or given scant attention in history books. Consequently, many children have grown up ignorant of the injustices and hardships these people have suffered, of the important contributions these minorities have made in the development of this country, and of the historical roots of the civil-rights movement. Should we wait until young people are in high school and already have firmly ingrained attitudes to teach them the truth? Why, if history is introduced in the upper elementary grades, should we not present the whole truth from the beginning, or at least as early as possible? Books such as Milton Meltzer's *Columbus and the World Around Him* (1990), Mildred Taylor's *The Friendship*

45

FIG. 3–4

(1987), or Laurence Yep's *Dragon's Gate* (1993) help to fill in the gaps left by history texts by presenting the struggles of minorities with much of the violence and suffering intact. Meltzer's biography presents not only the great accomplishments of Columbus, but also the details of his barbarous treatment of a peaceful native population in his ruthless pursuit of gold, as in the following passage.

> So he ordered all Indians from the age of fourteen up, to collect a fixed amount of gold every three months. Each person who delivered his tribute of gold was given a copper token to hang around his neck. Indians found without that token had their hands cut off and were left to bleed to death. (142)

Readers of *The Friendship* join the Logan children as shocked bystanders who watch a white store owner shoot an elderly African American for calling him by his first name. In the following passage from *Dragon's Gate*, Otter, a Chinese boy who has immigrated to the United States to work on the transcontinental railroad, is brutalized by Kilroy, the foreman, for threatening to quit.

> I didn't believe my ears when I heard the crack of the whip; but the next moment, I felt the fiery pain across my back. The heavy whip had ripped through even the thick padding of my coat and my shirt as if they were paper.
>
> With a scream of pain, I fell to my knees. I put a hand to my back and winced as I felt the wet stripe across my back. When I brought my hand in front of me again, I saw the blood. As I held out my hand to him, drops fell from my fingers to stain the snow. *"You hurt me."*
>
> This time when the lash struck, I had no strength in my legs, and its force sent me sprawling on my face.
>
> *"There's only one way down from this mountain and that's my way. You sabe me, John?"* Kilroy demanded. (174–75)

Few young people can read or hear these stories without reacting with indignation. History will speak to them. Because violent passages in excellent historical fiction and nonfiction help to give young readers a deeper, more complete understanding of the story of our past and its relevance to the present, the violence is justified. Because readers come to know and care about book characters and can see themselves in the characters, they will attend more to the social and political contexts of the characters' lives. In other words, they will learn the lessons that history has to teach. Aranka Siegal, author of the Holocaust memoir *Upon the Head of the Goat: A Childhood in Hungary, 1939–1944* (1981), states,

> I believe we all protect children too much. We say, don't tell the children. This is not good, because these [today's] children cannot take anything. They have to grow up in a world where terrible things happen, and if they don't have any experience in overcoming hardship, then they think they won't be able to face it when it does happen to them. (Natov and DeLuca 1988, 82)

Violence in Contemporary Realism

There are those who persist in their efforts to provide an illusory "protected" childhood for young people by trying to censor, ban, or rewrite anything controversial in children's books, including violence. Bardola (1993), on the other hand, makes a case for violence in children's books:

> There is good reason for modern children's writers to address violence in their books head on, to make it a topic of their work. Violence (as no one needs to be reminded today) is an almost daily part of children's lives, either directly—through war, civil unrest, or abuse at home—or through the all-pervasive media. . . . It is

47

not right that these children be left alone to deal with these uncomfortable subjects with no recourse to books which can lead them to reflection and deeper understanding. They need children's books that help them cope with the circumstances of their lives and the images in the media. (7)

As Adams (1986) points out, books can serve to broaden, refine, and balance the often simplistic messages given by the media, which seem to be dedicated to the glorification of violence. Unlike MTV and HBO, high quality contemporary realistic fiction probes the social and political causes and sad consequences of violence. Where television uses explosions (emotional, verbal, or physical) like fireworks, filling screens with visually exciting bursts of flame and anger that are pure entertainment, books such as *AK* (Dickinson 1990) take time to portray the long-term suffering or loss these explosions cause. Where television often uses child abuse to make suspenseful stalker movies, books such as *Staying Fat for Sarah Byrnes* (Crutcher 1993) emphasize the ways abused children can find help and can end the abuse. Where television concentrates on "colorful" homeless characters, books such as *Monkey Island* (Fox 1993) reveal the weaknesses in our social and political systems that allow or cause homelessness. Where the subtle violence of poverty is rarely dealt with on television shows that children watch, books such as *We Are All in the Dumps with Jack and Guy* (Sendak 1993) and *Secret City, USA* (Holman 1990) make children aware that many of their peers, through no fault of their own, go without adequate food, housing, health care, or schooling. Undoubtedly, some of the incidents written about in modern contemporary realism are harrowing. But if a harrowing vicarious experience will warn children away from actual experimentation with drugs, guns, gangs, or crime, or encourage them to recognize or find help for any form of abuse, or help them to be more sensitive to the problems of their less fortunate peers, the violence is justified.

Gratuitous Violence

By no means is all violence in children's books justifiable. The media's "Gore Is Good" product has its equivalent in the extremely popular children's and young adult horror formula books such as those churned out, or cloned, by R. L. Stine and Christopher Pike. In these books, violence and titillation are substitutes for substance and thought. "The Caretaker" in Pike's *Chain Letter 2: The Ancient Evil* (1992), for example, summarily kills or cripples a group of friends one by one. Kipp is drenched with gasoline and torched:

> The flames whipped up his legs all the way to his hair, and the scream that poured out of Kipp's throat rent Tony's heart. Kipp thrashed up and down like a demented scarecrow for several seconds in the worst imaginable pain a human being could experience. (116)

Brenda is forced to cut off her own index finger:

> Brenda sat up, her face a mask of fury and fear. "How could I save my life? It wasn't hard. I got drunk enough and got a knife that was sharp enough and cut it off. Then I put the finger in an envelope with the chain letter and—" (151)

Alison is nearly killed by a monster:

> She threw the car in reverse and backed out of the wall of weeds. But as she flew backward she hit something hard—maybe a body. . . .
>
> It was at that instant that the car door was ripped off its hinges.
>
> The girl stood in the moonlight three feet to Alison's left, dripping embalming fluid from her crushed guts and grinning from ear to ear. There was a tire mark across her tattered black blouse. . . .
>
> She reached inside the car and grabbed Alison by the throat. (186)

Who cares about Kipp, Brenda, or Alison, or any of the undeveloped characters in slasher and horror stories who serve as mere ducks in a shooting gallery for the real hero, Nameless Evil, to destroy? No one. Consequently, readers feel little or no remorse as one character after another is slashed, sawn, sliced, or skewered. On the contrary, readers look forward to the next bloodletting, since violence is the only feature in these otherwise featureless exercises in the banal. Violence thus used for its shock value as a device for entertainment is difficult to justify, particularly if this excess serves to blunt young readers' sensitivity to violence in all its forms.

Regardless of how adults may view any children's or young adult book that contains violence, banning or censoring it is no solution. Denying children free access to books is no way to teach them responsible choice or to promote their intellectual growth. For children to discover for themselves the inferiority of formula books to real literature and then to voluntarily choose the latter shows greater growth than does reading good books because they are the only ones available. Grappling with the issues and rooting out the causes of social problems found in controversial, yet well-written, stories gives children an important intellectual challenge and helps them to formulate their own beliefs and values. Parents, teachers, and librarians themselves benefit from the knowledge these books contain. Such reading may, in fact, give adults the confidence to discuss controversial topics with children for the first time. Rather than trying to protect children against any book that contains violence, adults would be better advised to seek out and read those that are worthy of children's attention and then offer these titles to children as alternatives to the trash.

Professional References

ADAMS, DENNIS M. 1986. "Literature for Children: Avoiding Controversy and Intellectual Challenge." *Top of the News* 42(3): 304–308.

BARDOLA, NICOLA. 1993. "The Sense of Violence in Children's Literature." Translated from the German by Jeffrey Garrett. *Bookbird: World of Children's Books* 31(3): 6–7.

FREEMAN, THOMAS. 1977. "Heinrich Hoffman's *Struwwelpeter*: An Inquiry into the Effects of Violence in Children's Literature." *Journal of Popular Culture* 10(4): 808–20.

GIBLIN, JAMES C. 1972. "Violence: Factors Considered by a Children's Book Editor." *Elementary English* 49: 64–7.

KEARNEY, ANTHONY. 1986. "Savage and Barbaric Themes in Victorian Children's Writing." *Children's Literature in Education* 17(4): 233–40.

MESSNER, RUDOLF. 1989. "Children and Fairy Tales—What Unites Them and What Divides Them." *Western European Education* 21(2): 6–28.

NATOV, RONI, and GERALDINE DeLUCA. 1988. "The Darkest Side: Writing for Children about the Holocaust: An Interview with Aranka Siegal." *The Lion and the Unicorn* 12(1): 76–96.

SCHOSTAK, JOHN F. 1986. *Schooling the Violent Imagination.* London: Routledge and Kegan Paul.

SCHWARTZ, MELVIN, and JOHN R. O'CONNOR. 1981. *The New Exploring American History.* New York: Globe Book Company.

SILVEY, ANITA. 1989. "The Serpent in the Garden." *The Horn Book Magazine* 65(1): 5.

Children's Literature

CRUTCHER, CHRIS. 1993. *Staying Fat for Sarah Byrnes.* New York: Greenwillow.

DICKINSON, PETER. 1990. *AK.* London: Gollancz.

FOX, PAULA. 1991. *Monkey Island.* New York: Orchard.

HOFFMAN, HEINRICH. 1845. *Der Struwwelpeter.* Rastatt, Baden: Favorit Verlag.

HOLMAN, FELICE. 1990. *Secret City, USA.* New York: Scribner's.

MARUKI, TOSHI. 1982. *Hiroshima No Pika.* New York: Lothrop, Lee and Shepard.

MELTZER, MILTON. 1990. *Columbus and the World around Him.* New York: Franklin Watts.

PERRAULT, CHARLES. 1991. *Little Red Riding Hood.* Illustrated by Beni Montresor. New York: Doubleday.

———. 1983. *Little Red Riding Hood.* Illustrated by Sarah Moon. Mankato, MN: Creative Company.

PIKE, CHRISTOPHER. 1992. *Chain Letter 2: The Ancient Evil.* New York: Archway.

RICHTER, HANS PETER. 1970. *Friedrich.* New York: Holt.

SENDAK, MAURICE. 1993. *We Are All in the Dumps with Jack and Guy.* New York: HarperCollins.

SIEGAL, ARANKA. 1981. *Upon the Head of the Goat: A Childhood in Hungary 1939–1944.* New York: Farrar, Straus & Giroux.

SPIEGELMAN, ART. 1973. *Maus: A Survivor's Tale.* New York: Pantheon.

TAYLOR, MILDRED. 1987. *The Friendship.* Illustrated by Max Ginsburg. New York: Dial.

YEP, LAURENCE. 1993. *Dragon's Gate.* New York: HarperCollins.

FOUR

The Disturbing Image in Children's Picture Books: Fearful or Fulfilling?

BARBARA KIEFER

As part of a unit on Japan third and fourth graders were studying World War II and the events surrounding the bombing of Hiroshima and Nagasaki. Their teacher had read *Sadako and the Thousand Paper Cranes* (Coerr 1977) to the class and had created a center with information books, periodicals, and copies of some primary source materials such as newspaper reports that children examined and discussed. However, it was not until she read Toshi Maruki's picture book *Hiroshima No Pika* (1980) that the children began to write and create art work that expressed important understandings and feelings about this critical event in modern history (Kiefer 1988).

The book is based on a survivor's account of the bombing of Hiroshima, and the vivid, expressionistic illustrations called forth powerful responses from the children. A fourth grader created a picture of the atomic dome in Hiroshima and wrote:

> As the evening sky turns to the dark night sky we light paper lanterns and let them float freely on the open pond with the spirits of our ancestors. The purples, pinks, and blues of the sky reflect onto the atomic dome which in 1945 August, the atom bomb blew up on top of. Today is August 6 1982 and we are celebrating peace day. I wrote on the lanterns the name of a dear friend and relative that died of the atom bomb.

A third grader created several watercolor paintings in response to *Hiroshima No Pika* and then wrote three pieces about the dropping of the atomic bomb. The first piece was a first-person account of the bombing, and the second was a brief book review of *Hiroshima No Pika*. Her third composition was a very personal reaction that seemed to synthesize her experiences with the study. She wrote:

A Solemn Wish for Peace

As the sun sets in the evening it leaves a blue and purple stain in the sky which is in good contrast to the lake as we free our lanterns into the water which is like a key, the key to our ancestors spirits. We see them dance in the water and pray it will never happen again. besides,

This is our cry, this is our prayer
Peace in the world

There can be no doubt that the children's responses to the study were deeply felt or that the illustrations in *Hiroshima No Pika* contributed to their personal understanding. One child talked about the colors used in the pictures in the book and explained that the "colors are dismal dark and gray and they make you feel almost terrified to see all those people dead and dying." Several children compared *Return to Hiroshima*, an information book with black and white photographs, to *Hiroshima No Pika*. One stated:

> First of all this [*Return to Hiroshima*] is photographs and this [*Hiroshima No Pika*] is almost chalky watercolors. Since these are photographs they have just the obvious shape of it and you can tell what it is. But these pictures [*Hiroshima No Pika*]— people really don't have certain shapes to them. They look sad because they didn't have much of a certain shape to them. If this was in a photograph you could just look through it but if you look at *Hiroshima No Pika* you can really look at the pictures to get a feeling of the story.

Another child agreed, "With photographs it wouldn't be that sad. I don't think the pictures give a setting to the story. It makes you want to *think* more."

A third grader who had been looking at the small vignettes and single-page illustrations present in the first part of the book remarked, "The colors are lighter and they're happier [at first]." Then she turned to a double-page spread with no printed text, done in tones of red, rust, and black. "It gives me the impression that the illustrator's just seen the bomb happen and she just choked and doesn't want to talk about it and she'll show you a picture of what happened." Thus, through their talk, their art, and their writing, these children revealed the ways in which a picture book informed their feelings and ideas and deepened their aesthetic understanding.

Initially, however, their teacher was hesitant about reading Maruki's *Hiroshima No Pika* to the group, afraid that this survivor's account and these stark images might prove too disturbing. Indeed, the children's reactions during and just following the initial read-aloud session were much quieter than usual. Instead of the enthusiastic talk that often accompanied read-aloud sessions in this classroom there were very few comments or questions. One child asked why they would call the bomb "Little Boy," and another tried to understand why the building underneath the explosion wasn't destroyed. After the teacher had finished the book the children talked about Maruki's reasons for creating the pictures and writing the book. One child remarked,

"The pictures were so sad like when he's coughing up blood and his hair was starting to fall out and he started turning purple." Another child said softly, "Do not read that again."

Indeed, many adults would not read to children any picture books that contain disturbing subject matter or that deal with sensitive issues. Kimmel (1982), for example, wondered if books like Maurice Sendak's *Outside Over There* (1981) or Molly Bang's *The Grey Lady and the Strawberry Snatcher* (1980) weren't more suitable for adults than for children. In many cases books that contain troubling or distressing images are the subject of censorship efforts. As a result, many elementary classroom teachers worry about using anything but the least controversial picture books in their classrooms.

Despite misgivings on the part of adults I believe picture books such as *Hiroshima No Pika* can lend a powerful impact to classroom studies and can engender deeply felt responses on the part of children. In the remainder of this chapter I will describe how art has a unique meaning-making capacity and how illustrators can mediate difficult messages for children through the choices they make in illustrating stories about war, death, and the Holocaust.

The Meaning-Making Power of Art

Picture books are singular art forms in which images and ideas interact to create an experience that is more than the sum of individual parts. Any art form can be seen as a form of communication (Langer 1942; Kaelin 1989), yet each has a unique way in which meaning is symbolized. For example, while both language and visual art have a meaning-expressing potential, the two are not identical and cannot be matched at a "word" or "sentence" level. Gombrich (1982) argues that while both language and visual images have the capacity to express, arouse, and describe, the visual image is most effective in evoking emotions while it is unable to match "the statement function of language" (138).

This lack of specificity in pictorial images, however, may be what lends them their emotional punch. While an author can be more unequivocal about meanings through word choice and composition, an artist can enhance our affective response to a book through the choice of elements of art, knowing that there are emotional associations we bring to certain configurations of line, shape, color, texture, and value. We may feel, for example, that wavy lines convey serenity while angular, jagged lines convey tension or excitement. The children talking about *Hiroshima No Pika* were responding to these affective meanings when they talked about shapes and colors that made them feel sad or terrified. In addition, the artist chooses principles of composition and layout and certain historical and cultural conventions that also may be highly effective in expressing meaning and evoking emotion. In a picture book even technical choices relating to book production such as the original medium, the design of the endpapers, or the typeface can enhance the impact of the book. When the illustrator's choices regarding the elements of art, the principles of composition, and the technical elements of book production work with the author's words to extend and enhance the meaning of the work, we have an art object that can evoke complex emotional and intellectual responses (see Kiefer). Such an art object can provide the reader with an important aesthetic experience, an experience that will be qualitatively different from viewing a television news report of an incident or seeing a photograph of a scene.

Images of War, Death, and the Holocaust

Our present century has seen horrors that are hard to conceive in both scale and savagery. In telling the story of the bombing of Hiroshima in *Hiroshima No Pika*, Toshi Maruki highlights a single story, a survivor's account that connects young readers to the horrors of the event without overwhelming them with the unthinkable immensity of the occurrence. In words and pictures Maruki depicts the daily life of young Mii and her family in Hiroshima just prior to the bombing. Maruki includes details of wartime preparations as well as aspects of the family's domestic life. Although the cover, which depicts figures engulfed by flames, is a clear signal of the book's disturbing content, the reader is not immediately overwhelmed by the story's emotionally charged content. We open the book to plain white endpapers and a title page with a small picture of the atomic dome. For the first eleven pages the images are placed on only one side of the double page spread, balanced on several of the first pages by small vignettes on the opposite page. The type, an unpretentious, nonthreatening serif design, is placed in orderly blocks in the middle of a white page. Colors, though toned down by the grey-brown background include cheerful blues and yellows.

Once the bomb is dropped, however, the lighter colors of the early pages give way to fiery reds and charcoal blacks, a visual reminder of the fires Mii and her family try to escape and a foretelling of the charred city that Hiroshima will become. The pictorial layout also changes, moving across the gutter or center of the book to encompass two-thirds of the page, then back to a single page, then to a full double-page spread. This layout, used throughout the rest of the book, sets up a subtle visual rhythm and gives us a sense of the pulsing nature of the firestorm.

Two double-page spreads contain no printed text at all. These are the scenes that show people fleeing the fire and survivors seeking shelter. In both cases words, in their precision, would lessen the impact of the tragedy. The third grader who said that the illustrator "just choked and doesn't want to talk about it and she'll show you a picture of what happened" understood that what is impossible to signify with words can be powerfully expressed by a picture.

As the story progresses and Mii and her family flee the center of the city, they encounter scene after scene of horror. Here, however, the artist's style moderates the impact of the written text. Maruki's elongated figures, the lack of details, the hazy contours, and the flowing brush strokes of the paint distance the reader, making it possible to read words that tell of floating bodies and dead babies.

As the story nears its end and the narrative takes us years into the future, Mii and her mother are pictured on a single page. The soft blues and lavenders of the figures and the return to large expanse of white page signal that the worst horrors are over. This is clearly the denouement and the point at which the reader can take a moment to regain control of overwhelming emotions. Maruki does not want us to forget the story, however, and at the book's end the picture of Peace Day remembrances takes up two-thirds of the page. A return to bright red and orange recharges our emotions and ensures that readers will remember Maruki's words, "It can't happen again, if no one drops the bomb."

In Eleanor Coerr's *Sadako* (1993) the bombing of Hiroshima is remembered in a different way. Coerr provides a new and shorter version of her novel, *Sadako and the Thousand Paper Cranes*. Ed Young's illustrations bring a new dimension to the story of a young girl who died from leukemia contracted as a result of the bombing. This story takes place in 1954 so the hazy edges created by the pastel chalk used in the original art serve to soften the horrors of the actual event of the bombing and instead focus our attention on the character of Sadako and on her story.

The book's dust cover is done in black and white chalk with a tiny touch of red. A double image of a crane with spread wings superimposed on a close-up of a child's eyes recalls the flash point of the bomb and the images engraved on thousands of retinas. The book's title is printed in a regal purple that is picked up in the endpapers and echoed throughout the book. This color unifies the overall design and suggests the great dignity and courage with which this child dealt with her life and death. If we lift the dust cover, however, we find that the bound cover has a repeating pattern of origami cranes, some in bright colors, drawn over a pale green muted pastel background. Here is a message of hope. The green color suggests new life and the cranes represent an important motif in the story in addition to a belief in a higher power. Thus this tragedy is imbued with a subtle sense of hope before we even begin reading the words.

Throughout the rest of the book Young uses elements of color and value rather than pictorial details to accentuate themes and intensify the mood. In the early part of the book when, full of hope, Sadako awakens on Peace Day the colors are soft blues and earthy greens and browns set on a large expanse of white page. On the next several double-page spreads, as Sadako awakens her family and sets off with her friend to the Peace Park, white continues to predominate but the colors are less vibrant. Dark browns and purples seem to foreshadow tragedy. Even the blue shadows cast by the two girls as they face the memorial recalls the shadows of the dead imposed on the cold concrete. When night comes and the people light candles of remembrance we see the Atomic Dome lit by candlelight and imposed against a solid black sky.

On the following page the color shifts abruptly to brilliant oranges and reds intermingled with green. These colors signify a return to Sadako's daily routine. We sense her excitement at being chosen to run on the relay team at school and the energy of her training. But coming so suddenly after the muted, softened colors of the previous pages these brighter hues also recall the firestorm of the bombing and anticipate the onset of Sadako's illness.

On subsequent pages the illustrations continue to predict tragedy. Even though the words tell of preparations for holidays and Sadako's continued passion for racing, the colors in the illustrations continue to darken. At this point Young does not blend his chalks but instead allows the rough texture of the pastel paper to show through, suggesting the terrible news that follows. By preparing the reader in this way Young lessens the emotional impact of the news that Sadako has leukemia. Indeed on the double-page spread where the text conveys the awful word, the colors of the illustrations return to muted green and yellow-green and the textures soften.

The colors continue to accentuate the meaning of the story as we follow the course of Sadako's illness and her hope that if she folds one thousand paper cranes they will carry her wishes to heaven. As her death approaches, however, the pages grow dark with thick layers of blue and black color and the typeface changes from black to white. When Sadako sees the faces of her family gathered around her bed and looks at the paper cranes hanging from the ceiling the predominant color of the double-page spread is predominantly black with slashes of brilliant color on the wings of the paper cranes. The text reads, "Sadako sighed and closed her eyes. How beautiful and free they were" (43). But the images tell us that she has died.

On the following page our belief is confirmed by the first sentence. "Sadako died on October 25, 1955" (45). But here the illustrations are done in soft, almost transparent layers of orange and blue chalk. Against this dawning sky are the hazy images of cranes in flight. The emotional impact of this change in color, texture, and perspective is intense. These two pages represent the climax of the story but also a message of hope. They serve to introduce the book's final pages, which tell of Sadako's statue in the Peace Park and the efforts of millions of children to remember her. The final picture on a single page picks up and intensifies the orange and blue-green color scheme to evoke the image of the statue and repeat the words carved on the base: "This is our cry, this is our prayer: Peace in the world" (48). Because of the impact of the illustrators' choices in books like *Hiroshima No Pika* and *Sadako*, children of today are not likely to be repelled or terrified by these tragedies. Instead they make this plea for peace their own.

Hiroshima No Pika and *Sadako* tell of the overwhelming destruction wrought by the atomic bomb. Although the styles of the two artists are very different, in both books artistic elements such as colors, shapes, elongated figures, a lack of detail, or an emphasis on the effects of paint or pastel serve to distance the reader to some extent from the actual events. At the same time they do not lessen the emotional impact of the story. In *Sami and the Time of the Troubles*, on the other hand, Florence Parry Heide and Judith Heide Gilliland (1992) tell of another type of conflict, the war in Lebanon. This war is characterized not by a single explosion and its devastating after-effects, but by never-ending hostilities marked by short periods of normalcy.

In this story the representational style of illustrator Ted Lewin is appropriate to convey a sense of reality to events that are far from most readers' understanding. The detailed, realistic pictures of Sami's life provide a different, although no less important, emotional accent to this story.

On the surface, *Sami and the Time of the Troubles* seems to be a simple story of a family's day-to-day existence. We are not told the details of battles, nor do we witness bombing or death firsthand as we did in *Hiroshima No Pika* and *Sadako*. Instead we experience the extremes of a seemingly endless war. Heide and Gilliland tell of the sad futility of Sami's father's death, of the family's fears of living with the unknown day after day, and of the sounds of nighttime bombs. Yet they tell also of better days: the joys of a visit to the beach on a "quiet day," a wedding procession, children at play, and the pleasure of a fresh peach obtained in the local market. These contrasts are emphasized and intensified by Lewin's artistic choices.

The cover picture of Sami sitting in his family's shelter surrounded by a lantern, a portable radio, and a brass vase summarizes the important elements of the story. The intricately patterned rugs that surround him are witness to the complexity of the war in which Sami and his family are caught. The intensity conveyed by the cover painting is continued in the endpapers where Lewin pictures a bombed-out street in Beirut. Indeed this sense of energy is maintained throughout the book on each of the fully illustrated double-page spreads. The type, set over the full page paintings, does not detract from the lively power of Lewin's full-color palette. Even Lewin's use of his watercolor medium conveys a sense of drama and heightens the story's dramatic oppositions. Unlike more traditional uses of muted watercolor wash, Lewin's watercolor brush is heavily saturated with pigment so that colors are intense and the values sharply contrasting. Yet the colors flow across the pages, and the bold brush strokes add further vigor to Sami's story, providing a sense of action and movement.

Lewin's ability to give three-dimensional form to his figures and scenes and his depiction of his characters' personalities bring the story to life and connect the reader to Sami's experiences. Thus, even though the last pages are overwhelmingly dark in tone, the reader is left with some hope and is fully sympathetic with the pleas of Sami and his friends who on "the day of the children" plead with their elders to "stop the fighting!"

Realistic depiction is also used in Christophe Gallaz and Roberto Innocenti's *Rose Blanche* (1985), but here it lends a horrifying irony to this story of the Holocaust as seen through the eyes of a child. Rose Blanche is a young girl living in Germany as soldiers arrive to take over her town. For half of the book she is the narrator of events. She tells of the small changes in her life and also relates some of its simple pleasures. But when she sees a young boy forced into a truck at gun point, she follows the truck and discovers people living behind barbed wire. This marks a major shift in her viewpoint, and she subsequently goes hungry to slip food to the inmates within the wires (it also marks a shift from first-person to third-person narration). Toward the end of the war as armies of liberation approach her town, Rose Blanche tries to get to the camp but becomes lost in the fog. The words of the story imply that she is shot by soldiers who mistake her for the enemy. The text tells us only that "Rose Blanche's mother waited a long time for her little girl" (30).

Rose Blanche is a very different type of book than the previous three. *Hiroshima No Pika*, *Sadako*, and *Sami and the Time of the Troubles* sought to inform, to tell stories of real people, or to give fictionalized accounts of real events. *Rose Blanche* is more clearly meant as an antiwar message. By telling the story from the point of view of a naive child the author heightens the irony of war's futility almost to the point of sarcasm. Moreover, the written text leaves out crucial details from Rose Blanche's story. The reader is not told that this is World War II; the words *Nazi*, *Jew*, or even *concentration camp* are never mentioned. Nor do we learn any details of suffering and destruction from the text. In addition, the narrative's faithfulness to real or even likely events are subsumed by the book's theme. Although the setting is a real place, it is unlikely that a German child would be as unaware of the war or of the Nazis as the narrator would have us think. It is even less likely that a young child could slip out of town and make it to a concentration camp to feed inmates day after day, year after year. Instead of choosing to detail particular or even possible events, the writer leaves it to the reader's imagination or to the illustrator's handiwork to fill in the gaps in meaning. The book thus assumes the character of allegory.

Indeed Roberto Innocenti's illustrations provide the weight of information in *Rose Blanche* in addition to conveying the emotional impact. The pictures are highly detailed with almost photo-realistic renderings of scenes and figures. These are alleviated only by a touch of caricature in some of the German figures. It is through the pictorial details that we identify the time of the story as World War II and the soldiers as Nazis. We see the yellow stars on the inmates' striped uniforms before Rose Blanche does and so identify the long wooden house she has found behind the barbed wire as a death camp. We see her touching a blue flower caught in the barbed wire as soldiers approach through the fog, and on the final pages we see the blue flower dried up, and pinched between the twisted wire. At first this detail is lost in the bright beauty of a sunny spring landscape. But if we doubted the implication that she has been killed, it is harder to ignore the final page of the book where the flower is highlighted in a small square frame surrounded by white. If some of the pictorial details can be understood only by a reader with the correct background knowledge, the awful irony of the story is available through the use of this floral symbol, a visual detail that provides the clue to the truth.

The use of color and layout also provides clues to the true nature of the story. The colors used are predominantly red and green. Normally these colors function as complements, that is, when placed next to each other, each appears brighter and more energetic. In *Rose Blanche*, however, the green is not the bright green of living things but the dull khaki of military uniforms and the grey-green of ash. This color scheme accentuates the somber and depressing mood, belying the smiling faces and the innocuous words of the early pages of the book and becoming more intense as the story unfolds. Except for the red used in the Nazi flags and arm bands, which is clear and intense, the overall red tones are also darkened and resemble the rusty red color of dried blood. This lends a sense of doom to the story, suggesting the pain and devastation of the war that the words never mention.

The visual design of the book is also oppressive. The printed type is placed at the top of every page. The pictures take up almost all the space on the pages, suggesting that this is where the important message really lies. Until the last eight pages of the book, the layout of the pictures alternates between a single scene shown on a double-page spread and two pictures separated by the white border at the center. The visual rhythm set up by this design is as relentless as the pounding of soldiers' boots.

Thus the depressing mood established by color and layout is unalleviated until the end of the book when suddenly the turning page shows a yellow-green field alive with bright flowers and blooming trees under a sky of springtime blue. This abrupt change hammers home the story's irony. We can view this scene with relief at being released from the intense emotions previously felt, or we can notice Rose Blanche's small blue flower hanging from the barbed wire fence that is rapidly being covered by new growth.

Conclusion

In *The Narrative Symbol in Childhood Literature*, Golden (1990) proposes five different relationships between illustrations and text in picture books that are based in semiotic theory (the theory of how signs convey meaning). In three of these relationships, she argues, the illustrations play a complimentary, extending, or highlighting role but the text can be read separate from the pictures without any essential loss of meaning. In the other two relationships that she suggests, the illustrations either provide information crucial to the written text or clarify and go beyond information in the words. In these last two relationships the pictures must be present if all information is to be obtained.

While such categories provide interesting ways to analyze information systems in picture books they do not adequately explain the deeper understandings possible in good picture books. In *Hiroshima No Pika, Sadako, Sami and the Time of the Troubles*, and *Rose Blanche* the pictures provide more than information, they provide the context for telling of human brutality in ways that do not repel or frighten but that evoke the deepest intellectual and emotional responses. If indeed the picture book is an art form that "hinges on the interdependence of pictures and words, on the simultaneous display of two facing pages, and on the drama of the turning page" (Bader 1976, 1), we see that partnership evolve in different ways in the four books discussed here. In *Hiroshima No Pika* and *Sadako* there is an interaction between pictures and text that heightens our emotional response without overwhelming us with feelings we cannot handle. In some pages of *Hiroshima No Pika* and *Sadako*, words hold back from telling us what the images and colors suggest. On other pages, pictures mediate or soften the blow of details made clear by the words. Thus a subtle emotional equilibrium is maintained without diminishing the author's message.

In *Sami and the Time of the Troubles* the realistic depiction and strong design work closely with the story to heighten our emotional involvement. This is possible because the words describing the destructiveness of war keep the horrors at a distance; we do not meet bodies lying on the streets or face death with the main character. In addition, Lewin's illustrations may allow the Western reader to more deeply understand and empathize with the plight of children in a far-away country.

In *Rose Blanche*, on the other hand, the illustrations take on the major burden of storytelling. Innocenti's highly realistic paintings and his skillful use of elements and principles of design provide the cruel details and intensify the mood of hopelessness. However, the reader may be distanced from despair because the words tell so little. Thus a young child will simply not have the background knowledge to understand the full horror of the Holocaust. Older readers who are more knowledgeable still have the option of ignoring the evidence that Rose Blanche has been killed, very possibly by the soldiers sent to liberate the concentration camp's inmates. Here the book's cruel message is mediated both by the capacity of the pictures to arouse our emotions and by the pictures' inability to match "the statement function of language" (Gombrich 1982, 138).

Thus in looking at picture books that present difficult issues to children we must consider the range of choices available to the artist in expressing visual meaning. In reflecting on the artist's choices we must examine the ways in which visual elements can add to the intellectual understanding and emotional engagement with the book. For it may be that by understanding the ways in which the illustrations mediate, enhance, or intensify these messages, teachers and children alike can come to better understand their own responses to the books and to the ways in which they connect us to our world and to our future.

With these understandings about the meaning-making potential of illustrations and the ways in which the pictures interact with the text, therefore, teachers and children should not be uncomfortable reading picture books that deal with difficult topics. In a book such as Margaret Wild's *Let the Celebrations Begin!* (1991), illustrated by Julie Vivas, for example, they will find a very different story of the Holocaust, one imbued with hope rather than horror. In Eve Bunting's *Fly Away Home* (1991), with illustrations by Ron Himler, and in Maurice Sendak's *We Are All in the Dumps with Jack and Guy* (1993) they will learn about issues of homelessness. As writers and illustrators continue to use their art to explore and question their world, teachers and children will find other picture books that challenge their assumptions and engage their passions.

Maxine Greene has argued that "art education, like aesthetic education, can create domains where there are new possibilities of vision and awareness. . . . Educators can help awareness feed into an expanding life of meaning, can make increasingly available moments of clarity, moments of joy" (1978, 196). Picture books such as those discussed here call for sensitive examination, careful discussion, and thoughtful responses that are possible for teachers and children of any age.

Whether the illustrator seeks to heighten or soften the impact of a painful message for children, the result need not be one that traumatizes or terrifies. Instead the experience of engaging with a work of art can be transforming. The experiences of reading, talking about, and responding to picture books, no matter what the subject matter, can allow children to feel deeply and think fully about human issues, and then to consider the world around them as if it could be otherwise.

Professional References

BADER, BARBARA. 1976. *American Picturebooks: From Noah's Ark to the Beast Within*. New York: Macmillan.

GOLDEN, JOANNE. M. 1990. *The Narrative Symbol in Childhood Literature*. Berlin: Mouton de Gruyer.

GOMBRICH, E. H. 1982. *The Image and the Eye: Further Studies in the Psychology of Pictorial Representation*. Ithaca, NY: Cornell University Press.

GREENE MAXINE. 1978. *Landscapes of Learning*. New York: Teachers College Press.

KAELIN, E. F. 1989. *An Aesthetics for Art Educators*. New York: Teachers College Press.

———. 1995. *The Potential of Picturebooks: From Visual Literacy to Aesthetic Understanding*. Columbus, OH: Macmillan.

KIEFER, BARBARA. 1988. "Picture Books as Contexts for Literary, Aesthetic and Real World Understandings." *Language Arts* 65(3):260–71.

KIMMEL, ERIC. 1982. "Children's Literature Without the Children." *Children's Literature in Education* 13(1): 38–43.

LANGER, SUZANNE K. 1942. *Philosophy in a New Key*. Cambridge, MA: Harvard University Press.

Children's Literature

BANG, MOLLY. 1980. *The Grey Lady and the Strawberry Snatcher*. New York: Four Winds.

BUNTING, EVE. 1991. *Fly Away Home*. Illustrated by Ronald Himler. New York: Clarion.

COERR, ELEANOR. 1977. *Sadako and the Thousand Paper Cranes*. Illustrated by Ronald Himler. New York: Putnam.

———. 1993. *Sadako*. Illustrated by Ed Young. New York: Putnam.

GALLAZ, CHRISTOPHER, and ROBERTO INNOCENTI. 1985. *Rose Blanche*. Illustrated by Roberto Innocenti. Mankato, MN: Creative Education.

HEIDE, FLORENCE PARRY, and JUDITH HEIDE GILLILAND. 1992. *Sami and the Time of the Troubles*. Illustrated by Ted Lewin. New York: Clarion.

LIFTON, B. J. 1970. *Return to Hiroshima*. Photographs by Edward Hosoe. New York: Atheneum.

MARUKI, TOSHI. 1980. *Hiroshima No Pika*. New York: Lothrop.

SENDAK, MAURICE. 1993. *We Are All In the Dumps with Jack and Guy*. New York: HarperCollins.

———. 1981. *Outside Over There*. New York: Harper & Row.

WILD, MARGARET. 1991. *Let the Celebrations Begin!* Illustrated by Julie Vivas. New York: Orchard.

PART TWO

The Changing World of Girls and Boys: Exploring Family Values and Children's Roles

What images are being offered to children in literature? Shirley Ernst explores this question through the lens of gender, while Deborah Thompson explores the same question by taking a look at African American families in the past twenty years. Authors Judith Heide Gilliland and Charlotte Huck offer their perspectives as children's authors. Ernst's ultimate concern is for the need for balanced collections that show both males and females in a variety of roles. Her analysis of recent Caldecott and Newbery winners and honor books and titles published in the 1990s suggests an ongoing trend in children's literature that highlights active male protagonists. Her suggestion that relegating girls to second-class citizenry is achieved by treating males as the dominant gender is shocking and difficult to challenge when one looks at the figures. Even if newer books are beginning to address this imbalance the bulk of books available to children in libraries and classrooms reflects decades of accumulated literature. The problem is not going to disappear soon. As I suggest in my chapter on fantasy, classics we hold dear are riddled with gender stereotypes

Charlotte Huck's discussion of her depiction of Princess Furball, a feisty female in traditional folklore, and Anita Lobel's accompanying illustrations are a startling contrast to the hundreds of angry letters that accuse Huck of animal abuse and insensitivity to ecological issues. While critics gave Princess Furball starred reviews, animal activists were furious over what they termed the casual killing of animals to make Furball's coat. This chapter could easily fit in with the first section on censorship; however, Huck's Cinderella is an independent contrast to the widely known Perrault and Disney versions that show Cinderella as a passive victim, and therefore, belongs in the middle of a discussion of children's roles in literature. Furball has spunk, energy, and uses her wits to succeed.

Deborah Thompson's chapter picks up where Rudine Sims Bishop's research ended in 1979. Thompson takes a look at the African American family in books for children written between 1974 and 1993. Because the topic is so broad she limits her analysis to picture books written and illustrated in the past twenty years. Thompson is a skeptic. She sees the imbalance in the portrayal of black families in literature as revolving around many issues. Violet Harris reports that the total number of books about African Americans rarely exceeds two hundred of the five thousand books published annually. Many show black children growing up in nuclear and/or middle-class families. Thompson points out that nuclear families were the norm in the African American community prior to the 1980s. She also gives a different perspective on what has become a slur in political circles: single-parent families are not stigmatized in black communities. Furthermore, Thompson points out that single-parent families are on the rise in all segments of the population, not just African American communities. Her analysis of African American picture books is thorough and full of insight.

A recent development in picture books shows children in other parts of the world. One of Judith Gilliland's characters spends much of his time hiding from bombs in a basement in Lebanon. A prevalent theme in the book is how children long for peace and freedom in the midst of civil war. Another book about Ahmed, a child of modern day Cairo, is equally controversial. First, Gilliland is an outsider writing about cultures of which she is not a part. Is her voice authentic? Rudine Sims Bishop and Violet Harris might challenge her right to write *The Day of Ahmed's Secret* or *Sami and the Time of the Troubles* based on race alone. Gilliland is an outsider looking in. She hasn't experienced the culture from the inside and most likely has missed important aspects of Egyptian and Lebanese culture and thinking. Second, this book has been challenged as not being representative of modern-day Cairo. I have used this book in many presentations with teachers, and it has been challenged as not reflecting the lives of children today. Some claim that Ahmed would be in school, not working all day long, while others praise the book for accurately depicting the life of a child in Egypt. Few books like these exist, so I applaud authors like Gilliland, Baillie, Bunting, Isadora, McMahon, Laird, Hoyt-Goldsmith, Reynolds, Williams, and Stock for bringing us pictures of the lives of children in other parts of the world. What the controversy suggests strongly is that we need to see and hear many voices providing stories about children from all over the world. Authors and illustrators like those mentioned above have opened up the dialogue and have provided pictures of children from many cultures.

I would like to conclude with the following questions about children's books. Where are depictions of single-parent families? Where are the families living on welfare? Below the poverty line? Where are the images of children dodging bullets on their way to school? If picture books are tackling realistic issues, why are there so few voices for millions of children in this country who face war zones every day? If Kozol and Kotlowitz are correct in their images of millions of children, where are these children in children's literature? Gilliland closes her chapter with the following words: "Of course, all children's books don't need to be 'instructive.' There are, thank God, still just plain fun books, books with no message, no moral, no agenda. Now if we'd just turn off our TV sets, we'd have time for them all!" She's probably right, but I wonder if the books that endure don't have some special quality that Gilliland might call a message, moral, or agenda!

FIVE

Gender Issues in Books for Children and Young Adults

Shirley B. Ernst

Everything we read, from sexist advertisements and women's magazines to romance novels and children's books, constructs us, makes us who we are, by presenting our image of ourselves as girls and women, as boys and men.

Mem Fox

Reading continues to be one of the most criticized components of a child's learning experiences. Arguments about phonics, literature, basal readers, reading groups, and methodology flare up in faculty rooms, professional journals, political circles, popular magazines, and newspapers. When it comes to reading everyone is an expert. While most of the emphasis has been on the actual process of learning to read, there are those like author Mem Fox (1993) who have grave concerns about the gender messages we send our students via the content of what they read. This is hardly a new topic; issues related to gender roles have been part of educational research and hot debate for at least thirty years. With the advent of the whole language movement and literature-based programs in the 1970s one can step into almost any elementary or middle school classroom today and find children's literature in the curriculum. What kinds of books are our children reading? What images are we offering boys and girls in the literature they read?

In this chapter I will take a look at some of the pivotal gender studies of children's literature in this century. I will also take an indepth look at the Newbery and Caldecott books of the 1990s. Has literature for children changed significantly? Are current award-winning books offering images for children that show girls taking chances, making important decisions, building houses, practicing medicine, or climbing mountains? Studies from the 1970s indicate that girls were not typically perceived as risk takers, being physically active, or having professional lives. Girls were generally relegated to the background as nurturers, supporters, whiners, or weak-kneed whinnies who depended on men for guidance and salvation.

Studies of Gender

Research conducted in the 1970s and early 1980s focused on sex role stereotyping. While much of this research examined basal reading series, children's literature was also included. Researchers focused on the extent to which main characters were male or female, while others examined the treatment and image of male and female characters (*Women on Words and Images* 1972; *Feminists on Children's Literature* 1971; Weitzman et al. 1972). The books examined were typically award-winning literature such as Newbery and Caldecott medal books. These studies essentially found that males were represented more than females. Stereotyped behaviors such as girls working in the kitchen and boys riding bikes were also prevalent, with the images of males frequently more positive than those of females. Boys were generally shown as independent, problem solvers, active, and in charge of situations while girls were often portrayed as dependent, problem causers, passive, and followers. With the number of children's books published each year numbering well over three thousand during the 1970s, however, the books examined in these studies constituted a proverbial "drop in the bucket" in terms of what was available. (An overview of this research can be found in textbooks written by Rudman and Huck, and in professional books written by Frasher, Nilsen, and Swann.)

Grauerholz and Pescosolido (1989) examined Children's Catalog listings for over two thousand books published between 1900 and 1984 that had been identified as "Easy books." They found that males in books outnumbered females nearly three to one; male animals outnumbered female animals six to one; adult males outnumbered adult females four to one; boys outnumbered girls almost three to one; and human males outnumbered human females over two to one. While these figures varied over the years, these imbalances persisted for eighty-four years. How many children read these books and concluded or still conclude that boys were more important than girls? How easy it is to relegate girls to second-class status when they are seen as second-class citizens, or not seen at all.

Peterson and Lach (1990) sampled 136 picture books selected from *The Horn Book* during 1967, 1977, and 1987 to determine whether there was any change in the number of books about boys and about girls. They selected these years to represent the current period (1987), a period when early research was at its height (1967), and a period halfway between these two (1977). They relied on *The Horn Book* because it was one of the "primary resources used by pre-school teachers and librarians . . ." (1990, 186). They found that while there were still significantly more males in books, the main characters were more evenly balanced by 1987. Their samples, however, were small and rather selective, which might have accounted for their findings.

Hypothesizing that one of the considerations in the selection of Caldecott books included a nonsexist view, Kortenhaus and Demarest (1993) examined 125 nonaward-winning picture books (selected at random from five different libraries) and twenty-five Caldecott winners or honor books (selected according to availability). They analyzed twenty-five books selected for each decade between 1940 and 1980 for eight characteristics: females in titles, males in titles, females in central roles, males in central roles, females in pictures, males in pictures, female animals, and male animals. They also examined the activities in which the characters engaged and categorized them as dependent and independent. The researchers theorized that there would be less sexism evident in the Caldecott books, and a trend toward less sexism in all books over the fifty-year period. What they found, however, was that there was no significant difference between Caldecott and nonaward books. In all cases (titles, roles, pictures, animals) males outnumbered females, and while there was a gradual decrease in gender imbalance over the decades it still existed in the 1980s. In addition, they found that males were more likely to be portrayed as independent (249:54) while females were more likely to be portrayed as passive and dependent (249:29). While girls were more likely to be pictured as active in books published since the 1960s, males still were portrayed as active three times as often as females. Girls were four times as likely to be portrayed as passive than were boys. This research is scary. It is hardly surprising then that a five-year-old girl remarked during a class book discussion in 1994 that girls can't be astronauts.

While the *number* of females in books *has* increased, research indicates that the stereotypical behaviors with which they have been portrayed have not changed. How can girls build positive images of themselves when the books they read reinforce passive and dependent roles? Why don't these books portray females in "real-world" roles?" For example, Kortenhaus and Demarest found only one working mother in their sample of books published since 1960. Contrast this image to the 60 percent of women who have children under the age of fourteen and are in the work force. What a sad commentary!

Christensen (1991) studies gender images in children's books with groups of high school students as a regular part of her curriculum. She suggests that "children's literature is perhaps the most influential genre read" (1), and that "the stereotypes and world view embedded in these stories become accepted knowledge" (15). Her students examined popular classics such as "Cinderella," "Sleeping Beauty," and "The Little Mermaid" and drew conclusions about the way women and girls are portrayed. They found that most often these are stereotyped images—girls who are young and pretty simply want to catch their man while those who are smart are ugly, and if they are old and pretty they are also mean because their looks are leaving them. Christensen challenges her students to be critics of gender images in that literature and urges them to draw their own conclusions.

Gilbert (1989) also explored gender issues in literature, specifically from a beginning reader perspective. She examined two different programs of reading materials used in Australian schools. The first program, The Story Box, is a series of books written specifically for instruction in classrooms where whole language theory informs practice. The idea is to have materials that are authentic, contain natural language, and are interesting to readers. Gilbert found that gender bias was not a consideration when these materials were written. She predicts that among the hypotheses children might form from reading these materials are the following:

- Men fix things.
- Animals are male or neuter.
- Women rarely have jobs.
- Fathers make decisions.
- Women serve food but don't eat food.
- Girls have dolls.

The second program that Gilbert examined was the Core Library, which consists of a set of books previously published specifically for children and not for classroom purposes. Each set was put together for a particular age/grade range with the level of difficulty noted. Gilbert found that many of these books represented diversity, but they also included many titles that were published over twenty years ago. In a sampling of one of the sets Gilbert discovered that there were twenty-five male characters as opposed to eight female characters, one hundred male animals and only twenty-nine female animals. In addition she found forty-eight different occupations or roles for men and only ten different occupations or roles for women. Men and women were represented jointly in only three roles. Men were portrayed as farmers, mail deliverers, police officers, and pilots while women were portrayed as witches, washerwomen, shop assistants, and office workers. What I find unsettling about the findings of Gilbert, Grauerholz, and Pescosolido is that gender bias exists in all materials used in reading instruction, both kits that are specifically designed for instruction and those made up of previously published books. While it is not appropriate to expect each and every book to portray both boys and girls, it is appropriate to expect gender balance across the materials. What are we conditioning our children to think?

An Informal Study

In most classrooms there is also a library available for supplemental and recreational reading. Are these collections of children's literature gender unbalanced? When I talk to teachers about how their classroom literature collections are developed I find that in most cases it is a haphazard process. There is little money allotted by the schools for classroom collections, so teachers often spend their own money on books, which are often selected based on price rather than content. They include books from tag sales, their own children's collections, and books from friends and acquaintances. They also ask parents to send books rather than cupcakes at birthdays. These collections can be rather random, and many of the books do not reflect high-quality literature and contain many examples of gender bias. To meet these standards would involve more money than is currently available to teachers.

That literature with gender biases finds its way into the hands of teachers, and thus into the hands of students, is supported by a study done by Luke, Cooke, and Luke (1986). They evaluated the selection of children's books made by a group of students taking a children's literature course in a teacher preparation program by asking students to select a book they liked and that children would like and benefit from. They found that of the fifty-four titles selected 59 percent were by male authors, even though 74 percent of the books were from the 1970s and 1980s, a time, they explain, when women authors were well accepted in children's literature production. They also found that 74 percent of the books selected had males as the main character, 19 percent had female main characters, and the remaining books had both male and female main characters. They also found that stereotypical images were used by the students to describe the main characters, whether they were male or female. Males were described as being "strong, imaginative, adventurous," "noisy," and "hungry, sly, clever." Girls were described as being "naive, cute, petite," "elegant princess," and "old spinsters." Conflicts were overwhelmingly resolved by male characters; female characters' problems were generally resolved by males to whom they had some connection. Problems resolved by female characters involved stereotypical ways, such as the return of a father, engaging in a marriage, or being saved by a brave prince. When questioned about how they selected their book most of the students reported that they paid no attention to gender issues. Is it any wonder that books for children continue to reflect gender imbalance when those who plan to teach children are unaware of their own gender biases?

Because teachers make many of the decisions about what children read, it is critical that we recognize the importance of balanced collections. In my own college classes I have tested these theories by asking students in my reading classes to bring in five picture books randomly selected from a library near their homes. My students are instructed not to specifically select books, but rather to pick them randomly from five different shelf areas. This eliminates personal biases and gives us a random selection of children's books. While this selection may not be representative of the total books available to teachers, it appears to be somewhat representative of the way classroom libraries are constructed.

The students are divided into five small groups with each group randomly selecting ten books from their piles, thus setting up a "classroom library" of fifty books. This number represents more than some classrooms have, fewer than others, and certainly nowhere near the three books or more for each child that Veatch (1959) has recommended. At this point I explain that we need to examine our collection in terms of ethnic and gender variables. The "findings" I share here are from a recent class, but I have used this activity for over ten years now and the results are always similar. I will share only the gender findings.

In this investigation we examined the books based on how many were about male characters, female characters, and gender-specific animal characters. Of the fifty books, 36 percent focused on male characters, 14 percent on female characters, 18 percent included both on a fairly equal basis, 16 percent were about male animals, 2 percent had both male and female animals, and 14 percent had no characters (human or animal) that could be identified by gender. There were no books with female animals in this set. The students were most amazed at the way in which animals were used to portray stereotypical views of males and females. Clothing, hair, and names were some of the ways in which it was easy to tell the gender of animals. There was a great discrepancy in terms of gender representation in this collection. The fifty books we examined could easily represent a typical elementary classroom library. What I hoped to accomplish was an understanding that the students would need to consider gender as a factor when they selected books for their classroom collections.

Books of the 1990s

With over four thousand books for children and young adults published each year how are females faring in books in more recent years? One might expect some sort of balance; that, however, is not the case. Upon an examination of two thousand titles in *The Horn Book Guides* for July 1992 through June 1993, I found that males were represented 640 times and females only 354. I counted the number of titles that included a male name and those that included a female name. Any names that were not clearly male or female were not included (that is, Toto, Jintzi), but titles such as King, Princess, Emperor were included. *The Horn Book Guide* represents most of what is published in each six-month period.

Simply having a male or female gender tag in the title does not mean that the books are about characters of that gender, or that the portrayal is positive. For example, *Princess* (Wilsdorf 1993) is actually about a Prince, and while the ending is somewhat nontraditional we still have a male (prince) out on quest (seeking a princess) with most of the females being portrayed in unflattering ways (vain, fussy, and so on) Conversely, not having a gender tag in the title does not indicate a lack of gender images in the book. In *No Milk!* (Ericsson 1993) the main character is a male. These figures do indicate, however, a potential gender imbalance in books for children based on title alone. If children select books by titles, girls are less likely than boys to find stories about themselves.

Biographies for children provide information about their heroes and famous people. These people often serve as role models for children and provide guidelines about what has, and thus can be, accomplished by men and women, so it is important to look at the gender representations in these books. Since *The Horn Book Guide* organizes the reviewed books into categories it was easy to take a look at the biographies reviewed. There were more than twice as many biographies about male figures in the second half of 1992 than there were about female figures (79:34). In the first half of 1993 there were over three times as many biographies about males than about females (102:31). With this kind of representation in books, young readers may assume that men are more important than women and that men do more things that warrant being written about than women do. This imbalance also results in girls having fewer role models than boys.

Since much of the early research was done with award-winning books, particularly the Newbery and Caldecott medal books, and since many teachers with whom I am in contact make it a point to introduce these books to children as an attempt to share high-quality books with them, it is appropriate to take a look at recent titles and issues of gender. I examined all of the Newbery and Caldecott winners and honor books of the past four years—1991–1994. Taking a look just at titles, the Caldecott books include four titles with males and one with a female. The gender of the main character includes seven males and four females. If one includes other characters mentioned in the stories approximately 60 percent are males and 40 percent are females. What do these findings mean? One interpretation is that there is a gender imbalance in the books that receive our most prestigious medals.

In contrast to the Caldecott titles the Newbery winners have titles with four females, no males, and one that could be either male or female (*Maniac Magee*). Ironically, the main characters are largely male. Eight of the books are about males with only three about females. Supporting characters include forty-three males and twenty-three females. It seems that the male trend in books for children continues into the 1990s.

It is not enough to play a numbers game, however, as the figures are merely an indication of a possible problem. What do these characters do and say? Earlier researchers have pointed out the stereotypical ways that male and female characters are portrayed (*Women on Words and Images* 1972; Stitt 1988) and suggest that the traits given to males are usually more positive and desired than those given to females. With this in mind I will examine some of the main characters in the four Newbery medal winners of the 1990s.

In *The Giver* (Lowry 1993) Jonas, the main character, lives in a "safe" world where everything is determined in a logical manner. It is a world of sameness, regularity, and denial. It is only when Jonas is selected to become the next archive of memories that the reader realizes the problems that exist in this secure world. Jonas is quick to catch on to the fact that things are not really as they seem. He is ingenious and creative in working out a solution when his plans go awry. On the other hand his unsuccessful predecessor, a girl named Rosemary, could not handle the pain and disillusionment and was "released" (which is a euphemism for murder, or in this case suicide). There are, at the same time, some nonstereotypic portrayals here. Life work is determined in that society by one's interest and abilities rather than by gender. Jonas' father is a caretaker of young children—a role still considered "women's work" in today's world by many people. Lowry offers both gender-based stereotypes and examples of these stereotypes being fractured.

In *Missing May* (Rylant 1992) Summer is dealing with the death of her Aunt May. She misses May and is worried about her Uncle Ob who is taking the death hard. In the chain of events that occur she is a follower, going along with the plans of her uncle and a neighbor boy, Cletus. In fact, if any problem-solving is done it is Cletus who does it. Cletus finds the article that sends this little group off to consult the medium they hope will help them contact May. Cletus takes charge when they find out from the Reverend Young's son that the medium has died. Cletus makes the suggestion that Ob could sell his whirligigs in a gift shop, a suggestion that seemed to "fix" things for Ob. Summer, on the other hand, appears lost throughout the book. She is mourning her aunt's death and objects to chasing after the medium. She is portrayed as a dependent, passive, fearful, female. While this book is about a female character, it is not one that demonstrates to readers that girls can be self-reliant, capable, and problem-solvers. Rather, this book reinforces the passive female stereotype.

In *Shiloh* (Naylor 1991) eleven-year-old Marty gives refuge to a dog that is being abused by its owner, Judd Travers. Although he is afraid of Judd, Marty decides to try to buy the dog, and in going to Judd's house sees him killing a deer. He uses this event to make a deal to work to buy the dog. While Marty is portrayed as being afraid he is also portrayed as having the courage to deal with his fear. Throughout the book he is shown as creative and ingenious as he works on solving the problem of how to save the dog. He is successful as a problem-solver, persevering in his need to "do right" by the dog.

Maniac Magee (Spinelli 1990) is another example of a male character with many of the characteristics often ascribed to males and seen as positive. Maniac's athletic prowess is evident as he runs, climbs, catches balls, and hits home runs. He demonstrates ingenuity as he solves the problems of finding food and living quarters. He solves the problems that come his way, figuring out how to untie Cobble's Knot and how to get the McNab boys to go to school. He is certainly autonomous. On the other hand, he is caring about people, and develops relationships with a number of them, including Grayson, the Beales, the Pickwells and to some extent, the McNabs. Caring is often a trait ascribed to females.

In these four Newbery medal books there are three male characters who do not accept the world the way it is and go about doing something to change it, while the one female character is a follower who lets others make decisions for her. In the Newbery honor books only two of the five titles feature female characters: *Eleanor Roosevelt* (Freedman 1993) and *The True Confessions of Charlotte Doyle* (Avi 1990). Of the other six honor books, one is a collection of stories and the others portray boys, who in most cases are adventurous, persevering, somewhat autonomous, and brave as they solve the problems in their lives.

While some may claim that children reading these books have already acquired their views of what males and females do, it is also likely that these views are reinforced by the messages children read in books. And, if these books have been preceded by picture books with similar messages, they become one more piece of evidence to readers that boys do and girls watch. Therefore it is also critical to examine picture books with a focus on the illustrations since so much of the book's message is based on the illustrations. An examination of the Caldecott medal books illustrated between 1991–1994 follows.

Grandfather's Journey (Say 1993) is a family story told by the author about his grandfather's life. The grandfather is portrayed as a brave young man who leaves his home in Japan to travel to North America. The many people he meets are men and are portrayed as such. The women in the story include his wife, daughter, a few women pictured in the illustration portraying his friends in Japan, and a few girls in the group of children after the war. A young boy is shown in a soldier's outfit with a gun in hand. Thus the book not only reinforces gender stereotypes—males are self-sufficient, brave, adventurous, curious, and of course, soldierly—but also most of the illustrations show males.

In *Mirette on the High Wire* (McCully 1992) the main character lives a hundred years ago, so one would expect historical authenticity, which would include some gender stereotypes in order to portray the time accurately. Mirette wears an apron, as does her mother. The reader also sees a little girl who is brave enough to attempt walking on a tightrope because she has watched one of her mother's lodgers crossing the high wire and is entranced. When the great Bellini freezes upon a high wire it is Mirette who goes out on the wire in an attempt to give him courage. In this situation a girl is portrayed as domestic yet persevering, achieving, and brave. Her bravery is somewhat stereotypical in that she helps Bellini out of his fear, but it is Mirette who takes charge.

Tuesday (Wiesner 1991) has no main characters, but there are various supporting characters in the book. Only one of the six police officers is a female. Of the two humans "visited" by the frogs, only the man is aware of the situation, although he takes no action. The elderly woman sleeps through the event even though the frogs have physically invaded her space.

In looking at the honor books for this period, only two, *Tar Beach* (Ringgold 1991) and *Working Cotton* (Williams 1992), focus on female characters. Of the other eleven honor books, five focus on male characters, and the rest are either combinations, no gendered characters, or the gender of the character is not clear. It's clearly still easier to find books about boys than it is to find books about girls. In most cases the boys are more physically active than the girls or exhibit more problem-solving ability than girls, or any of the other more highly desirable characteristics such as being athletic, curious, and persevering (Stitt 1988).

Conclusion

With the overwhelming number of books for children about males and the disproportionate positive attributes ascribed to males, Mem Fox's quote at the beginning of the chapter is alarming. How does this imbalance continue to be supported by authors, illustrators, publishers, educators, and parents? How can this balance be changed? While many of us believe that such changes are necessary and should not be difficult, the fact is that the imbalance continues despite the attention it has received over the years.

Perhaps more authors like Mem Fox need to be consciously aware of the gender of their main characters and the ways in which they describe those characters and their actions. Fox (1993) writes that many of her books are deliberately "dominated by main characters who are either girls, female animals, or dynamic elderly women." She does this because she believes that "both genders have to be allowed to be as real in literature as they are in life" (85). With this in mind we might ask in how many of the books with male characters could we substitute a female and in how many books with female characters could we substitute a male? This would be an intriguing critical response to a book in which to engage our students in order to examine gender balance.

I do not wish to imply that all books need to include both males and females. Obviously this would be unrealistic, and authors need to write their stories without any restrictions placed upon them. I would like, however, to see more books with strong female characters who are active, inventive, and in charge of their own destinies. I'd like to see fewer passive, dependent girls portrayed with stereotypical actions and with ineffective language. It will take a conscious effort on the part of authors to develop an awareness of their own use of gender stereotypes and to reflect more balanced images of both boys and girls in their writings.

Publishing companies should be aware of these imbalances and need to consider developing an active network that encourages authors to include strong female voices in children's literature, even as they have begun to actively search for other diverse voices. In addition they can deliberately seek out authors for whom gender balance is an important consideration.

While it is important that authors and publishers take the gender issue into consideration, it is equally important that those of us who use books with children are more selective about what we choose. Whether we are librarians or teachers we need to be more cognizant of the gender issues as we share books with children. An awareness of books that offer girls and boys strong and diverse images can expand their potential rather than limiting options. As classroom collections are acquired and developed the question of gender balance and accurate and fair representation of females and males needs to be taken into consideration. For every book such as Paula Fox's *Monkey Island* (1991), which portrays a homeless young boy struggling to survive on the streets of a big city, there should also be books that portray girls in similar situations, like *The Beggars' Ride* (Nelson 1992). The bottom line is that hunger and poverty don't discriminate on the basis of gender. If *Little Brother* (Baillie 1992) becomes part of the collection, perhaps *The Clay Marble* (Ho 1991) can also be added. War affects females as well as males. Books such as *Going to See Grassy Ella* (Lance 1993), *Shizuko's Daughter* (Mori 1993), and *Haveli* (Staples 1993) are powerful demonstrations to readers that girls can be brave, adventurous, and capable of taking care of themselves even under adverse conditions.

The need for educators to take a positive stance toward books that offer many diverse gender images is given more urgency when parents seem to be so unaware of the problem. Peterson and Lach (1990) surveyed parents of young children and found that while most had reasons for selecting the books they did, gender fairness was rarely one of those reasons. Thus, children do not necessarily come to school having had books that portray both positive male and female roles. If teachers do not balance the books, who will?

That gender bias in children's books has occurred and that it is still occurring is obvious from the research. This is only part of the issue, however. Does literature simply reflect society? Aren't we just preparing children for the real world? I suspect that we could argue for some time about this chicken or egg question: Does literature reflect society or is society influenced by literature? For those who take a sociopsycho-linguistic view of language and literacy each piece of literature reflects the author's experiences and knowledge, which are shaped by society. As readers negotiate the text they bring their experiences and knowledge, also shaped by society, to the task. Readers may have their stereotypes and biases reinforced by what they read or they might use new information to revise their knowledge and beliefs. Perhaps it would be wise to acknowledge that there is much in literature that reflects the "way things are," but that this reflection reinforces the status quo. In fact, it has been suggested that changes in children's books often come long after they have been seen in reality (Grauerholz and Pescosolido 1989) and that these books find their way into classrooms even later (Gilbert 1989). Perhaps it is time to declare that now is late enough.

Professional References

CHRISTENSEN, LINDA M. 1991. "Unlearning the Myths that Bind Us." *Rethinking Schools* 5(4).

FEMINISTS ON CHILDREN'S LITERATURE. 1971. "A Feminist Look at Children's Books." *School Library Journal* 18: 19–24.

FOX, MEM. 1993. "Men Who Weep, Boys Who Dance: The Gender Agenda Between the Lines in Children's Literature." *Language Arts* 70: 84–88.

FRASHER, RAMONA S. 1982. "A Feminist Look at Literature for Children: Ten Years Later." In *Sex Stereotypes and Reading: Research and Strategies*, edited by E. Marcia Sheridan. Newark: International Reading Association.

GILBERT, PAM. 1989. *Gender, Literacy and the Classroom.* Victoria: Australian Reading Association.

GRAUERHOLZ, ELIZABETH, and BERNICE A. PESCOSOLIDO. 1989. "Gender Representation in Children's Literature: 1900–1984." *Gender & Society* 3(1): 113–25.

Horn Book Guide. 1992. Volume IV, 1 (July–December).

———. 1993. Volume IV, 2 (January–June).

HUCK, CHARLOTTE S., SUSAN HEPLER, and JANET HICKMAN. 1993. *Children's Literature in the Elementary School.* Orlando: Harcourt, Brace & Jovanovich.

KORTENHAUS, CAROLE M., and JACK DEMAREST. 1993 "Gender Role Stereotyping in Children's Literature: An Update." *Sex Roles* 28(3/4): 219–32.

LUKE, ALLAN, JANINE COOKE, and CARMEN LUKE. 1986. "The Selective Tradition in Action: Gender Bias in Student Teachers' Selections of Children's Literature." *English Education*: 209–18.

NILSEN, ALLEN PACE. 1977. "Sexism in Children's Books and Elementary Teaching Materials." In *Sexism and Language*, edited by Nilsen, et al. Urbana: National Council of Teachers of English.

PETERSON, SHARYL BENDER, and MARY ALYCE LACH. 1990. "Gender Stereotypes in Children's Books: Their Prevalence and Influence on Cognitive and Affective Development." *Gender and Education* 2(2): 185–97.

RUDMAN, MASHA KABAKOW. 1984. *Children's Literature: An Issues Approach.* New York: Longman Publisher.

STITT, BEVERLY A. 1988. *Building Gender Fairness in Schools.* Carbondale: Southern Illinois University.

SWANN, JOAN. 1992. *Girls, Boys and Language.* Oxford: Blackwell.

VEATCH, JEANNETTE. 1959. *Individualizing Your Reading Program.* New York: G. P. Putnam & Sons.

WEITZMAN, L. J., et al. 1972. "Sex Role Socialization in Picture Books for Preschool Children." *American Journal of Sociology* 77: 1125–50.

WOMEN ON WORDS AND IMAGES. 1972. *Dick and Jane as Victims: Sex Stereotyping in Children's Readers.* Princeton: National Organization for Women.

Children's Literature

AVI. 1990. *The True Confessions of Charlotte Doyle.* New York: Orchard.

———. 1991. *Nothing But the Truth.* New York: Orchard.

BAILLIE, ALLAN. 1992. *Little Brother.* New York: Viking.

BARTONE, ELISA. 1993. *Peppe the Lamplighter.* New York: Lothrop, Lee & Shepard.

BROOKS, BRUCE. 1992. *What Hearts.* New York: HarperCollins.

CONLY, JANE LESLIE. 1993. *Crazy Lady!* New York: HarperCollins.

ERICSSON, JENNIFER A. 1993. *No Milk!* New York: Tambourine.

FLEMING, DENISE. 1993. *In the Small, Small Pond.* New York: Henry Holt and Co.

FOX, PAULA. 1991. *Monkey Island.* New York: Orchard.

FREEDMAN, RUSSELL. 1993. *Eleanor Roosevelt: A Life of Discovery.* New York: Clarion Books.

HENKES, KEVIN. 1993. *Owen.* New York: Greenwillow.

HO, MINFONG. 1991. *The Clay Marble.* New York: Farrar Straus & Giroux.

LANCE, KATHRYN. 1993. *Going to See Grassy Ella.* New York: Lothrop, Lee & Shepard.

LOWRY, LOIS. 1993. *The Giver.* Boston: Houghton Mifflin.

MACAULAY, DAVID. 1990. *Black and White.* Boston: Houghton Mifflin.

MARCELLINO, FRED. 1990 *Puss in Boots*. New York: Farrar, Straus & Giroux.

MCCULLY, EMILY ARNOLD. 1992. *Mirette on the High Wire*. New York: G. P. Putnam & Sons.

MCDERMOTT, GERALD. 1993. *Raven*. San Diego: Harcourt Brace & Jovanovich.

MCKISSACK, PATRICIA C. 1992. *The Dark-Thirty*. New York: Knopf.

MORI, KYOKO. 1993. *Shizuko's Daughter*. New York: Henry Holt and Co.

MYERS, WALTER DEAN. 1992. *Somewhere in the Darkness*. New York: Scholastic.

NAYLOR, PHYLLIS REYNOLDS. 1991. *Shiloh*. New York: Atheneum.

NELSON, THERESA. 1992. *The Beggars' Ride*. New York: Orchard.

RASCHKA, CHRIS. 1993. *Yo! Yes?* New York: Orchard.

RINGGOLD, FAITH. 1991. *Tar Beach*. New York: Crown Publishers.

RYLANT, CYNTHIA. 1992. *Missing May*. New York: Orchard.

SAY, ALLEN. 1993. *Grandfather's Journey*. Boston: Houghton Mifflin.

SCIESZKA, JON. 1992. *The Stinky Cheese Man and Other Fairly Stupid Tales*. New York: Viking.

SPINELLI, JERRY. 1990. *Maniac Magee*. Boston: Little Brown.

STAPLES, SUZANNE FISHER. 1993. *Haveli*. New York: Knopf.

WIESNER, DAVID. 1991. *Tuesday*. New York: Clarion.

WILLIAMS, SHERLEY ANNE. 1992. *Working Cotton*. San Diego: Harcourt Brace & Jovanovich.

WILLIAMS, VERA B. 1990. *More More More Said the Baby*. New York: Greenwillow.

WILSDORF, ANNE. 1993. *Princess: Based on Hans Christian Andersen's "The Princess and the Pea."* New York: Greenwillow.

YEP, LAURENCE. 1993. *Dragon's Gate*. New York: HarperCollins.

YOUNG, ED. 1992. *Seven Blind Mice*. New York: Philomel.

SIX

Princess Furball: The Writing, Illustrating, and Response

CHARLOTTE S. HUCK

As a child my favorite fairy tale was the story of "Furball." I loved this variant of Cinderella, which portrays a spunky young girl who uses her own ingenuity to change her life. When her father insists upon marrying her to an ogre for fifty wagons of silver, Furball sets conditions that she is certain he cannot meet. She demands three dresses, "one dress as golden as the sun, another as silvery as the moon and third as glittering as the stars." In addition she asked for a "coat made of a thousand different kinds of fur, one piece from every animal in the kingdom." When her father meets her demands and sets the marriage day, Furball's only choice is to run away. Wearing her coat of many furs, she trudges all night through a heavy snowstorm until she safely reaches another kingdom. Not afraid of hard work she becomes a scullery-maid in the castle. Here she must be a servant to all the other servants until she devises a plan that will help her capture the attention and love of the king and take her out of the kitchen forever. Princess Furball is as clever as she is lovely and as capable as she is beautiful.

Why, I wondered, had I never seen a picture-book edition of this dramatic story? In researching the background of this tale, I found my answer. Of the over five hundred variants of "Cinderella," the most popular version involves the lost slipper and fairy godmother motifs. The second most popular grouping of tales employs a "hated marriage theme," some of which are incestuous. The Grimms' version of Furball titled "Allerleirauh" or "Many Furs," includes the scene in which the father will only marry someone as beautiful as his deceased wife; he finds her when he looks upon his grown daughter. Now I knew why "Many Furs" had not appeared as a single picture-book edition.

However, the story I remembered from childhood had substituted an ogre for the father, thus retaining the psychological truth of incest. In illustrating *Princess Furball* (Huck 1989), Anita Lobel showed a portrait of the ogre. A closer look reveals his resemblance to the father-king himself.

The third large grouping of these Cinderella tales begins with the father asking each of his three daughters how much they love him. The first two give insincere flattering answers, while the youngest answers truthfully with an honest metaphor. She says she loves him as much as "meat loves salt." The older sisters laugh at her answer, and her father is so disappointed that he sends her away from his house. The girl becomes a maid in a nobleman's castle and attends three parties as does Furball. This is the story that Shakespeare used for the beginning of *King Lear*. The early English tale on which this is based was know as "Caporushes" (Steel 1962). Perrault (1993) retold this version as "Donkeyskin" while William H. Hooks (1987) found it as a Southern traditional tale and retold it as *Moss Gown*. In all these versions, the youngest daughter has a helper, from a fairy godmother in "Donkeyskin" to the slender black gris-gris woman, named for the chant she tells Candace to use if she should ever need her, in *Moss Gown*.

But in my book, Princess Furball is all alone after her loving and caring nurse dies. By using portraits of Furball's deceased mother, the illustrator suggests her spiritual presence, but in no way does the mother intervene for her daughter. Furball drops the three golden trinkets that belonged to her mother into the king's soup to obtain his attention. But these objects have no magical qualities. Only Furball's determination, hard work, and ingenuity change her life and bring her the happiness she deserves. This was the version I remembered and wanted to retell.

The decisions I faced in the retelling were challenging. First of all I had to decide whether to include the incest or not. With the rise of incest in our society, one could argue that it should not be eliminated from the story. While I do believe that somewhere in the sexual education of a child, he or she should learn about incest, I do not think such information should be derived from a fairy tale! Since I had found the versions that eliminated it in the retelling, I decided not to include it.

What about the coat of the thousand furs? That demand was made by a desperate princess who was convinced that her father couldn't fulfill it. The coat and the three dresses were in every version of this story. In order to be authentic and respect its traditional origin, I decided to retain this motif. I credited children's intelligence enough to realize that during the time period of this tale, people had to kill animals for food and to use their skins for warmth.

The hunt scene was a problem for the illustrator also. How could she portray the hunt for one thousand furry animals without showing a blood bath? She wisely distanced the viewer from the scene and showed tiny animals and hunters in a tapestrylike setting. The hunters have their cross-bows drawn but not a single animal has been killed.

The fur coat suggested the setting for the story. It would need to be in a cold climate, probably in northern Germany where the Grimm brothers may have recorded it. When the princess is forced to run away she puts on her coat of many furs and steps out into the deep snow. Anita Lobel as illustrator showed the changing seasons and the passage of time. The waxing moon peeping in the various windows of the palace show the time between the three balls. When the moon is full, the princess sheds her fur at last and the King declares his love for her. Their wedding is held under an arbor on a sunlit day in June when the roses are in bloom.

The nurse was my addition to the story. How, I wondered could the princess ever love her king if she had never known love herself? Also the nurse would see to her proper education as a princess, providing her with a tutor and a dancing master. As a friend of the cook, the nurse could let the little princess learn how to bake bread and make soup. And since she was neglected by her father, the nurse also provided her with village playmates. This surrogate mother helped to make Furball the capable lovely person she became as an adult.

Just as I added the nurse to the story, Anita Lobel added two silent sentinels to mirror the young king's growing confusion and gradual awareness. While they do not appear in the text, they are pictured some eleven times in the illustrations and always with the king. They look at the princess with admiration for her beauty when she appears at the first ball. As the story continues, they watch with puzzlement and then knowing smiles.

All of the characterizations reflect the story and move the action forward. With just four illustrations, the artist creates the loving caring personality of Furball's nurse. The father-king is portrayed as an evil scheming man in his portrait and in real life. The cross cook is seen grumbling and shouting orders in every one of his pictures. With just a raised eyebrow and a slight smile, the young king himself is seen as beginning to guess the true identity of his scullery-maid. And Furball's face reflects her satisfaction that all is happening as she planned.

The illustrator has given the same careful attention to the early Renaissance setting of this tale as she has to the characterization. Her rich use of reds and turquoise glow with the colors seen in the medieval paintings of the Book of Hours. The nurse's headdress on the title page recalls a Dürer painting of the period, while the snowy hunt scenes remind one of Brueghel landscapes. The many varied architectural pillars and black and white tile floors suggest vast and wealthy castles, all appropriate to the time setting.

Anita Lobel faced other artistic challenges in illustrating this tale. How could she make the three ball scenes different? In order to avoid repetition, she varied their staging. In the first scene, she showed the king and the princess meeting each other at the entrance to the palace. At the second ball, they are shown dancing with the whole court behind them. The focus in the third scene shifts to the king's hands as he slips a ring on Furball's finger. Only the musicians, who had been asked to play the longest piece they knew, are shown in this scene.

The artist's skillful use of color is seen throughout this tale. She started the story with the funeral of the queen. In the midst of the dark and gloomy graveyard, she portrayed the nurse holding the baby princess as a strong life-force dressed in red. Later she dressed the princess in blue, the same color the dead queen is wearing in her black veiled portrait. When the princess first meets the young king, he appears in green, a hunting color. In the next two balls, the artist implies that he wishes to please the princess by wearing a costume of the same color as her dress in the previous ball. And the last picture completes the artist's portrait motif by showing a picture of Princess Furball, her husband the king, and their three children each wearing colors that have been shown throughout the story. Hidden in the frame itself is a picture of Princess Furball's mother. I thought the bottom picture was her nurse, but a closer look reveals a jester, who represents the artist's personal statement on the traditional ending of fairy tales: "They lived happily ever after."

The illustrator's use of light reflects the action of the tale. The illustrator said she saw Princess Furball entrapped in her palace with long dark halls and no exits. After she runs away and meets the king, a window appears. More windows are shown at each ball until the king proposes to her and the full moon is seen through five windows. Finally, as previously stated, they are married outside under a sunlit arbor.

The artist has tapped the deeper psychological meanings of this story. She said she saw a series of imprisoning enclosures that the princess passes through on her journey from darkness to light. The tall dark columns within the palace and the trunks of the trees in the forest all reflect the psychological imprisonment of the princess. The hollow tree in which she takes refuge becomes the womb of her new life where she is reborn and becomes free of her frightening father. Only her own skill and cleverness take her out of the fiery kitchen and into the arms of the king.

The responses to this tale have been gratifying and frightening, positive and negative. Critics applauded it, children loved it, and animal activists wanted it withdrawn from library shelves. What follows is a sample of their comments.

From *The Horn Book* review of *Princess Furball*:

The text is direct, unpretentious and appealing, embellished only with the kind of details one might expect from a traditional tale. . . . By the alchemy of words and pictures, this princess seems very real and quite deserving of her good fortune. The text reads smoothly; the illustrations handsomely reflect its tone and theme. (1989, 779–80)

From ALA *Booklist*, a starred review:

Huck gracefully retells her favorite story which, despite its traditional motifs, contains some strong feminist elements. This princess is independent, practical, and clever thanks to a caring palace nurse. Lobel's accompanying paintings are richly evocative. . . . A handsome and substantive retelling. (1989, 74)

From *Publishers Weekly*:

Huck deftly retells a variant of the Cinderella story. . . . [Her] princess is not only beautiful but clever, and the solutions to her problems are of her own devising. Lobel's elegantly composed paintings in vivid Renaissance colors are as lovely as the princess herself. (1989, 67)

From *School Library Journal*, a starred review:

Author and illustrator have created a strong female character; particularly endearing in her coat of fur, she is resourceful and charming throughout. The Princess' reliance on her own abilities and the absence of obvious magical help make this a fresh and satisfying addition to library collections of all sizes. (1989, 240)

Princess Furball was included among the ALA *Booklist* Editor's Choice for the year and in the *School Library Journal* Best Books of the year. The International Reading Association placed it on their Teachers' Choice for 1990, and it was a Parents' Choice Honor Book. Scholastic purchased it for one of their paperback books, and it was published in Japanese and French. Weston Woods made a video/film of the story.

This approval by knowledgeable critics contrasts sharply with the many letters and postcards sent to Greenwillow by animal activists who were appalled that I would write a book in which in their words "a princess casually asks for a coat of one thousand furs." The two words "casually asks" were included in almost all of their letters, suggesting the book was on some kind of disapproval list. The letters came from all over the United States and Canada for a period of about two months after publication. Some typical samples follow:

To Greenwillow Books:

I am shocked and thoroughly disgusted to learn that in your book *Princess Furball*, 1000 animals are casually killed to clothe a princess.

This is an obscene act of cruelty and teaches children that killing is just fine.

You are to be soundly condemned for putting out such material. I shall NEVER buy any book you published.

Pomona, CA

To the editors:

I am astonished that you chose to publish "Princess Furball"! I couldn't believe my eyes when I saw it. I teach elementary school and I am constantly on the lookout for books for my students and my classroom. This is not literature! This is a promotion for the fur industry. Children love animals—they don't want to hurt them, especially for clothing!

Just the suggestion of killing animals is wantonly harmful. I assume you are not familiar with the studies from Yale University on childhood cruelty to animals and violent behavior in later life. You are inducing a violent action in the minds of young children. Shame on you.

Your book should not be on the shelves of children's books. I suggest you recall it. It will not be used in my classroom or in my home and I am putting an announcement in every teachers' mailbox in my school.

Alco, NJ

To Greenwillow Books:

I am appalled by your book "Princess Furball" and the casual killing of 1000 animals to clothe a princess. Obviously you are hardened to the intense pain and suffering involved in fur being skinned from an animal's body to adorn a human. How *ignorant* and *callous* and *barbaric* to instill these hideous values in children! You should be ashamed. This book should be banned or buried with the real animals that have suffered in this way.

Gloucester, MA

Several letters were signed by ten or more persons, several were duplicates of others, all demanded an answer. The senior editor at Greenwillow replied to each letter thanking them for sharing their views, then stating the following:

> PRINCESS FURBALL is a classic folktale that has endured and been loved for generations, and we do not believe in re-writing classics. We regret that the story is open to misinterpretation, but like all folk and fairy tales that deal with the impossible, it is not to be taken literally.
>
> When the Princess asks the king for the sun, moon, and star dresses and the coat of a thousand furs, she believes she is setting him tasks that he can never accomplish. It is the evil king who is the villain. The story does not approve the wanton killing of animals. It is a tribute to the Princess's ingenuity and determination. . . .

As the author of the story, I was appalled that few of the persons writing had read the book or understood the reason the Princess desperately (not casually) asked for a coat of one thousand furs. The letters showed no understanding for the authenticity of fairy tales or for the time setting of traditional fairy tales. Instead they applied today's values against the unnecessary killing of animals to a time period when it was essential to kill them for food and warmth. Children know this difference and are more discerning than the persons writing these letters. The tone of most of the letters was threatening and vicious and represented the tunnel vision of persons fighting for a cause. It is disturbing that all letters were addressed to the editor in an attempt to control what is published by that company. Many of the writers threatened that they would not buy any books from Greenwillow or its parent company, Morrow, until *Princess Furball* was pulled from the publisher's list. This seems to be a particularly insidious form of censorship and attempted control. Fortunately, Greenwillow stood behind their publication and ignored the threatening letters, although they did reply to each one.

What difference did this attack on *Princess Furball* make? We have no way of knowing. The book has sold well to individuals, schools, and libraries. I do know that one publishing house in England was considering publishing *Princess Furball* and did not do so, but it could have been for many other reasons. Both Japan and France did publish translations. The entire episode was particularly interesting to me. For years I have been concerned with censorship; now I've been in the midst of it.

The most satisfying aspect of publishing *Princess Furball* was to see children's response to it. I have read it aloud to over eighty second and third graders and held the whole group enthralled. Teachers tell me and write to me saying how much children enjoy this fairy tale. I have received a photo and letter from one child in Laramie, Wyoming, who dressed up as Princess Furball for Halloween. Another child sent me a Furball Christmas decoration for my tree. I have received many letters about and illustrations of Princess Furball. Some of my favorite quotes from their letters with their original spelling follow:

Your book reminded me of the golden sun. . . . I like the coat of one thousand anamils. I want you to come to this school. I wanted to complement you on your book. . . .

Lindsay

I am seven years old. Do you have a dog or cat that has furballs? Your story is kind of like Cinderella. I really liked your story.

Kerry

I thot yore story was very good story and the title was strange.

Curtis

The best part I liked was when she was all curled up in the tree. How long did it take you to make the book? How did you get the ideas to make the story? The reason that I liked when princess furball was curled up in the tree was because I like bears and she looked like a bear to me. So thats why I liked it.

Dinah

I like you book Princes Furball. My best part was wanh she woke the gowns to the ball. Why was the cook so menh? It wod be be nice if you came to our school and talk about your book. Do you like my writing? I like it. You are a good writer. I tinkeh you are a fabeus writer. You no jusst wate to write. . . .

Elizabeth Jane

After years of teaching children's literature and writing a text about children's literature, it is a tremendous satisfaction to have rewritten a fairy tale that gives children this much pleasure. It is the children's responses that matter the most. If *Princess Furball* helps children to find joy in reading and to discover the traditional truth of fairy tales that hard work and goodness succeed, then I shall be richly rewarded.

Professional References

Booklist. 1989. Review. American Library Association, 1 September.

DUNDES, ALAN, ed. 1983. *Cinderella: A Casebook.* New York: Wildman Press.

The Horn Book. 1989. Review. November/December: 779–80.

HUCK, CHARLOTTE, and ANITA LOBEL. 1989. *About Princess Furball.* New York: Greenwillow.

Publishers Weekly. 1989. Review. 29 September: 67.

School Library Journal. 1989. Review. September: 240.

Children's Literature

GRIMM BROTHERS. [1944] 1972. "Allerleirauh." In *The Complete Grimm's Fairy Tales.* New York: Random House.

HOOKS, WILLIAM H. 1987. *Moss Gown.* Illustrated by Donald Carrick. New York: Clarion Books.

HUCK, CHARLOTTE. 1989. *Princess Furball.* Illustrated by Anita Lobel. New York: Greenwillow.

PERRAULT, CHARLES. 1993. "Donkeyskin." In *The Complete Fairy Tales of Charles Perrault*, translated by Neil Philip and Nicoletta Simborowski. Illustrated by Sally Holmes. New York: Clarion Books.

STEEL, FLORA ANNIE. 1962. "Caporushes." In *English Fairy Tales.* Illustrated by Arthur Rackham. New York: The Macmillan Company.

SEVEN

Family Values and Kinship Bonds: An Examination of African American Families in Selected Picture Books, 1974–1993

DEBORAH THOMPSON

Today one can browse the shelves of any library or bookstore and find children's books featuring African American characters—going to school, taking a lone walk on a beach, or visiting a favorite aunt or grandparent. The characters who populate children's books are far more diverse than they were nearly thirty years ago when Nancy Larrick (1965) wrote in a *Saturday Review* article about the absence of African American[1] characters in children's books. In the article, she noted that virtually every character in children's books was white despite integration's being the law of the land. One librarian stated categorically that the book publishers were performing a "cultural lobotomy on America's readers" (1965, 85).

Much has happened in the world of children's books since Larrick's article. There are more African American authors and illustrators of note. Two African American authors have won the Newbery award, and several others have won the Newbery honor position. African American illustrators have won the Caldecott award and its honor medals. The establishment of the Coretta Scott King Award ensures that African American illustrators and authors will have their work recognized annually. One African American, Virginia Hamilton, has been awarded the Hans Christian Andersen award for the body of her work. Yet, as I revisit a topic I was first interested in twenty years ago—the portrayal of the African American family in books for children—I wonder if that cultural lobotomy has successfully been reversed. Perhaps this feeling is due to publishing statistics on books for children. Harris (1990) notes that of the thousands of children's books published each year

---

[1] Where possible, the term *African American* will be used, even in instances where *Negro*, *Afro-American* or *black* were used originally.

(approximately five thousand per year according to the 1993 Bowker Annual[2]), the number of books by or about African Americans or African American experiences rarely surpasses two hundred.

A Brief Retrospective: Studies of African American Family Life in Children's Books

The search for fair representation of African American family life in children's books has been an ongoing search for decades. In the early forties, Charlemae Hill Rollins assembled "a reader's guide to Negro life and literature for elementary and high school use," *We Build Together* (the earliest edition on record at the Library of Congress is thought to have been copyrighted in 1941). This annotated bibliography, prepared for the National Council of Teachers of English, contained books that (1) portrayed African Americans in realistic settings—including family situations, (2) furthered democratic concepts, and (3) reflected achievements of African Americans. This highly successful publication has been revised many times since its initial publication. Today, it still serves as a valuable historical resource.

The portrayal of family life in juvenile literature has been the focus of many graduate theses. For example, Hall (1972) examined family life in realistic juvenile fiction published between 1950 and 1971. She found a decline in the number of juvenile characters (mainly white) living in nuclear families. In an analysis of selected children's books published between 1951 and 1963, Glancy (1969) found African Americans were portrayed with a variety of characteristics ranging from contented slaves (although fewer and fewer books had such characterizations) to family life in suburban settings. Thomas (1972) found that most family relationships in children's books were unrealistic. She argued that in the typical children's book, Mother always took Father, who carried a briefcase and wore a suit, to the train station in a station wagon. She also argued that authors treated single-parenthood like "the plague," and therefore, single-parent families were virtually nonexistent in books for children.

In 1974, I conducted a modest study of children's books. I examined twenty-five books, published between 1963 and 1972, for the purpose of examining how the authors portrayed the African American family and its individual members. There were five specific research questions:

1. How many books would have nuclear families?
2. What percentage of families portrayed would be single-parent matriarchies (now known as single-parent, female head of household)?
3. How many families would be extended families?
4. How many single-parent, male heads of households would there be?
5. Into which socioeconomic status group would the majority of the families fall?

---

[2] *The Bowker Annual* is the almanac of the library and book trade.

A content analysis of the twenty-five books was conducted. This analysis yielded interesting (albeit limited) findings. Of the twenty-five families portrayed, sixty percent or fifteen of twenty-five were nuclear families. Eighty percent of the single-parent families were headed by females (eight of ten); two of ten were headed by males. There were few extended families (three of twenty-five). Seven of the fifteen nuclear families were classified as being middle class based on father's occupation/income. Four of the remaining families were classified as being middle class based on the full employment of both parents. Other data gathered included an evidence of racial pride (Black is beautiful, and so forth), but there were still characters who felt inferior because of their complexions and facial features, such as lips, noses, and texture of hair. For example, in *Patricia Crosses Town* (Baum 1965), the protagonist, Patricia, clearly believes she cannot read well due to her dark complexion. Furthermore, she thinks her neighbor is "book smart" because she has a light complexion and long hair. On the positive side, intelligence was often used as a characteristic, and standard English was the most commonly spoken dialect (Thompson 1974).

Although I have made no attempt to replicate the previous study, many of the same questions guided me as I examined the books for this chapter—mainly picture books, published between 1974 and 1993. While representing only a small percentage of the books in a twenty-year span, many of the selected titles have won prizes, have been on lists of notable selections, or otherwise lauded. Those not so lauded, simply tell a good story. All of the titles are readily available in school libraries, public libraries, and well-stocked bookstores.

The Title Selection Process

Titles selected for this chapter were compiled from several sources: *The Black Experience in Children's Books* (The New York Public Library 1989); *The Afro-American in Books for Children, 4th edition,* (District of Columbia Public Library Children's Services 1992); *Teaching Multicultural Literature in Grades K-8* (Harris 1992); and *Children's Literature in the Elementary School, 5th edition* (Huck, Hepler, and Hickman 1992). In addition to these published sources, I tapped my expertise, as well as that of the reference librarian[3] at the Children's Literature Center of the Library of Congress. The titles selected for this study met the following criteria:

1. They were published between 1974 and 1993.
2. They have twentieth-century settings.
3. They are classified as fiction—contemporary, realistic, or historical with one exception (a biography).
4. They are for children in grades K-8.

---

[3] I would like to thank Peg Coughlan at The Children's Resource Center of the Library of Congress for her invaluable help.

Occasionally throughout the chapter, I will refer to books as being either melting pot, socially conscious, or culturally conscious titles. These terms are derived from Sims' (1982) comprehensive analysis of children's contemporary fiction reflecting the African American experience. Socially conscious books present the African American to the white middle class—titles in this category tend to center on stories showing the reader how "we all get along." Culturally conscious books reflect the trials and tribulations of being African American, for example, fighting discrimination, racism, or urban or rural poverty. Sims labels as "melting pot" those books having universal themes, for example, a family picnic, a day at the zoo, the birth of a new sibling. These books show that African American children are just like other children with the exception of complexion and physical features. Most of the picture books surveyed for this chapter fell into the latter category. Picture books lend themselves to universal themes. And just as Sims discovered in her work, most of the African American characters in the books for this survey lived in nuclear families. Sims cited many reasons for this phenomenon, one of them being the middle-class family is one symbol used to represent the homogeneity of America.

It is the homogeneity of children's books that creates a high level of comfort in the average middle-class reader. Reading about the young boy following the trail on the Summer Island in *Where Does the Trail Lead?* (Albert 1991) or about the little girl's dilemma about being a bug in the school play in *The Best Bug to Be* (Johnson 1992) offers few readers chances to examine personal prejudices, misconceptions, or discomforts toward persons who look differently from them. Indeed, in both books, the fact that the protagonists are African American is only incidental to each story. The protagonists could be from any ethnic background, and the stories would be the same. Given the contentiousness in many school communities, the homogeneity in melting pot books makes them easy choices for teachers to bring to the classroom. (At a multiethnic literature workshop I conducted at a local school, several teachers requested that I send them bibliographies containing more books that celebrated our sameness rather than our differences. We all feel comfortable with other people when we discover they do some of the same things we do, or we share some of the same or familiar experiences—getting new shoes or finding lost stuffed animals or wishing for a new lunch box.) Although many melting pot books (mostly picture books) do little to inform the reader of the strengths and values of African American families, Harris (1990) notes they do serve several important functions: the amelioration of ignorance about African Americans, the portrayal of African Americans as possessing universal values and sharing universal experiences, and the provision of aesthetic experiences.

African American Families: Some Statistics

What constitutes the "model family unit" in the African American community has often been distorted in the venues of public policy and politics and in the minds of the general public. The predominant family structure in the African American community, according to the popular opinion, is the single-parent, female head of household. Census data have shown that only within the last decade has that opinion been based on fact (Billingsley 1992). The public's perception of the African American family is constantly fed by the popular press and the nightly news. Moreover the major progenitors of the female-dominated African American family characterizations often do not come from the ranks of the informed, but instead from the ranks of politicians whose agendas include influencing and shaping both public opinion and public policy with or without accurate data.

For example, during the sixties Daniel Patrick Moynihan, then a Labor Department official now a U.S. senator from New York, focused attention on the "crisis in the black family due to an excessive dependence upon the income of the African-American female" (1970, 299). Moynihan's characterization became talking points for those who needed to explain away or shift blame for the social unrest witnessed in Watts, Detroit, Newark, and so on (Gresham 1989). For after all, had not the Civil Rights and Voting Rights Bills become law with the help of legislators from the states of California, New Jersey, and Michigan? These states were not like George Wallace's Alabama or Ross Barnett's Mississippi, where exercising one's right to vote could be a life-threatening activity. Clearly the rioters had to have come from dysfunctional families, especially those in which the mother was the dominant figure.

Nearly three decades later in April 1992, when frustration over a miscarriage of justice in a Simi Valley courtroom spilled into the streets of Los Angeles, the assault against African American families, again mainly the female, single-parent units, was lead by the then vice president of the United States. He stated that the cause of the 1992 Los Angeles riots was "fundamentally a poverty of values in the inner city, where too many mothers were having babies out-of-wedlock, treating such a decision as 'another lifestyle choice.'" He continued by saying the "best anti-poverty program was marriage" (Jehl 1992; Yang and Devroy A1, 14 1992). Whether by accident or by design, the vice president's criticisms were later made to appear to be aimed at a fictional white female character on a popular TV sitcom instead of at African American families headed by females. Such a shift made the vice president appear to be merely insensitive to the struggle of single-parent families instead of being both insensitive and racist—a far greater liability in the political arena.

The irony of both, especially the Moynihan report, is that the majority of African American children did live in nuclear, two-parent homes until the 1980s (Billingsley 1992). Economic forces and other cultural upheavals created a climate that did little to support any but the strongest two-parent families, not only in the African American community but also in other ethnic communities as well. The frontal assaults on the African American family miss the true strengths of these families. Those that fault the family wholesale have failed to focus on what makes all African American families so hardy—their traditional family values. These family values are nothing so maudlin as respect for the flag, although there is a healthy streak of patriotism in most African American homes. Instead these are values that have carried African

American families from the Middle Passage through slavery and reconstruction into the twentieth century and now on the threshold of a new century. These values can be found in almost every group of African Americans that considers itself family.

In studies of what makes for strong and stable African American families, there have been several recurring characteristics. Gary and Gary (1986) found that such families typically had a strong economic base, a strong achievement orientation, a strong kinship bond, strong coping capabilities, love, resourcefulness, and family unity. Hill (1972) listed strong kinship bonds, a strong work orientation, adaptability of family roles, a strong achievement orientation, and a strong religious orientation. Billingsley (1968, 1992) cited spiritual values, educational achievement, family ties, and economic independence.

Whether in the form of the model middle-class family or a struggling single-parent family, many of the families in the books discussed here exhibited at least one or two of these African American family values. At times as the main theme, at others as subtext. Overall, the community of families in the books selected for this chapter is a showcase for the ideal nuclear families. Some are extended, others are not. The strengths of the selected titles abide in—as with any well-written piece of literature—their themes, characters, and settings and the background and skill of their authors.

Books That Bridge the Ethnic Gap With Universal Themes

Family values that are universal are easily found in many books that appeal to mainstream readers. These values can be found in the model middle-class family that is the focal point of three books featuring Jamaica: *Jamaica's Find* (Havill 1986), *Jamaica Tag-Along* (Havill 1989), and *Jamaica and Brianna* (Havill 1993). In all three books, Jamaica, an adorable little African American girl who lives with her dad, mom, and big brother in a typical nuclear family, learns and practices the lessons of two very universal themes—honesty and friendship. The reader is introduced to Jamaica in *Jamaica's Find*. While playing in the park, Jamaica finds a hat and a stuffed dog by the slide. She gives the hat to the park attendant, but she keeps the stuffed dog. Once at home, her parents remind her that there probably is an owner for the dog, too. So being an obedient child, Jamaica returns to the park the next day and gives the dog to the park attendant too. When she returns to the slide, she finds a little girl searching the area. Jamaica ascertains that the little girl is the owner of both the hat and the stuffed dog, so she takes her to the park attendant to recover both items. Jamaica learns (and so do her young readers) the value of honesty, a very necessary and color-blind lesson.

In *Jamaica Tag-Along* Jamaica tags along after her brother who is doing his very best to avoid her as he goes to meet his friends at the neighborhood playground. She begins playing by herself only to be "disturbed" by a little boy, younger then she. She immediately treats him just as her brother had treated her. Realizing that her treatment of the little boy is unnecessary, Jamaica befriends him and they enjoy the day. In *Jamaica and Brianna* Jamaica and her best friend, Brianna, are at odds as to who has the best boots. Harsh words are exchanged. Feelings are hurt. Amends are made. Jamaica and Brianna are friends again. As a group, the Jamaica books portray family life at its homogeneous best. Illustrations show the family engaged in ideal middle-class activities: Father is reading the paper, Mother, a book, and big brother is talking on the phone. Also, Father appears to be a professional, and all evidence points to Mom's being a stay-at-home mother. Jamaica and her brother represent the best in sibling and peer relationships. The universality of these three books makes them accessible to the middle-class reader of every ethnic group.

Another universal theme is the fear children have of being forgotten by a parent. In *You're My Nikki* (Eisenberg 1992) Nikki worries that her mom will forget her when her mom goes to a new job:

"I'm me," her mother laughed. "I'm the same Mama as this morning, the same Mama who just pressed her going-to-work skirt, the same Mama who just washed her hair."

"Then who am I, same Mama?"

"You're my Nikki. I'd know you if you were wearing two circus tents, and you sounded like a hoarse nanny goat."

"But what if you forget me at your new job tomorrow?"

Her mother shook her head. "No way!" I've only got one Nikki. . . . (4)

When after a harrowing day at work Mom does appear to forget Nikki's favorite activity, Nikki is crushed. After dinner is served and Mom recuperates, she talks to Nikki and explains how difficult her new job is:

"You forgot, and you forgot me too."

"It only seemed that way, honey. I was busy and tired, but I can't really forget you—ever. . . ." (29)

Nikki feels reassured by her mother's talk and life goes on. This book has all the trappings of middle-class life with one glaring exception—no father is mentioned or pictured, nor is there an explanation as to his absence. Mother is going to a new job, but the reason for the new job is never explained. Given the rise of single-parent families, especially in the ranks of the middle class, the author could have maintained the universality of the book and addressed an absentee father at the same time.

The fear of being replaced in the affections of the parents because of a new baby brother or sister is very widespread among young children. In the case of *Daniel's Dog* (Bogart 1990), the protagonist has a problem dealing with a new sibling, so he acquires a "ghost dog":

"Are you feeling mad at me, Daniel?" his mother asked one night as she tucked him in. "I'm sorry I haven't been spending as much time with you lately. Things will get better soon."

"I'm all right," Daniel told her, and smiled a little. "I'm just fine since Lucy came."

"Who is Lucy?" his mother asked.

"Lucy is my dog," Daniel explained. "My ghost dog. She always has time for me, no matter what."

"Oh, I see," Daniel's mother said. "Is she here now?"

"Right here next to my feet. She's nice and warm, and she likes it when I read stories to her." (10–12)

Lucy, the "ghost dog," helps Daniel adjust to the new baby by giving him someone to love and on whom he can concentrate his energies. According to the jacket note, the author was inspired by African American tales of ghost dogs, yet there is little in the story to suggest these ethnic roots. Bogart has written a simple book that helps children relieve the fears of being forsaken for a new family addition. Just like other books of its kind, *Daniel's Dog* provides young readers from any ethnic group (and with new siblings at home) someone with whom they can identify. However, in a disturbing resemblance to *You're My Nikki*, this book has no father present. He does not appear in the story at any time, not even incidentally. There is no explanation for his absence, when there should have been, given a new baby has just arrived home.

Instead of a ghost dog, the protagonist in *Jimmie Lee Did It!* (Cummings 1985) has an imaginary friend—Jimmie Lee. For every unexplained or annoying event that happens in the book, the response is "Jimmie Lee did it." Dirty room? Jimmie Lee did it. Toys strewn over the floor? Jimmie Lee did it. Sister's plaits are tweaked? Jimmie Lee did it. The book should delight every child whose exploits constantly get them into trouble.

Pat Cummings has also teamed up with Mildred Pitts Walter to give young readers books that focus on the relationship between a bigger sibling and younger siblings—*My Mama Needs Me* (1983) and *Two and Too Much* (1990). In both books, readers see middle-class African American children at play with their younger siblings or helping their mothers with chores. The stories are universal and unlike the books by Eisenberg and Bogart, fathers are present in both books. While neither father plays a significant part in furthering the story line, each appears to be supportive.

The presence of strong African American families in melting pot picture books can be due to the family background of the illustrator. Such is the case of books illustrated by Pat Cummings, whose warm family illustrations usually portray African American nuclear families. Family members are often models for her illustrations (Cummings 1992). By personalizing her illustrations, Cummings gives young readers a sense of strong family bonds (especially between and among siblings). In addition to the two books with Walter, Cummings has written and/or illustrated several books with universal themes that celebrate the joys of family life. Among them are *Clean*

Your Room, Harvey Moon! (1991), *I Need a Lunch Box* (Caines 1988) and *Willie's Not the Hugging Kind* (Barrett 1989). Each of these books gives the reader a slice of middle-class life with African Americans in the starring roles. In *Willie's Not the Hugging Kind*, the protagonist, Willie, struggles with his need for hugs and his best friend's remarks that hugs are silly. What's a body to do when he so wants to be hugged, but yet can't quite bring himself to admit it?

> Willie watched each morning as his daddy hugged first his mama and then Rose. He remembered how safe and happy he always felt with his daddy's strong arms around him.
>
> He remembered how good it felt to put his arms around his mama. She smelled a little like lemon and a little like the lilac powder in the bathroom. She felt big and lumpy and a little bumpy. She also felt soft and safe and warm.
>
> One morning Willie went into the kitchen and everyone was hugging everyone else. But no one hugged Willie. They didn't even see him. Willie waited hoping someone would put their arms around him. If they did, maybe he wouldn't slip away.
>
> But no one tried. Rose just said, when she saw Willie watching, "You know that Willie says he isn't the hugging kind now. He says it's all too, too silly." (17–18)

As with the Walter books, Cummings' illustrations exude warm family feelings that invite readers into the homes of middle-class African Americans. Finally, even though the immediate family is not the focus of *Just Us Women* (Caines 1982), the pleasures of being together with a favorite aunt are just as satisfying:

> Saturday morning is jump-off time.
> Aunt Martha and I are going to drive
> all the way to North Carolina
> in her new car.
> Aunt Martha says,
> "No boys and no men,
> just us women." (7)

This leisurely visit to see Southern relatives is made all the more enjoyable with Cummings' use of her sister and niece as models for the two travellers.

Bridging the Ethnic Gap with Eloise Greenfield and Lucille Clifton

Take one universal theme—for instance, a new baby come home from the hospital or a father's coming home from the army. Add the skills of an Eloise Greenfield or Lucille Clifton. Mix thoroughly and one has masterpiece. Perhaps better than any authors for children, Clifton and Greenfield capture in their writing the trials and joys of the young. The language each uses gives the books life. For example, Kevin in *She Come Bringing Me That Baby Girl* (Greenfield 1974) is completely outdone when he discovers that his new sibling is . . . a girl!

> I asked Mama to bring me a little brother from the hospital, but she come bringing me that little baby girl wrapped all up in a pink blanket.
>
> I was glad to see Mama even if she didn't bring me what I wanted. When she got out of the car, I ran to the door to meet her.
>
> Mama hugged me hard. She was glad to see me, too. But she only had one arm to hug me with 'cause she didn't put that little girl down for a minute. (6–9)

The reader can feel the disappointment Kevin feels—a girl—no football buddy or any good "boy" activities. Even worse, his father says he's a big brother, something that's definitely not to his liking: "I don't want to be a big brother to no girl." His parents are patient with him. His mother tells him she was once like his little sister. Kevin ponders this tidbit of news. He is really surprised when his mother tells him she expects his help. Eventually he decides that perhaps having a little sister is not so bad after all, just as long as his mother has one arm free to give him a hug. Compared to *Daniel's Dog, She Come Bringing Me That Baby Girl* is a fifty thousand kilowatts clear channel station.

Children who create invisible alter egos have already been examined in two earlier books, but the Greenfield touch makes *Me and Neesie* (1975) an extra special read:

> It was a good thing for Neesie that Mama couldn't see her, or she would have got a good spanking.
>
> Mama couldn't hear her either, but I could. All the time Mama was cornrowing my hair, Neesie kept calling me and waving her arms around, trying to make me look at her. After a while, I got tired of it.
>
> "Stop it, Neesie!" I said. I couldn't play with her all the time, even if she was my best friend.
>
> Mama pulled my head back around. "Keep your head still, Janell," she said. "And stop talking to yourself."
>
> "I was talking to Neesie, Mama," I said.
>
> "Nobody's in this bedroom but you and me, you talking to yourself."
>
> "Your mother don't know nothing," Neesie said. She made a face at Mama. (6–9)

Children delight in reading the passage where Neesie "disses" Janell's mother—quite the reason to have an imaginary friend who can do those things no respectful child would ever do.

Amifika (Clifton 1977) is a humorous but gentle story that focuses the fears of a child who thinks he is about to be discarded. Amifika knows his father is coming home from the army, because he overhears his mother talking to Cousin Katy about it. He also hears his mother talk about making room in their small apartment. Her solution is to discard things he will not remember so therefore will not miss. Needless to say, Amifika thinks he will be among the discards; since he cannot remember his father, surely his father will not remember him:

> Amifika turned his head and closed his eyes tight and tried to remember his Daddy, but he couldn't. Just something dark and warm that kept moving in his mind.
> "If I don't remember him, how he gon' remember me?" he thought. "I be what Mama get rid of. Like she said, he can't miss what he don't remember. I be the thing they get rid of." (13)

Again through skill and a thorough understanding of her characters, Clifton brings a very satisfying and joyous closure to Amifika's story:

> "Wake up boy." The man looked at Amifika's face.
> "Do you remember me?"
> "You my own Daddy! My Daddy!" he hollered at the top of his voice and kept hollering as his Daddy held him and danced and danced and danced all around the room. (26, 30)

In every listing of traditional African American family values, strong kinship ties are cited. These ties are evident in all of Clifton and Greenfield's writings. In one of Greenfield's most recent books those strong intergenerational ties are at work. *William and the Good Old Days* (1993) is the story of William, a small boy of about seven or eight, who reminisces about the "good old days" when his grandma was doing okay and feeding the neighborhood at her restaurant. We can see in his description of the day before his grandma gets sick the importance of his grandma to him and to the neighborhood. Also in the passage, in addition to the grandmother, are other elders in the neighborhood on whose wisdom and strength the neighborhood depends:

> Yeah, I'm mad. That's because I *still* think it was that fly that made my grandma sick. . . . I was sitting on this tall stool in Grandma's restaurant, eating my good dinner. Granddaddy and Mr. Frank were sitting on the other stools, and Miss Betty and Miss Lucille were sitting in the big chairs, and Grandma was standing at the stove, stirring the bean soup. Everybody was laughing and having a good time. (4–5)

Greenfield's story of William and his grandma captures the essence of intergenerational ties that have always been a staple of African American families and communities.

Lucille Clifton has given us a series of prose poem books that gently portray the story of a single mother and her son, Everett Anderson. This series of books began in 1970 and introduced readers to Everett Anderson, a lively little boy who loves his mother but misses his father in *Some of the Days of Everett Anderson* (1970). We laugh with Everett Anderson as he gets a new neighbor—a girl no less—in *Everett Anderson's Friend* (1976):

> Someone new has come to stay
> in 13A, in 13A
> and Everett Anderson's Mama and he
> can't wait to see, can't wait to see
> whether it's girls or
> whether it's boys and
> how are their books and
> how are their toys and
> where they've been and
> where they go and
> who are their friends and
> the people they know,
> oh, someone new has come to stay
> next door in 13A. (6)

We celebrate Christmas with Everett in *Everett Anderson's Christmas Coming* (1991). *Everett Anderson's Year* (1974) is a year full of fun. Everett's Mom meets Mr. Perry, and they get married in *Everett Anderson's 1-2-3* (1977). Subsequently there is a new baby in *Everett Anderson's Nine-Month Long* (1978). Finally, Everett has to deal with the death of his biological father in *Everett Anderson's Goodbye* (1983):

> Everett Anderson holds the hand
> of his mama until he falls asleep
> and dreams about Daddy
> in his chair, and
> at the park, and
> everywhere.
> Daddy always laughing or never,
> just Daddy, Daddy, forever and ever. (9)

Whether writing about single-parenthood or getting a new neighbor, Clifton treats each character with respect. She writes nothing that stigmatizes Everett Anderson's mother for being a single parent nor Everett Anderson for being fatherless. Single-parenthood was and is a fact of life in all ethnic communities. African Americans have always viewed the single-parent unit as one type to build on not to stigmatize (Billingsley 1992). Clifton's books reflect that view.

Both Greenfield and Clifton write fondly and skillfully about all types of African American families. The parents are loving and caring. The situations about which they write are realistic and never condescending. There is a strong male presence in almost every book—whether that male be father, stepfather, or grandfather. Each author respects her readers with accurate portrayals of African American families who honor the traditional family values that are a natural part of growing up African American.

Other Looks at Single-Parenthood

As subject matter for picture books has become more culturally and socially conscious in the last decade, authors have broached more sensitive topics, among them single-parenthood. In some of the books, the authors portray the difficulty some women have raising children alone as in *The Black Snowman* (Mendez 1989). In this story, Jacob is a lonely and angry boy who resents being poor and being African American. He can think of nothing to cheer about even though it is near Christmas. He can only think of his family's poverty:

> Jacob dressed quickly and followed delicious breakfast smells coming from the kitchen. His younger brother, PeeWee, was standing beside their mother at the stove.
> "Can we go shopping today?" PeeWee asked.
> "Well, not today," Mama said.
> "Not today or any day," Jacob interrupted. "Poor folks like us can't afford Christmas."
> "Now Jacob . . ." Mama spoke, trying to smooth over the hurt she saw rushing into PeeWee's eyes. (11)

The story, while not directly focused on a mother-only family, does show how being a single parent often impacts on the family's financial situation.

In other books there is a lighter touch as in *What Kind of Baby-Sitter Is This?* (Johnson 1991). The single mother in this book is going back to school, so she has to find someone to care for her child. He is very surprised to discover that the baby-sitter his mother has hired, an older woman, is quite a sports fanatic. *Jenny* (Wilson 1990) features Jenny, a girl who delights in her world, enjoys her grandparents and mother, but really misses her daddy. This book has a very universal appeal because it deals with one of the major reasons for the increase of single-parent families—divorce.

In perhaps one of the most striking picture books ever written with a single-parent, female head of household, *Amazing Grace* (1991), Mary Hoffman and Caroline Binch underscore how the family's values and beliefs are more important than the family's structure. As an only child, Grace is a girl who loves stories (obviously, she reads and is read to often). When she isn't being read to or told a story or when she is not reading herself, she acts out the adventures with the help of her trusty cat. She plays folk characters like Anansi, the Spiderman. She plays historical figures like Hannibal and Joan of Arc. Grace loves adventures and acting so much that she decides that Peter Pan is the character she wants to be in the class play. But naysayers Raj and Natalie say she cannot be Peter Pan because she is neither a boy nor is she white. Grace goes home a very sad little girl:

> "What's the matter?" asked Ma.
> "Raj said I can't be Peter Pan because I'm a girl."
> "That just shows what Raj knows," said Ma. "A girl can be Peter Pan if she wants to be."
> Grace cheered up, then later she remembered something else. "Natalie says I can't be Peter Pan because I'm black," she said.
> Ma looked angry. But before she could speak, Nana said, "It seems that Natalie is another one who don't know nothing. You can be anything you want, Grace, if you put your mind to it." (16–17)

Nana solves Grace's problem with wit and style. Her solution reveals to us all how much a person can accomplish through belief in self and perseverance.

African American Families Facing Social Injustice

As previously stated for years, picture book authors rarely tread in waters that publishers or the public deem controversial or discomforting. Most culturally conscious books are chapter books, whose reading clientele is older and perhaps more sophisticated. More recent picture books have had more "adult" themes. There are picture books that portray homelessness, examine the ravages of war on children and the consequences of being "discovered" by explorers. Picture books that portray the bigotry that African Americans face have been practically nonexistent until recently. There are still very few of them, but those authors who do tackle this subject have done so without being pedantic. Each examines the imperfect world that is the United States of America where there still are people who make rules that discriminate against racial, ethnic, and religious minorities.

In the Caldecott honor book *Tar Beach* (1991), Faith Ringgold's Cassie Louise Lightfoot wishes to be free to go anywhere she wants and buy the union building her father is working on:

> Daddy took me to see the new union building he is working on. He can walk on steel girders high up in the sky and not fall. They call him Cat. But still he can't join the union because Grandpa wasn't a member. (16–18)

The "grandfather clause" was the subtle way northern unions (and southern state and local governments) prevented ethnic and religious minorities from becoming members of unions (and in the South to keep African Americans from voting). Ringgold also addresses how the lack of being in a union forces Cassie's father to look for work away from his family. This causes undue stress on her mother, who cries all winter because Dad is not at home.

Li'l Sis and Uncle Willie (Everett 1991) is loosely based on the life of African American painter William H. Johnson. Johnson was born in the South, trained in New York, and fled to Europe to work and live because the people there were "friendlier to black people." The story focusses on one of his visits down South. Li'l Sis, a young girl, enjoys his visit, marvels at his artistic accomplishments, and is saddened when he returns to New York. Surely, she thinks, New York must be a most wonderful place. But hearing about job riots changes her mind, and she decides that perhaps she is better off living in the South.

Uncle Jed's Barbershop (Mitchell 1993) is the story of a very determined man whose dream is to own his own barbershop. We meet him in the 1920s. African Americans have no local barbershop to which they can go, so Uncle Jed goes from house to house giving kin and neighbors alike haircuts. Uncle Jed painstakingly saves his money. However, two unforeseen disasters threaten Uncle Jed's dream. The first is a medical emergency. The narrator, a young girl, is critically ill, and the only way her life can be saved is with an operation. Uncle Jed comes to the rescue. Once again, Uncle Jed begins to save his money, but this time the Great Depression affects African Americans and whites alike. Uncle Jed loses his money when the banks crash. Uncle Jed perseveres. Finally at the age of seventy-nine, Uncle Jed opens his barbershop. He does not live long after that, but he lives long enough to realize his dream.

From Miss Ida's Porch (Belton 1993) examines the effects that segregation had on even great African Americans like Duke Ellington and Marian Anderson. In this nostalgic story, neighborhood children gather on Miss Ida's porch to listen to the stories of some of the older neighbors who have wonderful names like Poissant and Shoo Kate. One story that many of the adults sitting on the porch begin telling is the famous story of Marian Anderson, the Daughters of the American Revolution, and Constitution Hall. (African American history being relived right there on Miss Ida's porch.) After the DAR refused to let Marian Anderson sing in Constitution Hall, her concert was moved to the Lincoln Memorial, and among those attending the concert was the First Lady, Eleanor Roosevelt, and one of the neighbors on Miss Ida's porch.

During the 1920s, hundreds of thousands of African Americans fled the prejudice and bigotry of the South for a better life "up North." This "great migration" has been captured in art by Jacob Lawrence (1993). Because of this great migration, it is not unusual for many African American families to have strong roots in the South. Many picture books focusing on African American family life highlight the return home to see relatives who remained in the South. In *Back Home* (Pinkney 1992) Ernestine goes "down South" to visit relatives. *Bigmama's* (Crews 1991) is autobiographical. The author tells of the wonderful summers he and his family had when they went to Florida to visit Bigmama. Perhaps Crews sums up the excitement of going South to visit grandparents best when he wrote:

Everybody sitting around the table that filled the room—Bigmama, Bigpapa, Uncle Slank, our cousins from down the road, and all of us. We talked about what we did last year. We talked about what we were going to do this year. We talked so much we hardly had time to eat. (29)

The African American family is alive and flourishing both in children's books and in real life. For the most part these families exhibit very strong kinship bonds and very traditional family values. Just as in real life, there are families that are affected by outside forces, and just as in real life, families are coping with, teaching, honoring, and adhering to these values—a far cry from the portrayal of African American families in the public's eye.

Professional References

BARR, CATHERINE, ed. 1993. *The Bowker Annual, Library and Trade Almanac. 38th ed.* New Providence, NJ: R.R. Bowker, Co.

BLACK EXPERIENCE IN CHILDREN'S BOOK COMMITTEE. 1989. *The Black Experience in Children's Books.* New York: New York Public Library.

BILLINGSLEY, ANDREW. 1968. *Black Families in White America.* Englewood Cliffs, NJ: Prentice-Hall.

———. 1992. *Climbing Jacob's Ladder: The Enduring Legacy of African-American Families.* New York: Simon and Schuster.

DISTRICT OF COLUMBIA PUBLIC LIBRARY CHILDREN'S SERVICES. 1992. *The Afro-American in Books for Children,* 4th. rev. ed. Washington, D.C.: District of Columbia Public Library.

GARY, LAWRENCE E., and ROBENIA B. GARY. 1986. *Searching for the Strengths of Black Families.* Presentation at the 16th annual conference of the National Black Child Development Institute, Miami, FL: ERIC ED 277 463.

GLANCY, BARBARA J. 1969. "The Changing Characteristics of the American Negro in Children's Fiction of 1951 through 1963." Master's thesis, Ohio State University.

GRESHAM, JEWEL HANDY. 1989. "The Politics of Family in America." *The Nation* (24–31 July): 116–22.

HALL, KATHRYN L. 1972. "A Comparative Analysis of Problematic Situations and Behavior Patterns in Realistic Juvenile Literature from 1950–1971." Master's thesis, Ohio State University, Columbus, OH.

HARRIS, VIOLET J. 1990. "African-American Children's Literature: The First One Hundred Years." *Journal of Negro Education* 59: 540–55.

———, ed. 1992. *Teaching Multicultural Literature in Grades K-8.* Norwood, MA: Christopher-Gordon Publishers.

HILL, ROBERT B. 1972. *The Strengths of Black Families.* New York: Emerson Hall.

HUCK, CHARLOTTE S., SUSAN HEPLER, and JANET HICKMAN. 1993. *Children's Literature in the Elementary School.* 5th. ed. Fort Worth, TX: Harcourt Brace.

JEHL, DOUGLAS. 1992. "Quayle Deplores Eroding Values; Cites TV Show." *Los Angeles Times*, 20 May, A1, A14.

LARRICK, NANCY. 1965. "The All-White World of Children's Books." *Saturday Review* (11 September): 63–5, 84–5.

MOYNIHAN, DANIEL PATRICK. 1970. "The Ordeal of the Negro Family." In *The Family Life of Black People*, edited by C. V. Willie. Columbus, OH: Merrill.

ROLLINS, CHARLEMAE HILL. 1941. *We Build Together: A Reader's Guide to Negro Life and Literature for Elementary and High School Use*. Chicago: National Council of Teachers of English.

SIMS, RUDINE. 1982. *Shadow and Substance: Afro-American Experience in Contemporary Children's Fiction*. Urbana, IL: NCTE.

THOMAS NIDA. 1972. "Out of the Melting Pot." *Library Journal* 97: 3421–3.

THOMPSON, DEBORAH L. 1974. "The Portrayal of the Black Family in Selected Children's Books, 1965–1973." Master's thesis, Ohio State University, Columbus, OH.

YANG, JOHN E., and ANN DEVROY. 1992. "Clinton Finds New Voice of Emotion; Quayle Decries 'Poverty of Values': Vice-President Urges Firm Hand in Cities." *Washington Post*, 20 May, A1, A14.

Children's Literature

ALBERT, BURTON. 1991. *Where Does the Trail Lead?* Illustrated by Brian Pinkney. New York: Simon & Schuster.

BARRETT, JOYCE DURHAM. 1989. *Willie's Not the Hugging Kind*. Illustrated by Pat Cummings. New York: HarperCollins.

BAUM, BETTY. 1965. *Patricia Crosses Town*. Illustrated by Nancy Grossman. New York: Knopf.

BELTON, SANDRA. 1993. *From Miss Ida's Porch*. Illustrated by Floyd Cooper. New York: Four Winds Press.

BOGART, JO ELLEN. 1990. *Daniel's Dog*. Illustrated by Janet Wilson. New York: Scholastic.

CAINES, JEANNETTE. 1982. *Just Us Women*. Illustrated by Pat Cummings. New York: HarperCollins.

———. 1988. *I Need a Lunchbox*. Illustrated by Pat Cummings. New York: Harper & Row.

CLIFTON, LUCILLE. 1970. *Some of the Days of Everett Anderson*. Illustrated by Evaline Ness. New York: Henry Holt.

———. 1974. *Everett Anderson's Year*. Illustrated by Ann Grifalconi. New York: Holt.

———. 1976. *Everett Anderson's Friend*. Illustrated by Ann Grifalconi. New York: Holt.

———. 1977. *Amifika*. Illustrated by Thomas DiGrazia. New York: Dutton.

———. 1977. *Everett Anderson's 1-2-3*. Illustrated by Ann Grifalconi. New York: Holt.

———. 1978. *Everett Anderson's Nine Month Long*. Illustrated by Ann Grifalconi. New York: Holt.

———. 1983. *Everett Anderson's Goodbye*. Illustrated by Ann Grifalconi. New York: Holt.

———. 1991. *Everett Anderson's Christmas Coming*. Illustrated by Jan Spivey Gilchrist. New York: Henry Holt.

CREWS, DONALD. 1991. *Bigmama's.* New York: Greenwillow.

CUMMINGS, PAT. 1985. *Jimmie Lee Did It!* New York: Lothrop.

———. 1991. *Clean Your Room, Harvey Moon!* New York: Bradbury.

———. 1992. *Talking With Artists.* New York: Bradbury Press.

EISENBERG, PHYLLIS ROSE. 1992. *You're My Nikki.* Pictures by Jill Kastner. New York: Dial.

EVERETT, GWEN. *Li'l Sis and Uncle Willie.* 1991. Paintings by William H. Johnson. New York: Rizzoli & National Museum of American Art/Smithsonian.

GREENFIELD, ELOISE. 1974. *She Come Bringing Me That Baby Girl.* Illustrated by John Steptoe. Philadelphia: Lippincott.

———. 1975 *Me and Neesie.* Illustrated by Monetta Barnett. New York: Crowell.

———. 1993. *William and the Good Old Days.* Illustrated by Jan Spivey Gilchrist. New York: HarperCollins.

HAVILL, JUANITA. 1986. *Jamaica's Find.* Illustrated by Anne Sibley O'Brien. Boston: Houghton Mifflin.

———. 1989. *Jamaica Tag-Along.* Illustrated by Anne Sibley O'Brien. Boston: Houghton Mifflin.

———. 1993. *Jamaica and Brianna.* Illustrated by Anne Sibley O'Brien. Boston: Houghton Mifflin.

HOFFMAN, MARY. 1991. *Amazing Grace.* Illustrated by Caroline Binch. New York: Dial.

JOHNSON, DOLORES. 1991. *What Kind of Baby-Sitter Is This?* New York: Macmillan.

———. 1992. *The Best Bug to Be.* New York: Macmillan.

LAWRENCE, JACOB. 1993. *The Great Migration.* New York: HarperCollins.

MENDEZ, PHIL. 1989. *The Black Snowman.* Illustrated by Carole Byard. New York: Scholastic.

MITCHELL, MAGAREE KING. 1993. *Uncle Jed's Barbershop.* Illustrated by James Ransome. New York: Simon and Schuster.

PINKNEY, GLORIA JEAN. 1992. *Back Home.* Illustrated by Jerry Pinkney. New York: Dial.

RINGGOLD, FAITH. 1991. *Tar Beach.* New York: Crown.

WALTER, MILDRED PITTS. 1983. *My Mama Needs Me.* Illustrated by Pat Cummings. New York: Lothrop.

———. 1990. *Two and Too Much.* Illustrated by Pat Cummings. New York: Bradbury.

WILSON, BETH P. 1990. *Jenny.* Illustrated by Dolores Johnson. New York: Macmillan.

EIGHT

Living in Sami's and Ahmed's Worlds: Picture Books Explore Children's Lives in Other Countries

___

JUDITH HEIDE GILLILAND

One of the most exciting things that has been happening in children's literature is its exploration of various cultures here and around the world. More than ever, an understanding and respect for human diversity is vital not only to our well-being, but to our very survival. By learning about the lives of other people we gain tolerance, different perspectives on how we live our own lives, and new possibilities for dealing with old problems. And we increase our chances for peace.

We now have a growing selection of children's books about Native Americans, Hispanics, African Americans, Chinese, Japanese, Indians, Africans, Latin Americans. Many of them are thoughtful, sympathetic pictures of people living, working, and playing.

I remember some of the "multicultural" books from my childhood. They often featured children in various strange costumes, wooden shoes, bizarre hairstyles, doing extremely odd things, like the Japanese boy who bowed his head all the way to the ground without bending his legs! "Different" was the byword. And different is wonderful. However, I think today's best books celebrate not only those wonderful differences, but also our samenesses, our common humanity.

For children—for adults too—different can be interesting, but it can also stir feelings other than interest: contempt, fear, alienation, ridicule, boredom. For many children, "differentness" is like a wall without windows or doors, an impenetrable barrier. Often, it is the small things, the little details, that help a child begin to see through it.

When I was a girl my grandmother, who was also a writer and passionately interested in the world, insisted that all of us children learn to count to ten in several languages. And to say "please" and "thank you," "yes" and "no."

Knowing just that much opened for me a small crack in the wall, a little window.

It made me feel a certain ownership, a special relationship. Spain and Spanish were not impossibly strange; after all I could count to ten! I could say yes and no! Its sounds were sounds I could make. The same with French and German and Russian and Italian and Danish.

Recently I spoke to a group of high school students about writing children's books. I noticed that one girl, in particular, was very interested in what I had to say about the Middle East, where two of my books take place. Afterwards she came up and confided that years ago someone had taught her to write her name in Arabic. That window had been opened a crack for her, and Arabic and the Middle East will never be entirely strange to her; she will always feel that special "ownership."

Usually children's multicultural books attempt to do just that, to help make more likely a child's lasting interest in and sympathy for another culture. By spending some time with another child, by wearing his or her shoes for a short while and seeing the small events of that life, even if only between the pages of a book, our children may be able to remove some of the barriers that cause misunderstandings and worse.

Promoting tolerance and goodwill is not the only benefit of exploring the lives of children in other countries. Multicultural books for children can give us—children *and* adults—perspective on our own lives. They can lead us to question some of our own assumptions about what is important. We can learn that maybe we do not have all the answers, that we may find something of value outside our own small world. We may learn to be less judgmental.

The Day of Ahmed's Secret (1990) comes from the years I lived in Cairo while my husband was a diplomat. From the moment I returned to the United States after four years in the Middle East, my mother wanted to write a book with me about some of my experiences. She is Florence Parry Heide, the author of many books for children. We both felt that children needed to know more about the Middle East, to learn that there is more to that part of the world than mummies, Aladdin, and fighting.

Ahmed was our first collaboration. It is the story of a little boy of modern-day Cairo who has the difficult job of delivering heavy canisters of cooking gas, "butagaz," to people in the city. As he goes about his job Ahmed thinks about how he can't wait to tell his family his secret. "Today I have a secret, and all day long my secret will be like a friend to me. Tonight I will tell it to my family, but now I have work to do in my city" (1).

He also thinks about the city, and the things his father has told him about Cairo, about its great age and importance. What his father tells him about life stays with Ahmed, like the sand off the desert. "The sand is a part of each day, like the noise, like the colors of the city, like the things my father has said" (20). He meets friends, talks, philosophizes, works, and finally goes home. "Everyone is waiting for me," he says. At last he can tell his secret, which is that he can write his name, which he does, in Arabic.

We had several reasons for writing *Ahmed*. We wanted children to meet Ahmed, to admire him, to see his differences, and to notice that in many ways he is like them. We hoped they would reflect on how precious literacy is to him. And we wanted to help counteract the awful stereotypes of Arabs that children are presented with in many and subtle ways in cartoons, in sitcoms, in comic books, even in commercials: Arabs as bloodthirsty fanatics who wave scimitars around, Arabs as rich sheiks driving around in Cadillacs, Arabs surrounded by harems of seductive veiled women, Arabs as terrorists, as bad guys.

I think one of the reasons these stereotypes have prevailed is that there have been few, if any, children's books about the Middle East to counteract them. And part of the reason for that, I'm afraid, was that publishers were fearful of giving offense. The words *Middle East* have so long been identified with the word *politics* in American minds that it has been hard to separate them. When we first sent out the manuscript of Ahmed, for instance, it was returned with the comment that it was "probably too political."

Ahmed has very little, materially. He has no TV, no Little League. He has to work hard as a boy. He will have to work hard all his life. But he is secure in his world. He is appreciative of the everyday things around him, the bustle of the city, the sound his cart makes, the shade the old walls of the city provide. And he is proud of himself, of who he is.

He says, "Everyone is going somewhere. Like me, everyone has something important to do. I know [my city] would not be the same without me" (2). Why is Ahmed so confident?

First, I would like to say that he is real, that I met many Ahmeds in Egypt. The philosophical nature of even the children impressed me. Ahmed knows who he is. He is the son of loving parents he in turn loves and respects, the brother of siblings who honor him, the cousin of cousins who see him as a brother. He contributes in a real way to the well-being of his family. He has plenty to eat, but not much more. He is busy, as is his family. But they are not too busy to share the stories of their lives. He listens to his family, they listen to him, and every story is important.

After a long day of working, when it is finally time for Ahmed to share his secret with his family, he shows them what he has learned. He says, "I write my name over and over as they watch, and I think of my name now lasting longer than the sound of it, maybe even lasting, like the old buildings in the city, a thousand years" (30).

Ahmed feels like a complete person. Not all children feel like this. In fact, low self-esteem among children of all economic circumstances in America is an issue of great concern to parents and educators. Many children feel needy and unfulfilled. There are probably many contributing factors to this, but I believe one of them is television and its commercials.

From the earliest moments of life, the American child who watches commercial television is professionally and skillfully directed to this conclusion: "I am an incomplete person. Without those shoes (that soft drink, those pants, a body like that person's) I cannot be as attractive, or popular, or happy as everyone else. Look at *them. They* belong, *they* are happy. *I am missing out!*" This is the purpose of most advertising, of course, to make listeners feel that they need something, that without it they are lacking, they are somehow inferior. Many of our children hear this message over and over again every day of their lives.

In the words of a recent ad: "I need it, I want it, I gotta have it!" Without the right shoes, I am nobody.

We, as adults, try to tell the children that they *are* somebody. But who do they believe? Whose message will prove to be more powerful? Children's assumptions about themselves and the world around them are arrived at in many different ways: from parents, teachers, friends, television—and books. We cannot tell children what their conclusions must be, but we can certainly guide them to look beyond manipulation and slogans. We don't always do that. Having been well-trained by Madison Avenue ourselves, we all too often present serious issues to our children in the form of platitudes and phrases. "Be Proud of Yourself!" In presenting the "issues of the day" we resort, almost by reflex, to the methods and images of the electronic marketplace, losing sight of the larger issues and neglecting to lay the foundations of truth.

For instance, is the world a good place or a bad place? How does a child answer that question? How do we answer that question?

One answer we sometimes give is that the world is a mess, and we human beings have made it so. We present our lesson, often in the form of cute phrases: POLLUTION IS THE SOLUTION—NOT! First graders draw pictures of garbage heaps and dying animals and a choking planet.

But is that our first answer—the world is a mess!—the one we start with? How can you believe that the planet is worth saving if you don't know why? It seems to me that the first answer might be, the world is a good place. Can we show our children that it's so?

With the tremendous amount of confusing, disconnected pieces of information fired at children in machine-gun fashion, we cannot assume that their underlying assumption *is* that the world is a good place. I think it is entirely possible that one of their impressions is that this is a world of pollution, extinction, violence, death, fear, and meaninglessness. Television, newspapers, the radio all seem to tell them so.

Books, though, can look past the news and the horror story to the deeper stories of courage and hope. They can explore the lives of other people in "real-time" in a way no other medium can. The best ones are not slick and slogany; they give real glimpses of life, offering small truths and insights in small servings. There is time to think about them.

Today, with children "witnessing" war and violence and environmental threats everywhere they turn, the need grows for books that address these issues sensitively.

All of these thoughts, and more, were ones my mother and I had before writing *Sami and the Time of the Troubles* (1992), a book about a boy living through the civil war in Beirut. It begins: "My name is Sami, and I live in the time of the troubles.

It is a time of guns and bombs. It is a time that has lasted all my life, and I am ten years old" (1).

This is a book my mother and I did not think at first we would write, or could write. I lived in Beirut at the beginning of the war there, where my husband was a diplomat. I knew Sami. Like him, I listened many long nights to the sounds of artillery shells crashing into nearby high-rises, and to the radio, our link with the outside world.

After each round of fighting, we would emerge from our homes almost dazed. The sun would be shining brightly—the sun always shines brightly in Beirut—and the world would look beautiful, a little dusty, but beautiful. The air would fill with the noises of normal life: cars honking, people calling, and children playing, glad to be outside.

Sami lives in this world of "good" and "bad" times, referred to as "The Troubles" by the Lebanese. On bad days, Sami stays in the basement with his mother, sister, grandfather, and uncle. His father was killed in a bomb explosion earlier, but Sami remembers him well. Sami's mother has insisted they surround themselves with some of the beautiful things they have:

> My uncle brought the carpets here [to the basement shelter] from our house, because my mother says there must be nice things around us to remind us of the good days, to remind us of how it used to be. This is the reason we have, here in the basement, the big brass vase that was a wedding present to her and my father.
>
> "There is so little space, why do we need this?" my uncle asked as he carried it. My mother did not answer him, and the vase stayed. (6)

When it is quiet and Sami is allowed to go outside, he says,

> The air is dusty, but the sky is blue. I had forgotten the blueness of it! And there is more green. Each time we go out, there is more green. My uncle says nature is trying to cover up the sad ruins of the buildings, trying to cover up what the fighting has done. (16)

Sami plays war with his friend Amir:

> I find a piece of wood that looks like a gun and help Amir find one, too.
> "My brother has a real gun," he says.
> We run, we hide, we pretend to shoot, we pretend to die. I see my mother at a stall buying flowers, and she frowns at me. She does not like for me to play this game.
> After a while, we stop to rest. Amir says, "When we are older, we will have real guns."
> I shake my head. "The fighting will be over then. It cannot last forever."
> "But who will stop it?" asks Amir. (22, 24)

This book is partly about Sami's answer to that question, who will stop it?

Should a children's picture book about war be written? Does this only contribute to the notion that the world is a bad place? This is a question my mother and I thought much about. War and children do not mix. And yet, in many countries on this planet, war and children do mix. In some ways, even in America.

Children in America know about war. What do they think about it?

While we discussed these issues, back and forth over the phone and in letters, my mother heard a report on the radio that radio announcers in Beirut were counseling parents to smile at their children as they hid in their basements, as a way of reassuring them. It was that report, in a way, that decided us. We thought about the images America's children have of war. In a way, Sami would be a way of reassuring them that hope and love live on in the worst of times.

What are those images children have, and where do they come from? They see "the real thing" on the nightly news, graphic footage from the world's hot spots. They see movies. They know all about war.

War is terrifying. Images of blown-apart homes confront children in their living rooms, suffering faces of distant strangers stare out of the front pages of morning papers, and the radio delivers the news of more death every hour on the hour. The world is a scary place, and there is nothing we can do about it. We are potential victims.

War is glorious. Smart bombs seek out faceless victims through the windows and doors of their offices. Anonymous "others" are zapped, pulverized, disappeared. Other people in faraway places can die. They are not like us, so maybe it's OK.

War is inevitable, like the weather; it happens all the time and there is nothing you can do about it.

War is boring. War and violence are the everyday ingredients of life. People die. Ho hum. With a steady diet of violent pictures can a child become untouched by human misery?

Sami knows what war really is. He hides in the basement with his family as the world falls apart outside. He knows what it is like to be afraid for his life.

But he knows something else: that in the midst of all the hatred and fear outside, he is loved and cherished by his family. He has dignity, hope, and even a kind of serenity.

We do not explain, in the text of the book, that this takes place in Beirut, Lebanon, for several reasons. What happened and happens in Beirut is a complicated story, the details of which are not important to Sami. War is war. Fighting is fighting. And although this is a story about Beirut, it is just as much a story about Somalia, Nagorno-Karabakh, Bosnia. Sami is every child: he wears blue jeans and red tennis shoes, he lives in a city of high-rises and cars, he builds sand castles and forts and plays war and goes to school.

I think of *Sami and the Time of the Troubles* as a book of hope. It is a book that celebrates, I think, the strength of the human spirit.

It is a story of courage and optimism, of small beauties in the midst of a large ugliness, of love existing in a world of hatred. Sami's life consists of little pleasures: the taste of a peach, the sound of a song, the blueness of the sky, the safe sound of hammers and honking horns, of memory and stories.

Mostly, though, *Sami* illustrates the power of love. Sami learns firsthand about violence and death, but he is, nevertheless, surrounded by love. The love of his family is his strength, his reality.

As the war in Beirut raged on, many psychologists feared for the mental health of the children, and for good reason. There is no question that the effects of war have taken their toll on the children of Lebanon, especially on those who lost close family members. And yet, I have spoken to people who have been to Lebanon since the war, who have visited with young adults who experienced the civil war for most of their lives, and they have expressed surprise at their spirit, at their hopefulness for the future. These are the children whose families held them, loved them.

I think of some of the children of the inner cities and elsewhere in America, the ones for whom violence is a fact of life, the ones for whom violence comes from those who should love them. And in some ways, I think Sami was better off.

For Sami, stories are what connect him to the past and the future, and what make sense out of the present. He remembers the stories his father used to tell him about the peach orchards, and he wonders if the orchards are still there. When his mother brings home a peach on one of the quiet days, Sami says, "I think again of the orchards of peach trees my father loved so much. Now I know they must still be there. Someday I will go to see them. Someday, when the fighting has stopped" (30). He laughs with his family at the funny stories his uncle tells them as they wait in their basement. And, throughout the book, he ponders the meaning of the story his grandfather has told him many times.

It is the story of the Day of the Children. That was the day, years before, when children marched in the streets, carrying signs that said "Stop the fighting," "Please! No more war!" This, like many of the details in *Sami*, is true. I saw the children march. This is what happened.

It was after a week or two of exceptionally heavy fighting. We were all tired; no one in Beirut had slept much during that time. It was early morning and another cease-fire had been announced. The guns had stopped. We opened our windows and the doors onto the balcony overlooking the street. The air smelled of jasmine. And then we heard a commotion. It was coming from down the street and we ran out to our balcony to see what it was. It was the sound of hundreds of children marching towards us, and they were carrying signs in Arabic and French and English. As we stood there watching them we could see that many other grownups stood on their balconies, like us, and wept, like us. We all believed, a little, that maybe those who were fighting would listen. They didn't. At least not that time.

Sami comes to realize that maybe now it is time to march again, that maybe this time "they" will listen. He does not feel powerless.

Sami explores war from the point of view of the people who live it. War is not exotic. The victims of war are real people who care about their lives and about the lives of their loved ones. It is too easy for children to think, "They are not like us, they care less about life than we do, they are used to death and violence." And it is too easy for adults to think that, also. Our children will be adults someday. Our hope for peace depends on their ability to understand what war is and what its real consequences are and that it's up to them to stop the fighting.

Books like this are, I think, a good way to introduce classroom discussions on why people fight and on approaches to conflict resolution.

Sami and Ahmed come from very different worlds, different from each other's and probably very different from the world of the reader. Still, their humanity, I hope, makes them almost familiar. We can identify with them. Their stories are worth hearing.

Of course, there are five-and-a-half billion other stories on this planet, all of them worth hearing. Writing a multicultural book is like writing any other book: you cannot say everything. Ahmed is representative of only some people in Cairo. He is not a girl, he is not rich or of the middle class, he is not an adult. And yet, since there are so few books about, say, the Middle East, there is the danger that those few will be taken to be the only truth about that part of the world. That is why we can never have too many stories! All of us, children and adults, need to hear them, and see them, the more the better.

There are more and more children's books appearing every year—and they are being taken more seriously. Many of them are exploring ideas and issues in new ways, ways new not only to children's literature, but to books in general. Picture books, in particular, have become a new medium of expression for many writers. They have found a medium that gives them a broad range of expression, one that doesn't tie them to the conventions of the past. Large ideas can be condensed into small scenes, into poetry even, and they can be accompanied by illustrations that bring them to life. The result is a new kind of book, a book not only for children, but for everyone.

Of course, all children's books don't need to be "instructive." There are, thank God, still just plain fun books, books with no message, no moral, no agenda. Now if we'd just turn off our TV sets, we'd have time for them all!

Children's Literature

HEIDE, FLORENCE PARRY, and JUDITH HEIDE GILLILAND. 1990. *The Day of Ahmed's Secret.* New York: Lothrop, Lee & Shepard Books.

———. 1992. *Sami and the Time of the Troubles.* New York: Clarion Books.

PART THREE

Themes of Freedom
and Oppression:
New Grit in Historical
and Realistic Books

Inviting the voices of Allan Baillie and Minfong Ho brings the book full circle. Why would authors choose to write about topics that are so serious, so politically volatile? What compels an author to sit down and write a book for children about forced labor camps and refugees? In this section two authors explore their motives for writing about topics that many would reserve for adult books. My study with fourth-grade children suggests how children interact and respond to books like these. Joel Taxel brings a third perspective, that of political correctness and multiculturalism, two terms widely used by educators today. He creates a context for exploring the use and abuse of both terms and their relation to children's literature. Taxel places the controversy within a historical framework, thus broadening our understanding of what multiculturalism is and is not, and why political correctness has attempted to adjust for past injustices.

NINE

Fourth Graders Read, Write, and Talk About Freedom

SUSAN LEHR

Untamed Responses

> In the book *Kiss the Dust* my favorite part was when Tara, Daya, Baba, and Hero were on the mountains and joined the Peshmurgas and got bombed.
>
> *Ellen, age 9*

After spending six weeks reading *Kiss the Dust* by Elizabeth Laird (1991) with three fourth-grade children, Ellen's response shocked me. The book is set in northern Iraq and tells the story of Tara's family, Kurds who must flee to the Zagros Mountains because the secret police have linked them to the Peshmurga rebels. While Tara's family is hiding in a mountain village Iraqi planes bomb and kill many of the villagers. Eventually Tara's family escapes to a detention camp in Iran and resettles in England. Laird's account is vivid and carefully researched.

I asked James, Peter, and Ellen to write their overall impressions of the book. All three children went off to separate tables in the library and began writing. After twenty minutes Ellen shared what she wrote:

> In the book Kiss the dust my favorite part was when Tara, Daya, Baba and Hero were on the mountains and joined the Peshmurgas and got bombed. I thought it was a very interesting book since they went to so many places and did so many different things.

I paused before responding, many thoughts racing through my head, none of them very positive. "Go back and write why the bombing was your favorite part of the story." Ellen did and this is what she wrote:

> The reason why when they got bomed was my favorite part was because I thought it was real neat how they all were hiding in the cave and how so many people could get hurt just by being bombed.

I didn't find this encouraging. It was such a crass and heartless response to this Kurdish family's plight. My instincts of wanting to use literature that would link these nine-year-old children to children in other parts of the world seemed noble on paper but in reality was taking me and the children to places I hadn't anticipated. The literature is untamed, but so were their responses.

So Ellen and I sat down and talked. "The part about bombs was neat. I never knew what bombs could do." As she talked she explained that she was relieved that Tara and her family escaped in the cave. She found the whole chapter scary and full of suspense. When the bombs dropped and Laird described the destruction, Ellen learned with Tara what bombs can do to people and their homes. It took some time and persistence on my part to find out what Ellen's writing meant. I already knew what bombs could do, but Ellen didn't.

Taken at face value, her thoughts about bombs seem callous, her response to the book shallow; however, that description does Ellen a disservice. She identified strongly with Tara, a girl a few years older than her. One of Ellen's earlier written responses to the book mentioned how Tara had bought her younger sister crayons when she had the chicken pox. Ellen noticed the veiled women and the vegetable stalls in the market, taking in the differences of another culture, but she identified with Tara in ways familiar to herself. Younger sister. Crayons. Chicken pox.

Children talk their own talk; they have their own agendas. Adults often impose adult agendas on children looking for adult answers and adult perspectives. Researchers often impose research paradigms on children. Newkirk (1992) writes about the tendency in research to highlight the superlative. If we think of response as being on a continuum, then it is misleading to report only the best and the brightest responses and unrealistic to expect them. It also sets the stage for failure when teachers read about the ideal and experience the mundane. I'm excited by the fact that Ellen zeroed in on chicken pox and crayons even as Peter and James were talking about women's rights, CNN, the Persian Gulf War, and Tara's confusion about being a Kurd. Consider the contrasts. It is enticing to report the sophisticated conversations that Peter and James had while ignoring Ellen's unique encounter with the book. Ellen hooked up with a real person, a girl she could relate to. I wonder what impact this will have on Ellen over the years. I'd like to think that real encounters with characters in literature help one define oneself and one's relation to others. I know that knowing Anna Karenina as a teenager shaped my thoughts regarding choices. Reading Ayn Rand freed my thinking with regard to systems and institutions. Knowing the Little Engine that Could challenged me to reach for the stars. Johnny Tremain freed me from thinking that girls couldn't be spies or catalysts for revolution, because I was Johnny Tremain.

Response to literature is not a tidy predictable process as Ellen's writing and thinking illustrates. Stephen Simmer (1992) writes:

When stories are wild and untamed we react hysterically—we need distance, like those who stand on a chair. So long as stories are in cages, marked Children's

Literature or Folklore, they are safe for us to have as pets. Outside these intellectual cages, we are terrified that they might crawl inside us, but it is inside us that they belong. (60)

Laird's story crawled inside Ellen. She experienced what Tara experienced with an honest reaction. This is probably why children's literature scares so many people and is censored in so many places. The personal transaction that occurs is not prescribed; teachers cannot know what will happen when children begin reading and talking about real events, real problems, real episodes from history, spiritual journeys, and reflections as found in fantasy, historical fiction, nonfiction, realistic fiction, and poetry.

Charting New Territory

My journey with Ellen, James, and Peter began while on sabbatical when I went back into the classroom to work with two fourth-grade teachers. I spent two months in the classrooms watching, observing, teaching, talking with children, reading new books, and immersing myself in this team-taught situation. Sharon Scavone and John Milne share a wall that has been partly removed so children, teachers, and talk flow freely between the two rooms. I became a part of that rich environment. I wasn't an outsider, and the children soon came to see me as a positive part of the woodwork. Sharon and John invited me to explore some new books with the children. This was an open invitation, and I thought about the kinds of books I might like to introduce.

I had just finished reading Elizabeth Laird's *Kiss the Dust* and had watched Tara's safely structured world in Iraq collapse. I had read many stories about children living under oppression and fleeing oppression. Minfong Ho's story, *The Clay Marble* (1991), about Dara who lives in the middle of a Cambodian war that just doesn't end, had connected with me to the point where I was advocating strongly for that book on an award committee. Allan Baillie's *Little Brother* (1992) was hauntingly similar to Minfong Ho's book, and I couldn't put it down until I finished, until I knew that Vithy was safely resettled in Australia. I was less hopeful for Dara in *The Clay Marble*, who returned to her village with her family ready to make new beginnings with bags of seeds for planting. I had also just read *Goodbye Vietnam* by Gloria Whelan (1992). Through Mai's eyes I began to experience the dangerous journeys people will take to find freedom. *Journey to Jo'burg* by Beverley Naidoo (1985) was another book that had touched me and taught me about apartheid in South Africa. For several years I had used *Journey* with my college students. All of these stories, all written for children, all teaching me so much about the world, all crawling under my skin. What would children do with books like these? How would they react, respond? Would they get involved? Would they be bored? Would they care? Would the books open up their eyes in new ways? Were the books even appropriate for children? I decided to get as many copies of the books as I could and to work with the children in a loosely structured format.

I got permission from all of the fourth-grade parents, and Sharon and John helped match readers and books based on ability and difficulty. I know that this is a controversial statement in an age of choice, but there are times when teachers can act as catalysts for linking children and books. Most of the children who began with a particular book stayed with that book. Initially, there were some changes. The children were given the freedom to leave a book or to advocate for a new one based on availability. Three children read *Kiss the Dust*, one child read *Goodbye Vietnam*, seven children read *Little Brother*, and six children read *Journey to Jo'burg*. I could not get multiple copies of *The Clay Marble* and also felt that it might work better with older children. *Kiss the Dust* was a gamble in terms of length and difficulty, but I decided to pilot it with three children, all of whom were strong readers.

I met with the children every day for about an hour over the course of six weeks. The children did not read at the same rate, nor did they finish the books at the same time. The children read individually and occasionally in pairs based on personal choice and preference. We did not read aloud. We met in small groups several times a week to talk about the books. Sometimes I asked questions and invited children to respond in their reading logs. Their writing acted as a catalyst for discussions. Samples of questions included: What did you learn that was new to you? How would you describe [character]? What would you have done if you were in a similar situation?

Maps, globes, encyclopedias, and nonfiction books were important resources for our discussions. Our early discussions focused on talking about what they were learning that was new, what they didn't understand, and discussing the plot. We took out the globe frequently during discussions. I videotaped and audiotaped our discussions.

Culminating projects were completed in class during daily work time. Students researched, referred to their books, and created illustrated maps and timelines on large butcher-block paper, which summarized and sequenced important events from their stories. The projects were designed by the children, and the groups ranged from an individual to pairs to a group of three children. The projects were displayed in the hallway, and the unit was completed when the children presented information about their books and projects to the class. Two girls decided not to complete projects, and two boys abandoned their projects after a week. I had misgivings about this, but decided that the four children had been deeply involved with the reading, writing, and discussions of the books and that making them complete a project went against my instincts as a teacher and learner. The children who participated in the projects wanted to and took ownership of their work.

Through talking with the children regularly and reading entries in their reading logs, I discovered that the books not only entertained, but more importantly increased the children's knowledge about the world, expanded their personal views about freedom, and provided shocking glimpses of social injustice. In the following pages

117

I will provide a glimpse of how fourth-grade readers interacted with and responded to the plights of children escaping to freedom.

Living in Great Confusion

> She lives in great confusion. She is confused because she doesn't no why every one hated Kurds.
>
> *James, age 9*

> Tara
> I come from Sulmaniya even though I am in village town because I am being chased down by Iraqi troops. Som my mother decided to go into the mountains. We have just gotten bombed so my mother just decided to head farther north
>
> *James, age 9*

> It is hard being Kurdish, having to watch people die. and seeing a terrible In town a boy got shot later we moved to the mounytains although it was nice it was hard when bombers came and bomed are village.
>
> *Peter, age 9*

The world is a confusing place for Peter and James as evidenced by excerpts from their reading logs. It was less confusing before they started reading *Kiss the Dust*, and I suspect that reading this book added to their confusion. In the opening chapter Tara is walking home from school with a non-Kurdish friend. Both girls see a young Kurdish teen shot by the secret police because he and his friends had been reading and distributing subversive reading material. This incident made a lasting impression on Peter and James. It is something they referred to again and again over the course of six weeks.

In an early conversation Peter said: "We decided that in Sulamaniya you can't turn around without being watched. Like rocks or and like guns and bullets blood everywhere. Help. Cries and screams. Every hour. Every minute. Every second." Peter's dramatic reaction to my invitation to describe what was happening in the book is an indication of his involvement with the book. He identified strongly with the harsh situation in which Tara found herself. Tara essentially had a normal middle-class existence in northern Iraq, when suddenly her world shattered.

As her world unravelled Peter and James both shared in her shock and confusion. James' words "she lives in great confusion" are also an indication of his confusion. He initially had trouble even conceptualizing what a Kurd was. My explanations and comparisons to Asian, Italian, or Irish Americans were useless, and James essentially thought that all people were Kurds. I gave up and told him that he would eventually understand what a Kurd was. He did the next day. And from that point on James and Peter lived with a globe or a map in their hands. Once they discovered that Tara had real roots in a real world they were hooked on her history.

Both boys were totally absorbed so I cut them loose with reading. When they took six days off to make a bas-relief map of Kurdistan, I left them alone. They worked through Tara's and their own confusion. They were eloquent. They were model students. They were the reason I loved sharing literature with children. It took them in at one level and left them at another. I hypothesized that gifted students don't need to leave the classroom once a week for ninety minutes. They only need to get hooked on substantive books and to be cut loose to explore them. At many given points over the course of the six weeks one could find the two boys huddled together over the book, reading, sharing, making new discoveries, or bent over maps and globes.

I acted as a resource person and a catalyst. I asked good questions occasionally and provided more maps of Kurdistan. Their map of Kurdistan was drawn in yellow and was superimposed on Iraq, Turkey, and Iran. It's a land drawn from history. The boys were intrigued with the concept of a displaced people who had no country. Tara made the trip eventful and real for the two boys. Their research was their own; they were the ones who planned it and shaped it. I hadn't anticipated asking them to do this research. It arose out of their own confusion about countries that don't exist, police that can shoot and kill teenage boys, and school girls who must escape in the middle of the night out the back door as the police are pounding on the front. I knew when to leave them alone, and I tried to interrupt only when I wanted to stretch them in new ways of thinking about Tara's escape from Iraq. They spent six weeks living in Vygotsky's (1978) zone of proximal development, pushed into new ways of thinking about the world even as I scaffolded the event for them.

In contrast, what was Ellen doing during this time? She had trouble getting started with the reading and was easily distracted. I occasionally found her wandering about the room talking to anyone who would listen. After three or four days I thought that she might choose to drop out of this particular literature study, although she had initally volunteered to read. The book is almost three hundred pages long, which is quite a stretch for a fourth grader. Knowing that Ellen could not concentrate, I took her to the library, put her at a table in the corner, and left her with the following friendly instruction: "Read as much as you can." This was her last chance to read this particular book. I wanted her engaged with something that would hold her interest, but this didn't seem to be the book for her. About an hour later Ellen was at my elbow beaming. "This is really a good book. I really like it." Thus began a pattern that lasted for two weeks. Ellen went off to the library for an hour to read while Peter and James worked on other matters.

After Tara and her family escaped to a Kurdish village in the Zagros Mountains Peter, James, and I had a conversation about women's rights. My question was basically geared toward a response about Tara's treatment as a woman in Iraq. I had my own agenda as an adult female. Peter had his own agenda as a young male. As you read this transcript notice Peter's confusion, his sorting through of ideas, his mix of history and fact. He is in a formative stage regarding women's issues. He quickly left Tara behind and began exploring his ideas regarding women's and men's rights in the United States.

PETER: If you were male, you would get treated, you had to become a peshmurga. And you would, and as a female, er, and females aren't allowed to be peshmurgas.

TEACHER: They're not allowed to be?

PETER: Dreamer is saying "Oh well, the men have to go out and like fight for their country while the women stay home and like wash clothes and everything." And she's really mad about that.

TEACHER: Tara's mad about that?

PETER: Yeah.

TEACHER: Why?

PETER: Because she just, she thinks women should have a right too, to choose.

TEACHER: OK. And why don't they?

PETER: Same thing with men. They have a right to choose. They should have the right to choose. Just like a while ago. Right here in the United States. You weren't allowed . . . women weren't allowed to vote. But people fought and fought and fought. Women fought and then finally they said "Hey, we can't, I mean, sorry but we have to do this because we're going to have riots and get all. . . ." Like some of the times it seems like, it doesn't seem right to kill females but then when you go up to a male you can just punch him and nothing will happen, but you can't do, it's like you feel different when sometimes you do that to a female.

TEACHER: What do you mean you feel different?

PETER: If you've ever heard the expression "you shouldn't hurt females" whatever or something like that. When you do that in real life that theory still exists. It just doesn't seem different. So, therefore, women should have rights in doing this. That's probably why they don't want them.

TEACHER: When did women get the rights you're talking about in this country?

PETER: I think they got them in the seventies, sixties.

TEACHER: What kind of rights did they get?

PETER: They got the right to vote.

JAMES: Yeah.

TEACHER: Oh, you think they got the right to vote in the 1970s?

PETER: Um, maybe, maybe a little bit farther back.

JAMES: Well you still haven't, well in this story they still haven't got the right to vote, to be in the army yet.

TEACHER: OK. In what country though?

JAMES: In Kurdistan and Iran.

TEACHER: OK. OK. So you're saying that we have these rights in our country but they don't have those right in their country?

PETER and JAMES: Yeah.

James brought the conversation back to Tara. He was an interested listener during this conversation. His final comment brought the conversation full circle and built on Peter's earlier statement about Tara's anger at not being able to join the military. Peter's explorations included his views on men's rights. He talked about their lack of choice with regard to joining the military as being onerous. He identified so strongly with his topic that he included his voice when he spoke about women not being allowed to vote. He instantly backed off and corrected his reference: "Just like a while ago. Right here in the United States. You weren't allowed—women weren't allowed to vote." He sympathized with women's issues, particularly the right to vote, but also touched on violence to men and women. The idea that it's all right for men to punch each other was troubling to Peter, and he realized that in our culture violence toward women is treated differently.

In this conversation one can see the nine-year-old mind in action. Peter tried on new ideas. He reflected about women's issues and the history of voting for women in the United States. His information is confused, but one can see the ideas taking shape. What about men? They have to become Peshmurgas. Shouldn't men have choices too? The conversation comes full circle. We began with a discussion of Tara's rights as a woman in *Kiss the Dust* and ended with James' observation that women still don't have the right to vote or be in the army in Iraq. Many voices. Many perspectives. Many stories. Tara's is only one voice, one story, therefore the conversation can include much more than the book. Peter can freely explore his thinking about women and their struggle to gain rights and freedoms. Oppression happens here at home, so reading *Kiss the Dust* does not limit thinking to Tara and her personal struggle for freedom.

The boys were working on a variety of issues simultaneously in relation to their own culture, as well as issues that spring from the book. One can see why discussion and reflection are critical parts of the daily regimen. The teacher's role is that of catalyst, prod. I see my role frequently as that of wasp under the saddle. Why? What makes you say that? How is Tara's life different from yours? How is Tara's life in the village different from her life back in the city? Those kinds of questions invite learners to sort through information, explore Tara's environment in relation to theirs. Notice who did most of the talking in the above conversation. Peter. Not me. Not James. Peter had center stage, and he was given the time to think his thoughts out loud. What were all of the other students doing? Some were reading. Some were writing journal responses to similar questions for their books. Some were devising time lines of events for their stories. While the three of us were talking for ten minutes the other children were off working independently and in pairs. Sometimes larger groups of students got involved in conversations, but at this particular point in time Peter had James' and my complete attention. We wanted to hear his views on women's rights. Think about the power of that for learners.

On the last day you'll recall that I invited the three children to write their overall impressions of *Kiss the Dust*. James wrote a stirring response to the book, which needs no explanation:

Kiss the Dust

I loved the book! It was weird how Elizebeth Laird decribed the things that happened. It made me think of how lucky I am to have this much freedom, I never thought having freedom was so special. I now feel sorry for all those people that don't have freedom. At first I personaly thought this book would not be so interesting, how wrong I was. One thing is that at the end of the story she was in kind of a day dream, thinking back to when she saw a boy being killed for no reason, and she dreamed of seeing him right before being shot putting his head on the ground and kissing the dust, the dust of Kurdistan, and that, at that moment I felt the sorriest for the people mostly in the middle east. Although this was my second 200 or more page book it felt like it was the best one I would ever read. One other thing is that it was weird how they had so little money but traveled so far. They started out in Iraq, went up into the Zangros Mountains which are mountains in Iran, then they went to a camp just north of the Zangros, then they escaped from that camp, stayed at a relatives house then they flew to England and stayed at a younger relatives house whoem was there for a Phd class, and in England they stayed living their lives the way the English do rather than the Sulaimanian ways.

James' first written words about Tara were that she lived in great confusion. This final unedited piece of writing speaks eloquently as to how James is beginning to sort through his and Tara's confusion.

No Comforting Landmarks

The daily experiences of the fourth-grade children were far removed from the oppressive and dangerous situations faced by characters in the books. Could the children empathize with children who were not free? Some of their early writings defining freedom in response to a survey included phrases like "to be free and open and to do what you want," "to have rights and not have someone boss you around all the time," "to live the way you want to live," "no restrictions, no put-downs, to have equality," "it means to be free and not ordered around or be a slave," "to live without being whipped when you do something wrong." Philip wrote that you could be "free from another person's/country's power." Karen summed it up by saying freedom means "being able to make your own choices and to live without being chained up." These are concrete responses about the concept of freedom. Many children wrote about being able to do what you want with no one telling you what to do. One can sense their place in the scheme of things, being ordered about by parents, older siblings, relatives, teachers and a host of adults. When asked to list the kinds of freedoms they had, children typically used action words: free to do, to be, to have, to make, to live, to play. From the perspective of a nine-year-old freedom involves choice and movement, being able to stay up late, watch TV as long as one wants, fight with a brother, go to school, go to the field across the street, ride a bike, vote, go to the store, and go over to people's houses. When asked to list countries having freedom like the United States children responded widely and included Canada, Australia, Great Britain, Africa, Asia, North Pole, South America, Hawaii, Laos, Florida, California, New York, Syracuse, Boston, Spain, France, Europe, Brazil, and "no other countries." The list is haphazard.

When asked about countries not having freedom like they do, the children included Iraq, China, some of Africa, Cambodia, Laos, Vietnam, Cuba, Bosnia, Russia, Somalia, Africa, South Africa, Iran, Asia, South America, Quebec, Europe, Greece, Mexico, Australia, and Japan. The idea that secret police exist was mentioned by six of the children when asked how the freedoms in these countries were different from theirs. Slavery was also mentioned by six of the children. The children have a lot of information, but it is confused and confusing to them.

For the most part they are not sure where these countries are located, what their relation is to the United States, and what freedom is like in that country. Many of them are aware that recent wars have occurred in Iraq, Iran, Bosnia, Somalia, and Vietnam. One child mentioned Saddam Hussein as being a "real bad leader," and one connected the "Persian Gulf War, oil fields, and Saddam Hussein." Another child identified greed as being Iraq's motivation. Several children identified being black and being poor as the extent of their knowledge of Africa. Two children identified South Africa as having slaves.

What this survey revealed is that the children had very little background knowledge about Cambodia, Iraq, South Africa, and Vietnam, the countries explored in the books. Their notions regarding freedom for the most part were locked into their daily lives and were based on immediate actions and events. I wondered if they would be able to relate to characters in stories about events in other countries. Would they begin to understand the concept of oppression?

Journey into Apartheid

Naledi, the main character in *Journey to Jo'burg*, like Tara in *Kiss the Dust*, lives in great confusion, and like Tara, her world is suddenly shattered. Her younger sister is dying, and Naledi, along with her younger brother Tiro, walk from their rural village to find their mother in Johannesburg. Beverley Naidoo transports this young black girl and the reader into the heart of apartheid with each step. The children made connections to Naledi's character and through her eyes learned about apartheid for the first time. The children and I spent time describing Naledi and her brother Tiro. Words like *persistent*, *determined*, *smart*, and *strong* were mentioned in relation to Naledi.

> TEACHER: Oh, OK. What's Naledi's problem, her biggest problem facing her? Anyone can answer that, anyone at all. Kurt.
>
> KURT: Trying to keep the baby alive.
>
> TEACHER: OK, and then, so the way she determines to do that is?

KURT: To walk to Jo'burg to find her mom.

TEACHER: So her mom is the one who she thinks can solve the problem. OK, what other characters did you pick to describe. Kurt?

KURT: I picked Toro something like that.

TEACHER: That, I call him Tiro, I don't know what his name is exactly.

KURT: I was glad they were hungry, cause when they were in the orange field and he kept shoving oranges into his mouth.

TEACHER: OK, oranges.

KURT: Small, and worried.

TEACHER: Oh, you think he's worried?

KURT: Yeah.

TEACHER: OK, what gives you a clue to that in the book?

KURT: Because in the beginning of the book, when they were going, he wasn't sure about going there because the police and things might see them and things, and do away with them.

TEACHER: OK, does he know that in the beginning of the book, that the police might see him, and do away with him?

KURT: No, his sister tells him, and reminds him that we have to be careful of police.

TEACHER: OK.

KURT: [Pause] And they're dangerous.

TEACHER: Secret police?

STUDENT: Yeah.

TEACHER: And they're dangerous?

MEGAN: Because, like they're dangerous.

KURT: Someone named, well, a song.

TEACHER: Hmmm?

STUDENT: You need a pass.

KURT: Someone in Naledi's class wrote a song about police . . .

TEACHER: [Pause] Why would you have to worry about the police? I mean, we don't have to worry about the police here.

MEGAN: Oh, I just . . . I wrote that down.

TEACHER: If you see a policeman on the corner, is that the first thing you do, hide?

GROUP: No.

DANNY: Cause you need a pass to go to different places. Without that you can't go.

TEACHER: Do you know what a pass is?

KAREN: Like a passport?

TEACHER: Yeah, its similar to that. Yeah, it really would be.

MEGAN: Something that you need to . . . to like um . . . you have to bring it with you, like if you're going on a, like um, like [pause].

KAREN: Long trip?

MEGAN: Yeah, like a long trip, and um, you need that, uh to get into the towns, and stuff.

TEACHER: OK, why do you need that pass? Karen?

KAREN: Because, if you don't have the pass they might take you away, and like whip you really bad. [*Pause*] Just beat them.

TEACHER: OK, is that in the book?

MARY KAREN: Yeah.

DANNY: Yeah. Somebody got whipped so bad they couldn't walk.

MEGAN: Couldn't walk.

KURT: Couldn't stand up, and so they couldn't stand up.

TEACHER: And the secret police did that?

STUDENT: Yeah.

STUDENT: Yes.

TEACHER: OK, do we have to carry a pass in this country?

GROUP: No.

TEACHER: Can you go . . .

KURT: Unless you go to another one.

TEACHER: Unless you're going to another one. OK, then you need a passport, right. But in this country you don't need a pass?

KAREN: No.

The fourth-grade children understood that the immediate problem was saving Dineo's life. Kurt identified with Tiro's size, confusion, and hunger. I directed the children back to the book to support their answers. The conversation quickly moved to the heart of the real dilemma, however, which was to get past the police safely. The children understood that needing a pass in South Africa is different from needing a passport in the United States. Karen and Danny referred to an example from the book to support this fear of police: "Because, if you don't have the pass they might take you away, and like whip you really bad. Just beat them." "Somebody got whipped so bad they couldn't walk." Two students added to their statements. Clearly this was new information to the children, and they understood that basic rights are different for Naledi and Tiro in South Africa.

The idea of when this all takes place is important because the children have studied Colonial times in the United States and have learned about slavery, which was mentioned by children reading *Journey to Jo'burg* and *Little Brother*. I wondered if they would have an understanding of recent history in relation to events that took place in the distant past.

TEACHER: OK. Do you know when this story takes place?

KURT: A long time ago, cause, um, cause it says the blacks cannot live in the cities, um, a family of blacks cannot live in the cities, cause they won't go by the white peoples' rules.

DANNY: I think it takes place now cause their clothing is, the truck wouldn't of picked them up if they were . . .

KURT: Trucks have been around a long time.

DANNY: Oh yeah.

TEACHER: So you [Danny] think that the truck and their clothing make it seem like it's more now, then, and you [Kurt] think it might be a long time ago?

KAREN: Not that long time, he . . .

KURT: Not very long, but maybe in two decades, twenty years ago.

Kurt started by saying that the book happened a long time ago because blacks weren't allowed to live in the city. By his reckoning this dated the book, because what he knew about his own country was that people can live anywhere they want. Danny observed that the type of clothing and the use of a truck placed the book in modern times. Karen concurred with Danny and Kurt, who decided that a long time ago is about two decades. Kurt basically led this conversation, and the input from Danny and Karen seemed to alter his thinking. I gave some background information on the situation in South Africa and asked if the children had ever heard of apartheid. Kurt had some knowledge of what has happened in South Africa and was aware that gold is a motivation for oppression.

KURT: I know.

TEACHER: It's like "apart-ness."

KURT: Only white families live in the cities, and black have to live out of the city—the whole family.

TEACHER: Yeah. All of the things that you're reading about fall under what was called apartheid, and a lot of those things have been gotten rid of, but in South Africa today, blacks still don't vote. They still are not allowed to vote, and all the white people are still in power, and the blacks are still fighting to make that change.

KURT: They were there . . . [pause]

TEACHER: But the whites are still saying "no, we want to keep the power, we don't want blacks in power."

KURT: They were there first, so why are we taking it away from them?

STUDENT: Yeah.

TEACHER: That's true, yeah, they were there first.

KURT: So we just go there to get the gold, you know, it's their land, they had it first.

STUDENT: Yeah.

TEACHER: And you're right about that, that's what made it attractive to us for one thing.

KURT: Cause all of the gold and everything is there. There's lots of mining in places down there though.

KAREN: They were there first.

KURT: . . . but that so many people came there just for that, and so many people came and took over.

Kurt had more background information than the others and consequently he had some strong views on domination and economics. In the next segment the children discussed an event in the book that involved police violence toward children. Danny was unclear as to what had happened, and the children helped him untangle the plot. The children concluded that the situation was crazy. We then explored the reasons for treating people differently, and Karen shared an insight.

TEACHER: Why do you think that happened in South Africa? Why, why would they treat people that way?

KURT: It's 'cause they're different from us.

TEACHER: OK, Karen, you want to add to that?

KAREN: Maybe people don't like the idea of someone being different, they didn't want 'em to, they wanted everything the same, they didn't want any changes.

TEACHER: What would they want the same? What is it that's different?

KAREN: Their skin color.

Karen understood that blacks are treated differently because there's a difference and that people don't like difference and they don't like change. That's quite an insight for a nine-year-old.

An invitation to describe Naledi's village evoked a wide range of observations.

KURT: Strange, 'cause they had to go buy water.

MEGAN: Um, its really weird, 'cause I mean, they have, like a, its like, most their huts, they have huts and they build it out of like, mud and straw. And, and they don't have, like, they, they don't have like electricity down there and stuff.

KAREN: In my book they didn't, they were like really, [Tiro] kept flashing on and on, on and off with the light, when he finally saw where the light was, he kept turning it on and off.

MEGAN: But they don't have enough money.

KURT: Yeah, they have to go to a store to buy water.

DANNY: The river's dried out.

Although there are few familiar landmarks in this book the children were empathetic to the main characters and made many observations about the lives of Naledi and Tiro. By comparing their lives to those of the main characters and thinking about the problems facing Naledi, the children were able to situate themselves in the book thus creating familiar landmarks to guide their reading.

Building a Framework for Understanding

In contrast, children reading *Little Brother* had more difficulty relating to the main character, Vithy; Cambodia; the Khmer Rouge; and the concept of forced labor camps. Vithy's experiences were perhaps too far removed from those of the fourth-grade children, so providing a framework for understanding the flight of this child from a Khmer Rouge work camp to a refugee camp in Thailand presented a different challenge.

Based on his experiences working in a refugee camp in Thailand, Allan Baillie, an Australian, has written about the escape of a child in Kampuchea living under the Khmer Rouge. As *Little Brother* begins, Vithy and his brother are escaping from the Big Paddy into the jungle, shot at by soldiers, and immediately separated. As a reader, I wanted to know who this boy was and why soldiers were shooting at him. The author does not explain what Big Paddy is. One must piece together the clues explaining that Vithy is escaping from a forced labor camp in which children and adults work long hours in rice paddies with little food, have no personal freedom, and experience constant fear of violence from the soldiers. Baillie provides glimpses of what happens in a forced labor camp through painful flashbacks, but the information remains sketchy. Baillie's book is successful because he keeps the action immediate. As a reader I saw through Vithy's eyes, understanding his confusion and fear.

The seven fourth-grade children reading and responding to Vithy's story were hooked on the strong narrative action of the plot. They often referred to the book as being "exciting." At first the children found the unfamiliar names and Cambodian words uncomfortable to read: Vithy, Mang, Khmer Rouge, Phnom Penh. Children were intrigued by the different names and places that Baillie introduces. Our early discussions focused on talking about what they were learning that was new, what they didn't understand, and the plot. They were not familiar with Cambodia, and we spent time locating the country on world maps and globes. I read a nonfiction book about Cambodia, *The Land and People of Cambodia* (Chandler 1991), in order to be the resource person when questions arose. We took out the globe frequently during discussions. Eventually, two of the children made a time-line map showing Vithy's journey to freedom, a concrete response to an unfamiliar experience.

Children made connections between the work camp in Kampuchea and slavery in the United States, linking information learned in social studies about Colonial America and their assessment of Vithy's experience in the Big Paddy. Children identified with Vithy's quest for freedom and viewed him as an escaped slave. Mandy wrote in her response log that "they live in Khmer Rouge and they are used as slaves. Little bro's name is Vithy. And olders name is Mang. The people killed Mang so Vithy is on his own." Katie wrote: "There isn't much peace in this country. And if you talk at The Big Paddy you could be risking your life." Nikki offered the following during a group discussion: "They [Khmer Rouge] held kids and their parents like prisoners and they had to work all day." When asked why the Khmer Rouge rounded up people and placed them in work camps Phil responded with "Well, they came down to take people and make them work in rice paddies so that, to make money for them." He added: "It was like slaves. They weren't allowed to talk. They weren't allowed to think." The written and oral statements of the children show that they are beginning to think about the theme of oppression in *Little Brother* and that they are linking this new information to what they already know about oppressed people.

Through brief flashbacks Baillie describes the horror of the forced labor camp and why an eleven-year-old would risk escape and death. When Vithy thinks about his brother's advice for surviving in the labor camp, Vithy reveals his role as victim:

> Mang had told him, many months ago, that the only way to survive in the Big Paddy was to be careful and dumb. Work hard, never let them know that you can read and write and handle arithmetic. Always remember your kid sister, Sorei. And above all, never think. But now he had to. (Baillie 1992, 15)

I didn't think children would grasp what this chilling piece of advice really suggests—that a character has been conditioned not to think in order to save his life merited discussion. The children and I spent one session just talking about this passage. The concept of not thinking and acting as if you were dumb was hard for them to grasp at first; the children weren't sure why Vithy's brother had given him this advice. To create a context for understanding this passage in the book, I talked about how the Khmer Rouge gathered many of the educated people from the cities and villages and how many were killed. The children speculated why this might have happened and decided that knowing too much meant that you would teach others how to leave the work camps, a concrete response to an abstract concept. The children then decided that if the Khmer Rouge were in charge in our own city their fourth-grade teachers and I would be among the first to disappear. We then talked about how the cities were literally emptied of people, how people were forced simply to walk out of cities and eventually put into forced labor camps.

After rereading this passage and discussing the idea of not allowing yourself to think, Mandy took on Vithy's perspective and wrote a brief letter to Mang in her reading log.

Dear Mang,

  Im very scared to be out here alone. It's not like the Big Paddy. You can do what ever you want. I want you to be with me. Im at the Phnom Penh. The King of this city is here. I miss you alot.

your brother,
Vithy

Mandy's words "you can do what ever you want" indicated that from her perspective the idea of being on your own—fending for yourself, making all of your own decisions—was what really frightened Vithy. Mandy understood that Vithy had suddenly been left to his own devices and that he needed Mang's support as big brother.

In her letter Mandy also mentioned the "King" who was an abandoned street-wise child who had learned to fend for himself in the emptied city of Phnom Penh. All of the seven children mentioned the King at some point in their journals. His ability to survive in style appealed to these children. They identified strongly with the King's ability to be independent. In a recent letter to me, Baillie wrote that his Vithy really did meet a character like the King.

Through Vithy's eyes the children and I saw abandoned cities and began to understand the Khmer Rouge's ruthless abhorrence of modern cities, the forced return to an agrarian society, and their mistreatment of people. I never really grasped the situation in Kampuchea as an adult until I saw the land as Vithy traveled through it.

Vithy and his brother long to be free and are willing to die finding freedom. The "it" is vague to Vithy because he doesn't really know what freedom is. At the beginning of the book Vithy is separated from his brother and thinks he is dead. Baillie spends time developing this sense of aloneness and shows Vithy's initial inability to think. He has been numb too long. "But he knew what it meant. It meant that he had no one, no friend, no family, nobody left. He was terribly alone" (1992, 13). His brother's last bit of advice was to "follow the lines out of the war." This metaphor guides Vithy in a type of underground railroad flight to freedom out of Kampuchea, which other authors have described in books for children.

Understanding Opposing Viewpoints

By linking stimulating literature and discussion or role playing Kohlberg (1981) found that children's moral thinking could be changed. He further hypothesized that left alone without discussion or role playing children would proceed with their normal attitudes. Through discussion, role playing, and writing, children in Kohlberg's study were able to understand two opposing points of view, because they were able to empathize with one character, while condemning the behavior of another. As mentioned earlier, children reading *Journey to Jo'burg* spent time talking about Naledi's problems and describing her as a character. They liked Naledi, and their responses indicate that they were not only supportive, but also empathetic. Donaldson's (1979) research suggests that in empathetically relevant situations young children seem capable of taking on other points of view. In earlier studies related to the child's developing sense of theme (Lehr 1985; 1988; 1990; 1991) I found that children as young as age five can understand or consider the actions of characters, and that by the fourth grade children can easily take on the perspectives of characters in stories and talk about themes in abstract terms.

I read a passage from *Journey* that described the meeting between Naledi and Mma. In this passage the children knock on the front door of a large intimidating house where their mother is a servant.

There it stood. A great pink house with its own grass, lawn, and trees in front. Even its own road leading up to the front door. The two children stopped at the wide iron gates looking up to it. The gates were closed with a notice on them. Beware of the dog.

"Are we allowed in?" Tiro whispered.

"We must go in," Naledi replied, opening the gate a little.

Nervously they slipped in and slowly walked up the drive to the large front door. Before they dared to knock, they heard a fierce barking from inside, which made them grip each other's hands, ready to run back to the street. Then they heard a sharp voice inside call out in English. "Joyce? See who it is."

The door opened.

As Mma gasped, the children flung themselves at her and she clasped them in her arms, hugging them. Tears welled up in her eyes, as the children sobbed against her.

"What is wrong? What is wrong?" Mma cried softly.

"Who is it, Joyce?" came a brisk voice from behind. The dog was still barking.

"Be quiet, Tiger," ordered the brisk voice, and the barking stopped.

Mma stifled her sobs.

"Madam, these are my children."

"What are they doing here?" asked the white lady.

"Madam, I don't know, they haven't told me yet."

"Dineo is very ill Mma," Naledi spoke between the sobs. "Her fever won't go away. Nono and Mmangwane don't want to trouble you, but I told Tiro we must come and bring you home."

Mma gasped again and held her children more tightly.

"Madam, my little girl is very sick. Can I go home to see her?"

The Madam raised her eyebrows.

"Well, Joyce, I can't possibly let you go today. I need you tonight to stay in with Belinda. The master and I are going to a very important dinner party."

She paused.

"But I suppose you can go tomorrow."

"Thank you Madam."

"I hope you realize how inconvenient this will be for me. If you are not back in a week, I shall just have to look for another maid, you understand?"

"Yes, Madam." (Naidoo 1985, 29–32)

After reading this powerful scene aloud I invited the children to think of words to describe their feelings toward the white Madam. The children used examples from the excerpt to support their choices. Karen decided the woman was mean because she threatened to get rid of her maid and was just going to drop her, not caring if she ruined her life. She added later that the woman was selfish. Megan described her as being bossy because of the way she talked to Mma. Danny described her as being lazy and demanding because she wouldn't answer the door and she wouldn't hold Mma's job open while Mma went to tend her daughter. Kurt thought the woman was like his sister who is very demanding.

Next I invited the children to role play by pretending to be the white Madam and to tell their husband about the incident at the end of the day or to write a letter to a friend describing the incident. The children wrote and then shared their responses.

KAREN: [*Reading with disgust*] I can't believe she would let her children come one foot in the house. I can't believe she wanted a whole week off. I look at the numbers for the other maids. Those children are so dirty and disgusting, and demanding. They wanted my lazy maid to go just because of that. How bossy!

TEACHER: What was her thinking about how that woman looked at those children when she was standing at the door looking at those children?

KAREN: Disgust.

TEACHER: Disgusting and dirty. Someone else like to share?

DANNY: [*Reading in a sneering voice*] Why should I let you go? Who would do all the work. Fine, go away, but you won't get paid. And kids? They are filthy. So what if one dies. They are useless. They're not important like me!

TEACHER: What were some of the things that he said that captured her feelings about black people?

KURT: Hated 'em.

TEACHER: Doesn't it come through loud and clear? They're useless.

KURT: So why did she have a black servant that's doing all the work for her? Cause she wants to know she's better. They're probably better physically fit than them.

KAREN: Probably like, a hundred pounds.

KURT: More! Five hundred!

DANNY: Hmmm . . . three thousand.

TEACHER: So, you figured she must be big and fat because she has someone else doing all the work?

KURT: She's too lazy.

GROUP: Yeah.

KAREN: The way she, she probably sits down like with a bag of potatoes just in front of the TV.

KURT: She probably looks like Homer Simpson.

MEGAN: Or if she's not big and fat, she's very, very um, like, she likes to dress up in fancy dresses and, and really like, she really shows off a lot.

TEACHER: So you think she could actually be very conscious about how she looks and just takes care of herself all day long.

KURT: Bet she never fixes a flat tire.

TEACHER: You don't know do you? What did, what did you come up with?

KATIE: Umm. Let's see. [*Reading in an indifferent tone of voice*] When I saw those two children at the door, and when I heard that my maid had to go see her daughter, because she was ill, I could not let her go today. The master and I were throwing a dinner party.

TEACHER: Ooh, so you were really preoccupied with your dinner party. Notice how you've all read it so far? What did you put into your voices?

DANNY: Uh, expression.

TEACHER: A lot of it, too. What kinds of things would you say would describe the way your voices are sounding? What kind of words, how would you describe your own voices, the way you're reading with expression?

KATIE: Hate?

TEACHER: OK, what else?

KAREN: Strong.

TEACHER: Strong. Yeah, this is not a weak person talking.

KURT: Fat.

TEACHER: It's someone whose going "listen," right? What else?

KURT: Uh . . . fat.

TEACHER: Fat? OK, you're kind of hung up on fat. What else? Remember the words you described before? Demanding, impatient, mean. Does that all come through in the way you're writing? I think I hear it.

KAREN: I used the um, same words up here, like she was describing the other kids is the way she really was.

KURT: [*Reading in a bored tone of voice*] I was surprised. I just hope the kid doesn't die, she might make a great servant. Those two other kids might make good servants, too.

TEACHER: Now, what did he do, totally different with his thinking than what you guys did? Totally different. What did he come up with?

KAREN: He didn't want the kids to die; he wanted to use them as servants instead.

TEACHER: So you thought they might be useful, but for your use, huh? Megan, do you want to read what you wrote?

MEGAN: [*Reading with disdain*] These kids are really gross, why should I let them in my house? So what if her kid is sick? She's my maid and I can tell her what to do.

KURT: How much, do those, get paid?

TEACHER: What?

KURT: How much do these people get paid?

TEACHER: You know, I don't know the actual price, but it's, it's not very much. Were her kids allowed to come stay with her then for the night?

STUDENT: No.

TEACHER: Where'd they have to go?

KURT: They had to go back to . . .

STUDENT: Grace's.

TEACHER: They had to go back to Grace's. Why couldn't they stay with their mom in her room?

KURT: They . . . there wasn't enough room?

TEACHER: Not enough room, that's an idea? What's another?

KURT: They might get in the way.

TEACHER: They might get in the way?

STUDENT: It says the big house.

TEACHER: It's a big house? But that doesn't, so maybe there . . .

STUDENT: It says big, pink house.

TEACHER: So, maybe there would be room? So why can't they stay? Karen?

KAREN: Maybe the maid didn't want her house to get all dirty because of the children and, and . . .

TEACHER: But who's the maid though?

KAREN: Um, no . . .

TEACHER: Oh, you mean the Madam?

KAREN: The Madam, yeah.

TEACHER: That's possible. The children might, if you said they're disgusting, and you said they're filthy . . . someone said they're filthy.

STUDENT: I did.

TEACHER: OK, so wouldn't they be able to stay there? Does the book tell you at all?

STUDENT: No.

STUDENT: No.

TEACHER: No?

STUDENT: Yeah, I think mine does.

TEACHER: There actually were, I think there's actually a reason given in the book. Can you find it? And there's a, there's another reason actually, and I think it's in the book somewhere. Do you remember anything about the fact that blacks weren't allowed to stay in the city?

GROUP: Oh!

TEACHER: What, do you know anything about that?

KURT: Oh, yes, 'cause they won't, they wouldn't accept it.

DANNY: They had to have passes.

KURT: And they told, they told, and Grace's story about that in the chapter, that the blacks were, at the villages, 'cause the whites were always shooting at them.

TEACHER: And Danny said they had no passes. What's, so why can't they stay at the Madam's house?

STUDENT: They don't get a ride home.

STUDENT: They'll get arrested.

This conversation was based on several days of reading and discussing the book. I included it as a whole piece so as not to disrupt the flow of the children's thoughts and observations. From previous conversations based on Naledi's motivation for going to Johanesburg, the children identified with her dilemma and identified with her as a character. From the conversation above, one can see that the fourth-grade children understood the white woman's disdain of Mma and her children. The fourth graders also perceived that Madam placed little value on the life of Dineo. In the eyes of the children a party and baby-sitting services were more relevant to Madam's life than the life of a black child. Although the children understood Madam's perspective they were not sympathetic to it. Their conversation reveals their disdain and disgust for her viewpoint. They assume that she's fat, lazy, and demanding. Their words also suggest a self-importance that they do not feel is warranted. The fact that Karen based her letter on the words brainstormed in the initial conversation illustrates the pivotal role of extended conversation prior to writing. Her writing was much richer as a result and probably shaped her thinking with regard to taking on the role of the white Madam.

Because there are few familiar markers in the concept of apartheid, the fourth graders do not understand why Naledi and Tiro cannot stay with their Mma. Consequently they must be led into new ways of looking at the world, harsh ways. Even then the children have difficulty understanding apartheid's position of separation. Without the character of the white Madam I do not think the children would have been able to identify with one aspect of white apartheid's point of view. As a concept it is too far removed from their reality. Megan's attempts to say that the children would dirty the house are somewhat confused. The fact that Naidoo has given prejudice a face and a personality helps the children to see another point of view. Their final comments indicate that they are far from understanding apartheid. Danny talks about passes and Karen talks about getting arrested, but the children did not arrive at these conclusions without my prodding. The concepts are new and not firmly established. They are not able to articulate that because Madam thinks the children are dirty and disgusting she would not want them to touch anything in her house. Kurt's initial reaction is still that the house must not be big enough.

Making the Strange Familiar

The odyssey of Southeast Asian refugees reaches a conclusion in books like *Hoang Anh: A Vietnamese-American Boy* (Hoyt-Goldsmith 1992), which is a photo-picture book about a child in junior high, living in San Rafael California, whose family escaped from Vietnam. This kind of book tells us what became of characters like Vithy and Mai after their escapes to freedom. That children might know a Vithy or a Mai and meet them in their neighborhoods or schools can be cause for celebration. Hoyt-Goldsmith suggests, however, that there are cultural differences between Vietnamese and Americans and that embracing or cringing from new ways is experienced on both sides. Hoang Anh is a Vietnamese American who embraces both heritages, the old and the new. His parents escaped from Vietnam in 1978, after the war.

The eight children who read *Little Brother* and *Goodbye Vietnam* discussed this book over the course of two days. It was too lengthy to read aloud even in two sittings, because children had many comments to make relating *Little Brother* and *Goodbye Vietnam* to this picture book. Joseph predicted that the reason Hoang Anh's family came to the United States was because "the police was starting trouble with them." When asked why, he added that "they were prisoners working hard in the paddies . . . and they wanted to try to get away." Bobby added that "they wanted to be free." Children in this setting knew where Cambodia and Vietnam were located on the map. They had ideas about why Hoang Anh's family wanted to escape and identified freedom as a motivation for leaving another country. Children identified the conflict that Hoang Anh's father was involved with as being the Vietnam War. Philip decided that the family wanted to leave because the communists took over and "they wanted to get out before something could happen." When I read that the new government acted harshly toward its people in 1975 Joseph volunteered that harsh meant "you're acting bad to your people. It's setting laws that they can't get out." Nikki added that "the people over there, whatever, the communists, they were being mean to the people that were, that originally lived there. They were being harsh."

When asked to link Hoang Anh's situation of escape to Vithy's escape in *Little Brother* two students made no connection while one student talked about how the escape and relocation were identical. The two students immediately saw the connection, but it had to be made explicit for them.

In exploring the photos of Hoang Anh's family the children noticed the different names, the different country, and the difference in the people's appearance. One boy suggested that they had different problems than we have. Joseph elaborated by saying that we don't have to move to places where there's always freedom and stuff like that. His words were eloquent because Joseph understands that we move because we want to or need to because we already exist in a place where freedom is. The children were able to sympathize with Hoang Anh's immersion in an unfamiliar culture because they made connections to the book characters' and this real child's experiences in relation to their own life experiences. Sandy talked at length about her friend who was moving to Puerto Rico. "She sort of wants to [move] but not. She doesn't want to leave her friends. She doesn't want to leave our team, the gymnastics team." I asked her how it would be different. "Heather's gonna have to speak a different language." Phil added that there would be a warmer climate and that it would be wetter. They were able to take on the perspectives of the characters best when they put themselves in similar situations and thought about how they might respond in unfamiliar situations.

Our first conversation ended with talk about chopsticks and eating crabs, fish, and hot dogs. The photos acted as a catalyst for exploring different foods. On the second day the children talked at length about how Vithy and Mai would feel coming in to our culture, using standard words like *scared, afraid, strange, weird.* At first it was difficult for them to imagine how western customs might feel strange or unfamiliar to others. Knowing how absorbed they were with the topic of food, I asked them how often they ate fish. After exploring their perspectives I invited them to consider Hoang Anh's point of view by asking them how Hoang Anh's family would feel about using forks. Hoang Anh eats fish or seafood frequently. Children offered "strange," "weird," "like we do using chopsticks," "sort of like the wrong way," "it would be hard for them." I suggested that the idea of using hands was unfamiliar and unhygenic to a person coming from China. A student suggested eating a hamburger with chopsticks. The children discussed food and eating habits for thirty minutes, making comparisons to Hoang Anh as well as to each other. There were giggles when talking about new unfamiliar foods, like crabs and live fish in the bathtub. Children hypothesized concretely about how frustrating it might be to give up hamburgers, hot dogs, and pizza for a Vietnamese diet with fish as the main meat. Children talked about moving to new countries and leaving forks and knives behind in exchange for chopsticks.

TEACHER: Would you start using chopsticks? Or would you keep your forks?

NIKKI: I'd use chopsticks.

KRISTI: I'd bring my silverware over.

NIKKI: I'd try.

PHILIP: I don't know. I'd bring a fork over. I could use them [chopsticks]. I'd take the fork just in case.

MANDY: I couldn't get anything in my mouth.

JOSEPH: I'll do both and occasionally I'll have a burger.

PHIL: Well, I'd only bring a knife and a spoon because well I could use the chopsticks, I only use chopsticks to stabbing the food and the putting it in my mouth.

STUDENT: How can you stab rice?

TEACHER: What about you Bobby?

BOBBY: I don't know. I'd bring a bowl. Couple spoons, just in case.

NIKKI: If you're gonna live there for like the rest of your life, you'd better learn how to do it, because it's gonna, it's a custom there sort of. I'd bring a fork anyway.

TEACHER: All right. So you'd feel that you'd go with the custom of the country you were living in.

NIKKI: Yeah, and you'd learn how to do it.

This conversation is revealing about nine-year-old children. First, it illustrates that they like to talk about food and forks and chopsticks. Their concerns are concrete and tied to real objects, day-to-day celebrations, trials, and trivia. Their beliefs about the world are reflected in their thoughts about moving to a new country and taking on new customs. Their responses range on a continuum from no risk to try anything. Most are practical and want a backup, such as a fork or spoon. Nikki suggested taking on new ideas and ways of doing things: "You'd better learn how to do it." The conversation continued about particular foods Hoang Anh and his family ate and eventually turned to gender roles in the kitchen. As Newkirk (1992) suggests, the book is one story, and in conversations there are many stories waiting to be told. In this instance the book acted as a catalyst and brought many stories to the surface. I read: "In Vietnam [this will be new to you] only women work in the kitchen" (Hoyt-Goldsmith 1992). Responses were swift. "My dad works in the kitchen." "All the time." "No way." "What's he do?" "He cooks." "He cooks all the time." "How do bachelors get food?" "My dad just sits on the couch." "My dad cooks, he cleans everything too." "My dad can't cook. He's lazy." The conversation meandered into children's responsibilities. "I don't do anything in our house. I don't even clean my bedroom." "I eat and occasionally clean." "I know how to cook. Scrambled eggs and macaroni and cheese." I continued reading from the book. "But here my family has adopted an American life-style. Everyone in our household knows how to cook. My mother has a full-time job outside our home. . . . Because she doesn't get home until quite late in the evening, we all help out. Sometimes my father makes dinner" (1992, 11).

Conversations. Reflections. Stories. The children continued talking about being different, going into a Korean house with unfamiliar smells, smells of food that the nine-year-old didn't like. A girl shared a story about her Italian grandmother and how people made fun of her accent and about her wheelchair. The conversations are untamed because there is no way to plan how books will interact with readers and listeners. Each child brought new information and their own reactions and values systems to the conversation. One could argue that the book caused children to think about new ideas and new ways of looking at Hoang Anh and his family. I mentioned earlier that Kohlberg found that discussions like these can alter a child's moral thinking. I would guess that is true.

My final questions asking if the children had any thoughts on how it might be for Vithy in a new country got no response. Children wandered all over with comments about pronouncing names, how skinny Vietnam looks on the map, and what Mung beans are. I was looking for a profound end to a stimulating conversation. The children were tapering off; their business was complete. I learned that it is important to follow the children's leads and that no amount of repeating a wonderful question is going to catch a response that doesn't want to be answered. Perhaps there is no such thing as closure.

Links to Today's World

What makes the children's responses to these survival stories unique? They link children to today's events through powerfully written literature. These stories narrate children's struggles to survive, struggles to escape, struggles to gain entry into free countries, and struggles to learn about and to understand new cultures. Hoang Anh is a junior high student in San Rafael now. Someone like Vithy is in his mid-twenties in Australia now. Tara's Kurdish relatives still live in Iraq today. Boat people are still making their way across water to find freedom in Southeast Asia and in the Caribbean. Kurds are still in jeopardy. The Khmer Rouge are still seeking power by using violence in the State of Cambodia, although the last of the Thai refugee camps was closed in March 1993. These books are too valuable not to be shared with children.

Multicultural children's literature lets children experience the lifestyles of others and thus affects their attitudes and values (Aoki 1992). Berg-Cross (1978) and Monson and Shurtleff (1979) have suggested that listening to literature has an affect on attitudes of readers. Aoki (1992) suggests that discussing the values found in these books is just as important. The connections that the children made between characters in *Little Brother* and *Hoang Anh* indicate that the discussions helped them to make real-life connections to the journeys of people escaping from oppressive political situations and the difficulties of moving to a new culture. Gimmerstad and De Chiara (1982) have written about the importance of leading children in discussions so that they might empathize with characters and identify with their problems as the children did while talking about Naledi and her journey to bring her mother home. A comparison of what the children knew about freedom in the initial survey to the knowledge gained by reading these books indicates a shift in attitude, the ability to locate, explore, discuss, and respond to the struggles of people living in distant places. Substantive books with substantive themes. Extended dialogue about the characters and their problems. Time for reflective writing and discussion. Concrete projects that helped the children to sort through information by re-creating a chronology of events. All of these things combined became an integrated experience in which children learned a bit more about their world and expanded their own views about the people in it.

Professional References

Aoki, Elaine. 1992. In *Teaching Multicultural Literature in Grades K-8*, edited by Violet J. Harris. Norwood, MA: Christopher-Gordon Publishers.

Berg-Cross, L., and G. Berg-Cross. 1978. "Listening to Stories May Change Children's Social Attitudes." *The Reading Teacher*: 659–63.

Donaldson, Margaret. 1979. *Children's Minds*. New York: Norton.

Gimmerstad and De Chiara. 1982. "Dramatic Plays: A Vehicle for Prejudice Reduction in the Elementary School." *Journal of Education Research* 76: 45–9.

Kohlberg, Lawrence. 1981. In *The Child and the Book*, edited by Nicholas Tucker. New York: Cambridge University Press.

Lehr, Susan. 1985. "A Child's Developing Sense of Theme." Doctoral dissertation, Ohio State University, Columbus, OH.

———. 1988. "Classroom Research Explores the Child's Construction of Meaning." *Reading Research Quarterly* 23: 337–57.

———. 1990. "Literature and the Construction of Meaning: The Preschool Child's Developing Sense of Theme." *Journal of Research in Childhood Education* 5(1): 37–46.

———. 1991. *The Child's Developing Sense of Theme.* New York: Teachers College Press.

MONSON, D., and L. SHURTLEFF. 1979. "Altering Attitudes Toward the Physically Handicapped Through Print and Non-Print Media." *Language Arts*: 163–70.

NEWKIRK, THOMAS. 1992. *Listening In: Children Talk About Books (and Other Things).* Portsmouth, NH: Heinemann.

SIMMER, STEPHEN. 1992. "Psychological Interpretations of Stories: On Catching Mice." In *Stories and Readers: New Perspectives on Literature in the Elementary Classroom*, edited by Charles Temple and Patrick Collins. Norwood, MA: Christopher-Gordon Publishers.

VYGOTSKY, LEV S. 1978. *Mind in Society.* Cambridge, MA: Harvard University Press.

Children's Literature

BAILLIE, ALLAN. 1992. *Little Brother.* New York: Viking.

CHANDLER, DAVID. 1991. *The Land and People of Cambodia.* New York: HarperCollins.

HOYT-GOLDSMITH, DIANE. 1992. *Hoang Anh: A Vietnamese-American Boy.* New York: Holiday House.

HO, MINGFONG. 1991. *The Clay Marble.* New York: Farrar Straus & Giroux.

LAIRD, ELIZABETH. 1991. *Kiss the Dust.* New York: Dutton Children's Books.

NAIDOO, BEVERLEY. 1985. *Journey to Jo'Burg.* New York: J. B. Lippincott.

WHELAN, GLORIA. 1992. *Goodbye, Vietnam.* New York: Alfred A. Knopf.

TEN

The Shaping of The Clay Marble

Minfong Ho

There is a massive, old white pine that grows in a corner of our backyard here in upstate New York. Its boughs shade a sandbox where our two toddlers played, its lower branches held a precarious tree house they built, and its needles provided a soft bed where I could read. Its effortless symmetry hinted of a stability and permanence that has always calmed me.

One winter morning, after a heavy snowstorm, the lowest branch of this old pine suddenly broke off, under the burden of the new snow. From the kitchen window, I heard a loud splintering sound, then the crash as it hit the ground, tearing apart the tree house, crushing the little sandbox. I rushed outside to look at the tree. There, in the tree trunk where the branch had ripped off, was a dark, deep rot, so soft that I could have plunged my hand in and scooped out moist pulp. It looked as if the tree was rotten to its core. I stared at it and thought: that's me.

Why?

After all, hadn't things been going well for me: graduate school, marriage, children, and now our own house? So why did it feel so wrong?

If I had to answer that in one word, I would say now, "Cambodia." But I did not realize it then. That winter, Cambodia was as hidden and buried in me as the rot in the old pine tree.

I am not Cambodian, had not even ever set foot in Cambodia all the first fifteen years that I grew up in neighboring Thailand. All I had done was to do some relief work on the Thai–Cambodian border in 1980, when the first influx of refugees from the harsh Pol Pot regime started to straggle into Thailand.

The work itself was straightforward enough. I was supposed to help set up supplementary feeding centers for the severely malnourished children in the ring of refugee camps along the Thai border. Basically, this consisted of buying truckloads of fresh vegetables and rice and charcoal, getting the stuff to the thatched kitchens at far-flung sites, and overseeing the distribution of the cooked food to the long lines of children waiting under the hot sun. It was time-consuming work, and tiring, but not particularly difficult. Plenty of other people—the surgeons and nurses, the UNI-CEF field staff, even the military patrol—had much more grueling jobs, which they seemed to perform efficiently, unflinchingly.

And yet I hadn't been able to do my work properly. I remember being erratic, moody, angry, morose, an emotional minefield. Most nights I would cry myself to sleep, and later I took to drinking glasses of Mekong, a very strong Thai rice whiskey, to get any sleep at all.

Eventually I quit and returned to graduate school at Cornell, and resumed "normal" life.

Until the big old pine tree broke.

My husband called up his good friend Robin, a tree surgeon. I sought out another friend, Rachel, a motherly Jewish therapist who had fled her childhood home in Europe just before the Second World War.

Robin the tree surgeon took a look at the tree and said: let it be, it's strong and tough, it'll heal itself.

Rachel the therapist took a look at me and said, predictably enough, "Talk."

It was very difficult to talk about Cambodia, about the Cambodian refugees. Without my having acknowledged it, I had been sucked into the conspiracy of silence that is so often generated by absolute misery. The Cambodian refugees themselves had not spoken much of their own suffering. How could I? One does not talk about such unspeakable things.

I remembered, yes, but I did not want to, could not, talk—about the dead and the dying, the starving and the shooting, the pain and the suffering, and most terrible of all, the total senselessness of it. Why had it happened? Why was it still happening? And why was it inflicted onto even the children? How could such things be talked about?

The Cambodians that I saw were for the most part themselves silent. Especially in the malnutrition "wards," no more than makeshift thatched huts, where I spent a lot of my time, the children were too weak to cry, their mothers too stoic or perhaps too tired to talk. It was a terrible thing, this silence, like some thick web that had descended and choked everyone underneath.

Only very rarely was the silence ever broken. And when that happened, it too would be terrible. I remember once hearing some screaming outside the ward I was working in. Two Cambodian women were standing in the fierce noonday sun, fighting and screaming at each other. One of them had evidently been a Khmer Rouge cadre in the Pol Pot regime, while the other was someone who must have suffered horribly under that same regime. The latter was crying: how could you have killed so many of us, how could you have been so cruel? The Khmer Rouge ex-cadre was screaming back, in equal anguish: how could you have *let* us do this to you?

Nothing made any sense, not the silence, not the screams.

"But you don't have to be silent," Rachel said, "and you don't have to scream. Try talking." And so I started talking.

I told her how seeing the Cambodian refugees on the Border had shaken me to the core of my being. Growing up in Bangkok I had often seen beggars on the streets, or malnourished babies of nomadic hill tribes in northern Thailand, but never, never in all my life had I seen such absolute misery, on such a massive scale.

In one border camp there had been tall watchtowers of split bamboo erected. If you climbed to the top of this watchtower, you would see thousands, hundreds of thousands of people, like a churning brown ocean, stretched out in every direction as far as the eye could see. All of them uprooted, helpless, and silent. It was overwhelming.

Yet seeing the refugees somehow confirmed one of my most deep-rooted fears: that one's regular, mundane life could be so suddenly and drastically disrupted. Growing up in a Chinese immigrant family as I did, I was used to hearing stories of how, for example, my mother had left her childhood home in Shanghai blithely one summer and was never able to return, because the Japanese had taken it over. When she was finally able to go back, almost forty years later, the house had been razed to the ground. She had not even been able to locate her mother's gravesite. Most of our friends and family of her generation have similar stories to tell. Or I would be told how after I was born in Burma, my parents left Rangoon "temporarily" with me so that my mother could give birth to my brother in the relative comfort of Hong Kong and how we had never gone back to Burma because of the political turmoil there. As a result, neither my mother nor I have many photos of ourselves as young children, because our childhood photographs, together with other family possessions, had all been irrevocably left behind.

The lives of these Cambodian refugees had been disrupted in much the same way. Like us, they had been living quietly one day, with the rumblings of war only a distant reality, and the next day everything had changed. They had to move, and they had to leave behind not only a lifetime of possessions, but everything they were familiar with—language, culture, religion, country. In a very literal way, none of us could ever go home again.

I think, in retrospect, I had always felt a dread of such sudden disruption in my life. It meant that I could have very little control over my own destiny, because the big things—when I might be uprooted and where I might be able to go afterwards— were completely beyond my control. This is not humility; it is a sense of enforced helplessness.

Then, too, I felt that the fate of these refugees touched close to home because they were very much like people I grew up with in neighboring Thailand. I speak Thai, and can therefore understand many Cambodian words that have the same Sanskrit-based roots. And their clothing, the dances, the Buddhist religion, all seemed familiar to me because they were so closely linked with Thailand's own traditions. And, basically, I identified with them simply because I looked like them.

There was one camp that I visited early on during my time on the Border that was secluded and heavily guarded, because many of the refugees inside it were ethnic Chinese from Cambodia. Since my own mother-tongue is Chinese, I had felt an instant rapport with these refugees, listening to their stories of escape and loss. The afternoon passed quickly, and before I knew it the Thai security guards were ushering out the handful of foreign relief workers in preparation to locking up the camp. My colleagues all left, but the security guards wouldn't let me out because they thought, quite understandably, that I was one of the refugees. No amount of argument on my part, whether it was in Thai, in Chinese, or in English, would persuade the guards that I actually belonged outside. It finally took one of my fellow relief workers, a white man—and therefore visibly foreign—to vouch for me and to insist that they let me go. As I walked out and the gates slammed behind me, I remember feeling a great disquiet, that perhaps I really belonged in there with Them instead of outside with the foreign Us.

That same sense of dislocation stayed with me after I left the Border altogether: what was I doing in upstate New York, pretending that the Thai–Cambodian border and the refugees never existed? Why wasn't I back there with them? Why did my life now seem a farce, unreal and shadowy, when the nightmare of the Border by contrast seemed so real?

I talked and talked, as Rachel listened. Once in a while she would murmur something. "Post-Traumatic Stress Syndrome," she said once. "Read Eli Wiesel," she suggested.

Post-what?

Eli who?

Eli Wiesel. There was a whole shelf of his books at the public library. I took out the first one of the lot ("Accident, The"). All I knew about him was what it said on the dust jacket of the book, that the author had survived the Holocaust at Auschwitz as a young man. The story opened with someone who narrowly escaped death after being hit by a car but who felt afterwards that he had really no right to be alive. I don't remember details, just that I could not stop reading, could not stop crying. By the end of the book it was dusk, the box of tissues was all used up, and I was exhausted.

But also more at peace. There was a feeling of overwhelming relief, that someone else had actually felt this way, had felt so devastated by death that life could seem only an obscene mockery of it. Yet there was a shaft of hope—the very fact that this writer, this survivor, had voiced his deep despair with such control hinted at some indomitable wellspring of strength and yes, even beauty.

I understood then that between the silence and the scream, there could be a song.

More than anything, I wanted to find the song in the refugee camps of the Border. And to do that, I had to face the refugees again.

I pulled out cardboard boxes of journals I had haphazardly written in while I was working on the Border, looked at photographs I had taken of the people there. I opened myself to the people in my notebooks, in my photographs, and in my memory. I let them talk, and I tried to hear what they might be saying to me.

It was the children who spoke to me most directly. They had made me so uneasy for so long, keeping their silent vigil in my mind. I didn't know, still don't know, what it was that made them stay there, waiting, watching. Were they sad? Angry? Sullen? Envious? What did they want of me? Why did they want to talk to me? Did they want me to understand, to remember, to give them voice, movement, life? What was it in them, in me, that wouldn't let them just gently disappear? Did they hate me? Did I hate them? Did I love them? What if they needed me? Why did I need them? Why couldn't they talk to me?

What could they have said? I hate you I need you I hurt I can't bear it I am bearing it go away stay come back touch me hold me leave me alone? And how could I have said any of that either? Even while I was with them at the Border, I had been unable to really talk to them. Instead I had cooked and trucked food around and fed them, maintaining that silence, that unbridgeable distance. And every day that I kept it up I had known it was a sham. I was ashamed, ashamed of being so useless, so weak, so well-fed myself. How could I live with so much, when they had nothing?

And yet, of course, there was really no Them, no Me. I was Them, each child, each barefoot, snotnosed child. I had been so much like them, when I was little. I knew them, was familiar with them, and most devastating of all, I liked them, liked their gumption, their spirit, their sudden giggles. If I had been ten or fifteen years younger, I would have wanted nothing more than to be friends with them. Instead, separated by a few years and an arbitrary twist of history, we had diverged into such different paths: they to endure war and famine, I to watch them endure. But they *had* endured, these sweet tough children, tougher by far than I could ever be. They had endured; I had cracked under the strain of just watching them endure.

It was this endurance, the memory of their resilience, that spoke to me now. I examined the faces of the children in my photographs, and surprisingly many of them were smiling, even laughing. I had never been able to bring myself to point my camera into the faces of the sick and miserable, since that would have violated what little they had left of themselves. But there amidst the images of ugliness and suffering that had haunted me, I found that there *had* been flashes of happiness.

Tenuous at first as the first blades of new grass after a hard drought, these memories of hope began to surface. I remembered the ingenious toys the children at the refugee camps had made: fish woven from strips of plastic IV tubes, trucks from tin cans, and everywhere the little dolls and animals shaped from clay.

And out of the dreaded silence I remembered some sounds of laughter. Once, in a malnutrition ward, I was sitting next to a stick-thin baby held in the lap of his older sister, herself no more than eight or ten years old. On her wrist were several rubber bands, and I had gently pulled one and snapped it against her arm. Playfully, she had reached over to the rubber band on my own wrist (which I used to tie back my hair) and snapped it against me. I laughed; she giggled. It was a lovely light sound, her giggle. Soon there was a small crowd of little girls gathered around me, taking turns to snap my rubber band and holding up their wrists for me to snap theirs. For a moment, the sound of their light laughter filled the ward. How had I forgotten that?

And, too, I remembered a gift another little girl had given me one day. For no reason that I could see, a ragged little girl had come over and slipped something into my hand. It was a clay marble, so smooth that she must have spent hours rolling it between her palms. Briefly, we linked fingers, our skin so much the same shade of brown that we could easily have been sisters.

And thinking of that marble again, I realized that if she could shape such a lovely round marble out of the chaos of her own life, then I too would try and shape something out of my own confusion.

And so I followed her example and started to shape my own clay marble.

Writing the story *The Clay Marble* was not an easy process, but it was a slow, healing one. I started moulding it around the girl who gave me her clay marble, naming her Dara, and eventually she took over the whole story. At the time I was writing, I had not known the word *empowerment*, but looking back on it, I think that was what happened to Dara, and through her to myself.

One of the deepest satisfactions came after the story was almost finished. My husband had accepted a job in Laos, and so we moved back to Southeast Asia, our two young children in tow. Living for over a year in Laos—Cambodia's Communist neighbor—I could sense for myself the basic peace and stability of the countryside.

I visited Cambodia too and spent time not only in its capital city of Phnom Penh, but also its surrounding countryside.

It had been over a decade since the turmoil of the Communist takeover there, after the vast outflow of refugees, and in the aftermath of the dislocation there was still widespread poverty. Yet both in Laos and in Cambodia life had resumed its age-old pattern. Men ploughed their paddy fields, young monks swept temple compounds, looms clicked as women wove checkered sarongs underneath stilted houses. And the children, like the children everywhere, were spinning tops, flying kites, making marbles out of clay.

It was in Laos that I finished up the revisions for *The Clay Marble* and wrote the final two pages. When I turned those in to my editor at faraway Farrar, Straus and Giroux, I said in my letter to her:

> It has been a gift, to be able to finish up the story here, with the swallows diving in arcs above the rice fields right outside my window, the mango trees a stone's throw from my desk. Everything is a seamless whole, the fields, the story, the past, the present, Dara, myself.
>
> I could not have envisioned before, how life goes on, after the misery and suffering I saw on the Border. The last glimpse I had, of children like Dara, was of their oxcarts, heading past the land mined forests, to a war torn country. And now, I have met them on the other end. The countryside here, behind the "rattan curtain" in Indochina, is very poor, but—and this makes all the difference in the world for me—I find the children playing here, as I did on the Border.
>
> I did not make it all up, it was not some solipsistic nightmare I had, shut up in a cold house in upstate New York. It all happened, it exists, it is all here. I have

come home again, and I have brought Dara and her family home with me. And now finally I can leave her safely here.

That was a couple of years ago, and now here I am back at that same "cold house in upstate New York." Instead of rice fields, my desk now overlooks that big old pine tree in the backyard.

We have taken the advice of the tree surgeon and let the old white pine alone, rather than dredge out the rot or seal over the hole with cement. And just as Robin said, it was a tough old thing; its trunk and its own root system keep growing, and it is healing itself.

All through this morning the snow has been falling heavily, and the world outside my window is a whirl of white. The massive boughs of the pine tree are completely covered now, and the lowest branch is so heavily weighed down with snow that the tips of it are touching the ground, forming a sort of lacy igloo under the tree. I will go out now and shake some of the snow off that branch.

Because, as Rachel maintains, even the strongest and toughest things can do with a bit of help, now and then.

Children's Literature

Ho, Minfong. 1991. *The Clay Marble*. New York: Farrar, Straus & Giroux.

ELEVEN

Pol Pot's Reign of Terror:
Why Write About It for Children?

ALLAN BAILLIE

"Family?" the Cambodian boy said. "Now or before? Before I have a father, a mother, four brothers and three sisters. Now I have a brother and a sister."

The boy's quiet words have stayed with me—it seems—for a lifetime. He was a Cambodian, speaking in a Thai refugee camp in 1980. His tragedy has been echoed ten thousand times in that camp and the ragged string of others on the Thai–Cambodian border, but it was his story that drove me to write about it.

But the roots of *Little Brother* (1992; 1985 in Scotland and Australia) go back a further eleven years—to the time I was wandering about Cambodia working on a tourist book. It was that sort of place, then.

In 1969 I sneaked into Prince Sihanouk's kingdom with a British passport that said I was an artist, although I cannot draw a straight line. I was in reality an Australian journalist, but any journalist from any country allied to the United States would never be allowed into the country. I spent some time in Singapore getting artist's materials and trying to sketch Bugis Street, but I needn't have bothered. Nobody was interested in my qualifications.

Oh, I found some justification for the prince's shyness with the Western press. Apparently ships were docking in the southern port of Sihanoukville, loading weaponry onto trucks that barreled along the U.S.-built Peace Highway to the jungles of the Vietcong. But the Vietnam War was beyond the mountains and of no concern to Cambodia.

In 1969 Phnom Penh was just about the cleanest, prettiest city in Asia. The single hill in the city, the Phnom, looked over the meeting of the Tonle Sap and the Mekong rivers. Below the Phnom the French had left parks, boulevards, fountains, grand houses, and a taste of French cuisine. The Chinese, the Indians, the Vietnamese bustled about downtown around the massive concrete dome of the market and had lunch in French–Cambodian restaurants. The green-shaded fruit market sold Australian apples, at one dollar apiece.

The green and gold roofs of Buddhist wats (temples) broke the pattern of the city, and monks in saffron walked their parasols along the tree-lined streets. Past the garish cinemas, stupas and symbolic dollhouses were made for the cemetery—where a sign asked people to refrain from kissing.

Sihanouk governed the country after Cambodia's first election, but to most Cambodians he was still a God-King, and nothing showed this so clearly as Phnom Penh's Festival of the Waters. This festival celebrated the Reversal of the Waters, or yearly flood. Normally the Tonle Sap river flows from the huge Tonle Sap lake to the Mekong. But when the monsoon rains hit South China, Laos, and northern Cambodia, the Mekong swells and pushes the Tonle Sap river backwards to fill the Tonle Sap lake, carrying rich silt and fish. When the rains stop the Tonle Sap reverts to normal. This is the time for Phnom Penh to celebrate—no, for Cambodia to celebrate.

Sihanouk stepped from his grand green and gold palace and was cheered by thousands to the river bank. At night a procession of illuminated floats drifted past the royal pavilion; during the day village crews of thirty raced their pirogues—long canoes—against each other and the royal pirogues. I don't know if any of the village crews ever beat Sihanouk's royal pirogues. In a downtown cinema Sihanouk starred in a romantic epic, and in a Russian-built theater a daughter danced with the Royal Ballet.

I got on well in Phnom Penh. I spoke bad French, and very many Cambodians also spoke bad French. A Frenchman muttered that I was conversing with Cambodians better than he was, and he couldn't understand what we were talking about. I liked the Cambodians, liked their gentle humor, their customs, their French-Chinese-Indian food, their way of life. I felt that I could live permanently in Phnom Penh.

And it was the same way around the country. There wasn't much money about, but there was no hunger and the life was relaxed and pleasant. Stilt-houses were besieged by ducks and geese, waterwheels or slow pedal power irrigated the paddies, but a floating village had tall TV aerials tuned to Bangkok. Night markets took over from day markets with delicious meals beneath hissing lamps.

I spent a week wandering around Angkor, a proud, ruined city being cut slowly from the jungle by French archaeologists and Cambodian teams. I spent a still night with the bats in one of the ruins and wondered at a woman singing alone in the heart of the forest.

I went up the Mekong on a creaking ferry run by a fourteen-year-old boy who smoked foul homemade cigars, so foul that the only time I could speak with him was when the wind blew from me to him. At the end of that trip I visited some Frenchmen running a rubber plantation.

They slapped a revolver in my hand and took me on a night hunt in the plantation. They warned me about careless shooting because we were going into an area controlled by a few bandits. Harmless, they said, and charming. The bandits were just sick and tired of the corruption of the Sihanouk government. Called themselves Khmer Rouge. We stopped, and I shot four coconuts.

The Frenchmen said they could see the Vietnam War from a nearby mountain top. They sometimes spent Sunday afternoons sipping mint juleps watching the bombers and the choppers over the jungle.

Eventually I went home.

But two months later Cambodia began to change. Sihanouk traveled to China and was deposed while he was away by one General Lon Noi. Lon Noi vowed to wipe out the Khmer Rouge bandits, and the rivers began to carry the bound bodies of Vietnamese villagers. The "bandits" of the Khmer Rouge were supported and trained by North Vietnam and became a formidable army. Civil war spread across the country. The American air war swept into the Cambodian highlands, and I wondered if the Frenchmen watched the bombs marching toward them.

Places I knew were battered, torn apart. A school in Phnom Penh was shelled near where I had eaten breakfast; Angkor Wat was shelled; the cigar-smoking youth's Mekong was mined. While I watched from safe Sydney, friends disappeared, Cambodia became Kampuchea. The war was lost and Phnom Penh went the way of Saigon, but at least the fighting was over. Cambodia could recover, rebuild, and perhaps recapture the easy life of 1969.

But a dull student of Marx and Mao, Pol Pot, gained control of the Khmer Rouge and used mines and soldiers to lock Kampuchea from the world. Stark, unbelievable stories began to leak across the border. Cities had been emptied, with hospital patients being wheeled in their beds along the highway. There was something about "Year Zero" and "Big Paddies" and killing, constant killing.

Then in 1979 some Khmer Rouge attacked villages in Vietnam, and North Vietnamese troops invaded Kampuchea, driving the Khmer Rouge into the forests and mountains. Thousands of starving, maimed and battered Cambodians ran the gauntlet of war and mines for the safety of the Thai border. Many of them reached the new camps—hastily set up by the Thai army and humanitarian agencies with food and medical treatment—only to die of starvation. They had not eaten for too long.

In 1980 I returned, not to the torn and forbidden Kampuchea but to the border camps. I had written and published a novel based on the far milder civil war in Laos, so I was supposed to be a writer. I would try to write an adult novel on the tragedy of Cambodia to pay a debt to the country and the friends I knew in 1969.

I learned the meaning of "Year Zero." It was an attempt to cut all knowledge from the people of Kampuchea beyond the dictum of the Khmer Rouge. And that could only be done in one way. You're a doctor? You're dead. A nurse, clerk, taxi driver, Buddhist monk, teacher, student? You're dead. A small child with soft hands, meaning you have—had—parents with money and knowledge. You're dead.

And "Big Paddies"? The Khmer Rouge leveled great swatches of land, using slave labor instead of machines, replacing the traditional small paddies. Very grand, but people alone cannot level large areas so exactly that the paddy will work. The water runs to flood a corner and leaves a section barren. Little paddies can survive on a shower and a light dip into the stream, but large paddies need a river and Kampuchea had endured a drought. The big paddies were not producing enough rice for the country, and most of this little rice went to the Khmer Rouge soldiers. The people growing the rice were slowly starving.

But there was little sign of this when I wandered through the camps. The agencies were delivering food to the refugees regularly; doctors and nurses from France, America, Australia, and other countries were working solidly in canvas hospitals. The worst was over—or so it seemed.

I went to the border camp of Nong Samet, called 007 by the Thai army. They said, with a wink, that Camp 007 was full of danger and intrigue, like James Bond. The Thai army had dug a broad channel beyond which no refugee could pass. One side was Thailand; the other was Kampuchea and 007. Camp 007 was a thousand shelters of orange plastic, a tent for a hospital, water tanks, a bicycle repair shop under a tree, a barren vegetable market—and a coffee shop. Cafe Boheme was clean, with pinned plastic on the tables, and displayed a large painting of Angkor Wat—but had no coffee.

Grinning youths played netball near the water tanks, but if you walked down any track the atmosphere changed. You met one-legged men carrying water in buckets, half-families, lone widows cooking rice and vegetables in battered pots outside the orange plastic shelter, perhaps with a mat and a piece of material. Everything they had, the buckets, the pots, the mats, possibly even the clothes on their backs, they owed to the agencies. They had lost nearly everything to the Khmer Rouge, and they had come to the camp in a last desperate bid to escape them.

But the Khmer Rouge were there. I saw them with their guns, sprawled in the middle of the camp.

They had come to the camp for the rice and for protection. The refugees could not move away because the Thai army said that the rice must be delivered there.

Under a Thai army directive I left the camp with the doctors and nurses before sunset one evening. Half an hour later Vietnamese troops attacked the Khmer Rouge. More than three hundred died that night, most of them refugees caught in the crossfire.

I went to the camp of Khao-I-Dang, fifteen kilometers into Thailand, safe and established. Here were bungalows being built in streets, a water tower, a crafts and community center, a loudspeaker system, and a canvas hospital. Here Cambodians were being interviewed, a process that might get them into a new country, a new home.

Kids on bent sheets of tin skidded down gravel humps, screaming and laughing. But there were other kids who sat in silence and just watched. I saw drawings by kids like these, showing kids killing kids in planned games. . . .

151

And here I met Vuthy. I walked into the shadowed brown hospital and saw Vuthy bandaging the shoulder of a dull Khmer Rouge soldier. The day before, Vuthy had saved the life of an American woman doctor by wrestling a pair of scissors from the soldier. The doctor introduced me to Vuthy and suggested I listen to his story.

I picked up other stories, many others, went home and tried to write a book about what I'd seen and heard. And failed. How can you write of people being starved to death in a rice paddy, schools becoming torture chambers, people being executed with plastic bags or staves to save bullets, little kids being trained to play games to kill. . . . How can you write of these and expect people to read the book?

My wife dragged me from the morass to write a children's adventure called *Adrift*, and then I remembered Vuthy and his sad words: "Family? Now or before? Before I had a father, a mother, four brothers and three sisters. Now I have a brother and a sister." And I remembered his story.

He had been a slave-laborer on a Big Paddy as the Khmer Rouge whittled his family from him. He was actually marched into the forest to be executed, but gunfire distracted the soldiers and he was able to bolt. He wandered into an almost deserted Phnom Penh and loaded rice trucks for the North Vietnamese.

Eventually he hid in one of the trucks and reached Battambang. Using a little hidden gold, he moved on with a cyclo-pousse (a rickshaw driven by a bicycle), then a buffalo cart and entered a forest loaded with mines and armed men at war. Finally he crossed the Thai border and became an orderly-interpreter at the comparative safety of the Khao-I-Dang camp hospital. . . .

And two years after speaking to Vuthy I began to realize what he had given me.

It was a good story, why not tell it?

More, why not use it to tell the story of Cambodia?

Tell the story of Cambodia through the eyes of a child.

And I stopped there.

Not an adult book, not an adult looking through the eyes of a child for adults. No, a book about a child's view of Cambodia for children.

Oh, there are limitations in writing a novel for children, fences you cannot climb, but these fences can actually help. With a children's story you don't tell the full horror. You can't. If you write about the obscenity of the plastic-bag executions the image will stay with the child in his bed and worse. But if you step back a little, the truth and the tragedy will still be there. You have only reduced the horror to a shadow.

But the child reader will see enough.

Forget about the Byzantine complications of the Khmer Rouge, the application of a warped Marxist philosophy, and deadly rice politics. A children's story must be basically simple, and that helps you get at the essence of what you are trying to say.

But why tell children about Cambodia? Because children like them suffered in Cambodia and maybe there is a Cambodian in the class. Look at that weird refugee kid, he might have gone through something like this. Maybe he's a bit nervous, doesn't talk much about his past, has trouble laughing. Understand him a little, give him some time. That simple.

But to reach children I *had* to make the book readable. I had to set up Vuthy's escape story as a trap, so the reader cannot retreat from the worst of it.

So Vuthy, fifteen and very shrewd, becomes Vithy, about eleven and afraid, dependent on his big brother. Start with Vuthy's real-life race for life to drag in the reader, and add the big brother. Take his brother away, to increase Vithy's desperation and give him a double quest. Vithy starts as a very *little* brother, but by the end of the book he will no longer be one, as with the thousands of other refugee kids. So in the last line of the book when the big brother says, "Hello, little brother," he is wrong. He hasn't seen what has happened to Vithy.

But the first person to be caught in my trap was me. I started writing a chase story, and I kept the fact that it is set in Cambodia until deep in the book, because the reader may not be interested in a Cambodian boy's story. Except that I had to start feeding a lot of information from that late revelation while trying to keep the story moving at the same time. And of course the publisher would blow my secret with the cover and the blurb. I went back and started again.

But the idea of reducing the Cambodian element—the Khmer element—of Vithy was still there. I realized I was writing something like H. G. Wells' *War of the Worlds*, where a Martian invasion has destroyed the way of life of England. Vithy has lost his family, his friends, his culture, everything. He is no longer a Buddhist-animist who dances the monkey-god at school and makes bamboo toys. He is simply a boy running for his life and so is universal. There are times when Vithy has enough time to be Khmer, but not enough time to dwell on it.

Vithy taught me that culture can be put on or taken off like a shirt. The person underneath is the same. I am a Scots–Australian, but when I wrote of Vithy I *was* Vithy, weeping with him of the lost Cambodia in Phnom Penh, running with him from the nightmare stirred by a bus queue.

I put the 1969 cigar-smoking ferry boy in the near-deserted Phnom Penh for a rare bright patch in a grim tale and because one character can survive, no matter how bad the situation. Vuthy went to Battambang, but Vithy went to Angkor instead, because it is the heart of Cambodia's culture and history, all that the world knew of Cambodia before Pol Pot—and because I had been there.

And then deep in the book, where the reader cannot leave, I tell the depth of Vithy's tragedy, as with many, many others—father taken away in a bus never to be seen again, mother starved to death while growing rice for the soldiers, little sister killed for knowing arithmetic.

At that point I realized that I was not writing about Cambodia anymore. Vithy could be a child in Burma, Iraq, Somalia, Beirut, Bosnia, Afghanistan . . . nice little global village we have, haven't we?

And I wasn't writing to stir sympathy from the reader for the refugee boy in the classroom or on TV anymore.

I was writing *Little Brother* to make a boy from Utah feel he could *be* the boy in Cambodia. By a casual spin of the coin.

Children's Literature

BAILLIE, ALLAN. 1991. *Adrift.* New York: Viking.

———. 1992. *Little Brother.* New York: Viking.

TWELVE

Cultural Politics and Writing for Young People

Joel Taxel

Few issues in today's contentious social and cultural environment evoke as much heated debate as do the subjects of political correctness and multiculturalism. In the most general sense, multiculturalism or multicultural education refers to education that addresses the interests, concerns, and experiences of individuals and groups considered outside of the sociopolitical and cultural mainstream of American society. The term often is interpreted as a reference to groups such as African Americans, Native Americans, Asian Americans, and Hispanic Americans. More expansive definitions emphasize the notion of diversity and include gender, sexual orientation, and other kinds of "difference." The call for multiculturalism in children's literature is a reaction to a central reality in the history of American children's literature: "Until quite recently, people of color have been either virtually excluded from literature for young people, or frequently portrayed in undesirable ways—as negative stereotypes or objects of ridicule" (Sims Bishop 1993, 39).

More recent controversies have raged around books about African Americans written by white American authors. In some of the more highly publicized instances of this phenomenon, *Ben's Trumpet* (Isadora 1979), *Jake and Honeybunch Go to Heaven* (Zemach 1982), *Sounder* (Armstrong 1969), *The Cay* (Taylor 1969), *The Slave Dancer* (Fox 1973), and *Words by Heart* (Sebestyen 1979) all were reproved for either their dubious cultural authenticity or for more subtle stereotyping by critics who raise issues that go beyond those typically articulated in most discussions and reviews of books for young people (see, for example, Banfield and Wilson 1985; Moore 1885; Sims 1980; Taxel 1986; Trousdale 1990).

Political correctness (PC) was defined in an article in *Time* as a movement that seeks "to suppress thought or statements deemed offensive to women, blacks or other groups" (Allis, Bonfante, and Booth 1991, 13). Advocates of PC are said to favor the banishment of unfavorable speech, opinions, and attitudes about women and

---

An earlier version of this chapter was published in the Spring 1994 issue of *The New Advocate*.

minority groups from college campuses and from the pages of children's literature. PC has been labeled "the enforcement arm of multiculturalism" (Ozersky 1991, 35). It is important to keep in mind the relation between multiculturalism and PC because in most assaults on political correctness, "the bogyman is multiculturalism" (Foner and Weiner 1991, 163). Minsky (1992) suggested that although most assaults on PC are presented as a defense of free expression and speech, they actually are attacks on multiculturalism (32). Close examination of the controversies surrounding political correctness and multiculturalism in literature, art, curriculum, and culture in general reveals that they are concerned with how we define ourselves as individuals and understand our nation's past, present, and future possibilities. As Carton (1991) noted, the war on multiculturalism expresses increasingly unsettled "American assumptions about the nature of personal and national identity" (40).

Clearly, PC debates become passionate and polemical because they represent challenges to deeply held beliefs and myths that are basic to this country's sense of itself. PC debates raise other serious issues for those involved with children's literature, including questions about the relation between sociocultural and political perspectives and the more strictly aesthetic considerations critics claim are utilized when selecting books for young people. Perhaps most apparent from even a cursory review of the growing literature on political correctness is the deeply felt commitment of the disputants to their respective positions that often precludes reasonable discussion and discourse. The lamentable result is that the sides often talk past one another.

Is There Really a PC Problem?

One of my basic contentions is that the very existence of this article is testimony to the remarkable success of conservative, reactionary forces in convincing the public that there, in fact, is a PC crisis. The term *PC* is not new. It originated in the late 1940s in reference to political debates in the U. S. Communist Party where it was an approving phrase to denote someone who toed the party line (Kohl 1991, 33; Berman 1992, 5). Most current discussions of PC, however, speak of it in relation to developments on college and university campuses. D'Souza (1991), one of the best known and often cited critics of PC, spoke of "thought police" on the left who are taking over college campuses and bent on the destruction of intellectual freedom, a charge repeated regularly by media gurus like George Will (1993). Kimball's (1990) best-selling conservative call-to-arms charged that "tenured radicals" have taken over college campuses and are subverting traditional notions of curriculum. The objective of these radical professors, according to Kimball, "is nothing less than the destruction of the values, methods, and goals of the traditional humanistic study" (xi). In response to these and similar claims, Kohl (1991) suggested that the term PC has been appropriated by right-wing intellectuals "to disparage students and professors who advocate multiculturalism and are willing to confront racism, sexism, and homophobia at the university" (34). Central to the tactics of those who attack

PC is the accusation that students (or professors) who insist that the voices of women and people of color be included in the curriculum are "making rigid, oppressive demands that constrain academic freedom" (1991, 34).

The perception that the purveyors of PC are exerting an undue influence on children's literature also has widespread public acceptance. A review of recent children's books in *Newsweek*, for example, began with the observation that "kids' books" had fallen "into the clutches of the politically correct, the multiculturalists and every other do-gooder with an eat your spinach attitude." While noting that it's "tough . . . to knock" the emphasis on "being good—respecting others, respecting yourself, allowing for cultural differences," Jones (1993) wonders "whatever happened to old fashion fun like gluing your sister's hair to the bedpost" (54). Far more serious are the charges of Rochman (1993) in *Against Borders: Promoting Books for a Multicultural World*, a book containing a passionate, compassionate, and exceptionally literate plea for "great books from all cultures" to "break down apartheid" (12). Despite her laudable embrace of the multicultural ethos, Rochman begins a chapter entitled "Beyond Political Correctness" with the following declamation:

> Multiculturalism is a trendy word, trumpeted by the politically correct with a stridency that has provoked a sneering backlash. There are PC watchdogs eager to strip from the library shelves anything that presents a group as less than perfect. The ethnic character must always be strong, dignified, courageous, loving, sensitive, and wise. Then there are those who watch for authenticity: how dare a white write about blacks? What is a gentile doing writing about a Jewish old lady and her African American neighbors? The chilling effect of this is a kind of censorship and a reinforcement of apartheid. . . . But the greatest danger from the politically correct bullies is that they create a backlash, and that backlash is often self-righteous support for the way things are. Whether we are weary or indignant, we wish the whiners would just go away. (17)

In light of my thesis that attacks on PC are attacks on multiculturalism, Rochman's denunciation of PC is contradictory and troubling indeed. Her book is a laudatory call for multicultural children's literature that is of the highest quality. I resonate to her belief that good books can break down barriers and "make a difference in dispelling prejudice and building community." I also agree that we need to resist those who insist that all books need do is provide "role models and literal recipes," that a book be deemed good simply because it is multicultural (19). Nevertheless, her presumption that there is an army of PC enforcers, like that of Jones (1993), is a distortion of current reality. Not only do Rochman and Jones fail to provide evidence to support their claim that PC "watchdogs," "bullies," and "whiners" are imposing a new censorship on children's book publishing, but they also fail to place the actions of those who have protested the historic exclusion and distortion of the culture and experiences of minorities and women—alluded to earlier by Sims Bishop (1993)—in a context that would help us understand it. While my guess is that there

157

is a new cautiousness on the part of many authors and editors when dealing with certain subjects and themes, I prefer to think that such caution is born of a new-found respect that the parties feel when writing about the experiences of historical oppressed and powerless groups. Finally, Rochman's charge that protests against the racism and sexism in children's literature are responsible for the reaction of those who resist change is among the more distressing instances of blaming the victim in recent memory. Like those who see the fabric of the universities threatened by those who advocate a more inclusive, multicultural curriculum, Rochman's attack on PC is a logical outgrowth of her lack of historical perspective and her failure to situate these controversies in the context of the ongoing "culture wars" (e.g., Gates 1992).

Basic to the case of those who attack PC on campus is the belief that prior to the recent present, universities were places where disinterested scholars, free of the taint of political and ideological interests, simply and without constraint pursued "immutable, transcendent truths" (Beyer, in press). By making oppressive demands that threaten academic freedom and the dispassionate quest for knowledge, advocates of PC are said to threaten the very fabric of the university itself. The parallel claim is that there are "politically correct" bullies seeking to impose an orthodoxy of children's literature and in so doing, limit the ability of authors to write about whatever they choose in whatever fashion they deem suitable.

I believe the historical record suggests a tale quite different from that told by conservative opponents of PC. Schrag (1993), for example, recently challenged the widely held conservative view that "American education is on the direct road to hell."

> When was the golden age from which we supposedly declined? Was it in the years before World War II, when Jews and blacks were not only systematically excluded from the better medical schools but subject to rigid quotas in most private undergraduate college admissions as well? Was it in the 1950's, when William F. Buckley Jr., the dean of all conservatives, was already complaining that Yale and other Ivy League colleges were hopelessly under the domination of liberal professors?. . . . Was it in the McCarthy years, when "politically correct"—had the phrase existed—would have had an entirely different meaning? Was it in the early years of this century, when . . . all minority groups, white as well as black, with the exceptions of English, Scots, Germans, and Scandinavians were negatively portrayed in American textbooks—when Jews, Italians, Chinese, and blacks were mean, criminal, immoral, drunken, sly, lazy, and stupid in varying degrees? (638)

Pointing out that universities historically were afflicted with the racism and bigotry found in the rest of society is not to deny that angry and dogmatic individuals and groups are to be found on many college campuses and that there have been incidents where such groups and individuals have shouted down others for making remarks deemed racist and sexist. A number of universities have developed speech codes that are designed to curb "hate speech." What often is left out in most reporting of these developments is their relation to the alarming rise of violence against minorities on college campuses and incidents like the "burn a fag in effigy" rally on one campus, and a fraternity slave auction where the services of dancing pledges in blackface were sold on another (Carton 1991, 44). Whether the curtailing of such outrageous activities (an abridgement of free speech?) will inhibit the intellectual growth of the students, which is believed to depend on free expression, is a matter worthy of discussion that goes deeper than the tendentious claim that students' right of expression is being limited by campus thought police (Perry and Williams 1991).

Despite these caveats, I personally am unaware of any universities being taken over by the "tenured radicals" conjured up by Kimball and others. This is so despite the fact that "the universities are the one place in America where liberal and left-wing thought has flourished," especially in History and Literature departments (Stansell 1991, 53). Nevertheless, the real power at most universities hardly lies in English or History departments but rather in the business schools and in the "hard" sciences that rarely are hotbeds of radical thought. Further, the insinuation by neoconservatives that egalitarian democratic demands actually are authoritarian, orthodox, and even communist influenced when they oppose racism, sexism, and homophobia can be seen as "a way of diverting the issues of bias within the university to issues of freedom of speech without acknowledging that the right to question professorial authority is also a free speech matter" (Kohl 1991, 34). In short, "the university described in the literature on political correctness is a fantasy, and the pseudo-debate has nothing to do with higher education" (Carey 1992, 64).

PC, Children's Literature, and the Selective Tradition

I cannot imagine anyone seriously arguing that authors of children's books, whether past or present, operate in a political and ideological vacuum and pursue their artistic vision without constraint or limitation. Like other cultural artifacts, children's literature is a product of convention that is rooted in, if not determined by, the dominant belief systems and ideologies of the times in which it is created. Literature for children always has had its conventions, boundaries, and taboos. Many were shattered with the advent of the "New Realism" in the sixties when previously taboo subjects and themes (family discord, violence, sexuality, drug abuse, and so on) began entering the world of children's literature. While the total elimination of boundaries and conventions in writing for young people surely is not desirable, one hopes there always will be writers and editors who challenge convention and extend the boundaries with sense and aesthetic sensitivity. In any event, it undoubtedly is the case that although boundaries and conventions change, they never are eliminated altogether.

A recent example of the breaking of a long-standing convention occurred during the Columbus Quincentennial. While the response of American children's book publishers to the Quincentennial, on the whole, was disappointing, it at least did bring us a handful of books that, for the first time, broke with convention and presented the often-told story of Columbus' voyage from the Native American point of view (Taxel 1993). For example, Dorris' *Morning Girl* (1992) provides a glimpse of the lives of Taino children that ends in the arrival of the Nina, the Pinta, and the Santa Maria. Yolen's *Encounter* (1992) is a fictionalized account of the arrival and initial interactions between Columbus and his crew and those whose lives ultimately were destroyed by the Spanish invasion. Meltzer's (1990) biography of Columbus is notable for its balanced attempt not only to give voice to the Native American viewpoint, but also to situate Columbus in the context of fifteenth-century Europe. On the other hand, despite a growing number of books written about the war in Vietnam that have focused on its horrifying reality, none to this date has departed from the convention that precludes discussion of the complex and controversial political issues that underlie that tragic conflict. Books like Emerson's *Echo Company Series* (1991a, 1991b), Graham's *Crossfire* (1972), and Myers' *Fallen Angels* (1988) exemplify books that focus on the dehumanizing brutality of the war while eschewing meaningful discussion of the politics of American involvement in it (Overstreet 1994).

It is widely understood that narratives about the past, whether history or fiction, often reveal as much about the era in which the books were written as they do about the period they re-create. The striking discrepancies between such fictionalized accounts of the antebellum south and slavery as Mitchell's *Gone With the Wind* (1936), Lester's collection of short stories entitled *Long Journey Home* (1972), and Haley's *Roots* (1976), for example, involve far more than the obvious, immediately discernible white-black differences in point of view and perspective. Similarly, the radically different perspectives on slavery in Yates' *Amos Fortune, Free Man* (1950), Hamilton's *Anthony Burns: The Defeat and Triumph of an Escaped Slave* (1988), and Lyons' *Letters from a Slave Girl: The Story of Harriet Jacobs* (1992) provide as much insight into the evolving societal attitudes toward African Americans as they do information and understanding of the tortured lives the authors seek to portray. In the time of its creation, Yates' Newbery-winning biography was read as a work with liberal, progressive sensibilities. More recent readings (for example, MacCann 1985; Trousdale 1990) deem it racist, a point that makes it clear that changing social values and attitudes influence the way readers read as well as the way writers write. A final illustration of how sociohistorical context shapes cultural creation is revealed by a comparison of the patriotic viewpoint of the classic Revolutionary War novel *Johnny Tremain* (Forbes 1943) and the antiwar perspective of novels such as *My Brother Sam Is Dead* (Collier and Collier 1976) and *The Fighting Ground* (Avi 1976). The differences in the way these novels explain the Revolution probably tell us as much about the attitudes of their respective authors toward World War II and the Vietnam War as they do the war that led to the founding of our nation (Taxel 1983).

My point is that it is impossible to understand the evolution and development of children's literature without situating the books of a given era in the sociocultural and political milieu of that period. Pressures and forces, both direct and indirect, subtle and not so subtle, influence the writing, publication, and review of books and are a part of the social landscape that includes the culture of publishing. Present-day concerns with the representation in literature of the historic victims of oppression simply are the latest manifestations of this phenomena. There is a direct and hardly surprising relation between the civil-rights and women's movements and the push to include more women and African Americans and other racial and ethnic minorities in children's books and to question the nature of their representation in existing books. "Interpretative wars" over these issues are at the heart of PC controversies and are illustrative of efforts of the historically marginalized and powerless to challenge the equation of history and literature with "the narratives of the people in charge" (Cockburn 1991, 691).

Values, beliefs, ideological structures, traditions, boundaries, forms of representation, visions and versions of the past and present of each era constitute a "selective tradition" (Taxel 1981, 1983) that both encompasses and extends beyond what we commonly refer to as the "canon." The concept of selective tradition reminds us that social power is represented in literature, art, film, in all of culture, and must be seen as a critical factor in the process by which certain groups maintain their power. Beyer (in press) describes the selective tradition as "sanctioning forms of knowledge, interpretations of events, and perspectives or world views that are tied to the interests of those with social, economic, and cultural power in the wider society." Therefore, the opposite of this proposition is the belief that "those who lack cultural power, or interpretations not in keeping with 'official' versions of events, tend to be excluded" from literature, curriculum, and other important forms of cultural representation.

This is not to suggest some grand conspiracy at thought control, the flip side of that conjured up by conservative opponents of PC. Rather, it is to point out that in all societies, there is a direct relation between the control of social, economic, and political power and the control of the society's dominant cultural institutions and forms of representation. Attacks on "politically correct" thought by long-time conservatives, one-time radicals and academics are best seen as a manifestation of the anger at and resistance to the growing influence of large numbers of women and minorities on college campuses and other centers of intellectual and cultural significance by those whose power and privileges have been challenged (Foner and Weiner 1991, 163).

Understanding the important relations between knowledge and power, between how specific social groups are represented or excluded from literature, in no way precludes recognition of the tremendous progress made over the past several decades in giving voice and recognition to artists and illustrators from, for example, the African American community. Citing the "unprecedented artistic and literary excellence" of the literature created in the 1980s and 1990s, Harris (1993) suggested the dawning of a "golden age in African American children's literature" (59). Despite this progress, Sims Bishop (1991) points out that of five thousand books published in 1990, only 1 percent were written by African Americans. Even when one considers nonblack authors writing about African Americans, the number does not increase appreciably. Sims Bishop concludes that "over the past few years, the total percentage of books published each year featuring African Americans has been hovering somewhere between one and two percent" (1991, 34). Unlike the books of previous decades, most current books about African Americans are written and illustrated by African Americans. There are, of course, exceptions, and she notes that most of the criticisms and controversies related to African American children's literature are focused on these exceptions.

> Controversies arise because the long, sad history of U. S. race relations, coupled with the tradition of negative images of Blacks presented in children's books, make African-American readers and other knowledgeable critics sensitive to even the most subtle manifestations of racism, negative attitudes and prejudice. (34)

We all can be thankful that the most abhorrent and loathsome of the caricatures and stereotypes (for example, Harris 1993) of the racist and sexist history of American children's literature are absent from most contemporary books. We also must acknowledge the decisive role played by the activism and protest of the women's and civil-rights movements in fostering the consciousness that led to the eclipse of these noxious representations. However, a number of newer, more subtle stereotypes and representations lacking in cultural authenticity still are to be found in books for young people as well as in films, on television, and throughout popular culture.

Isadora's *Ben's Trumpet* (1979), for example, was criticized because of its negative representations of an African American family. Moore (1985) stated that the family in this Caldecott Honor Book was "stratified and isolated from each other . . . and that there was no indication of human feeling, life or energy in the depictions" (185). The "lack of specifics in the text," according to Moore, invites the "smear of generalization" such as the existence of a " 'sickness' or inadequacy in the black family" and the belief that "a lack of material wealth equates with a lack of familial love, caring, and responsiveness" (186). Banfield and Wilson (1985) suggested that books like *Jake and Honeybunch Go to Heaven* (Zemach 1982) contribute "to the cultural repression of black people by appropriating and misrepresenting important cultural symbols." They charge that in her portrayal of heaven, Zemach "has not used one culturally authentic clue about heaven as understood by generations of Black people" and that "those symbols she has appropriated have been distorted" (198). Finally, Trousdale's (1990) analysis of *Sounder* (Armstrong 1969) and *Words by Heart* (Sebestyen 1979) reveals a "submission theology" that applauds behavior in black characters "that is docile, submissive towards whites, and accepting of justice and oppression." For the characters in these award-winning novels, growing up "involves acceptance of a submissive attitude along with an inferior position in society." Trousdale's article is especially useful because she contrasts the underlying "models of social action" in these books with those contained in *Roll of Thunder, Hear My Cry* (1976). In Taylor's Newbery-winning novel, a "submissive attitude is presented as a practical necessity when survival is at stake, but one which must be balanced by the need for identity, integrity, and self-respect" (Trousdale 1990, 137).

The present moment obviously is one of heightened sensitivity and pressure to move beyond stereotypes of this sort. There also is growing impatience with the slowness of some to take such criticism seriously and to recognize the less readily apparent, difficult to discern manifestations of racism, negative attitudes, and prejudice. The persistent willingness of critics to protest and lobby against these and other perceived forms of bias in children's literature surely was a factor provoking Rochman's and Jones' condescending allusions to PC "watchdogs" and "do-gooders."

None of this is to deny that there are academics, critics, writers, and editors who are extremely sensitive, at times angry, and occasionally didactic and dogmatic in their views of what literature for young people should be like. Some of their criticism can be simplistic, and at times it reflects limited understanding of the historical issues that underlie current controversies as well as their relation to the more strictly aesthetic considerations basic to good writing (Taxel 1986). Recognition of the existence of such excess, however, is a far cry from the alarmist rhetoric of Rochman or the dubious claim of author/illustrator Diane Stanley that American children's literature is in the grips of the "doctrine of political correctness." Stanley's comment, made during a symposium entitled "Is This Book Politically Correct?: Truth and Trends in Historical Fiction for Young People" held during the 1993 American Library Association Annual Convention, essentially argued that the current climate limits the ability of authors to tell the stories they choose to tell in the way they see fit. Walter Dean Myers, another panel member, offered a quite different interpretation of our current situation, one that parallels that offered in this chapter. Myers contended that the present moment is not one where the freedom of authors and illustrators is being restricted, but rather that writers now (finally) are being asked to show more care and respect when writing about the experiences of minorities and women.

In *Loose Canons: Notes on the Culture Wars* Henry Louis Gates (1992) suggested that no past exists without "cultural mediation" and that however worthy, the past "does not survive by its own intrinsic power." A crucial function of literary history, Gates concludes, is to disguise that mediation and "to conceal all connections between institutionalized interests and the literature we remember" (34). Given the complicity of children's literature, and the rest of society's cultural apparatus, in providing legitimacy for racial and gender-related injustice and oppression, why are we surprised that there are those who are sensitive, angry, and occasionally dogmatic. How could it be otherwise? Does anyone truly believe that the progress made in the past few decades would have been possible without the loud voices of those determined to unmask the disguised connections between institutional interests and literature? Does change in any deeply rooted institutional pattern or practice occur without the efforts and energies of those willing to offend? A central thesis of this article is that attacks on PC are essentially a backlash against multiculturalism and those who have argued and protested forcefully for long overdue changes in campus life, in children's literature, and throughout society. It is disturbing that otherwise thoughtful critics choose to focus on occasional excess rather than on the enormous contributions of those who, after all, simply are asking that their cultures and experiences be treated with sensitivity and accorded the respect they deserve.

If there is a real threat to the future health and vitality of children's literature, I doubt very seriously that it comes from those concerned with the accuracy and authenticity of representations of women and minorities. Rather, the threat lies in the crass commercialism, the hucksterism, the bottom-line mentality that is ubiquitous to our mass culture. This phenomena has its roots in the profound changes in the economy, including the publishing industry, that finds enormous multinational corporations gobbling up smaller companies so quickly that it is impossible to know from one moment to the next who owns what. These changes deserve far more attention than they have been given and have led to a transformation in the nature of publishing. While thankful for the growing number of marvelously innovative authors and illustrators who are encouraged by bold and innovative editors willing to take chances, I am deeply troubled by the remarkable amount of junk published that reflects the desire to play it safe, to appeal to a lowest common denominator, to capitalize on the latest fads, to publish sequels or copies of somebody else's best-seller, and so on that has become generic to television and films. The skyrocketing price of books also threatens to make purchase of the best of children's literature impossible for an increasingly large portion of the public. If unchecked, this trend will virtually assure the proliferation of the worst of the series and other mass-market books that take up all but a fraction of the space in mall bookstores and supermarkets. Again, the threat to children's literature today lies in these largely ignored developments, not from those who express consternation or outrage over the persistence of stereotypes or hackneyed clichés in writing about minority cultures.

What Does All of This Mean?

Despite what even the liberal media would have us believe, there is no conspiracy to impose politically correct thought on college campuses or to prescribe an orthodoxy on children's literature replete with guidelines and a new censorship. My guess is that the alleged proponents of PC wish they had even a fraction of the power ascribed to them by both their conservative and liberal critics. Viewed in historical context, current debates about PC and multiculturalism are best understood as part of a larger struggle over questions of how we understand our nation's past and present, as well as our possibilities for the future. Above all, it is about the insistence of peoples from many of the diverse cultures that comprise our multiracial, multicultural nation to have their history and culture treated with respect, dignity, and sensitivity.

These hardly seem to be unreasonable requests, and the dividends to be derived from taking them seriously already have begun to accrue. Are we not better off because the protests that commenced during the buildup to the Columbus Quincentennial derailed many of the insensitive, even mindless, celebrations that were being planned? Is there any doubt that the Quincentennial resulted in some desperately needed reflection, discussion, and research and writing on a subject that for centuries had been shrouded in arrogance, ignorance, and an almost willful historical amnesia?

Does anyone seriously dispute the contention that protest played an important role in the demise of the virtually all-white world of children's books and helped pave the way for the likes of Mildred Taylor, Gary Soto, Virginia Hamilton, Walter Dean Myers, Patricia McKissack, Floyd Cooper, James Ransome, John Steptoe, Pat Cummings, Faith Ringgold, Lucille Clifton, Donald Crews, Jerry and Brian Pinkney, to name only a few?

Debates about PC and multiculturalism in children's literature, to a significant degree, are debates about social responsibility. This is a complex issue in and of itself that has been discussed previously by, for example, Little (1990), Meltzer (1989), and Taxel (1990). While we must continue to insist that books for young people be literature and not propaganda, I find it impossible to imagine anyone arguing that those who write for young people do not have a special responsibility. In light of our painful national history, I believe this responsibility is especially acute when writing about groups that have been denied access to the full promise of the American dream.

Social responsibility cannot be legislated and, like Hazel Rochman, I abhor the idea of any attempt to prescribe what writers should write or illustrators should illustrate. In an article entitled "Cultural Politics From A Writer's Point," Katherine Paterson (1994), one of our very finest, and socially responsible, writers eloquently expresses her views on the dangers of simplistic and mechanical application of notions of what is "right and proper" representation of particular individuals or groups. Paterson, along with Mildred Taylor, Jane Yolen, Gary Soto, Virginia Hamilton, Walter Dean Myers, and others have demonstrated consistently that there need be no conflict between aesthetic excellence and more honest, inclusive, and culturally authentic portrayals of the diverse peoples that comprise our nation.

Raising issues of this sort connotes an understanding that what children read in books is important and that authors need to be cautious in creating characters, developing plots, articulating themes, and so on that deal with subjects about which certain groups have every right to be sensitive. Clearly, there is a precariously thin line between this position and the need for authors to have the kind of freedom to create what Katherine Paterson (1994) pleads for. Straddling this line is not now and never will be easy, and I'd prefer to err on the side of giving authors more freedom, rather than less.

My confidence in this position is born of my experiences and those of countless others who share books with young people on a regular basis. West, Weaver, and Rowland (1992), for example, concluded their account of sharing several controversial books about Columbus with children with a plea that reading should "be regarded as exploration, a voyage of discovery, as invitation, rather than as a tool of didacticism or moralizing" (262). I share their conviction that it is possible, even essential, to read and discuss stories that "challenge our expectations, that force us to confront new ideas and to grapple with long held beliefs." Having older, more mature students wrestle with the complex issue raised by some of the controversial books mentioned earlier is an extremely effective way to begin addressing some of the difficult issues raised in this article. Comparative reading of Sebestyen's *Words by Heart* and Taylor's *Roll of Thunder, Hear My Cry*, for example, leads to discussion not only of the many striking similarities and differences between these books, but also of a host of important literary and political issues as well. Experiences of this sort illustrate that response to literature is never easy to predict. Encounters with literature such as those described by West, Weaver, and Rowland demonstrate that young children are strong, resilient, and that with the guidance of caring and skillful teachers, are capable of handling complex and controversial issues when presented in a developmentally appropriate fashion.

I am convinced that through gross overstatements of fact and outright distortion, the focus of debates about PC have been deftly turned into attacks on multiculturalism and on the important progress made by the women's and civil-rights movements of the last several decades. The responsibility of those who work with children and with literature is to urge publishers to build on the encouraging progress made in recent years in creating a literature that accurately and honestly reflects the rich cultural mosaic that is the United States, as well as the very highest literary and artistic standards. As teachers, we need to create conditions in our classrooms that encourage students to read, discuss, and write freely about these books. Finally, we need to be steadfast in our resistance against conservative critics who claim to be advocates of a free and open society, when their real objective is to roll back the progress made in the long and painful struggle for justice and equality.

Professional References

ALLIS, SAM, JORDON BONFANTE, and CATHY BOOTH. 1991. "Whose America?" *Time*, 8 July, (1): 12–17.

BANFIELD, BERYL, and GLORIA WILSON. 1985. "The Black Experience Through White Eyes—The Same Old Story Once Again." In *The Black American in Books for Children: Readings in Racism*, 2d ed., edited by Donnarae MacCann and Gloria Woodard. Metuchen, NJ: Scarecrow Press.

BERMAN, PAUL. 1992. "Introduction: The Debate and Its Origins." In *Debating P. C.: The Controversy of Political Correctness on College Campuses*, edited by Paul Berman. New York: Laurel.

BEYER, LANDON. In press. "The Curriculum, Social Context, and 'Political Correctness.' " *Journal of General Education.*

CAREY, JAMES. 1992. "Political Correctness and Cultural Studies." *Journal of Communication* 42(2): 56–72.

CARTON, EVAN. 1991. "The Self Besieged: American Identity on Campus and in the Gulf." *Tikkun* 6(4): 40–47.

COCKBURN, ALEXANDER. 1991. "Bush & P. C.—A Conspiracy So Immense." *The Nation* 252(20): 680, 690–91, 704.

D'SOUZA, DINESH. 1991. *Illiberal Education: The Politics of Race and Sex on Campus.* New York: The Free Press.

FALUDI, SUSAN. 1991. *Backlash: The Undeclared War Against Women.* New York: Crown.

FONER, ERIC, and JON WEINER. 1991. "Fighting for the West." *The Nation* 253(4): 163–66.

GATES, HENRY LOUIS. 1992. *Loose Canons: Notes on the Culture Wars.* New York: Oxford University Press.

HALEY, ALEX. 1976. *Roots.* New York: Doubleday.

HARRIS, VIOLET. 1993. Contemporary Griots: African American Writers of Children's Literature. In *Teaching Multicultural Literature in Grades K-8*, edited by Violet Harris. Norwood, MA: Christopher-Gordon Publishers.

HURST, LYNDA. 1993. "Censorship for the Kindergarten Set." *World Press Review* 40(6): 46–47.

JONES, MALCOLM. 1993. "Kid Lit's Growing Pain." *Newsweek* 122: 54–57.

KIMBALL, ROGER. 1990. *Tenured Radicals.* New York: Harper & Row.

KOHL, HERBERT. 1991. "The Politically Correct Bypass: Multiculturalism in the Public Schools." *Social Policy* 21(1): 33–40.

LINDREN, MERRI, ed. 1991. *The Multicultural Mirror: Cultural Substance in Literature for Children and Young Adults.* Fort Atkinson, WI: Highsmith Press.

LITTLE, JEAN. 1990. "A Writer's Social Responsibility." *The New Advocate* 3(2): 79–88.

MACCANN, DONNARAE. 1985. "Racism in Award-Winning Biographical Works." In *The Black American in Books for Children: Readings in Racism*, 2d ed., edited by Donnarae MacCann and Gloria Woodard. Metuchen, NJ: Scarecrow Press.

MELTZER, MILTON. 1989. "The Social Responsibility of the Writer." *The New Advocate* 2(3): 155–7.

MINSKY, LEONARD. 1992. "The Politics of Political Correctness." *Education Digest* 58(2): 31–33.

MITCHELL, MARGARET. 1936. *Gone with the Wind.* New York: Macmillan.

MOORE, OPAL. 1985. "Picture Books: The Un-text." In *The Black American in Books for Children: Readings in Racism*, 2d ed., edited by Donnarae MacCann and Gloria Woodard. Metuchen, NJ: Scarecrow Press.

OVERSTREET, DEBORAH. 1994. *Winning Children's Hearts and Minds: The Vietnam Experience in Adolescent Fiction.* Department of Language Education, University of Georgia.

OZERSKY, JOSH. 1991. "The Enlightenment Theology of Political Correctness." *Tikkun* 6(4): 35–39.

PATERSON, KATHERINE. 1994. "Cultural Politics from a Writer's Point of View." *The New Advocate* 7(2): 85–91.

PERRY, RICHARD, and PATRICIA WILLIAMS. 1991. "Freedom of Hate Speech." *Tikkun* 6(4): 55–57.

ROCHMAN, HAZEL. 1993. *Against Borders: Promoting Books for a Multicultural World.* Chicago: American Library Association.

SCHRAG, PETER. 1993. "Class Warfare: A Review of *Inside American Education: The Decline, the Deception, the Dogmas* by Thomas Sowell." *The Nation* 256(18): 638–9.

SCOTT, JOAN. 1992. "The Campaign against Political Correctness: What's Really at Stake." *Radical History Review* 54: 59–79.

SIMS, RUDINE. 1980. "Words by Heart: A Black Perspective." *Interracial Books For Children Bulletin* 11(7): 12–15, 17.

———. 1984. "A Question of Perspective." *The Advocate* 3(3): 145–155.

SIMS BISHOP, RUDINE. 1991. "Evaluating Books by and About African Americans." In *The Multicultural Mirror: Cultural Substance in Literature for Children and Young Adults*, edited by Merri Lindren. Fort Atkinson, WI: Highsmith Press.

———. 1993. "Multicultural Literature for Children: Making Informed Choices." In *Teaching Multicultural Literature in Grades K-8*, edited by Violet Harris. Norwood, MA: Christopher-Gordon Publishers.

STANSELL, CHRISTINE. 1991. "Liberated Loutishness." *Tikkun* 6(4): 52–54.

TAXEL, JOEL. 1981. "The Outsiders of the American Revolution: The Selective Tradition in Children's Fiction." *Interchange* 12(2–3): 206–28.

———. 1983. "The American Revolution in Children's Fiction." *Research in the Teaching of English* 17(1): 61–83.

———. 1986. "The Black Experience in Children's Fiction: Controversies Surrounding Award Winning Books." *Curriculum Inquiry* 16(3): 245–81.

———. 1990. "Notes from the Editor." *The New Advocate* 3(2): vii–xii.

———. 1991. "*Roll of Thunder, Hear My Cry*: Reflections on the Aesthetics and Politics of Children's Literature." In *Reflections from the Heart of Educational Inquiry: Understanding Curriculum and Teaching through the Arts*, edited by William Schubert and George Willis. Albany, NY: SUNY Press.

———. 1993. "The Politics of Children's Literature: Reflections on Multiculturalism and Christopher Columbus." In *Teaching Multicultural Literature in Grades K-8*, edited by Violet Harris. Norwood, MA: Christopher-Gordon Publishers.

TROUSDALE, ANN. 1990. "A Submission Theology for Black Americans: Religion and Social Action in Prize-winning Books about the Black Experience in America." *Research in the Teaching of English* 24(2): 117–40.

WEST, JANE, DERA WEAVER, and RUTH ROWLAND. 1992. "Expectations and Evocations: Encountering Columbus through Literature." *The New Advocate* 5(4): 247–63.

WEXLER, PHILIP. 1982. "Structure, Text, and Subject: A Critical Sociology of School Knowledge." In *Cultural and Economic Reproduction in Education: Essays on Class, Ideology and the State*, edited by Michael Apple. London: Routledge and Kegan Paul.

WILL, GEORGE. 1993. "'Compassion' on campus." *Newsweek* 121(22): 66.

Children's Literature

ARMSTRONG, WILLIAM. 1969. *Sounder*. New York: Harper & Row.

AVI. 1976. *The Fighting Ground.* New York: Harper & Row.

COLLIER, CHRISTOPHER, and JAMES COLLIER. 1976. *My Brother Sam Is Dead.* New York: Scholastic.

DORRIS, MICHAEL. 1993. *Morning Girl.* New York: Hyperion.

EMERSON, ZACK. 1991a. *Echo Company #1: Welcome to Vietnam.* New York: Scholastic.

EMERSON, ZACK. 1991b. *Echo Company #1: Hill 568.* New York: Scholastic.

FORBES, ESTHER. 1943. *Johnny Tremain.* Boston: Houghton Mifflin.

FOX, PAULA. 1973. *The Slave Dancer.* New York: Dell Publishers.

GRAHAM, GAIL. 1972. *Crossfire.* New York: Pantheon.

HAMILTON, VIRGINIA. 1988. *Anthony Burns: The Defeat and Triumph of an Escaped Slave.* New York: Alfred A. Knopf.

ISADORA, RACHEL. 1979. *Ben's Trumpet.* New York: Greenwillow.

LESTER, JULIUS. 1972. *Long Journey Home.* New York: Scholastic.

LYONS, MARY. 1992. *Letters From a Slave Girl: The Story of Harriet Jacobs.* New York: Scribners.

MELTZER, MILTON. 1990. *Columbus and the World Around Him.* New York: Franklin Watts.

MYERS, WALTER DEAN. 1988. *Fallen Angels.* New York: Scholastic.

SEBESTYEN, OUIDA. 1979. *Words by Heart.* New York: Bantam.

TAYLOR, MILDRED. 1976. *Roll of Thunder, Hear My Cry.* New York: Bantam.

TAYLOR, THEODORE. 1969. *The Cay.* New York: Doubleday.

YATES, ELIZABETH. 1950. *Amos Fortune, Free Man.* New York: E. P. Dutton.

YOLEN, JANE. 1992. *Encounter.* San Diego: Harcourt, Brace, Jovanovich.

ZEMACH, MARGOT. 1982. *Jake and Honeybunch Go to Heaven.* New York: Farrar Straus & Giroux.

PART FOUR

Heroes for Children: Battling Good and Evil

Children's authors like Tamora Pierce, Grace Chetwin, Donna Jo Napoli, Sherryl Jordan, and Monica Furlong have tackled themes of freedom and oppression by creating heroes who battle social injustice; frequently these heroes are isolated females who can't seem to find their proper places in society. These authors pursue the infrequently asked questions: How do children who are different survive on a day-to-day basis? What is society's response to poor children? Orphaned children? Minority children? What is the promise of society for them? How does a woman who wants more than staying at home with babies and dirty dishes survive in a man's world? Are there other options? How does an oldest child cope with not inheriting the kingdom based simply on her gender? Are there broad inequities in society based on gender? Do some societies attempt to achieve gender balance and equity while others blatantly strip women of legal rights?

In this section Grace Chetwin and I open up the dialogue by exploring these questions in depth and at times with passion. Chetwin writes about ethical heroes who muddle through life, face daily obstacles, and struggle to belong. Her characters are often outcasts, children who, by virtue of being different, are not a part of the fabric of the village. Sometimes they are children with special gifts, who stand out from other children. These children are reprimanded, hidden, contained, punished, ignored, and even thrown out.

Sherryl Jordan, an author from New Zealand, explores similar themes in her book *Winter of Fire*. Jordan's main character, like many in Chetwin's books, cannot accept the role given her based on race and gender. Elsha is like a chrysalis who must eventually emerge. In Jordan's world there are racial structures coupled with gender structures that limit freedom and institutionalize oppression. In books like these the peers and the adults surrounding the heroes do not know how to cope with difference and cannot conceive of changing institutions that oppress. They may not experience contentment or satisfaction within their limited societal roles; nonetheless, they are unable to envision or support change. Like Jordan, Chetwin explores the nature of the hero in her books, while showing the reader how her own rich literary background prepared her for creating questing and questioning heroes for children.

Grace Chetwin grew up in England, under the shadow of Sherwood Forest. Legend flows in her blood. Her rich evocation of what a hero is suggests that children desperately need solid heroes with whom to identify. Her heroes live in fantasy books, but Chetwin shows how heroes are fantasies in every genre. Grace Chetwin is alive with the mythology of the ages in both realistic fiction and fantasy as well. She reminds us that heroes are all mythic and that her Gom Gobblechuck is as real—or not—as any hero of realistic fiction. Her presentation of the hero's potential is boundless, and she does so with verve through an analysis of her own works. Her heroes are touchable, and her themes matter. Through a blend of looking back at her own childhood heroes and at the "ninth-grade nobodies" she taught in New Zealand, Chetwin offers a poignant and literary look at the concept of hero and of children's potential.

Following on the heels of Chetwin's definition of hero, my chapter became a personal and uncomfortable odyssey. It began as an overview of fantasy and ended as a view of the female hero in children's literature. I've read hundreds of children's fantasy books in preparation for writing this chapter. The links between Ernst's struggles to explore the lines of gender in books for children resound in this chapter with pain and a bit of paranoia as I explore the past century of the female in fantasy. Taking another look at the classics—favorites written by Lewis, L'Engle, Alexander, McKinley, Bond, McCaffrey, and Cooper—the conclusions are startling. Women have not fared well in fantasy for children. The books we cherish have girls taking back seats, being kidnapped, fainting at the whiff of danger, watching and worrying as boys take charge. What we hold as dear and noble is open for new interpretation. Having just reread a personal favorite, Nancy Bond's A String in the Harp, it is difficult to realize that there is an alarming pattern of active males juxtaposed beside reserved females who worry while they fix tea and learn to cook, or miss out on the adventures because they are told to stay at home. In contrast, Menolly in McCaffrey's Harper Hall Trilogy is a risk taker and a talented musician, yet she is beaten by her father and purposely maimed by her mother when she tries to break the pattern for women. The price women pay seems to be extraordinary.

The message is that it is still a man's world. The successful quests of women are often merely battles to succeed as men or in male domains. Women as victims proliferate. In the last section of my chapter, rather than mentioning many books superficially, I have analyzed several strong new voices in fantasy for children. These authors have new perspectives and have presented fresh themes for children to ponder—diverse voices that interpret the female experience for children. Chetwin writes, "Fantasy should reflect our past, scrutinize our present, and help us shape our future." A troubling premise is that fantasy mirrors real life. There exist more troubling similarities between realistically written contemporary books like Shabanu by Suzanne Fisher Staples or *The Clay Marble* by Minfong Ho and Tamora Pierce's fantasy *The Woman Who Rides Like a Man* than dissimilarities. Staples' and Ho's females resemble real-world women who are struggling to find a voice and a place in the world, one in Pakistan, the other in Cambodia; their quests are not fantasies, yet their perilous positions in the world are very similar to the women that Pierce writes about in fantasy. Fantasy tackles social issues of oppression and injustice on the offensive.

Imaginary heroes abound in children's literature. Children identify strongly with these mythic boys and girls, who come from real worlds, who dream in epic proportions, and who manage to save the day. In the third chapter Brian Jacques is the hero of his own essay. This remarkable and successful author grew up poor in Liverpool. He is not unlike the gifted children of which Grace Chetwin writes about in *Child of the Air*. Jacques dropped out of school at the age of fifteen and joined the Merchant Marine. In his own words he is a self-educated man who has held many many jobs. He had a gift for writing early on, but did not live in an environment in which that gift was a plus. Getting his voice included in this book meant getting past a critic reading my book proposal who found his chapter potentially exploitative because his books are popular with children and filled with violence. I built a case for including Jacques' voice based on the quality of his writing, the fact that deleting his chapter would be a form of censorship, and that I was the ardent fan who first invited him to the United States in 1988 to speak at NCTE in Baltimore.

In Part 5 of this book two teachers talk about sharing *Redwall* with fourth graders. These teachers offer some of the children's responses to the violence in Jacques' books. Their interactions with Jacques' heroes and each other indicate that the children identify strongly with Matthias and the cause of Redwall Abbey. They neither embrace evil nor flinch when it is crushed, yet they clearly enjoy the quest, the battle, and the final clash. They know they are in a fantasy world, and they wish to see evil crushed. Don't we all. These children know that there are no safe enclaves. Jacques reflects that sentiment with his depiction of Mossflower Wood and images from his own life. His strong sense of good and evil pervades his forests. He's known all of the characters in his books. His evil is straightforward. He doesn't believe in situational ethics, yet one can't help but notice that Cluny the Scourge is an evil character with many layers. Readers want him to fail, but Jacques' depiction is so full of vitality that one understands Cluny's dementia and has sympathy for his evil paranoia, even as one wants to see him destroyed. Jacques' view of good and evil is less simple than he would have us believe. For the first time he offers a candid view of his own roots and inadvertent struggles to become an author.

In the final chapter Susan Hepler offers an essay on a trend in children's literature that continues in contemporary fiction, folklore, and fantasy. Dragons as heroes and villains permeate books written for children. One finds Bruce Coville's *Jeremy Thatcher, Dragon Hatcher*, a good romp and read, side by side with Patricia Wrede's series of four dragon books, all with a spunky female who cooks, cleans, and catalogues

173

for the dragon queen. The recent immigration of Asian Americans has perhaps given rise to more folktales on the theme of dragons. As Hepler shows, Eastern dragons differ vastly from Western dragons. Dragons are everywhere. What are their roots? Why do they continue to appear in so many books for children? What makes them good or evil? Are they heroes or villains? As the title of this book suggests we continue to battle dragons.

THIRTEEN

Creating Ethical Heroes
Who Know How to Win:
Or Muddling Through

GRACE CHETWIN

Out of the Primal Pot

I am composing this essay as a (relatively) new fantasy *author*. I emphasize the last word because although, like Malvolio, this office was thrust upon me and only recently at that, I was born a storyteller. I cannot recall how it came about, but as far back as elementary school, the teachers would dispatch me to troubled classes in some crisis to spin a story on the spot and keep the peace. Since then, I have continued to share my tales with my nearest and dearest, until now, when through the written word their messages go around the world in many different tongues. And it is gratifying to learn from correspondence that for all the differences among those people and their customs, they and my heroes and heroines in their fantasy worlds have common coign.

Why this common coign? How is it possible that so many different cultures can find echo in people from worlds that do not physically exist? And how and why do I create these alien people and their fantasy settings? How do they *know how to win?* And what makes them *ethical?* I'll answer these questions throughout this chapter.

All heroes and heroines help express something about this planet that the author needs to say. They also reflect the author's view of the world and the human's place within it. But even if these protagonists pop up overnight in the author's imagination (as they do many times in mine), they have not formed instantaneously, but have arisen after long gestation from a sort of elemental soup in the author's primal pot. This primal pot, this crucible of the psyche and its contents, is what determines the kind of heroes the author will create, and the sort of stories that he or she will spin. The pot's contents are the sum of the learning and life experience of the author to date; as this data is absorbed, it moils around, blends and realigns into a psychic gestalt. Such is the stuff within the primal pot. What makes this stuff? What determines this gestalt's constituency? The answer is the pot, the crucible itself—and this is the most important factor of all. For the pot's shape and nature, representing the author's temperament and viewpoint, this idiosyncratic perspective, is what generates and shapes a work, whether it's a philosophical treatise or a manual on gardening.

Thomas Hardy, a poet of skill and sensitivity, wrote novels of unmitigated pessimism. Witnessing the downfall of his people was to me a feat of endurance, an act of self-inflicted emotional torture. An eternal optimist, I believe in individual redemption; in my books the hero must always win. This does not necessarily entail a Pollyanna ending. In *The Atheling* (Chetwin 1987), the hero dies horribly at the hands of his own brother—yet in dying, he ultimately wins. For what has rendered Torc vulnerable to fratricide is his own self-conquest: a brute creature spawned of Hobbes, he dies as Rousseau's noble savage.

Together with the most frequent questions from readers—"Where do you get your ideas?" and "Where did Gom [or some other character] come from?"—I'm also asked "How long did it take to write such-and-such a book?" To that I answer that in one sense it took me two weeks, two months, two years, or whatever. But in another sense, it took a lifetime.

When I was eight I remember lying on my grandmother's hearth rug reading books I found around her house or ours: *The Pickwick Papers*, *The Old Curiosity Shop*, *The Pilgrim's Progress*, *Vanity Fair*, *Just So Stories*, to name a few that I recall distinctly. Besides assorted novels, I found poets, both English and American (I could recite them all by heart—Christina Rossetti's *Goblin Market*, Browning's *Pied Piper of Hamelin*, Noyes' *The Highwayman*, Whittier's *Barbara Frietchie* . . .). At the same time, and this is important, I came across the folk element: *Brer Rabbit* and the fairy-tale collections of Grimm, Andersen, and Lang. Into this brew went *Wind in the Willows* and *Doctor Dolittle*, *Rupert Bear* of the daily comic strips, *Toytown* of the radio; and, on Saturday afternoons, regular infusions of Roy Rogers, Laurel and Hardy, Abbott and Costello, Flash Gordon, and Tarzan. Great food for the imagination, all of it, and what better place than the children's matinees to learn how to prompt a laugh and how to keep a story taut?

No sooner did each ingredient hit the pot than it was drawn into the vortex to blend into the rest. To this in high school was added Chaucer, Shakespeare, Milton, Hardy, Tennyson, Wordsworth, Shelley, Coleridge, Keats, and many other poets, old and new. Biweekly theater tickets to the Nottingham Rep, and in went dramatists: Eliot, Barrie, Shaw, Goldsmith, Sheridan, Synge, Wilde, Tennessee Williams.

In college, I meant to study mainly English and French—until I signed up for Philosophy I. It was love at first sight. To an eighteen-year-old raised in a monolithic British society, the array of metaphysical systems devised by these great human minds proved irresistible: Socrates, Aristotle, Leibnitz, Kant, Spinoza, Locke, Berkeley, Hume, and others, each touting his own metaphysical house of cards, every house poised precariously on a different base.

A study of ethics taught how, within a global sense of right and wrong, there was marked variation. To some minds, *right* was a fixed ideal, to others, it had a sliding scale, while to still others it was a matter of convenience. An action considered morally correct in one culture might be condemned in another, or even in that same culture over the passage of time.

I emerged from all this a scoffing freethinker, for one brief period, knowing it all. But within the primal pot lay the embryos of future heroes and heroines, their origins safe in the genetic pool. I didn't dream it then, of course. But no matter— time and experience would bring them to term.

Fantasy: Philosophy in Peter Pan Costume

In its highest form, fantasy is pure metaphor, its purpose metaphysical. Like a poem, a work of fantasy may be interpreted on many levels. It is absolutely not escapist fiction but an exposition of deep and timeless truths about the human heart and soul. In fantasy, it is dangerous to take things at face value: beneath the plot, story, adventure, quest, concrete visible objects, or names of people and places (in allegory, for instance) are symbols that treat with matters internal and quite abstract. If it be true to its roots, a fantasy tale must always have a moral—yet in the telling, should entertain primarily and *never* preach. At its worst, when it is created to manipulate the masses, it is merely propaganda: at its most sublime it is as enlightening as an ethical or metaphysical tract, and as uplifting as any great poem.

Fantasy should reflect our past, scrutinize our present, and help us shape our future: of our private thought, of our national ethos, and of our cosmic view. The singers, bards, wise ones—the keepers of the flame—have known this since the earliest days when *society* comprised a single tribe or clan, bound together by blood ties or the communal need to survive. Their songs, their tales maintained the unit, reinforcing the blood ties, keeping tally of the people. Songs of the seas and winds and moon and stars made sense of the natural forces around them, while epic sagas of those who died hunting or in battle kept their memories alive and established a shared concept of ideal conduct—in other words, a tribal moral code or ethos.

Sad to say, I have discovered during extensive visits to libraries, schools, and colleges as a fantasy author, this root function of fantasy is largely overlooked, or even actually forgotten. The old, traditional folk and fairy tales, the ancient Greek legends, are considered as quaint stories of the past, their true import ignored. Answers to a questionnaire I deliver at the start of a talk reveal that in modern Western culture they are viewed largely as juvenile entertainment.[1] Much of what is created in the name of fantasy today is a debased form; a story's bizarreness is for novelty's sake, and its incidental trappings have no functional value. In true fantasy, this could not be further from the case. These devices, these marvels and wonders serve as tools for the writer's great "What if. . . ."

In Plato's *Republic* Socrates tells of a Lydian shepherd, Gyges, who finds a ring that renders its wearer invisible. By means of the ring, Gyges kills his king and marries the widowed queen, thus becoming topmost person in his country. Intriguing as the ring is, its magic is incidental to the tale. For it is really a teaching tool; by its means, a moral question is examined—Is virtue an intrinsic quality regardless of appearance, or is it the result of social pressure? In other words, if no one were looking, would we continue to steer straight? A perennial and important ethical question, it continues to be argued—and by writers of fantasy—in a similar way.

When Wilde created Dorian Gray's picture, the aim was not to beguile the reader with yet another magical device. The portrait serves much the same purpose as Gyges' ring: it enables its owner to commit depraved acts without fear of detection. When Gray discovers that he can live a life of debauchery without its telltale ravages marking his face, he takes license to perform deeds of ever greater wickedness.

Arresting fantasy stories, both of them, featuring intriguing devices. But, again, both these devices, the ring and the portrait, and others like them, are created solely as tools to make a moral point. Today these kinds of trappings are featured in stories—especially in the medium of film—as ends in themselves; as light diversion in escapist fiction; junk food for the mind requiring little, if any, mastication.

People ask me often what is the main difference between fantasy and *realistic* fiction.[2] I used to answer that realistic fiction deals with topics local to its time and setting, whereas fantasy deals with timeless metaphysical themes: that realistic fiction is literal and direct whereas fantasy is wholly metaphor. But this does good fiction a great disservice. Good literature of all kinds examines our past, our present, and our prospects for the future. It all sings songs of the people that will help weave us into a single nation, even a world community, enabling us to find a common identity without surrendering those differences that nourish and enrich a rapidly evolving human race. The characters of all worthy literature transcend barriers of time and place, and there is use of metaphor, often extended throughout the length of the work.

What does distinguish the two different forms then?

Whereas in realistic fiction, the writer by definition confines his or her working palette to the realm of possibility, in fantasy, the writer is under no such restriction; none is expected or required. In reading or in listening to a work of fantasy, the reader suspends disbelief as a matter of course and anything is possible: whereas realistic fiction addresses the reader's conscious mind, fantasy cuts straight to the unconscious, using the language and symbols of our dreams—which we instantly recognize. In the crudest, most primitive of epic sagas full of he-man violence and monsters to slay, the hero represents a highly simplistic symbol of our super-ego; the monster, our id. But in more complex works, symbols can express (as in allegory) abstractions such as single states of mind, or journeys and ordeals within the main plot. In the third book of my Ulm tetralogy, *The Crystal Stair* (1988), the hero Gom has to climb a series of narrow and transparent glass steps leading way up into the sky. There is no handrail, no room to turn around on that stair: once he begins his climb, he cannot turn back. And so he goes on up, terrified of the increasing height, and risk, expecting at every moment to slip or lose his balance and topple to the ground. In *The Riddle and the Rune* (1987), the second book in that same series, Gom is forced to dance at the crack of a whip for horsemen who, finding him lurking around their camp, have dragged him to their bonfire. I receive letters about Gom not only from children, but also from adults of all ages, including some very senior ones. One librarian wrote me about the difficult times she had recently endured—deaths in the family and an adolescent gone rampant—and expressed gratitude for Gom's steadying hand during this climb up her crystal stair. And another correspondent, having just gone through turmoil at work, shared with me how she also had danced to the whip and the fire.

Just as in dreams, the people of whom we dream are often really ourselves; fictitious characters serve as surrogates for the writer—well, mine do, as I have discovered. In *Collidescope* (Chetwin 1990), three characters from three vastly different times and places meet again and again by means of a crystal timestone, and by trading perspectives, change one another forever. Hahn, an android (or so he believes), is a sort of intergalactic Greenpeace scout come to slap a quarantine sticker on Earth: he's come to save the whales, and the whales are us. Sky-Fire-Trail is a Delaware Woodland Indian who lived on the island of Manhattan fifteen hundred years ago in a primitive settlement at the edge of a marsh, roughly where Broad and Wall Streets meet today. As the book begins, he is born and immediately the object of an augury: that a great calamity is coming upon his people and only he can save them. The third protagonist, a high school girl from Valley Stream, Long Island, has problems of her own. Her world has disintegrated: her parents are divorced and, despite her most fervent prayers, will remain so. More, her mother is just about to become involved with a brand-new man. In wishing to reunite her parents, Frankie seeks to control her personal life, to order it according to herself. She is also obsessed with the wider world and looking for secure parameters, between preserving our past and clearing a path for the future, for instance. She wants to join Greenpeace and save the whales, while at the same time wanting to join the NASA astronaut program. She wants to save the forests and yet admires a model of some stark future city comprising towers of steel and glass.

Those three channeled my angst over a number of issues arising when I wrote that book: increasing racial violence, in particular in my neighborhood of Long Island; the growing threats to those working to preserve the rain forests in Brazil; commerce without due thought of the threat to our environment; and the rampant destruction of our past through real-estate development. The pressure in these areas was building fast; each was a disaster waiting to happen. It was only a matter of time. Shortly after I had written a first draft of a scene wherein Sky-Fire-Trail was stoned by white youths for being in the wrong place at the wrong time, a young black straying into an unfamiliar neighborhood—Howard Beach—was chased onto a nearby motorway and killed. While I was writing the second draft, a similar incident occurred, this time in Bensonhurst. There were times during the writing of this book that I began to get an eerie feeling that maybe the tail was wagging the dog. But the fact was that, as I just said, these tragedies were building like thunderheads and many thoughtful persons must have seen that they were on the point of breaking. On another front, after I expressed my fear of a major environmental disaster through the heroine Frankie, there came the Alaskan oil spill. As I worked on, there came the big one in the Gulf of Mexico, then another off the Carolina coast. And as I wrote that first draft, the man working to save the Brazilian rain forest was under fire; as I finished the book, he was dead. These events I could not avert personally. But my characters could. Each helping the other two, this trio ran their individual courses and conquered. Hahn saved Earth—and in so doing, learned that he was no android but a cyborg and, as Frankie pointed out, more human than a lot of people she knew. In learning of his own humanity, Hahn came to know how to use discretion and make choices, disobeying a scout's directive of nonintervention to help change the course of Sky-Fire-Trail's history and so enable him to succeed in *his* quest. And Frankie at last succeeded in controlling *something*—and an important one, namely preventing the Indian clan's extinction. While it was Hahn who made the change of history possible, it was Frankie who found the clan a safe place to go.

This was not Frankie's only success. She began to grow on many levels, learning to share another's viewpoint, and in sharing, to compromise, even to cede a stance entirely. By the end of the book, she has matured considerably and is prepared for the new life her mother's lover will bring. Yet all through the adventure, while all three underwent some (often painful) trade-off in their attitudes, they never wavered from their purpose. Somehow, they made it, and I was as surprised as anyone, for during the story's unfolding I couldn't see for the life of me how they could possibly pull things off. But I have learned to trust that, gravitating toward their goal as driven by some inner essence, my heroes will find a way.

In Gom's earliest days, as, perched between my children's beds, I pulled out the filament of Gom's escapades from my head each night, I'd complain: "That's done it; how is Gom ever going to get out of this one?"

"You got him into it, you tell us," they'd say. But the truth was, I didn't have the ingenuity, then or now.

"You got yourself into this mess, Gom, it's up to you," I say in my turn. And so far he's always managed to extricate himself, usually by his bootstraps.

So much for the raw stuff from which the hero and heroine are created and the general medium in which they function. In what kind of arena will their drama unfold, between what parameters will they perform, what rules will govern the unfolding?

As the mention of *Collidescope* and the Gom series has already hinted, the answers depend once again on the need and disposition of the creator.

The Hero's Exploits: Did He Jump or Was He Pushed?

> The fault, dear Brutus, is not in our
>   stars,
> But in ourselves, that we are underlings.
>   *Shakespeare*, Julius Caesar

J. M. Barrie based an entire play (*Dear Brutus*) on this premise. As I sat in the Nottingham Playhouse, watching an assorted group of lost souls given the chance to relive their past and correct wrong choices, I found this powerful and moving stuff. The image of the painter conversing with his might-have-been daughter shook me to the core and left an impression on me that influences my thought and action to this day. The suggestion that we have discretion, some measure of responsibility, some choice in shaping our lives and that when things go awry we have no one to blame but ourselves is a strong claim, one difficult to deny.

Not for Hardy, however. According to him, Fate is "ingenious machinery contrived by the gods for reducing human possibilities of amelioration to a minimum" (*The Mayor of Casterbridge*).

Is the hero a free agent, or are his actions governed by external forces against which he has no recourse? Hardy would have the latter, and further, that those forces are not simply neutral dispensers of one's lot, but comprise a capricious, malicious *deus ex machina* permitting no salvation. This concept has a long pedigree. In the medieval song cycle *Carmina Burana*, Fate, in the *Wheel of Fortune* song (*O Fortuna*), is conceived as a willful female deity whose "*vain and empty*" cosmic wheel controls our destinies, raising us up only to cast us down at whim. Finally, we are urged to eat, drink, and be merry while we can, for in the end, however much we strive, *Fortune always crushes the brave*.

So here we have two opposing viewpoints on the nature of fate from fine, wise men. Which of them should we believe is right? Should we believe in free will? Or in fixed fate? This decision is an important one. Without choice, where is there room for morality? Does our hero have discretion—or is he merely a puppet on a cosmic string? The answer to all these questions is complex.

Assuming a belief in reincarnation, Hindu philosophy lists three main types of Fate (*Karma*). The first is *Pralabdh*, that portion of actions or karmas that are allotted to our present life. This kind is fixed: like Hardy's Fate, it allows no excuses, no time off for good behavior. The second type, *Kriyaman* karma, arises out of new actions or karmas generated in this present incarnation. Here there is the choice of whether or not to act. The third, the seed or *Sinchit* karma, comprises the hoard of actions and consequences (reactions) piled up from our past and carried over from life to life until they are cleared. The only choice here is of how we conduct ourselves while working off the backlog. This account provides a neat and useful way to make sense of one's actions—at least, it would if we could only figure which karma was which.

A simple, homely, and useful expression of the truth is found in the verse that Alcoholics Anonymous adopted as its official prayer:

> God grant me the serenity to accept things I cannot change,
> Courage to change the things I can,
> And wisdom to know the difference.

When my heroes set out upon their quests, that is the way it goes.

Knowing whence heroes and heroines come and the measure of their free will, what are they like? For all their individual differences, are there traits common to them all—and if so, why?

The Hero: Man or Mouse?

What is a proper hero? Beowulf, maybe, armed and shielded, going out against a monster who has ravaged a king's hall? That is the stock image of epic literature. But, you know, however noble and strong and brave these characters are, no one sheds a tear for them.[3] Closer to the human heart—mine, anyway—is the youngest son in folklore; or perhaps Andersen's devoted tin soldier, who immolates himself trying to save his love, the little ballerina. One hero for whom I wept as a small child wasn't even human but a dog, Beth Gelert from the old Welsh tale. In it, the dog saves his master's baby from a wolf attack while the man is out. The crib is overturned, there is blood everywhere. The man returns home and, thinking the dog has killed the baby, shoots him dead, only to find the child safe beneath the cradle. Who could not but identify with the injustice of it all? How many of us have not at one time or another been hastily tried and punished without a chance to protest our innocence?

The noble Beth Gelert notwithstanding, the human hero close to my heart is as flawed and vulnerable as the rest of us, someone with whom we can readily identify. And someone who has to earn his or her title.[4]

Antoine de Saint-Exupéry never knew what fear was, which was as well, the risks he took in the early days of aviation. Once, so goes one anecdote, after he had flown a small plane from Africa to France with an uncaged lion breathing down his neck, he was hailed as a fearless hero. He replied that he was nothing of the kind, since he had not been afraid. A true hero, according to him, was one who dared in the teeth of terror.

For me, my protagonist must be wholly human with all the foibles and weaknesses of Everyone, an individual who muddles through from crisis to crisis, holding on because there is no other way. This is someone for whom I can root, with whom I feel some affinity, not some lantern-jawed, well-muscled automaton running through a set routine that reads like a video game.

John Bunyan created my kind of hero in his allegory *The Pilgrim's Progress*.

Christian was a modest, pious man, who, fleeing his city's imminent destruction, was propelled on a quest through perilous places in order to reach his goal. Those places, those states of mind for which they are named,[5] have been experienced also by the readers who then can empathize with his sufferings and take heart from his conquests over them. Christian affected me, an eight-year-old, more powerfully than any he-man decapitating some malformed monster.

I didn't analyze in those days, I was too young, so I didn't register consciously the great difference between The Pilgrim's quest and that of the heroes in the old sagas. Christian's was not to slay something but to save his very soul: his weapons were not sword and lance but faith and hope. Where only Beowulf, of all the heroes in King Hrothgar's hall, dares dive into the mere and slay the monster Grendel, Bunyan allows all common folk a surrogate, to suffer for them what they do not wish to suffer, going where they do not wish to go. This is the stuff of the heroes who come to me in vision, demanding that I sing their song. I do not require them to have muscles, a crown, or blue blood.

With Archibald MacLeish, I believe there is a hero within every one of us. A single mother, a crippled sportsman, a retired worker growing old: the soldier need not be Lee or Napoleon, but

> The blinded gunner at the ford—the rest
> Dead: the rest fallen: none to see:
> None to say the deed was well done: no one:
> None to praise or to withhold praise: none
> Ever to know or guess or speak his name . . .
> The responsible man, death's hand on his shoulder,
> Knowing well the liars may prevail
> And calumny bring all his days to nothing . . .
> The responsible man: teeth bad: sleep
> Difficult: tired tired tired to the heart:
> Carries the day to the next day and the next:
> Does what must be done: dies in his chair
> Fagged out, worn down, sick
> With the weight of his own bones, the task finished,
> The war won, the victory assured,
> The glory left behind him for the others. . . .
> *Archibald MacLeish,* "The Hero"

We Can't All Be Winners—Can We?

> For he that naught n'assaieth, naught n'achieveth.
> *Chaucer,* Troilus and Criseyde

If we are to accept with MacLeish that there is a hero inside every one of us, regardless of our circumstances, how can we all "know how to win"?

It all depends what is meant by *win*.

Torc, in *The Atheling*, returning from the holy mountain of Rm, was crowned king and should have ruled his country long. But shortly after his coronation, his brother murdered him. To all the nobles of his culture, he died a failure, too soft to govern. And yet in truth, he died victorious, not by having subdued his unscrupulous brother but by having transcended his own savage upbringing. Like Christian's, his was an inner quest, even if he did not recognize it at the time.

This inner quest, to me, is what fantasy is about. In all my books, the quest and its goal are largely allegorical; whatever happens on the surface serves as an analog or metaphor for some inner struggle. And what is this struggle, in its simplest terms? For all the outward differences, the answer is the conquest of the self.

An Ethical Hero—What Is That?

By *ethical hero* I do not mean simply one who lives by his culture's moral code. There is no drama, no conflict in that, and so there is no story. An ethical hero to me is one who dares fly in the face of some outworn cultural shibboleth according to some inner and overriding sense of right.

Gom Gobblechuck, my earliest hero, whom I created for my two young daughters when they were still in diapers, is perhaps the strongest example of what I mean.

In his early years, Gom suffers every grievance known to a growing child. Despite the devotion of a gentle, loving father, Gom encounters harsh judgment, intolerance, and unkindness from those who do not recognize his singular gifts; he suffers and learns to avoid the brutality of an envious, resentful brother; and he endures the terrifying attentions of a con-man who almost murders Gom for gold. On top of all this, he bears the burden of learning that his mother ran off the very morning of his birth.

An incipient *ethical hero*, Gom is born with qualities that will one day render him a savior of his world—if he can learn how to use them effectively. From birth, Gom displays a strong sense of right and wrong, of fairness and of justice. From the time he can walk, he not only can converse with all manner of living things, even abstractions like Wind and Sessery, the drafts beneath Windy Mountain, but he also cannot abide to stand by and see a man cheated or a bully trick his peers. If he came across you being set upon by thieves and muggers, he'd leap to stand beside you in a minute regardless of the risk to his own small self. But these qualities that will one day transform him into the greatest wizard of his world only bring him so much grief and hostility until he learns how to use them *with discretion*. For instance, during a visit down into town, Gom, incensed by Gaffer Gudgeon's cruelty to Stig, exposes the Gaffer's hypocrisy over secret nightly nips. Using yet another singular gift of inner sight, Gom describes the old man in his nightshirt sipping plum brandy, thus publicly humiliating him, for this practice apparently is considered less than respectable in Clack. As Gom learns, such satisfaction at avenging his father only brings him enemies. If he is to become the king-maker of legend, he must first learn to conquer his hasty tongue and to temper his prodigious gifts with wisdom. This our ethical hero eventually learns after due suffering in the school of hard knocks. Only when a hero has conquered self can he or she effectively move on to larger quests elsewhere.

For Gom, this practice in the field is hard and long—luckily for him, or he might not have developed half so well. Those born with great talent and an agile wit, the so-called *child prodigies*, often vanish without trace after puberty. It's the Hare and the Tortoise syndrome. When things come easily in the early years, there is no need for the drudgery that builds discipline—the staff we fall back on in times of duress. Work is such a snap, it is hard for these quick, bright ones to realize life isn't so simple right across the board, and so, never having suffered the early pains of perseverance, of picking themselves up and starting over, they crumble when the real, grown-up world kicks in and things get tough. There is an analog for this common type of situation at the very beginning of *The Riddle and the Rune*—in fact, it is the book's premise. As Gom is setting out to find his mother, he is given a riddle to solve. Once he has the answer, so he is told, his mother will appear. At first, Gom thinks his travels are over. After all, he is so quick and clever, he should be able to sit down and simply solve the riddle on the spot. But his plan won't work, for this is not a mere play on words, but a *life* riddle: its terms must be experienced to be understood.

This is why Gom is given the riddle in the first place. Before his birth, Harga, his mother, at that point the greatest wizard in Ulm, knows that world will some day need someone not only having her great intellect and grasp of the magic arts, but also much more: one who will endure throughout generations without becoming blasé, or cynical, or corrupt; one who will never grow hungry for personal power, or so world-weary as to let the people's faces blur together. This is why she takes for mate the simple, steady, sensible woodman Stig: his kind and artless nature is a perfect complement to hers and will serve to balance the special child she needs to bear. (In the riddle, she is the Air, and Stig the Earth—a perfect way to put it.) When Gom sets out to find her, he is like today's child prodigy, and a true child of his quick and clever mother. That is not enough, for if he is to succeed Harga— supersede her, as she hopes—he needs to develop Stig's qualities, to be tried and tested until he grows into his father's strength. And so the life riddle to which there is no quick and easy mental answer. When Gom tries to solve the riddle and cannot, he has no alternative but to go on: to succeed and grow, or fail.

> From Air and Earth comes seed;
> By Fire and Water is tempered:
> In Wood is kernel's secret essence known,
> And purpose comes to light. (1986, 16)

Gom cannot possibly predict the ordeals through which that tempering will put him. A near-drowning under a deep, icy Sound; a deadly encounter with ruthless horsemen: a trial by fire, indeed. Only after he has undergone these and other difficult experiences will the meaning of the terms break upon him. Had he known how difficult his quest would be, would he have continued on across that first plain?

Things get worse the farther he goes, yet only once is he tempted to turn back from his quest. That temptation in itself is part of Harga's plan to prove him, I suspect. For while staying in the comfort of Hort and Mudge's farmhouse, he confronts head-on what he has only guiltily played with before: his deep-seated anger and resentment of his mother's abandonment. At last, it comes to boiling point and he rejects her. The rage is released, and at some point after that, the uneven, sporadic process of healing begins. Having come through that unhappy crisis, Gom is emotionally stronger and fitter to go on. And go on he does, the desire to find his mother overriding all other concerns, always, in the end. Like a lemming to the sea, or a bee to the honey, pulled, Gom is driven by his very essence to find the mother he has never known. And who cannot relate to that was never born of woman!

Did he know how to succeed? He certainly could not have sat down and given a written account of his plans, but, yes, he surely did on some inchoate level, and this innate sense, this deep instinct, is what got him through in the end. It's what gets us all through what we have to do in this lifetime on Earth, if only we'll stop rationalizing and admit it.

Since Gom, there have been other heroes and heroines, all faced with appalling odds, all propelled out to face them, and all succeeding, every one.

Child of the Air (1991) came to me during my early travels to schools and colleges. I would like to mention here that after graduation, I taught English and French in high schools in New Zealand and England. On account of my extreme youth and lack of seniority, I was given the classes no one else wanted to teach. Ah, my beloved rebel ninth-grade Nobodies! Quick of wit, indivisible by ten, they were the scourge of the school. Smart, streetwise, they could have been new Einsteins or Shakespeares (well, possibly) *if* one could only find the key to their interest and turn it: to make the *them* an *us.* I did. Teaching English made it easy. I took their term play text and, instead of merely reading it, had them audition, take roles, and perform before the school. The transformation in those children was amazing. From being rambunctious and troublemaking outsiders to the system, they became proud, card-carrying members. They carried off every class prize in their year—even for flower arrangement! I continued to use drama this way in subsequent years there, then back in England, every time with stunning success. To this day, the image of those changed children haunts me. Because for those whom I helped, there are thousands more whose latent talents are not even recognized. Instead, those qualities that are their greatest assets (any resemblance to Gom is absolutely not coincidental) are those for which they are punished. To me, these are the *gifted and talented* children, not those who get A's for neat, correct work; punctuality; and orderly behavior. Enough, this is not the subject of our discussion. I wanted you to know that I have had a great deal of experience with these clever and often troubled children; that I wept with them in the classroom after school as they poured out the details of their troubled lives, and I gave some of them rides to violent homes or to latchkey homes with absentee parents.

These children, then, became one of my preoccupations; my concern for them and their uncertain futures has never died. Going around the country giving talks in schools revived memories as I recognized those same children here and in this time. Grieving for them, as I did for Sky-Fire-Trail and his lost descendants, I promised them that I would sing their song. And so *Child of the Air* came about. Ostensibly, it is about children who are born with the gift to rise and ride the winds. Really, it is about the terrors of being gifted, gifted in ways not yet recognized by one's culture; gifted in ways that bring nothing but trouble. The dreamers, the ones whose ears are tuned to music of the spheres are different, and being different is a curse.

In order to point up their predicament, I first had to create a hostile environment, and so came up with Pyra, an egg-shaped world whose northern and southern hemispheres are separated by a thermal band punctuated with high, barren mesas that are swept at the height of summer by deadly firestorms. Creating a world and an ecosphere arising naturally out of it, for me, is a most enjoyable part of writing high fantasy. Everything must not only work, but, thanks to the influence of writers like Bunyan, it must also mean something. (Turned on its side, Pyra resembles the left and right hemispheres of the brain.) Severing those hemispheres, preventing any normal traffic between them, the mist-enshrouded mesas are thought to be totally devoid of life. But one of them is inhabited. Its people have developed into a rigid, myopic society with strict, authoritarian rules. There is no judgment implied in this: their ethos is determined by enforced isolation on a mesa whose barrenness affords only a meager subsistence. The thermal mists to them are *wyrth*, or spirit, and their dead are committed to the wyrth's keeping by sliding them with due rite and ceremony off the mesa's edge (the end of the world).

The two children in the book, a brother and sister, suddenly find that they can rise and ride the winds. When they are discovered doing this, they are brought before the magistrate, who sentences them to die by fire for presuming to do what only spirits should.

This gift of rising is an analog for having the power to transcend the narrow limits of society to take a broader view and to describe what lies beyond. These children of the mesa are our Earth visionaries: future educators, artists, scientists, and statesmen whose dreams—if recognized and nurtured—serve in time to enlighten, to connect, and to leaven us all. On Pyra, those who rise, *athlynder-skyrr*, have the most vital function in that world: these *messengers of the air* literally connect the two hemispheres, dispersing news and information, even physically transporting people from one to the other across the mesa belt.

When first the children secretly rise, Brevan expresses misgivings. Humans are not meant to rise, only wyrth. We might be ill, or even cursed, he says. Not so, his sister, Mylanfyndra, answers. "Rising's not bad. It's wonderful, and quite special" (103). But Brevan, cautious, skeptical, is not convinced. Still, Mylanfyndra, the positive, confident one, holds out, suggesting that their gift might even have been bestowed upon them by the wyrth. When they stand before the magistrate, and Brevan, cowed, capitulates, she states defiantly "We are not evil! . . . What we did felt good and right!" (116). But even she, beaten down by relentless condemnation, at last asks Brevan, "Do you really think we did wrong? Do you think us sick and possessed with evil?" (115). This is Mylanfyndra's lowest point, not because death seems imminent, but because for one brief moment, she doubts herself.

As for the townsfolk who judge them: again, this author is not into blame, only understanding. In that grim society, discipline and obedience to the law is vital to survival. The children, in obeying the dictates of their flowering gift, in succumbing to their inner imperative, flout their culture's taboo and so are called to pay the price.

What follows next is part chance, but largely the result of previous kind actions on their part. When released from the cage to flee, first they are driven by forces beyond their control, then after, they opt to follow their destiny. Blown by firestorm off the mesa, which their people believe to comprise the entire world, they set out to discover that which is vital to us all: a valid, valued place in the order of things.

In spite of several perilous encounters, they will not be deflected from their goal. As with Gom and the trio from *Collidescope*, they hug close to them a blind and undeniable trust that they will, somehow, somewhere succeed: they have to, because to fail is unthinkable.

This is not the usual kind of knowing, but it works.

In my concern for gifted children at risk, I consider another aspect of the problem in *The Chimes of Alyafaleyn* (1993). The chimes are *heynim*, golden spheres that float through the air, chiming incessantly. At a certain time each year, clouds of new heynim float across the skies of that world and the people snag them, that is, catch, summon, and hold them with mind power to bob and chime around their heads. After this power becomes active at puberty, people of average ability can eventually snag up to a dozen each but cannot tune them, and so there are no true harmonies in these modest clusters, only random chiming. Above-average persons can snag and hold around twenty or so and can alter their heynim's pitch to tune a *faleyn*, or true harmony. These more talented people have special functions in the community, such as regulating the weather for crops or healing sickness. This world, after all, is *Alyafaleyn*, the Region (*Alya*) of Harmony. The chimes, and the harmonies created by tuning them, lie at the root of everything: they keep the very world in existence.

In Fahwyll, a remote village in Alyafaleyn, a girl, Caidrun, is born with an unprecedented ability to pull vast numbers of heynim to her. (A dangerous power to possess without the discretion to wield it.) Before she is two years old, she suddenly pulls all the heynim in the village to converge on her like slingstones. A young boy, Tamborel, realizing what is about to happen, throws himself upon her and, shielding her from the full force of the strike, takes the brunt of it himself. He lies in a coma and almost dies. After Tamborel awakens, the villagers attempt to suppress Caidrun's use of the gift and end up maiming her emotionally. By the time she reaches adolescence, she is so filled with hatred and bitterness that she rushes off swearing vengeance and almost brings down total ruination on her world. Only Tamborel's devotion and enduring love for her averts the cataclysm.

Two protagonists: the boy, Tamborel, the girl, Caidrun. Heroes, both, but the quest is Tamborel's.

What is his quest? Is he ethical? And does he *know how to succeed?*

Tamborel is a sensitive, conscientious boy, inclined from his earliest years to be "good." A smile of approbation, a fond hug from his mother, these are as necessary to him as the light of the sun. This is a common enough kind of ethical practice: unexamined virtue, blind obedience to a social code for the sake of a pat on the head and the approval of one's community. Law-abiding Tamborel might have lived out his days thus in Fahwyll had it not been for a chronic conflict stirred up by Caidrun's gift. Therein lie the roots of his lifelong quest, though Tamborel never consciously perceives it as that. From the time of the near-disaster, it becomes a daily fight on Tamborel's part to protect Caidrun from both the enmity of those who fear her and harm from the clumsy, well-meaning folk who love her. Only he realizes her need and the kind of nurturing appropriate to her singular gift and lively, loving nature. But he is one small boy among a phalanx of authoritarian adults. Time and again, his attempts to champion Caidrun are thwarted, and yet he never gives up, such is his attachment to her, and such his distress to see the unfair, even cruel treatment meted out to her. Even so, he walks the fine line, championing Caidrun while obeying his parents' wishes—until the day that Caidrun scatters someone's heynim (a heinous crime) and runs.

Within hours, Tamborel flees family and home to go after her. Unable to find her, he turns aside and enters the Honfaleyn, the School of Harmonies, having been advised that a girl of Caidrun's prodigious ability must eventually gravitate there. While waiting, Tamborel works to develop his own not inconsiderable ability to tune the spheres. Years pass, and Caidrun still does not appear. When things begin to go awry—storms, ruined crops, increasing hunger and sickness—Tamborel knows in his heart that Caidrun is the cause. Learning in a dream where she might be, he flees the Honfaleyn to cross a forbidden plain leading to the edge of the world.

Breaking rules comes easy to some; for Tamborel it is a major act of courage. But both in Fahwyll and in the Honfaleyn, his inner convictions, his inner compulsion to act, override what is expected of him and drive him to strike out on his own.

Tamborel's quest is to save Caidrun, and his spur is his unconditional love. Does he know how to win? Like all my other heroes, he muddles along from pillar to post, no time to think, obeying the dictates of that inner pull. No amount of early-morning-hour anxiety can divert him from his purpose; mid-journey deliberations whether or not he will succeed are moot mind-play. Whatever Tamborel says or thinks, however many times he falters in his purpose, he ultimately presses on because he has no other choice. And like many others here on Earth, he does reach his goal.

The Quest: "To Pick and Not to Know . . . There May Be Danger in It."

I was three-quarters of the way through the first draft of *The Chimes* when I had the most extraordinary encounter with my next dream child. One Sunday night I went to bed in all innocence, little suspecting that within hours, along would come a young man who would have a tremendous effect on my creative life. His name was Jason; he made quite sure I got that. He was part-black or possibly Hispanic; poor, from some inner-city block, didn't matter which. He told me how he loved horses, all horses, and how he wanted me to give him a wonderful week of rides on some of the most fabulous of them all: Pegasus, Cheiron the Centaur, Poseidon's steeds; he wanted to ride the wooden horse into Troy, take a joyride on the ivory and ebony mechanical horse from the Arabian Nights. He wanted to meet a unicorn, and lastly, his secret friend Silver Star, a magnificent Arab stallion.

All this in a dream flash, all of it, complete yet inchoate.

In the pause between dreaming and waking, I knew but could not enumerate all of the above. I remember thinking "Hey, kid, get lost. I'm in the middle. I'll see you in a month or so, okay?"

And this I'll never forget. He fixed his large brown eyes on me and answered, "Walk away from me now and I'll never come back."

I turned on the light. Four A.M., the clock said. Around nine, I called my editor. "I've got a book," I said. "What, another one? You're doing the Chimes."

"I know, I know, but this kid won't wait." I told her of my experience, and without hesitation she told me to set aside the Chimes and deal with that importunate fellow. Such was Jason's power, his story was told while Tamborel and Caidrun's was left dangling.

This is not all.

As I began his tale, I knew what else I had to do, and this also issued from that bright, insistent energy that was Jason. I had at that time bought a Kaypro, my second computer, with a hard drive and a whole fifteen megabytes of brain. This kid wanted me to illustrate his story, not with pen and ink on treated acetate as I had done with previous books, but on computer! Despite the fact of my new computer with as much brain as I would ever need to write my books, despite the fact I knew nothing of computers in general beyond their being wonderful typewriters that saved me a lot of money in the local copy shop, and despite the fact that I could most probably ill afford it, New Year's Eve that year found me in a local Macintosh store, checking over a bewildering array of full-page color scanners, external hard drives, color boards, software packages such as Adobe Photoshop and Illustrator.

Jason got his way. By January, I was in possession of a complete desktop publishing system and teaching myself the mysteries of Photoshop at the rate of knots. The result is *Jason's Seven Magical Night Rides* (1994), complete with eight black and white illustrations and full-color jacket—all elicited by him. A most remarkable young man.

This is not all.

It was not until I worked my way through that first draft, pulling the dream stuff out into the waking world of time and space that I realized that his underlying aim, his true desire, had been not for a week of free joyrides, but to find his father. Living with his single mother in a high-rise inner-city apartment, he collected pictures and models of horses and dreamed about a father he had never known, and about whom his mother would not even speak. He was after two things, really. One, to know what it was to have such a person; two, to meet his own father at last. I have tried to imagine what he felt at embarking upon his quest. Excitement, fear, curiosity. Jason epitomizes all my heroes at the quest's beginning, not knowing consciously the full extent of either desire or task.

> The man took the card to the window. "Ah, you chose the mystery ride. A bold choice—even rash, maybe. But rewarding, if you're game. Are you?"
> "You bet," Jason cried, then added, "Game for what?"
> The man held up the card with a flourish. "For not one, but *seven* free rides. One whole week of glorious excursions on the most fabulous of steeds!" The man bent toward him, his dark eyes a-glitter. "There may be danger in it. Are you still game, Jason Kightly?" (4)

Here, he is given a choice between the relatively safe and known and that step that takes us off into the dark. Every ride he took during that magical week revealed to him a fresh aspect of *father*, and exposure to these various aspects changed him and his perspective on the world accordingly. As I worked through his adventures, I suspected that here was a hero who could not come through in the same triumphant way that Gom and Tamborel and Caidrun had. Here was a case where circumstances beyond Jason's control kicked in—the co-creator of the situation, Jason's mother. The nearer I got to the end of the story, the more certain I grew that Jason could never find his dad. And yet I had become so emotionally involved with this kid, and his influence on me was so powerful, that for a while I tried for his sake to cheat and make for him the happy ending that he wanted. I wrote it, and it sat between us. It wouldn't fly. I knew it. He knew it. And so, at last, the truth came out: he will never know his father in the flesh.

In the end, though Jason finds a mystical ground on which to meet his father, this is all that he can ever hope for. This is the crunch, and Jason has to make his peace with it; this he does, and in the doing, wins.

If ever that simple prayer belonged to any hero in this world or out of it, it's Jason:

God grant me the serenity to accept things I cannot change,
Courage to change the things I can,
And wisdom to know the difference.

Notes

1. I have been giving author presentations on fantasy to groups, both adults and children, for six years. In the beginning, I assumed the participants all had a common basic foreknowledge of fantasy, but after a while, it became clear that the majority, and that included educators at the primary, secondary, and tertiary levels, knew little about it. So I began to take a sounding at the beginning of my talks, a simple questionnaire comprising half a dozen questions, the first being "What is fantasy?" The members of the audience jot down the answers to my questions and set them aside until the end of my presentation. Then, I ask them to take a look and see if those answers are still valid. To that first question, the majority write that fantasy is "make-believe" or "escapist fiction." By the end of the talk, however, that misconception is cleared up, and a gratifying number of people express a will to start reading fantasy books.

2. A common question from students is whether I ever write about "real people." To that, I answer something like "OK, what 'real people' are you reading about now?" The student then says something like "John Doe" from *Fire on Main Street*. If the novel is set in a real city, I invite the student to look up John Doe's number in the phone directory. The ensuing dialogue reveals, of course, that it won't be there because John Doe is as imaginary as any of my off-world characters. Then we discover that when you get down to it, Gom Gobblechuck in the world of Ulm, for instance, is as real and three-dimensional a person as any in that audience—as is any self-respecting fictional character worthy of his or her salt.

3. John Gardner's *Grendel* (Vintage Books, 1971) is a most moving account of Beowulf's story, particularly of his dying moments, but it is a retelling of the old saga wrought in the first person, so it doesn't count.

4. Jos Smith, who painted the three Bradbury Press jackets for the Ulm series, said once of Gom that "he runs around with one foot stuck in a bucket." No one has ever put it better.

5. Christian flees the City of Destruction for the Celestial City. On the way, he passes through the Slough of Despond, the Palace Beautiful, the Valley of Humiliation, the Valley of the Shadow of Death, Vanity Fair, Doubting Castle, and so on. Along the way he encounters people with names such as Mr. Worldly Wise, Faithful, Hopeful, and the Giant Despair. I believe that reading fantasy, particularly allegory such as *The Pilgrim's Progress* when very young is akin to learning one's native tongue. There is a sort of mystical, elemental, one-to-one connection formed between the concept and the name that never comes with the adult mind. This nourishment of the developing psyche is, in my opinion, as vital to growth as proteins and vitamins for the body. When everything is laid down and the

formative years are over, no amount of back-tracking can make up for the loss. I am concerned to find how deprived our growing children are today for mind's nourishment, and appalled at their ignorance of such rich and varied cultural histories from all over the world.

Children's Literature

CHETWIN, GRACE. 1987a. *The Atheling.* New York: Tor Books.

———. 1987b. *The Riddle and the Rune.* New York: Bradbury Press.

———. 1988. *The Crystal Stair.* New York: Bradbury Press.

———. 1990. *Collidescope.* New York: Bradbury Press.

———. 1991. *Child of the Air.* New York: Bradbury Press.

———. 1993. *The Chimes of Alyafaleyn.* New York: Bradbury Press.

———. 1994. *Jason's Seven Magical Night Rides.* New York: Bradbury Press.

FOURTEEN

Wise Women and Warriors

SUSAN LEHR

Let me tell you why I think you are here. I won't talk much about it after today, so listen carefully. What I know about is power. Not the sort of power your father has with soldiers and armies and weapons, but a power that comes from knowing. . . . Seeing and knowing—and being very truthful about what you see and know . . .

MONICA FURLONG
Juniper

Women in high fantasy live in worlds ruled by men and must prove their "manhood" to succeed in those imaginary worlds. These females in children's literature continue to reflect the troubling gender times in which we live. Mirroring images in the newspaper, spouse abuse, sexual harassment, violence against women, rape, and incest are strong themes in fantasy for children.

Gender struggles have deep roots reflected in the mythologies of the world. Themes of male domination are common. In an ancient Brazilian myth of the Mundurucu, the origin of male domination is said to have begun with the woman's accidental discovery of the sacred trumpets (Bierhorst 1988). Bierhorst writes that men's worst fears were realized when women abandoned their roles as homemakers, spent all of their time playing these mysterious trumpets, and as a result, held power over the men in their tribe. The men were forced to gather wood, fetch water, make the manioc cakes, and hunt to appease the hunger of the clan ancestors. Once the men refused to hunt, the women were forced to relinquish the ancient trumpets of power and return to their original roles. "From that time on, things have been as they are today" (Bierhorst 1988, 44). The myths of the Tariana suggest that it is the root of sexual desire and the resulting faithlessness of women that are the cause of this separation of the sexes and the male conspiracy to dominate women.

Children's high fantasy is a mirror of males in today's world, who continue to dominate government, education, religion, and the corporate world. Although one still finds archaic systems worldwide, opportunities are beginning to exist for women if they are willing to fight or join the male systems under which they live. Even in liberal Western democracies such as Switzerland one finds women are not allowed to vote; two isolated women sit as a small minority on the United States Supreme Court. Gender continues to divide, even as women insist on sharing the power of the trumpets. For the purposes of this chapter I will address the evolution of female warriors and healers as mythic characters through a discussion of the role of the woman in children's literature. The term *fantasy* will refer to the body of children's books written as high fantasy, a definition of which follows in a section defining the genre. The term *heroine* will not be used since the cultural connotations of the word involve a particular bias that is distinctly different from the term hero. Joseph Campbell (1949), writing about the hero with a thousand faces, defines the role of hero as involving the exploits of a male or female. In this sense will I use the term.

A growing handful of authors in fantasy are gutsy risk takers who defy authority, convention, and the personal safety of their female characters. Their characters make new rules even as they continue to cook, clean, and pick up the kids. As a result, odd images juxtapose and make one wonder how far women have evolved in fantasy. That they are in the process of evolving is clear; where they will end up is less clear. Wrede's unconventional Princess Cimorene escapes the confines and conventions of palace life, only to cook and clean for a dragon queen; and once married and pregnant, she has to put up with the fussiness of those around her who want to limit her options. The matter rests with having and making choices, even for the privileged classes.

Female authors for children, like Ursula LeGuin, Sherryl Jordan, Donna Jo Napoli, Tamora Pierce, and Monica Furlong have begun to explore the hard social issues of our time through the lens of secondary worlds where women take on grand roles and quests at great personal cost and risk. Borrowing images from the real world, one could say that sometimes these heroes opt not to pay the social security of their illegal alien maids and lose their shirts; occasionally they yell foul when exploited by supreme court justices or long-term senators and are not believed; and in rare acts their rage explodes into insane bits of snipping at the male's anatomy— cutting off the organ that symbolically diminishes their personal freedoms. The authors are angry, impatient, and take deadly aim at themes of injustice against women. Their targets, not surprisingly, are frequently men.

How are these career witches and warriors coping with the stress of balancing family life, career, equal opportunity, sexual harassment, poverty, and the horrors of evil wizards? If fantasy is a mirror reflecting the social issues of our times (Lehr 1991), then the stories of these harried female heroes are vital voices in fantasy books because they offer diverse perspectives and options for children to consider. With that in mind, this chapter focuses on exploring the motives, choices, and morale of the modern-day versions of the Lucys, Susans, Megs, and Eilonwys, rather than the Tarans, Peters, and Geds.

What Is a Hero?

Mollie Hunter (1992), a leading writer of fantasy for children, has defined what a hero is *not* by talking about the heroes that are available for children today in the world of comic books, electronic games, movies, and TV. According to Hunter, Superman sweeping down from the skies, mouthing platitudes about saving the world, while using the same tactics as the bad guys, is as amoral as they are. "It has to be recognized that this presentation of the hero could also be pernicious rubbish in that its equation of might with right elevates the use of force to a prime ethos" (1992, 60). As a result, the lines between good and evil are considerably blurred, which "divorces that struggle from its true battleground—the human psyche." This, according to Hunter, is what a hero is not. I would add that the roles of women in these scenarios are appalling and frequently degrading. Although a Sean Connery movie, *The Rising Sun*, was accused of heaping disrespect and stereotypes upon the Japanese male, I read no similar outcries about the use of naked Caucasian women as dinner plates or the repetition of a scene involving the strangulation of a woman during coitus. One might forget the movie quickly, but the destructive images of women remain.

Joseph Campbell sees the hero as

> the man or woman who has been able to battle past his personal and local historical limitations to the generally valid, normally human forms. Such a one's visions, ideas, and inspirations come pristine from the primary springs of human life and thought. Hence they are eloquent, not of the present, disintegrating society and psyche, but of the unquenched source through which society is reborn. The hero has died as a modern man: but as eternal man—he has been reborn. His second solemn task and deed therefore is to return to us, transfigured, and teach the lesson he has learned of life renewed. (1949, 20)

Campbell captures the who and the why of the hero and reveals how myths are bound to the individual and his coming of age, his rite of initiation. Mythic strands connect humans to the spirit world and amplify the need for heroes and the need to be heroes. Myth reflects life's journey. That's why readers care passionately about journeys in fantasy and make connections to others taking parallel journeys, seeing how they process, struggle, interpret, and ultimately choose to live their lives. People cannot survive without heroes. That is also why the voices of women authors, writing for young females and males, offer fresh and vital visions of the hero's potential.

What Is High Fantasy?

> A hero ventures forth from the world of common day into a region of supernatural wonder: fabulous forces are there encountered and a decisive victory is won: the hero comes back from this mysterious adventure with the power to bestow boons on his fellow man. (Campbell 1949, 30)

Fantasy steps back from the familiar world and tells a hero's story, sometimes capturing just a fragment of that life. J. R. R. Tolkien defined the high-fantasy genre when *The Hobbit* was first published in 1937 in England. Tolkien was heavily influenced by George Macdonald's work in the late 1800s; however, no one had created a secondary world with such energy and thorough abandon before the appearance of Bilbo's and Frodo's Middle Earth. When fantasy is well done, its characteristics include common heroes any of us might have the capacity to become. The heroes are everyday folks, men who would rather be sitting at home with a good book and a cup of tea in front of a blazing fire. These heroes are all too frequently reluctant to leave the safe structure of their worlds to venture out into the unknown, what Campbell calls crossing the "first threshold," into a world typically fraught with danger. This is why tales like "The Three Little Pigs" and "The Three Billy Goats Gruff" continue to evoke primal responses from children at a young age (Lehr 1991). What do the stories teach you? "Never leave home." "Not to trust strangers." "Don't go across bridges." The themes of growing up, becoming independent, leaving one's home, and facing the world armed only with one's own resources are scary propositions. It takes a real hero to achieve that, but once completed he gets to the grass on the other side of the bridge and doesn't starve to death. If he happens to destroy an evil ogre along the way, then perhaps the world has become a safer place as well, and the hero will have stories of questing to tell his grandchildren around the fire at night. (The use of the masculine pronoun to refer to the hero reinforces that these stories have typically been about the exploits of men.)

Books of fantasy typically take the hero on a quest that outlines the struggles of the hero. The secondary world in which the hero quests must be believable to pull the reader into the adventure. If it's not believable we never sign on as readers and we never quite accept what occurs. Magic in fantasy is common and must adhere to basic rules; it is not to be used whimsically, and it is always used at great cost. Poorly written fantasy offers magic in a contrived fashion, with what I call the Santa Claus approach to life. It might seem appealing, but it's rarely reflective of life. Even the strongly written *Dark Is Rising* (1965) series by Susan Cooper portrays an easy magic with little personal cost. For example, Merriman, an ageless character similar to Merlin, reassures the three Drew children of *Greenwich*, particularly Jane, that at no time will they be in any personal danger. The struggle against evil does not parallel reality if confronting evil places one in no real personal danger. The message from fantasy is that there is no triumph without sweat and personal risk.

Frequently, helpful companions compose a loyal crew willing to struggle to the end, willing to give up their lives for the success of the quest. Gandalf was a wizard whereas Sam Gamgee was a gardener, both loyal companions to Frodo in Tolkien's *The Fellowship of the Ring* (1954). Both companions were predictably loyal, yet unpredictable when called upon to aid the hero. Both revealed inner strength and resources of which the hero was unaware, but which were necessary for the successful completion of the quest. Heroes do not stand alone.

Good and evil always define the quest because ultimately we all must define who we are, to whom we are aligned, and to what we are opposed. Hunter (1992) sees a force in both good and evil that is integral to human nature yet antagonistic to the other. The twin components either ennoble or degrade. Hunter's notion of the human psyche is that it is perpetually at war with itself. Fantasy is an extension of this war.

The wizards, witches, healers, heroes, and destroyers have been with us in reality down through the ages. Fantasy gives us that safe bit of distance. From the armchair we can meet Hitler face to face, the drug dealer who lurks in the city, or the bully who waits at the school gate. I believe we also see the bully in ourselves and the capacity for greater misdeeds. We decide to whom we are loyal, to whom we are opposed, and which risks are worth taking. Fantasy merely amplifies the quest. Fantasy is an inner journey that helps readers ponder the big questions about one's raison d'être. Those who think of it as escape have missed the point and have engaged only at the superficial level. Fantasy operates on two levels:

> There must be a surface one [tale] of incident engrossing enough to make the reader keep on turning the pages; but the incident must be conveyed through a form of writing that enables the story to operate also on the much deeper level of symbolism. And always, to create the essential meeting point of my own and the reader's mind, I have shown the heroic action being carried by a character with whom these readers could identify—an ordinary person drawing on some emotion common to all human nature, yet still one that enables my character to transcend ordinariness, and thus to become that inspired and inspiring figure, a hero. (Hunter 1992, 66)

Fantasy written with craft does not come easily.

A Brief History of Women in Fantasy

In the past, men have defined the images of fantasy, presenting readers with male heroes who quested and adventured in traditional ways, for the most part using women as accoutrements, sidekicks, and prizes. Sometimes the women were on pedestals; frequently they were valued. Yet the men quested, the men made the important decisions, the men took the risks, and the men generally saved the day. If they won women at the end of that day, it was considered their right, the right of plunder, rape, and reward. The journeys were long and arduous and included the searching and scrutinizing of one's soul. The heroes were often reluctant and sometimes dense. At times, the heroes were the problem. Through their arrogance or ignorance evil could be loosed. Death-defying acts and confrontations were always a part of this questing and again typically fit for men. Meeting one's dark side in an unlit cave was possibly the ultimate battle. But what of women? Where did they fit into the picture? Have their characters evolved over time?

The books discussed below all broke new ground in fantasy for female characters.

I discuss them frankly from the vantage of the 1990s, realizing that they are classics in children's fantasy. My criticism incorporates the fact that all books reflect the values of the time in which they were written. With that in mind, it is time to take a different look at these classics—for their representation of female heroes in children's literature. Do the authors portray women as independent humans who are active participants and adventurers? Do they treat women as intelligent and capable humans who battle beside their male counterparts against the forces of evil? Do the males in the stories accept females as equals or do they patronize and confine women to certain roles?

George Macdonald (1872), stretching the fairy tale into a new form in *The Princess and the Goblin*, gave the archetypal hero a personality that included a love of singing, a hearty appetite, and the Protestant work ethic. Curdie was brave, truthful, and pure of heart. His princess was a real person who pouted, was spoiled, and had a saucy tongue, a true heroine, rather than a hero. The goblins, who happened to have an abhorrence of songs, were suddenly fleshed out creatures, both male and female, with evil and detailed plans for storming the palace and forcibly wedding the princess to the goblin king's son. Who can forget the princess and Curdie foiling the goblin takeover in 1872? She and Curdie were a team, a child and a young man, both untested—echoes of "The Three Billy Goats Gruff"—trying to battle the evil ogre and make it safely to the other side of the bridge. Early in the story the princess' strong faith and an invisible ball of twine saved Curdie from the goblins. Consider the Victorian model of the angel in the house; the princess was spunky as a child, but she was also a good girl. As a young woman she would have to take on a new role and learn to control her childish impulses. She was spirited, but the reader knew that Curdie would take care of her, control her, and tame that saucy tongue. Macdonald, writing in the previous century, offered the female an active role in fantasy, but she was a heroine, not a hero. Like Alice in Wonderland and Dorothy in Oz, the princess was able to leave the house, enter a place of danger, save a friend, and become an important player in solving a problem. Nonetheless, the princess remained on a pedestal. No laudanum for her, she had the resources to find her "proper" place.

The princess stood alone until 1950 when C. S. Lewis gave us Lucy in *The Lion, the Witch and the Wardrobe*. None of the heroines since have been more innocent or pure in spirit than Lucy, a former princess of Narnia. She was strong, feisty, intelligent, and a true believer in Aslan, but she was forbidden to hold a sword in battle. She knew her place as a woman. Hers were the healing gifts, with drops of liquid given to her by Aslan. Lewis gave us strong women who quested and adventured, yet they always held back as he reminded his readers that women had certain roles, certain limitations, and were generally subservient to their male counterparts. In contrast, Edwin, her brother, embraced evil and even betrayed his sister; in the end, however, he was one with Aslan and ready for the final battle. Lewis' image of the female in fantasy was spirited, yet had many conventions that constricted her ability to function in a man's world. One never really doubted that Peter, the oldest and the male, was the brains and final authority of the four siblings, but again, the author was a male and a product of his times. Still, he offered readers a new vision of women in fantasy as the first author of high fantasy for children.

Ironically, Lewis' villain was a white witch, a nasty and capricious woman who turned characters to stone, as did the gorgon of Greek mythology. Her rage is reminiscent of the elemental earth forces, like that of the Celtic Morrigan who controls and frightens, and leaves one with the threat of impotence. Women as witches versus women as heroes are two separate strands in fantasy and mythology. Woman's power is different from man's power. When loosed in men's stories it is a frightful force that consumes. The elemental female force that terrifies perhaps causes men to tightly control their women.

Not until 1962 was the children's literary world ready for a strong questing female who battled against cosmic forces and won. Madeleine L'Engle's (1962) portrait of Meg Murray in *A Wrinkle in Time* was as refreshing as it was bold, a science-fiction fantasy with a classic confrontation between good and evil. Meg was every bit the equal of Narnia's Peter and Edmund, a potential hero. She battled It on Camazotz, a power that controlled through conformity; she saved her brother Charles Wallace and her father from evil control. She took on a boyfriend, and they were true partners. Her weapons of power were different from those of her male counterparts but no less valorous. Using love to overcome one's enemy is not unlike turning a dragon into a lamb as did St. Martha in mythology. The underlying theme of peace is essentially inexplicable—how can love defeat an enemy?—but effective, since filling up the void with harmony is one of woman's traditional gifts. Meg, as a successful, strong female character, sat alone for many years. But by the third book in the series Meg became a domestic woman, much more vulnerable and less willing to engage in battles. The message blurred as the image of traditional wife became stronger. The dialogue about a woman's role after marriage was as troubling as it was unclear, and it didn't hold much promise for those of us who grew up thinking that we could go out and battle with men against evil. Would marriage and children remove us from the battlefield?

As large numbers of women struggled into careers in the 1970s, authors began writing about women who had bite and sarcasm, women who were militant and unwilling to do as they were told; therefore, it is not surprising that these women emerged from traditional settings. Lloyd Alexander wrote about Eilonwy in the 1970s, a feisty princess who would have made Lucy blush. But the real battles were fought by Taran, common born. Eilonwy frequently had good ideas, but I always felt that the boys were merely patronizing the pretty blonde princess. She was a step in the right direction even though she came from a privileged background. She still had to contend with Lucy's conventions. Eilonwy had bite and sarcasm but usually irritated Taran who wanted to leave her at home where she belonged, even after she saved him from being imprisoned underground.

She was a woman in transition, who was beginning to question the notion of being a good girl and staying at home, but her creator was a male and ultimately didn't understand about questing princesses and equity on a horse. He made his female spirited within the confines of knowing one's rightful place. She had to beg and connive to be included in ventures, eventually returning to her father's castle to learn the etiquette of being a proper princess. Fluff and lace, manners and courtly games. Eilonwy was a bright beacon in a male world of literature, and we loved her even though she reminded us of Jo in *Little Women* or Caddy in *Caddy Woodlawn*. Tomboy for a season, and then it's growing up and settling down time. The reader is expected to like and respect Eilonwy, despite the fact that she's stuck in a place with limited options. Tunnell and Jacobs (1994) write that Eilonwy and Taran share top billing in the Prydain series, but also illustrate that Taran is the "protagonist and hero" in the books. The series is wonderfully rich with strong themes related to growing up, battling forces of evil, and building meaningful relationships with others. Tunnell and Jacobs present a compelling case for using this well-written series, but they ignore the gender issues that continue to empower men at the expense of women. Perhaps Eilonwy was strong in the 1970s, but I find her rather traditional in 1995.

Alexander's (1986) newest female creation is a true adventurer placed in a Victorian setting. She has spirit and is undaunted by any circumstance. She leads her male guardian on a string. Vespar Holly is a tall-tale figure, a legend come to life. In her character, Alexander has realized Eilonwy's potential, even within the constrictions of the Victorian era. Vespar represents women on the move, women who are exasperated and irritated by the Victorian molds. These fresh characters have no patience with convention and find many adventures.

In contrast to the development of women's roles in Alexander's books, action and adventure are primarily in the realm of the male as brothers and sister battle forces together in Susan Cooper's *The Dark Is Rising* series. The first book of the series, published in 1966, offers a portrait of a girl who functions as a little mother to her brothers. Jane worries and frets about dust, danger, making too much noise, seasickness, and asking too many questions, even as the boys talk about King Arthur and adventuring at sea. Her brothers cast aspersions on her gender constantly—"just like a girl"—as they move forward with the action. Jane's redeeming grace is that she is intelligent and uses her intelligence to solve some of the mysteries in the plot.

The second and fourth books of the series have no lead female characters. In *Greenwich* (1974), the third book, Jane is the only female of the four children, still isolated as she was in *Over Sea, Under Stone* (1966); however, the negative gender references from the first book have largely vanished, and Jane is the one who completes the quest successfully. Jane's wish, that the Greenwich might achieve happiness, culminates when she has a dream in which the Greenwich gives Jane the object needed to complete the quest. As Great Uncle Merry has assured Jane at book's beginning and reminded her at book's end, she and her brothers were never in any real danger: "The Dark will not touch any of you. . . . There will be protection. Don't worry. I promise you that. Nothing that may happen to Barney will harm him" (7). Cooper's quest presents a passive sort of adventure for Jane since the boys basically are the ones who venture into the woods, enter the gypsy caravan, become hypnotized, and swim the underwater domains of Tethys. When the boys ventured out for an early morning walk and did not return for breakfast, "Jane was almost in tears. 'But they couldn't just disappear! Something awful must have happened!'" (66). While eleven-year-old Will reassures the older Jane that her brothers are all right, he mentally signals Great Uncle Merry that the boys are in the clutches of the Dark. Jane, of course, must not be told; rather Will lies to her and suggests they go for a lovely walk. Jane exhibits all of the characteristics of a female stereotype through her constant worrying and agitated emotional state while Will epitomizes the male who feels the woman must be protected from the truth. Although Cooper's style of writing is strong, her depiction of the female is troubling for young readers as the boys continue to grab most of the active roles and patronize women.

All of the authors discussed thus far, both male and female, have created an evolution of sorts for the spunky female in fantasy as they continue to question and explore the balance of power and the distribution of labor between the sexes. The themes suggest that although the solutions are not ideal, the dialogue has been ongoing. What I find authentic about the significant contributions of these authors is the voice they give to the female experience in a society that continues to value men. These books reflect the struggle both sexes have in identifying where women fit in. In the remainder of this chapter I will examine the characters in current fantasy who begin to give voice to the woman's integrated role as warrior, healer, and self-sufficient being.

Woman as Warrior

The profile of the warrior reflects two opposing images, that of defender and that of attacker. Fantasy frequently explores the clash between the two and embodies that clash in themes related to struggles between good and evil, between gods and demons. Historically men have been the defenders. In contrast, both male and female images have assumed the role of evil usurper or attacker. Apart from that, women have remained in the background, often tucked safely at home as nurturers and bearers of babies. Women supply the soup, the soap, and the reason for keeping the village safe. Fighting has not been an option. The princess, Lucy, Meg, Jane, and Eilonwy were not warriors; they were nurturers.

History records the wars of men. Campbell refers to this necessary enterprise as clearing the field of the tyrants who are the cause of widespread misery. Infrequently one will find female warriors in mythology, like Saint Martha who goes against a dragon at the request of her people. Ironically, rather than bearing arms, her weapons are holy water and a crucifix. Rather than destroying her enemy she tames it as a lamb and puts a collar about its neck. The message is that women battle differently than men and have different purposes for overpowering an enemy.

As women's roles have expanded in fantasy, authors have presented female warriors who represent women struggling to succeed in male domains. Robin McKinley's *The Blue Sword* (1982) is set in a desert land ruled by Homelanders similar to the British Empire of the nineteenth century. The roles of men and women are parallel to the Victorian view of gender. Outlander women are limited in what they can hope to accomplish aside from successful marriage since men inherit estates and are responsible for penniless, unmarried female siblings. Natives are viewed by most of the Outlander military occupants as inferior, curious, primitive, and good servants, also similar to the British views of the last century. The main character, Harry, does not fit into this British scheme and experiences life with a strong undercurrent of dissatisfaction. We expect her to leap out of this outpost, or at least to radically alter women's options.

For this reason, the main female character is a curiously apathetic victim. When Harry is initially abducted by the King of the Hill People, her unexpected acceptance and passivity are troubling even though her dormant powers are awakening, and it is clear that she has a strong link and affinity to the native people. Her abductor is even more troubling in his depiction as an attractive, mysterious, and powerful man, a romantic who is forced to kidnap Harry because the inner voices tell him he must. Being swept away forcibly by a male in the middle of the night is not an attractive theme, and it never is resolved satisfactorily in the book. The book is superbly written, has adventure of the best sort, but again reflects society's troubling images with regard to the female. That Harry becomes a successful warrior after six weeks of training is also nettlesome because again there is no real personal cost; the power of kelar awakens the skills needed to be a woman warrior. The two threads of the story combine to make a strong female hero by book's end.

In contrast, the main character in Tamora Pierce's *Song of the Lioness* 1983–1988 series earns the right to be the Protector of the Realm because she hides herself as a man for eight years while training as a knight. To prove her manhood, Alanna binds her chest and takes on a male role as page, battling past what Campbell calls the "local historical limitations" (1949, 19), in this case, the fact that only men can be warriors. In Pierce's second book, *In the Hand of the Goddess* (1984), Alanna becomes a squire at the age of fourteen and continues to develop her skills as an emerging warrior. At book's end, she enters the Chamber of the Ordeal to emerge as a true knight who defeats an arrogant and destructive wizard who has underestimated her ability. Before the king and his court, she stands for the first time as a victorious woman but must leave because of the disgrace of her secret: she is a woman. Pierce makes this shame a powerful theme, a burden that Alanna cannot shed. Society has yet to be reborn. Alanna's world is not ready for a Joan of Arc.

In *The Woman Who Rides Like a Man* (1986), Alanna simply wants to be heard: "I think as a human being. Men don't think any differently from women—they just make more noise about being able to." Her guardian, Coram, replies with a chuckle: "Have you not discovered that when people, men and women, find a woman who acts intelligently, they say she acts like a man?" To which the leader of the desert tribe adds: "You frighten them. You are too new; you are too different" (Pierce, 49). Pierce's message is that powerful and successful women instill fear not only in the men around them, but also in the women. As Alanna takes on her new role as the tribal shaman, the women of the village continue to snub and ignore her. Ironically, the men of the tribe accept her as an aberration because she has proven her worth as a warrior.

In *Lioness Rampant*, Alanna's worth is finally self-evident, and she returns "transfigured" to teach the lesson she has learned of life, renewed although some still continue to challenge her claim as warrior. Pierce reflects real struggles of women who succeed in male domains. Upon the completion of my doctoral studies and dissertation in 1985, I was offered a job at a university. An adult student visiting from Nigeria told me during class that I had received the university position because I was a woman—quotas. My students gasped with disbelief. The words were like spears, symbolic of many similar experiences I have faced throughout my life as a woman. In my family, a girl like me was complimented with "you should have been the boy in the family," or "it'll take a strong man to control you." Pierce's themes resonate for me personally. Every step a victory yet a struggle. The themes are real. They relate to who and what we are if they are done with skill. Themes as powerful as these belong on the shelves of children so that they can begin to make decisions early on about who they will become.

The barriers that Alanna's character faced mirror the barriers that women face or have faced. If women want the opportunity to be warriors, then authors like Pierce have presented the complexities involved and have given young readers examples of successful women warriors. The image of Pierce's warrior goes beyond physical danger and fighting, however; her voice suggests the constant battle women face as they struggle to be seen and heard in many capacities and in diverse arenas.

An equally important theme in this fourth book of the series deals with Alanna's acceptance of her womanhood and the awakening of her sexual desire. In a conversation with one of her lovers, she is asked what her future plans are and if they include a husband and children. Alanna ponders the questions that many women today ask themselves: "Give up my shield after working so hard? Spend my time at court or on my husband's lands? I have no patience for that kind of life. Besides—I don't know anything about children. . . ." He responds, "I just wondered why you feel you have to be all warrior or all woman. Can't you be both?" (59). Liam's question cuts to the core.

The Desana of Brazilian mythology have a myth related to the Daughter of the Sun, who is responsible for offering the people two vital functions (Bierhorst 1988). The first shows the people how to live well through the teaching of survival and the domestic arts, which included the introduction of ceramics, basket weaving, the stone ax, husbandry, fishing, and the invention of fire. The second function occurs after the Daughter of the Sun boils over her cooking pot, urinates on the embers, accidentally burns her pubic hair, and spreads the exotic odor of sexual desire throughout the world. Alanna embodies the new woman who makes choices on the battlefield and in the bedroom. Her choices are not bound by convention, and her sexual desire is not limited to one mate.

Pierce explores a third point of view through the voice of a queen who has been dispossessed and who longs to be accepted as a person. "All my life I've been worthless, the one who should have been a male and an heir. My father was kind, in his way—I take after him in looks. But he never forgot I wasn't a boy. Every morning the Daughters of the Goddess and the Mithran priests have orders to pray for a jin Wilima in their daybreak services" (1988, 141). These are not whimsical themes. They bite deeply.

One could argue that these are dead issues, long solved, themes for a bygone era. But only two years ago a college student gave me her personal philosophy about women and men. She longed to return to her home state because she found the women of the small liberal arts college where I teach too untamed, too untraditional, too liberal. Her view of the male was that of a superior gender, smarter, more capable, the one who ought to be in charge. She left college and returned home a much happier woman. Her possibilities are limited by her vision of what a woman can be. She will one day pass this philosophy of limitation and inferiority on to another woman, probably her own child, or more troublesome, to a classroom filled with young children. Whether the children are males or females is of little consequence. Somewhere out there is a potential child who will either have an inflated sense of self or a poor self-image. I wonder if this woman I knew, or her someday child, will ever grow beyond this destructive view of women.

Alanna's real growth comes toward the end of *Lioness Rampant* when her companion, Faithful, snaps: "You want to be warrior and woman. You want to travel and serve [King] Jonathan. Can't you make up your mind about what you want?" Alanna replies: "Who says I can't have a little bit of each?" (256). Alanna's integration has begun. For the young reader going through puberty the themes are developed thoroughly enough that one must grapple with all of Alanna's decisions, frustrations, inconsistencies, and inner battles. Pierce has so many women going through so many different growth experiences that young readers must problem-solve even as they quest with Alanna and her associates. In the series' fifth book, *Wild Magic* (1993), Pierce successfully combines images of warrior, wife, and mother—marriage has not stripped Alanna's options—and introduces a new character who embodies the potential of woman.

Victims Emerge as Healers

> She'd been pushed into the fire while it was burning. I'd say maybe she fell, but if she'd been awake she'd have tried to save herself. They beat her and thought they'd killed her, I guess, and wanted to hide what they'd done to her. . . . (LeGuin 1990, 3)

Tehanu is a victim who has been raped and mutilated by men. LeGuin shows the violence, the pain, the raw ugliness of the scars. Raped. Beaten. Burned. Hidden. Left for dead. Charred on the face and hand to the bone. Her voice is a gasp, and it is long before she uses it. She doesn't trust men. I'd like to think that this child is a fantasy; however, she isn't. Tehanus have long been vulnerable to the violence of men. Seeing and knowing and speaking the truth about what is seen and known: this is what LeGuin has done. Out of the pain and vulnerability of being a victim comes Tehanu, who will neither be destroyed nor defined by the violence of men. Clearly she is not a warrior in training.

In *Tehanu*, the ways of the woman are rejected, held up for ridicule. Always battles to be fought. Always those who cannot respect the woman. "To her consternation she saw from their expressions that in fact they had not heard the name, Ogion's true name; they had not paid attention to her [Tenar]" (1990, 26). Perhaps the ultimate hurt is to be ignored, dismissed, to remain unnoticed. "'Oh!' she said. 'This is a bad time—a time when even such a name can go unheard, can fall like a stone! Is listening not power? Listen, then: his name was Aihal. His name in death is Aihal. In the songs he will be known as Aihal of Gont. If there are songs to be made any more. He was a silent man. Now he's very silent. Maybe there will be no songs, only silence. I don't know. I'm very tired. I've lost my father and dear friend'" (26). Estes (1992), author of *Women Who Run with the Wolves*, suggests that a woman cannot teach a man who is unwilling to learn who she is.

In Tenar's world a woman cannot achieve the status of wizard. A woman might become a village witch, but never can she receive the training of the mage, leaving her with "strength without art or knowledge, half frivolous, half dangerous" (1990, 32). LeGuin's final word on Earthsea in this fourth book is that men's magic is over—all changed. LeGuin has finally left the question of Ged, her Sparrowhawk, to others. Ged returns to Gont stripped of his magic; he has successfully battled evil, held it off for a time, and is now spent, his magic gone. Where does that leave us? Women are denied the use of magic, and the greatest mage of all time has lost his power. What will become of the world? In this fourth book of Earthsea, LeGuin offers a new statement of power and suggests that the old ways are worn, used up. She finally confronts the theme of women as potential. She offers Sparrowhawk as the mage who is willing to learn the deep ways of the woman, but this comes only after he has spent his own power. Estes (1992) writes that this willingness of the man indicates his readiness to learn the deep knowing of the woman.

The old village witch, Moss, is full of superstition and tells Tenar that when man's power is gone, man becomes empty. Nothing. But a "woman's a different thing entirely. Who knows where a woman begins and ends? Listen, mistress, I have roots, I have roots deeper than this island. Deeper than the sea, older than the raising of the lands. I go back into the dark. . . . Before the moon I was. No one knows, no one knows, no one can say what I am, what a woman is, a woman of power, a woman's power, deeper than the roots of trees, deeper than the roots of islands, older than the Making, older than the moon. Who dares ask questions of the dark?" (LeGuin 1990, 52). LeGuin explores woman's mystery and power as a force unknown and unexplained. It is different from man's power. Pierce's Alanna takes on a man's guise and is successful, even fulfilled, yet she is also a healer. Her old nurse warns her to balance healing with that of being a warrior, to give back some of what you take.

LeGuin writes of the emergence of a woman in her own guise. Tehanu achieves her identity through pain, through scarring, through the violence of men, and at book's end she is still a child. Her magic is unknown, untested. What will she become? LeGuin hints at woman's potential. The roots of which Moss speaks are deeper and older than the island. Mother Earth. Images of the life force suggest that the power of a woman comes from deep within, from the darkness inside her own body that is connected to the earth, both as a living tissue. What can men know of this power? LeGuin's truth accuses the men who fear this power, who would destroy and control woman rather than risking her release. This accusation is balanced by the threat or promise of the inevitable emergence of that new power. It cannot be held back. It will not be controlled.

Donna Jo Napoli's (1993) unexpected retelling of the traditional tale of Hansel and Gretel in *The Magic Circle* presents the witch as a hunchbacked outsider, who was midwife and later village sorceress. The Ugly One's descent into witchcraft begins with her role as outcast, a small craving for beautiful things, and listening to the voice of an untruthful woman. Eventually the healer stands within a magic circle and calls out the devils who inhabit the sick. A dangerous business, calling out devils. "I must be pure of heart, or no magic circle can stave off the devils" (Napoli 1993, 17–18). Napoli studied history, art, and religion to gain knowledge and provide a sympathetic stance toward the witches and wise women who lived in medieval Europe. While she weaves a supernatural tale based on historical motifs, she also explores the clash between Christianity and the older religions, between woman's healing and men's medicine. Her witch is symbolic of the many who were burned at the stake.

Napoli writes about fear, the fear people had toward women during medieval times and the lengths that were taken to still their voices. The witch in Napoli's story burns at the stake, along with her daughter. Maybe her strongest act of love is to accept the demon's offer to save the life of her child. Choices in life are rarely simple nor are motives. Told in first person by the Ugly One, *The Magic Circle* shows how one good woman was entrapped and enslaved by the demons all because of a bit of desire for a thing of beauty and a slight relaxing of one's vigilance. It hardly seems fair. The remainder of the book is spent not obeying the voices of the ruling demons. The theme is odd, unusual to the core, but the message is perhaps that all is not what it seems, that people are more complex than the stereotypes with which we label them. And, again, an author writes of the victimization of women in history, using fantasy as a bridge to those truths.

Who will read this book? A friend of mine, Deborah, would use this book with middle school children in an in-depth study of the Hansel and Gretel tales, talking with them about perspectives and choices. I feel this book is also written for women about a painful topic—stilling the odd female voice. Napoli certainly offers a peculiar twist on a familiar story, much like McKinley has done with her version of "Beauty and the Beast." Literature is filled with female victims, and Napoli's witch is no exception.

A Matter of Choice

Ironically, the women in these roles live in worlds where men's choices are as limited as women's. Monica Furlong's (1990) knight apparent longs to be a musician, not a warrior, although his mother would have it otherwise. The pressures to prove oneself as a man of strength can be equally constricting when one is a singer of songs and has the heart of a musician. In *Juniper*, Furlong presents a female heir to the throne and the wise woman who becomes her teacher. In a painful twist, Juniper outmaneuvers her aunt's plots to control the throne even as the queen gives birth to a baby boy, who, by virtue of his gender, has easily taken the throne from Juniper. Furlong suggests that some things are out of our control and that finding one's voice or position in life does not rest with man's power nor are the constricted choices restricted to women alone. Juniper's tormentor is a female who is willing to destroy her own son to achieve her dream. She is a thwarted female. Furlong makes the issue of male against female more complex. Women wish to dominate other women while some men have no wish to dominate. And what of women who experience injustice? Are their violent attempts to retake what they consider to be theirs acts of evil? Acts of insanity? Who's to judge?

Although Juniper cannot change the fact that a male heir is to take the throne, she is not governed by outside forces. Juniper's ultimate growth comes after her brother is born. "Questions and visions roiled in my mind. I felt myself coming to some difficult, reluctant decision. Something had to be surrendered or understood by me—I had to be different, but I did not know how" (187). Juniper struggles with the unfairness of a baby brother taking the throne from her, but in the end she decides that she is called to be a doran—a wise woman—like Euny, her mentor: "I want to travel, to see strange places, to learn more . . ." (197). The ending of this book is satisfying. Juniper will not be quashed into a mold nor will she have her voice stilled. Characters like these suggest possibilities, women who can be self-sufficient, even when faced with prejudice or limited choices. Juniper's world would be richer if the choices were broader, but reality frequently differs from the ideal. Juniper is more than a survivor. She will find peace and beauty in her world.

A Call for New Images in Fantasy

Women in fantasy have struggled to release their powers. Their voices are strong and varied. They have succeeded against a male backdrop and have fought past personal scars and destructive prejudices. The female hero in children's fantasy remains in mortal combat against images of arrogant and destructive men. Perceptive authors have offered images of arrogant and destructive women balanced with sensitive and caring men. The heroes are warriors, healers, wives, mothers, witches, and successful career women. And yet, I find a lack, a gap in fantasy for children. Most of the imagery in this body of literature is created out of a world in which men rule and women must fight to find their voices, where identity for women has been achieved through the struggle against a male heritage.

I long for a quest in which battling gender is not the ultimate theme or measure of success. Pierce, Furlong, LeGuin, and Napoli come closest to establishing new and wild mythological voices for women in children's literature. Their characters roam the woods, leap from the shadows, cross swords with foes, battle inner wounds, rely on primal instincts, and suckle babies. "The Wild Woman has been shadowing human women for years. Now we see a glimpse of her. Now she is invisible again. Yet she makes so many appearances in our lives, and in so many different forms, we feel surrounded by her images and urges. She comes to us in dreams or in stories, for she wants to see who we are, and if we are ready to join her yet" (Estes 1992, 456). The change, about which Estes and women who profile wild women in literature write, must come from woman. Woman must "shake out her pelt, strut the old pathways, assert her instinctual knowledge . . . proudly bear the battle scars of our time, write our secrets on walls, refuse to be ashamed, lead the way through and out" (1992, 460). And finally, Estes cautions lest we spend too much on anger—woman must use her cunning and feminine wits and most importantly "howl often."

Who is this woman in fantasy, this hero with a thousand faces? What does she look like? What business is she about? Is she still misunderstood, still burned at the stake, still dressed as a man, still enraged? I think not. This woman does not yet exist; I wonder if she has yet been born. This chapter has given an overview of the images of women in children's fantasy in the past century. We've witnessed the struggle of authors alternating between female characters who were submissive, docile, testing nonsexist wings, battling with the best of male heroes, trying on female voices, and coping with worlds in which males dominate.

Of what will this new woman be made? This hero will glory in her gender and will not apologize for being a woman. Nor will it be asked that she do so. Her quest will be that of achieving integration through her own voice and her own experience. Perhaps Campbell's initiation, separation, and return will not be applicable; his is essentially a male voice giving form to the experience of a male hero. The woman's voice is still emerging, still freeing itself from male images.

Will woman's power be a new expression? Will she battle the traditional battles? Will she battle at all? The image of war today is that of a male image. Women don't rape, pillage, and conquer. Did they? Will they? Could they? We simply don't know. If the Western woman achieves an evolving freedom how will she fare in a world that remains dominated by men? Our historic religious canons give men the power to rule, to make the decisions, even to beat women who are not submissive. It is unlikely that these holy rules will be eliminated. Men still carry the sacred trumpets. It is a pessimistic voice that I now offer, but I do so in the spirit of howling in a loud and strident voice, in the hope that children's authors will continue to offer new and troubling images.

To be heard in a sea of voices, the emerging voice for women must have the strength and aptitude for howling. The image of the lone wolf on an outcropping of rock in the wilderness night, challenging the full moon and howling to the emptiness, is one of satisfaction mingled with longing, anger, and communion with the stars.

Professional References

BIERHORST, JOHN. 1988. *The Mythology of South America.* New York: William Morrow.

CAMPBELL, JOSEPH. 1949. *The Hero With a Thousand Faces.* New Jersey: Princeton University Press.

ESTES, CLARISSA PINKOLA. 1992. *Women Who Run With the Wolves.* New York: Ballantine.

HUNTER, MOLLIE. 1992. *The Pied Piper Syndrome and Other Essays.* New York: HarperCollins.

LEHR, SUSAN. 1991. *"Fantasy: Inner Journeys for Today's Child."* Publishing Research Quarterly: 91–101.

TUNNELL, MICHAEL, and JAMES JACOBS. 1994. "The Prydain Chronicles by Lloyd Alexander." *Book Links* (March).

Children's Literature

ALEXANDER, LLOYD. *The Prydain Circle* series: *The Book of Three* (1964); *The Black Cauldron* (1965); *The Castle of Llyr* (1966); *Taran Wanderer* (1967); *The High King* (1968). New York: Henry Holt and Company.

——— . 1986. *The Illyrian Adventure.* New York: E. P. Dutton.

COOPER, SUSAN. *The Dark Is Rising* series: *The Dark is Rising* (1973); *Over Sea, Under Stone* (1966); *Greenwich* (1974); *The Grey King* (1975). New York: Atheneum.

FURLONG, MONICA. 1990. *Juniper.* New York: Alfred A. Knopf.

L'ENGLE, MADELEINE. 1962. *A Wrinkle in Time.* New York: Farrar, Straus & Giroux.

LEGUIN, URSULA K. 1990. *Tehanu.* New York: Atheneum.

LEWIS, C. S. 1950. *The Lion, the Witch and the Wardrobe.* New York: Collier Books.

MACDONALD, GEORGE. 1986. *The Princess and the Goblin.* New York: Dell Yearling.

McKINLEY, ROBIN. 1978. *Beauty.* New York: Harper Trophy.

——— . 1982. *The Blue Sword.* New York: Greenwillow.

NAPOLI, DONNA JO. 1993. *The Magic Circle.* New York: Dutton Children's Books.

PIERCE, TAMORA. *Song of the Lioness* series: *Alana: The First Adventure* (1983), *In the Hand of the*

Goddess (1984), *The Woman Who Rides Like a Man* (1986), *Lioness Rampant* (1988), *Wild Magic* (1993). New York: Atheneum.

TOLKIEN, J. R. R. 1937. *The Hobbit.* London: Allen & Unwin.

———. 1954–55. *The Lord of the Rings Trilogy: The Fellowship of the Ring* (1954), *The Two Towers* (1954), *The Return of the King* (1955). London: Allen & Unwin.

FIFTEEN

Describing the Fantasy of My Own Life

—

BRIAN JACQUES

I was born and reared in Kirkdale, Liverpool, at the north end of the docklands in what was once a great British seaport. The indigenous population of the area— "Scousers," a peculiar title given to Liverpool folk—was mainly of Irish descent. My father worked at the docks as a docker (longshoreman) as did I and my brothers in turn; it was once the main occupation for Liverpool men. Being the middle child of three brothers, I lived with my parents in an old brick-terraced house. We were a basic working-class family. I attended Saint Johns Elementary School, an ancient Victorian establishment for the Catholic children of the district. The learning process was openly rudimentary and enforced by strict discipline. I was endowed with the skill to write well and had a vivid imagination, which showed itself as early as my tenth year, though I do not recall it being encouraged, either by my parents or teachers. In my surrounding environment expressiveness and imagination were more a liability than an asset. I am not trying to enlist any sympathy by stating this, merely explaining a fact. I was no airy-fairy scholastic dreamer; on the contrary, bigger and stronger than most lads my age, I was a proficient swimmer and boxer, well able to take care of myself in a more than adequate manner. I lived in all, quite a rough and carefree existence, always ready to grasp any opportunity to make money, knowing every crease and wrinkle of Liverpool's streets. I made the most of life with little thought of the future, with no aspirations to becoming an author one day.

At the time it did not occur to me that we were poor, probably because never having been far outside of my environment, I had little idea of how better-off families lived. It was common knowledge among the kids of Kirkdale that wealthy people lived in one of three places: Buckingham Palace, out in the country, or in America. We knew because we had seen lots of feature films at the local movie houses.

Authors to me were dead men with impressive names, like Edgar Allan Poe, Sir Henry Rider Haggard, Robert Louis Stevenson, and Sir Arthur Conan Doyle. What room was there amid such illustrious personages for a Liverpool lad named Brian Jacques? The immortals who wrote literary tomes had never attended Saint

Johns Elementary School, Kirkdale. Besides, though I knew I was good at writing, the life of a pen pusher did not appeal to me. I wanted to be a sailor. Many Liverpool men followed the sea; it seemed a glamorous occupation from what I had read in books.

In the early 1950s circumstances dictated that on becoming fifteen, the boy became the man. It was the order of the day that you left school and helped support your family, usually by finding employment in some manual laboring job. Only if you were from a well-to-do family would your parents pay for further education—this was not the case with me. I bade a hasty farewell to Saint Johns and enlisted in the Merchant Marine as an A.B. (Able Bodied Seaman). It was hard, unprofitable, and not very romantic, with an all-pervading smell of fuel oil. Whatever happened to the palm-fringed coves, ancient temple bells at noontide, and distant sunkissed shores with mysterious names so prolific in the works of R.L. Stevenson and the poems of John Masefield? I suppose I am still sailing in search of them across the seas of my imagination.

Since then I have followed many different ways of making a living, jack-of-all-trades and master of none. Having no specialized skill or training in industry or commerce, I learned to duck and weave, go with the flow. Long-distance truck driver, policeman, construction worker, longshoreman, bus driver. . . . So many different jobs that now I have forgotten some of them. But through it all I still read insatiably, and wrote, just small things at my own personal whim, poems and prose, describing a place, person, or outlook. I was a student at the University of Life. What I value from those years are the characters, the faces, their attitudes and philosophies. Little did I suspect that one day they would be the grist to the mill of my books. Those people I worked side by side with, in the holds of ships, on the decks, on the building sites, in the warehouses, across the highways, and on the streets—both sides of the law sometimes—are the ones who abound in the pages of my works. I often wonder if the same wealth of humanity could have been observed had I gone on to further education. Would I have met them in the lecture halls of colleges or universities? I'll never know.

How strange it all seems now, being a middle-aged author, looking back over my shoulder at times past. Why should I, Brian Jacques, stand out as a man different from others of my social upbringing? A knockabout with no formal qualifications, not a single letter after my name. What magic was wrought to place my name in alphabetical order on library bookshelves with my heroes? Authors! The men and women who live forever through the works they created. I can only ascribe it to a number of influences, some lying dormant within me, awaiting the day they would be called upon.

Escapism was something I sought eagerly, the chance to be different. Never to be cataloged as a mere number in society, a face in the crowd, to see and learn of other horizons. Even today I long to be back in fabled times of romance and adventure, to transport myself awhile to some legendary age, where life was more simple and straightforward, where a person would be judged by basic tenets, outdated in the modern era. I become increasingly disenchanted with today's world of computerized technology. Some would say I am outdated, avoiding the age of software progress, but I prefer to think of myself as one who retains simplistic values, presuming everything reverts back to them in the final analysis.

It may sound slightly contradictory then to say that apart from books, the radio and cinema of the forties and fifties were an immense influence on my spirit. The movie palaces were an antidote, my bolthole from the depression of northwest England. Cocooned in warm darkness, I would be carried into realms of adventure, watching images, comical, sad, or stirring. From Robin Hood to the American Wild West, the Spanish Main to the Arabian Nights. While just beyond the exit doors Liverpool emerged from the Second World War—blitzed, rationed, unemployed, and squalid, in an age lost to the qualities of romance, where truth and loyalty together were pounded into the dust beneath the wheels of grim reality. Alas, there was little room for Sinbad the Sailor, Kit Carson, Captain Blood, or Richard the Lionheart amidst the debris of bomb-scarred docklands created by the juggernauts of twentieth-century warfare.

When there was no money available for cinematic safaris, and when my ingenuity at devising ways of stealing in to movies was exhausted, I loved listening to radio. Before the advent of television every home had its "wireless," a marvelous medium of information and entertainment. I recall winter evenings and rainy afternoons spent sitting by a coal fire's glow, listening to stories and plays unfold from the radio, voices relating tales, painting vivid pictures in my mind. Radio is the perfect vehicle for anybody with a spark of imagination. I have worked for many years as a presenter and broadcaster for BBC Radio Herseyside. I have no real need to at present, but I do it because I have a great regard and fondness for radio. Properly presented, it has a quality and enchantment of its own, sadly misused in today's commercial climate. I learned a lot from radio and am convinced that present and future generations could profit from its resurgence as an art form.

Music is my other grand passion. I feel I could not live without it, and my love for it is boundless. My tastes range from opera and symphony to folk music and golden-oldies nostalgia. There is a rich heritage of Celtic folk music in my family, and I have written many contemporary folk songs and made my living for a number of years as a professional folksinger/poet. Even as I write verse for my books, the music for couplets springs unbidden into my mind. I can recall every piece of music I have ever written, for books, stage plays, television, and radio plays. It was through writing music, monologues, and poems that I got my first real start as a writer, performing in folk clubs, being invited to take part in radio broadcasts, and finally getting a small piece in print with a university magazine. My early works were a mixture of comedy and social comment, designed to keep a smile on the face of the listener, while railing against government, working conditions, and the establishment with a healthy Liverpool Socialist disregard of sacred cows. In the late sixties I was approached by a small local publisher who invited me to compile my works into a slim volume. I was honored and delighted, more so when they agreed to pay me a minimal honorarium!

I realized that I had the talent to write things down that people would pay for the privilege of reading. I won't say that the money didn't matter; it did, because I was still a poor man, having been recently laid off when the firm I was driving a truck for had to close down. But what mattered more was the fact that I was now viewed as a serious writer, a professional!

The book was called *Get Yer Wack!* a Liverpool colloquialism meaning "make sure you get all that's due to you." It was an instant success throughout the region, being reprinted several times and having the dubious honor of being the most stolen book from the university bookshops; evidently the students showed good taste. Over the next decade six other books followed, all slim efforts, selling equally well, and all liberally salted with barbed comments on the injustices of the system. I was a protestor with some justification. I knew the dejection of spirit and mind that envelopes the unemployed, having been thrown out of work several times when companies folded. Even now the specter of being just another jobless statistic stands out starkly in my memory. Having a wife and two small sons to support and the rent to pay is no joke when faced with redundancy. (*Redundant* is the term used in Britain for being forcibly made unemployed.)

But life went on and so did Brian Jacques. I could duck and weave because I learned in a hard school, The University of Life. Though now I had an independent talent to utilize, and I did. Folksinger, radio broadcaster, raconteur, playwright (I was appointed writer-in-residence to the Everyman Liverpool Theatre for a year in 1981), I was also a columnist for a local newspaper, poet, after-dinner speaker, and part-time actor. Still, virtually speaking, a jack-of-all-trades and master of none, spread too thin along a wide front. Part of the reason being that it was difficult to break through the establishment, with my background and working-class attitudes. The inner circles viewed me for the most part with that lofty disdain they reserve for the self-educated, whose only qualification is the belief in their own ability. I realize now that I wasted a lot of valuable time in anger and frustration. At a certain point in my life I felt as if I was running on the spot and getting nowhere, with no goal in sight.

Then in 1983 I wrote *Redwall*. I had gained an amount of recognition in Liverpool and the County of Merseyside through my appearances as an entertainer and radio personality. I had also adopted a charity and was actively fundraising as a patron of the Royal School for the Blind in Wavertree (a Liverpool district). During the course of my visits to the school I became very friendly with both the staff and children. Often I would read fairy tales to the young ones, who sat riveted, listening eagerly to my every word. One day, having no immediate project to interest me, I decided to write a story to read to these blind children. But what kind of story? I thought back to the tales that had enchanted me as a youngster, yarns of high adventure and derring-do, which took place in far-off sunny lands, with heroes and villains, bravery and treachery, humor and pathos. A good old-style narrative of the sort that had been set aside for trendier subjects, such as modern-day teenage angst and junior science fiction. Would the child of today be interested in a timeless romance? I decided to put my theory to the test.

So, I bought three lined and margined office account books and six cheap ballpoint pens. It proved to be an investment I have never regretted. I chose to people my story with animals, because they are more readily identifiable to young minds. All through the old-world folktales and legends we see the sly fox, the slippery snake, the dirty rat, weasels, stoats, and ferrets—all identified as vermin, ready-made villains. Alternately the heroes and heroines would be the small and seemingly harmless creatures—mice, moles, squirrels, and hedgehogs—with protected and hunted species like badgers and otters as their friends. I deliberately used creatures native to the British Isles, animals that I have some knowledge of, much to the chagrin of certain young Texas readers, who are still awaiting the appearance of armadillos and rattlers. I avoided using creatures not from my country; there is too wide a diversity of species, and it would tend to complicate my story lines, which any reader will tell you are complicated enough by the fact that in any given plot I seem to have a dozen balls in the air together.

Definitely not any modern-day scenario inhabited by humankind, the place I chose was a nebulous medieval setting. This in itself limited the parameters of weaponry and dress (though sometimes the garb of certain characters could run from seventeenth-century corsair to Victorian military regalia). Armaments are firmly pretechnology; bows, arrows, spears, slings, swords, and knives being pretty much the limit. All in all, I was aiming for simplicity, resisting death lasers and jet-driven vehicles. The plot too was basic: an abbey (Redwall) inhabited by peace-loving creatures, threatened by evil vermin. Unskilled in the art of war, the Redwallers have to defend their home against a tide of villainous invaders who will stop at nothing.

There the simplicity ended. Caught up in the throes of my imagination, the plot spread and diversified. I had to keep a separate notepad so I could chart the demise of protagonists on both sides, work out and solve riddles, and rewrite rhyming verses until satisfied with their scansion. Then I began putting in the real characters I had met, giving them animal bodies. The longshoreman's union membership became shrews (G.U.O.S.I.M. Guerilla Union of Shrews in Mossflower). I gave a hare the characteristics of an old boss I had worked for (Basil Stag Hare. "Wot, wot? Absolutely jolly old chap!"). Truck drivers, cops, priests, teachers, seamen, school pals, even relatives, began popping up throughout my manuscript in various animal guises. I knew each of them well and could write about them with some authority. I made use of names by rearranging them in anagram forms, so they became other names. I love to play with words and especially delight in thinking up riddles, which I am sure my young readers enjoy solving or watching them be solved by the young heroes and heroines they like to identify with. I am a natural mimic and fond of regional accents; therefore, each group of characters had to have their own dialect, a lot of it picked up on my travels as a truck driver. Moles speak as old folk of Somerset (burr, oi, oo and arr, very bucolic and quaint). Otters have a nautical flavor of Merchant Marine (Ay matey). Snakes speak with a sibilance (sssooundsss like thissss!). Some of the dialects are invented, some taken from life.

Chapters I like to keep short and punchy to hold the reader's attention. They are much akin to my heritage of the Saturday afternoon movie serials—keeping the pot boiling by alternating the action between two factions. There is trouble at the abbey; the villains are tunneling in, unbeknownst to the Redwallers who are fighting off a diversifying attack. . . . Meanwhile in another part of the woodlands, our young hero, who is lost, has fallen from the rafters of an old barn right toward the gaping mouth of a huge cat! Back to the abbey and the tunnel plot. . . . Now read on!

Food plays a major part in my books too. Having survived a fairly frugal childhood and postwar rationing, I want to know what my characters like to eat. Simple! They dine on all the things I imagine a young person (and many an older one too by the mail I receive) would enjoy eating. When I read a book in my young days, I always felt frustrated. If the brave companions were given a royal banquet by the king, after which they sallied forth refreshed, what did they eat? Did it look nice? How did it taste and smell? Was there an ample sufficiency? So in my books I create basically simple but delicious fare, and then I tell the reader what fun and enjoyment our heroes had in consuming it. I relate the fare in fine detail, hoping that mouths will water in anticipation of the feast to come. The food and the preparations are all important to me. When I lecture in schools the kids eulogize about Redwall fare at question time.

Old fashioned as ever, I hold that any story must have a beginning, a middle, and an end. There must be nothing worse for youngsters than to finish a story wondering why or how or what really happened. I aim to give my readers a sense of continuity with no grey areas and at the conclusion, a feeling of enjoyment, sadness, or triumph with no puzzlement. I think that clouded conclusions and muddled middles are the fastest route to turning a young mind to TV and electronic games.

It is also my opinion that as an author I have moral obligations to young readers. There is a lot of talk about analyzing text and "reading between the lines," hidden messages and "what the author really means by. . . ." I resolved at the outset that no child would have to read between the lines of my work. The message is clear. There are no schizophrenic goodies and sympathetic baddies; no matter how long it takes and how hard the struggle, good defeats evil! My young animal heroes and heroines are sympathetic to young readers; they are small and inexperienced. But they learn the lessons of fortitude and courage, not by the aid of magic or technology, but by conquering self-doubt and fear, relying on their own willpower, pulling themselves up—literally by their own bootstraps—until they emerge as warriors. Not in any martial arts or Hollywood sense, but as creatures of strong moral fiber and good character, whom their peers can look up to and trust as true friends.

On the issue of violence. Yes, my books do contain the violence of death and war to a degree. So do the Bible and many, many other classics of real literature; life itself is a struggle for people the world over, throughout all the ages. Violence must not be gratuitous; sometimes a villain may kill another seemingly needlessly, but the writer's intention is to show the reader how wicked that villain is, what a thoroughly bad creature the peaceful ones are up against. What will happen to them if they do not have the courage to face up to such a villain? Often I have children who write to tell me that they were saddened by the death of a good or friendly creature; why did they have to die? I tell them that life and death are part of proper stories, the spirit of the good lives on through those they have touched, and we hold them dear in memory. Spring comes again, the earth flourishes and puts forth its abundance, young ones are born; we hope they will become good enough in time to replace those who are gone. Every life has its preordained and alloted span. Only in fairy-tale nursery books does everyone live happily ever after.

It took me six months to write *Redwall*, my first full-length novel. Then my life changed completely when fate took a hand. By a very fortunate accident, an old friend and mentor (Alan Durband, a widely published translator of Shakespeare for schools) borrowed my *Redwall* manuscript to read while on vacation. He enjoyed the tale so much that he sent it to his publishers (without my knowledge). They in turn appreciated it (with certain reservations) and called on me to make minor corrections—some of which I agreed to, others I flatly refused. Luckily they respected my views, and we reached a mutual compromise. A year later in 1984 *Redwall* was published. I had done it, Brian Jacques, an author!

Since then I have gone on to write other books, all well received as best-sellers, the original work having expanded into two Redwall trilogies, with a book of short ghost stories for the young in-between. I have won awards throughout the world, though the greatest award for me is to see a long line of children eagerly waiting to chat with me and have their books signed.

Reviewers have been extra kind when writing their summaries and penning lengthy critiques of my books, many of them taking pains to explain that a reader does not have to read Brian Jacques' works in sequence; they are not numbered Redwall 1-2-3 (perish the thought!) but can be picked up in any order and treated as a full story from beginning to end. I always thought it a bit of a swizz, making poor readers feel as if they are obliged to buy books three and four to have the complete set.

Awards and good reviews are all very nice, but to me it is the reader who matters in the end. I spend several months of each year lecturing in schools on both sides of the Atlantic, questioning and listening to my young readers. It is their opinions, and not that of judging panels and magazine critics, that really matter to me. The children always write or ask personally, "Brian, are you going to write more books about Redwall, Mossflower, and Martin?" My answer remains the same: "You keep reading and enjoying books, and I'll keep on writing them for you!" Secretly, it is also myself I write the books for. It is my escape from the modern world to retreat with pen and paper, or my huge old manual typewriter, round to the back of my garden in Liverpool (not far from my old neighborhood of Kirkdale). There I can transport myself from everyday cares for three months and go to live in the timeless places of the faraway long-ago world I created. It is therapy for my soul, and the spirits of my readers too I hope. I am especially delighted that I have captured the imagination of American children—America, land of my childhood movie yearnings. I travel there twice yearly now, thanks to my U.S. publishers and in particular to a lady named Patricia Lee Gauch, who had the foresight and spirit to believe in my work. (She is now a mouse scurrying through the pages of a certain Brian Jacques tale under an assumed name, with many other good pals I made along the way.)

I am completely happy and satisfied in what I do now. Author! A thirty-year overnight success. This is the first time I have committed my thoughts openly for others to read. I would not have been ready to admit these feelings publicly in former years, because where I come from they would have classed me as odd, or vulnerable in some fashion. So I kept it all inside, walking to the beat of my own drum. Now my attitudes have softened somewhat. I show more of my private face, particularly to children when I am lecturing, and it is gratifying to see their responses. Only infrequently do I find myself reverting to former feelings, mainly when in the company of pseudo-intellectuals and skeptics with patronizing attitudes. In a way I suppose I still wear my working-class heart on my sleeve for all to see, because I am not ashamed of my roots and I feel secure within myself. The worst kind of pretense to me is trying to be something, or somebody, that you are not. If I did this, I know that sooner or later folk would see through the deception; then I would feel diminished as a human being in their eyes, and more so in my own estimation.

What do I want from the future? What any good author wants I suppose—to leave footprints in the sands of time. By that I mean, in years to come when I am no longer here, some child will take from a library shelf a dog-eared book of mine, without an attractive dust jacket, and read it with enjoyment. How presumptious of me! That sort of thing just does not happen to someone with a name like Brian Jacques, who attended Saint Johns Elementary School in Kirkdale, Liverpool.

SIXTEEN

"Once They All Believed in Dragons"

Susan Hepler

The title of this article comes from Jack Prelutsky's marvelously varied collection of dragon poems, *The Dragons Are Singing Tonight* (1993):

Once they all believed in dragons
When the world was fresh and young,
We were woven into legends,
Tales were told and songs were sung,
We were treated with obeisance,
We were honored, we were feared,
Then one day they stopped believing—
on that day, we disappeared. (39)

Until recently, humankind did believe in dragons of one sort or another. It was probably with the advent of Mary Anning's uncovering of dinosaur skeletons in the first quarter of the 1800s that evidence finally buttressed our disbelief in dragons. Then humans had the scientific wherewithal to separate fact from fantasy, and dragons fell into disfavor as our fascination with dinosaurs and the proofs offered by scientists against dragons grew.

All along, though, dragons have been kept alive in children's literature in such classic works as Kenneth Grahame's *The Reluctant Dragon* (1938), J. R. R. Tolkien's *The Hobbit* (1938), Ruth Stiles Gannett's trilogy beginning with *My Father's Dragon* (1948), C. S. Lewis' *The Voyage of the "Dawn Treader"* (1962), Rosemary Sutcliff's *Tristan & Iseult* (1971), and Margaret Hodges' *Saint George and the Dragon* (1984). Dragons continue to appear in fantasy novels, lately in folklore with Asian anteced-ents, and in children's picture books as domesticated household pets. Whether we treat dragons with respect due them or declaw them for youngsters, it is almost as if we can't bear to let go of such an ancient symbol, this mighty sign of danger, cunning, greed, old wisdom, and power.

Where do dragons come from in our literature? Where might they have originated in reality? Where in the literature of childhood have they gone? What roles do dragons play in the stories in which they appear? And why, after all these years of storying, do dragons persist?

Old Dragons

A good place to start is *Dragons: Truth, Myth, and Legend* (1993) in which David Passes presents various dragon myths and legends from around the world. One of the oldest dragon stories, which may be traced back to Babylonia in the age of King Hammurabi or about 1900 B.C., depicts the battle between the powerful god Marduk and the dragon Tiamat, the female spirit of salt water and chaos. It was from Tiamat's split body that the victorious Marduk made heaven and earth. "And so order was made from chaos and the world was formed" (Passes 1993, 10–11; Hamilton 1988, 79–85). An Egyptian tale explained the sun's passage by telling how Ra, Lord of the Sky, sails from east to west across the celestial waters and is threatened by the dragon serpent Apep (Hogarth 1979, 26). Each evening Ra must fight back the powers of darkness and disorder that Apep (or Apophis) represents (Hamilton, 111–15).

The Greek myths tell of dragons named and unnamed. Cadmus slew a golden dragon, planted its teeth, and watched armed men arise from the ground. He set them upon each other and convinced the survivors to follow him in founding Thebes. A dragon guarded the Golden Fleece. As one labor, Hercules was sent to fetch the golden apples of the Hesperides guarded by a hundred-headed dragon (Low 1985, 105). For another, he killed the Hydra, a nine-headed dragon with poisonous breath, by cutting off the eight mortal heads, cauterizing each neck so that the head could not grow back, and then burying the severed immortal ninth one (Low, 97). Hercules later dipped his arrows in the Hydra's blood to make them poisonous, but this same blood, permeating a deadly shirt, became the cause of his death.

Serpentlike dragons were part of ancient explanations for the world's beginning. They came from before human time. They were often guardians of something a human needed in order to prove or improve himself. A puny ancient human alone might yet conquer one of these fearsome beasts with trickery, talismen, or good advice, thereby proving that size alone does not determine power.

Where Did Dragons Originate?

Most people agree that dragons never existed. A notable exception is Peter Dickinson who presents in *The Flight of Dragons* (1979) a well-reasoned and entirely plausible science. While the book looks like a coffee-table book for adults, children aged ten and over have been drawn to its lavish illustrations by Wayne Anderson and to its format, which includes numerous charts, graphs, and diagrams giving the book the familiar look of nonfiction. Dickinson suggests that in order to fly, the dragon possessed a digestive system including acid glands that continually reacted with its calcium bone structure to produce a gaseous self-supporting body in air. Naturally, its blood would dissolve metal or burn human skin; naturally, flame, heat, and dreadful breath would be a by-product of this internal combustion. Interspersed with outtakes from famous dragon stories, this book also answers such questions as to why we haven't discovered dragon hoards of jewels and gold or the fossil remains of these behemoths. Dickinson triangulates the true nature of dragons from a variety of stories asserting that

> no singular quotation carries much weight, but taken all together they build up a remarkably consistent picture, not only where they agree with each other, but also in the odd detail which nobody else has thought of but which still fits in. (132)

Another person fascinated with dragons is Avram Davidson who, in *Adventures in Unhistory* (1993), which is aimed at adult science-fiction readers, traces the possible paths humans may have taken to discover and believe in such mythical beasts as the phoenix, the basilisk, and the dragon. Like Dickinson, he cites ancient accounts to pull together a composite description of a dragon: "carbuncles" or jewels in its head; lives near and poisons water; guardian; terrible breath like noxious smoke; and so forth. By a series of interlocking and overlapping information, Davidson settles on the crocodile as the ancient's dragon. He discusses the fact that crocodiles swallow stones for keeping themselves in the water and that if their bodies decompose, the stones are nonetheless left. They may give off a vapory bad-smelling musk; they generally live near water into which anything ventures at its peril and when in the wild, dig a small cavelike depression. Davidson also discusses the possibilities that the ancients might actually have seen crocodiles in the areas in which dragon-bearing Greek myths occurred. So the dragon may not be an entire invented or imagined creature but one that began in reality and became embroidered over with our storying and our needs.

There are at least two distinct kinds of dragons: those emanating from Western tradition, and those that spring from Chinese traditions. Both kinds of dragons are found in literature for children.

Western Dragons

The Norse dragon Fafnir is typical of the Western dragons we have come to know. Fafnir guarded treasure stolen from dwarfs, giants, and others and lived in a cave. Sigfried (or Sigurd as he is called in some versions) slayed the dragon with advice from the Norse god Odin disguised as an old man. When he accidentally tasted some of the juices from Fafnir's cooked heart, he could understand the language of birds. From them, he discovered that if he ate the dragon's heart, he would acquire wisdom (Passes 1993, 18–19). Norse mythology also includes a dragon Nidhogg that gnaws at the roots of Yggdrasil, the world tree (D'Aulaire 1967, 50).

Other Western dragons include British ones such as the Lambton worm or wyrm, which was caught by John de Lambton who had skipped church to go fishing (Aylesworth 1980, 24–28; Passes 28–29). When he threw it into a well, it grew to such alarming size that it took up residence on a rock in the middle of a river and carried off animals, killed people, and uprooted trees. People even set out milk to calm its angry nature or distract it from more substantial human fare. Lambton eventually was able to kill the wyrm by promising to kill the next thing he saw after this dangerous deed. The next, however, was his father, whom Lambton could not kill, so the next nine heads of the house met violent deaths. A river-dwelling dragon very much like this wyrm appears in Janina Domanska's version of a Polish folktale, *King Krakus and the Dragon* (1979). This dragon is tricked by a lowly shoemaker who stuffs a false ram with sulphur and tar, which, when eaten, causes the thirsty dragon to drink until he bursts.

Perhaps the best known of traditional Western dragons is the one slayed by the English Saint George. Various versions of this story are told. One set in Eastern Turkey tells that George was a Roman soldier who protested the emperor's decree that all Christians must die by donning a suit of silver armor and a cross to seek adventure and spread the faith. This George found a dragon existing on sacrificed children, the last of which to be sacrificed was the king's own daughter. When George killed the dragon, the whole region was baptized into the Christian faith for which George was made a saint eight hundred years later (Passes 1993, 24–27; Aylesworth 1980, 20–24).

Margaret Hodges's version of *Saint George and the Dragon* (1984) is taken from Edmund Spenser's *Faerie Queen*. Trina Schart Hyman's Caldecott award-winning illustrations set this version in the fourth century rather than Spenser's Elizabethan times because she wished to depict the age when Christianity and pagan beliefs vied for possession of people's souls. Her borders depict this metaphorically with alternating pages framed with red-winged angels (red was the color of medieval royalty) or with spiky naked blue-winged fairies. Herbs of the times also enrich the borders with reference and allusion. For instance, on the page where the dragon carries off George, Agrimony, which is a charm against serpents or a cure for snakebite, frames the upright borders ("A Guide to the Flowers and Herbs Shown in the Borders of *Saint George and the Dragon*"). This horrible and terrible dragon features great clawed wings and elbows, red eyes, huge tooth-ridden jaws, spines, scales, fiery breath, and a bellow, "the like was never heard before" (19). By conquering it, George frees the countryside, brings Christianity to the people, and wins a wife, depending on how one reads the story.

So here, then, are an assortment of Western dragons. They are variously possessed of fiery breath; corrosive, poisonous or magical blood; lizardlike scales; claws; a forked tongue; the power of flight; long tails; and fierce roars. They dwell in caves or near bodies of water and feed on milk, cattle, children, and princesses. They represent chaos and disorder and wherever they are present evil results. Humans must conquer the dragon by facing the mighty power with their own poor talents, which, nonetheless, prove to be enough.

Eastern Dragons

Chinese dragons were first noted in about 1600 B.C. Like the naga, a creature of the Buddhist tradition from which the Eastern dragon may have stemmed, Chinese dragons were found near rivers, lakes, or the sea and could deliver rain or cause droughts. Like the Indian nagas, they carried a pearl of great worth, usually in their throats or under their chins. The pearl was able to bestow great fecundity upon whatever it touched or whoever possessed it. Four kinds of dragons, or *lung*, each had different responsibilities such as bringing rain, guarding hidden treasures, or holding up the mansions of the gods (Passes 1993, 42). Only very old dragons (of about three thousand years) became *ying-lung*, or winged dragons (Hogarth 1979, 49–53), a distinct difference from Western dragons that usually could fly. Neither did Chinese dragons breathe fire.

Eastern dragons were able to transform themselves into different shapes, often into young girls or old men. Jay Williams used this fact as the basis for his story *Everyone Knows What a Dragon Looks Like* (1976), one of the first children's books to depict Eastern dragons. Written before it became important that a tale be given its proper sources, footnotes, or provenances, this book was one of the first to introduce Western children to the Eastern dragon. In it, a fat old man with a white beard and bald head comes into the city following its prayers to the Great Cloud Dragon to help defeat the Mongol Wild Horsemen. A small boy is the only one who believes in the old man's assertion that he is a dragon. The boy treats the old man with respect and for his sake, the old man transforms into a dragon bringing a violent storm that blows the hoards away from the grateful city. Mercer Mayer's illustrations borrowed pictoral conventions from Chinese artwork in depicting trees, mountains, borders, and some incidental details, but his characters are pure Mayer-esque cartoons. Yet, in reading this book, children would discover facets to add to what they might already know about dragons, and the illustrations resonate with aspects of classical Chinese art.

What does an Eastern dragon look like? One of the most beautiful stories of the Eastern dragon is found in Julie Lawson's traditional tale of *The Dragon's Pearl* (1993), illustrated by Paul Morin. Lawson's afterword includes this description of a Chinese dragon:

> (He had) the head of a camel, the horns of a deer, the eyes of a rabbit, ears of a cow, neck of a snake, belly of a frog, scales of a carp, claws of a hawk, and soles of a tiger. His voice was like the jangling of copper pans. (30)

224

In Lawson's story, a poor boy from a drought-ridden area finds a dragon's pearl when he removes what he thinks is magic ever-growing grass to plant it on his own plot of land. When he and his mother hide the pearl in the near-empty rice jar, the jar overflows by morning. The pearl placed in their moneybox brings great wealth, which they share with the village, and all goes well until jealous neighbors attempt to rob them. The frightened boy pops the pearl into his mouth and is seared by an intense heat. Frantically, he drinks all the water in the house, rushes to the river and drinks it dry, and finally is transformed—into the dragon with the pearl embedded in his mouth. Julie Lawson's grace note to this tale is that the transformed boy returns, sometimes as a dragonfly, sometimes as the tinkling sound of water lapping on the shore. And he always brings this particular village rain. Paul Morin's highly textured paintings and collage textiles create an elegant setting for this traditional story, and his frequent use of gold echoes the fact that the dragon was the emblem of royalty. A person of great ability or courage was said to be dragonlike, the highest compliment one could pay another.

Another outstanding feature of Eastern dragons is their friendly and beautiful nature if revered by people. Temples and shrines have been built to honor them, usually along seashores and riverbanks. The Chinese name a year after dragons, and children born in the Year of the Dragon are said to enjoy health, wealth, and long life (Blumberg 1980, 30–31). These dragons are very fond of swallows and in some accounts, elephant meat. Chinese dragons dread iron, the centipede, the mong plant, and silk dyed in five different colors.

Dragons of all sorts have appeared in much of the world's traditional literature for well over three thousand years. These ancient characters have functioned symbolically in many ways and have endured to serve as foils for the honing of human knowledge. How do dragons fare in today's literature for children?

Dragons in Picture Books and Folktales

Dragons are alive and well in children's literature, especially in traditional folktales as we have seen. In picture books, however, they come in a variety of shapes, sizes, and powers. As one might expect, dragons in stories for the very youngest readers are usually household pets with only one or two of the distinguishing features outlined above. *The Dragon of an Ordinary Family* (Mahy 1992) shows what happens when a "fuddy-duddy" father brings home a pet dragon to his family. This one flies the family off to further adventures. In *The Magical Drawings of Moony B. Finch* (McPhail 1978), Moony discovers that he may need to sketch in just a little smoke and fire from his hand-drawn dragon pet that comes alive, in order to scare away his greedy neighbors. Books such as these often introduce young children to the character of a dragon but with few of its literal or metaphorical teeth.

Val Willis in *The Secret in the Matchbox* (1988) gives readers a little more to think about when a boy brings something to school in a matchbox. Readers don't know what it is except that Bobby is sure it will cause trouble, which it does when the tiny dragon escapes into the classroom. This dragon is able to grow suddenly, and soon its steamy breath has overheated the room, its wings are flopping over the desk tops, and its flight creates a maelstrom in the room. In true picture-book fashion, the adult does not notice until the end what the class has known all along—Bobby did have a secret and that it was indeed a dragon. John Shelley's paintings of school life are bordered by an ever-increasing complication of children's mischief and designs that gradually resemble Celtic knots and medieval windows. Unlike the previous picture books, this depiction alludes to dragonly antecedants and pictorial conventions, and child readers would suspect that dragons come from somewhere, even if they were not sure where.

The Knight and the Dragon (1980) is Tomie De Paola's humorous pass at dragons in a medievel setting. In two parallel picture-story lines, a knight prepares to do battle by practicing, getting his equipment ready, and generally gearing up. Alternately, a dragon prepares in much the same way. When both finally meet in a disaster of broken spears and charred trees, they agree to be friends. The ending pictures show the medieval hamburger stand with the dragon's breath frying the meat while the aproned knight serves the customers. Very young readers might see, however thinly, the connection between dragons, knights, and the Middle Ages.

This pacifist theme is not new: Kenneth Grahame's *The Reluctant Dragon* (1938), written two years after Munro Leaf's story of the peace-loving bull Ferdinand (1936), is another classic story to emerge following the Spanish Civil War. In this parody, a peaceful erudite dragon and a small boy conspire with an old St. George to stage a battle that the townspeople clamor for. When the dragon begrudgingly agrees that this is the only way to stop the hysteria, St. George warns the dragon that he will have to hold up his end:

> "I mean ramping, and breathing fire, and so on!"
> "I can *ramp* all right," replied the dragon, confidently; "as to breathing fire, it's surprising how easily one gets out of practice; but I'll do the best I can." (36)

When the fight is over, everyone is satisfied, and all adjourn to the village hall for refreshments, it is the dragon who charms everyone with his witty conversation. This novel has long endured as a humorous riposte to those who love a fight for a fight's sake.

Some of the same ground is covered, but for an audience even younger than those who appreciate *The Story of Ferdinand* and *The Reluctant Dragon*, in Margaret Shannon's *Elvira* (1993). This female dragon prefers dressing up and playing with daisy chains to eating princesses. After she is teased, she runs away to join a group of princesses and in her disguise of beautiful clothes is nearly eaten by her father. While stories of this sort appeal to early elementary-age children, they may not recognize the dragon conventions that are being played with. And, of course, the whole humor of *The Reluctant Dragon* depends upon one's prior knowledge of the story of Saint George.

Eastern Dragons have fared very well in recent literature for children. Perhaps because previously our literature neglected so much of what Asian literature had to offer young readers, publishers have rushed to catch up. Rosalind Wang's *The Fourth Question* (1991) presents a wise dragon who gives good advice and relinquishes his pearl to a needy boy when he ascends to heaven. Darcy Pattison's *The River Dragon* (1991) begins with a note about true Chinese dragons and presents a story of a humble blacksmith who must cross the dragon's bridge each time he goes to visit his betrothed. He always leaves a bowl of rice at the bridge, but he is worried about recrossing it this time because he has eaten curried swallows at his future in-laws' house and is sure the river dragon Ti-Lung will now eat him because of its inordinate fondness for swallows. But the blacksmith has found a centipede and uses it to frighten the dragon. On the second occasion of being served swallows, he escapes by waving his betrothed's five-colored silk scarf. But on the third, he has nothing with which to fend off the dragon and, instead, uses the old trick of pointing out the moon's reflection in the river, which the poor-sighted dragon mistakes for "the giant mother pearl, the Night-Shining Pearl" (27). Pattison disagrees with Peter Hogarth's informative book in which it states that Chinese Dragons did indeed have very sharp eyesight (1979, 54). Nevertheless, this sortie ends with the poor blacksmith in possession of the river dragon's pearl and, hence, great wealth with which to marry. The illustrations by Jean and Mou-sien Tseng, originally from Taiwan, possess vibrant color and narrative quality, and their dragon is within the boundaries of the traditional Chinese dragon as described above by Lawson. Yet, it holds its pearl in its hind leg and possesses a kind of eager, humorous quality not seen in other more weighty Eastern dragon depictions. The reader is almost sorry to see this one done in.

Two literary rather than folktale treatments of the Chinese dragon are found in Margaret Leaf's *Eyes of the Dragon* (1987). The story is based on a legend of an itinerant painter who painted three dragons on the walls of a temple in the present-day city of Nanking. When the painter added eyes to one, it broke loose from the wall. The other two eyeless dragons remain on the temple walls to this day (2). Ed Young's brilliant pastel illustrations echo the text so that one can almost hear the thunder and the dragon's scream that "sounded like the striking together of two copper vessels" (29) as it ascends from the now-broken wall to the heavens. An afterword speaks to the artist's obligation to portray dragons according to certain ancient harmonious principles, ones that Ed Young, who is himself of Chinese ancestry, has seemed to follow.

The second literary tale is Deborah Nourse Lattimore's *The Dragon's Robe* (1990), which uses a twelfth-century background and the paintings of the Sung dynasties to present a story of a young weaver's saving of her people. When dishonest employees of the emperor refuse to honor the dragon shrine, disaster results until Kwan Yin weaves a beautiful silk robe and the spirit of the rain dragon fills it and defeats the enemy warriors who have invaded the land. Unlike Mercer Mayer's illustrations for *Everyone Knows What a Dragon Looks Like*, Lattimore's pictures show the research that went into them, and her foreword note explains her sources. These afterwords, notes, and explanations of sources are a welcome relief to those who wish to understand how literature links to literature. They are indispensable, too, for teachers who can decide how much of this information is worth using to help children discover these important links.

Dragons have become part of picture books for older children, as well. In Robert San Souci's *Young Merlin* (1990), readers are introduced to a small piece of Arthurian legend that explains, via incidents surrounding Vortegern's tower, how Arthur's sign came to be a red dragon. Rosemary Sutcliff's *The Minstrel and the Dragon Pup* (1993) introduces a concept not yet discussed, that of a dragon's egg origin and its ability to imprint to the first living thing it sees, in this case a medieval minstrel. This dragon is exploited by evildoers, however, before it is returned to its rightful "owner." Jane Yolen has made a career out of her dragon knowledge. In her illustrated story *Dove Isabeau* (1989), a beautiful girl is turned by her stepmother into a fire-breathing, man-eating dragon and is cursed to eat her former suitors until one dares to kiss her three times. The catch is that then the brave suitor will be turned to stone. This dragon, loathsomely depicted by Dennis Nolan, weeps red tears as she goes about her business. When she is at last freed, and her suitor returns to flesh and blood, she has become a woman full of "spirit and fire," beloved by her husband who can appreciate this fierce, mighty, and glorious dragon queen. Yolen is well known for giving girls strong and bold heroines that defy traditional categories.

Dragons in Full Glory: Fantasy Novels

Jane Yolen's interest in dragons has led her to produce a wealth of stories and poems relating to the topic. In her series beginning with *Dragon's Blood* (1982), she has imagined a planet where dragons are bred to fight in dragon pits. A teenaged boy, Jakkan, whose job is to clean out the stables where the dragons are kept, steals a dragon hatchling and trains it for a year. (A swear word in this culture is *Fewmets!*, an old word for beast or dragon droppings.) The dragon, called Heart's Blood, is imprinted to Jakkan, understands human speech, and communicates telepathically with the boy via colors. Dragons have been bred here for centuries but some are still subject to Fool's Pride, a wounded dragon's demand to be killed and the victorious dragon's irresistible urge to kill. A sampling of Yolen's dragon works may be found in *Here There Be Dragons* (1993), which includes a compelling chapter from this novel. She has also played with the notion of a dragon as an all-knowing guardian and teacher of wisdom in her story of young Arthur's training to be king in *The Dragon's Boy* (1990). In it, Merlin assumes some of the aspects of a dragon, creating a mechanical apparatus to mimic a dragon's leg and voice, with which he woos young Arthur into a cave on the moors. Here he teaches Arthur in conversation and examples that gradually turn Arthur's fear into love and respect when he eventually discovers who the dragon really is.

Like Yolen, Anne McCaffrey imagines a society in which dragons and humans are deeply intertwined. On Pern, the deadly Thread falls from the sky and only flying dragons with the guidance of dragonriders can destroy the Thread. The dragons do this by devouring firestone, which is dissolved by their acidic digestion, and by belching the resulting gas they can quench the Threadfall. *Dragonsong* (1976), McCaffrey's first story in her series, concerns a teenaged runaway girl named Menolly upon whom a clutch of firelizards imprints. Through her bonding with these hatchlings and her fierce independence, she is able to achieve her goal of being a harper and one of the first female dragonriders.

In the Enchanted Forests of Patricia Wrede's quartet beginning with *Dealing with Dragons* (1990), the dragon king Kazul lives. In this humorous fantasy, a princess who is bored with her palace existence apprentices herself to Kazul and becomes a sort of cook and hoard cataloguer until wicked wizards threaten to take over the forest domain of the dragons. Wrede's dragon world is orderly and uncomplicated: dragons congregate to elect a new leader when one dies, but they seem more like background to the story, which is full of sly references to folklore in general.

Laurence Yep's dragon fantasy series begins with *Dragon of the Lost Sea* (1982), in which the dragon clan's home has been drained by an evil sorceress. Shimmer, the dragon princess, disguises herself as a human but notes how itchy and uncomfortable it is to squeeze all that dragon bulk of over three meters into such a small shape. Yep's dragon is true in spirit to Eastern ones: Shimmer can transform and has other magical powers; she can fly but with wings, making her an ancient water dragon. Her clan and she maintained a social structure and lived and played in the inland sea until it disappeared. Like Kazul, Shimmer has a sense of humor and a not very high opinion of humankind. However, humankind comes through in the end, saving the dragons in one way or other.

Shirley Rousseau Murphy's trilogy beginning with *Nightpool* (1985) imagines a society in which people have forgotten what freedom is. It is only through a human bard who can communicate with the ancient singing dragons that freedom can be restored. Another teenaged boy, Tebriel, is the agent to bring this about. Murphy's dragons can change shape, bellow, and create stormy winds with the stirring of their wings. They can communicate telepathically with humans and can create powerful images in human minds of what life used to be before the darkness overtook them. Murphy's imagined world is complex with overlapping societies of unhappy humans, talking animals, minions of the dark, the dark lord himself, and the dragon society.

The most powerful dragons are those created by Ursula LeGuin in her "Earthsea" stories. In the first of the quartet, *A Wizard of Earthsea* (1968), the mage or wizard Ged has gone in a fit of despair and impatience, to face the dragons on the island of Pendor. Here, an old dragon and his nine dragonlings have taken up residence in the castle of a now-dead piratical king. Ged is able to kill several of the dragonlings who, at the length of a forty-oared ship, are small. He keeps calling for the great dragon when he becomes

> aware that the highest tower slowly changed shape, bulging out on one side as it grew an arm. He feared dragon-magic, for old dragons are very powerful and guileful . . . but a moment more and he saw that this was no trick of the dragon, but of his own eyes. What he had taken for a part of the tower was the shoulder of the Dragon of Pendor as he uncurled his bulk and lifted himself slowly up. (88–89)

The dragon knows the old speech, is well versed in trickery, and can freeze its prey by staring at it. He scorns Ged, calling him "little wizard," but Ged knows the dragon's true name of Yevaud, which gives him bargaining power. Ged demands not gold from the hoard nor information about himself that he is seeking but that Yevaud and the remaining dragonlings depart. In LeGuin's masterful fantasies, dragons are a part of the old magic, in a time before time, and as such they do not bother with humans except as food sources. In appearance, they seem much like Western dragons but, as the story says, "no song or tale could prepare the mind for this sight" (LeGuin 1968, 89).

Jane Yolen, in *Here There Be Dragons*, quotes Ursula LeGuin as saying that we shouldn't banish dragons from our stories, as some would do, because then we banish the possibility of Saint George (1993, 1). Children need examples of what happens when someone small stands up to evil powers because so many more of our children are living in situations where they need this ability. Humankind in general deals with powers that were unheard of in Mary Anning's day: nuclear physics, genetic engineering, environmental manipulation, to name a few. Whether we recognize these powers by their true names and are able to use them for good or evil is one of the major questions for the next century. Jack Prelutsky's poem cited at the beginning of this chapter ends with the dragon's cry:

> We must make them all remember,
> In some way we must reveal
> That our spirit lives forever—
> We are dragons! We are real! (1993, 39)

Readers who discover the true spirit of dragons, who understand this great character in all of its diversity, may be better armed both as readers of some of literature's great folklore and fantasy and as more courageous dwellers, prepared for life in the twenty-first century.

Professional References

DAVIDSON, AVRAM. 1993. *Adventures in Unhistory: Conjectures on the Factual Foundations of Several Ancient Legends.* Philadelphia: Owlswick Press.

DICKINSON, PETER. 1979. *The Flight of Dragons*. Illustrated by Wayne Anderson. New York: Harper & Row.

———. 1993. "Masks." *The Horn Book Magazine* 69 (2).

"A Guide to the Flowers and Herbs Shown in the Borders of *Saint George and the Dragon*." 1984. Boston: Little, Brown.

HOGARTH, PETER, and VAL CLEARY. 1979. *Dragons*. New York: Viking.

Children's Literature

AYLESWORTH, THOMAS G. 1980. *The Story of Dragons and Other Monsters*. New York: McGraw-Hill.

BAUMGART, KLAUS. 1993. *Where Are You, Little Green Dragon?* New York: Hyperion.

BLUMBERG, RHODA. 1980. *The Truth about Dragons*. Illustrated by Murray Tinkleman. New York: Four Winds.

D'AULAIRE, INGRI, and EDGAR PARIN. 1967. *Norse Gods and Giants*. New York: Doubleday.

DE PAOLA, TOMIE. 1980. *The Knight and the Dragon*. New York: Putnam.

DOMANSKA, JANINA. 1979. *King Krakus and the Dragon*. New York: Greenwillow.

GANNETT, RUTH STILES. 1986. *My Father's Dragon*. Illustrated by Ruth Chrisman Gannett. New York: Random House.

GRAHAME, KENNETH. 1938. *The Reluctant Dragon*. Illustrated by Ernest H. Shepard. New York: Holiday House.

HAMILTON, VIRGINIA. 1988. *In the Beginning: Creation Stories from Around the World*. Illustrated by Barry Moser. San Diego: Harcourt Brace & Jovanovich.

HODGES, MARGARET, reteller. 1984. *Saint George and the Dragon*. Illustrated by Trina Schart Hyman. Boston: Little, Brown.

LATTIMORE, DEBORAH NOURSE. 1990. *The Dragon's Robe*. New York: HarperCollins.

LAWSON, JULIE, reteller. *The Dragon's Pearl*. Paintings by Paul Morin. New York: Clarion.

LEAF, MARGARET. 1987. *Eyes of the Dragon*. Illustrated by Ed Young. New York: Lothrop, Lee & Shepard.

LEAF, MUNRO. 1936. *The Story of Ferdinand*. Illustrated by Robert Lawson. New York: Viking.

LEGUIN, URSULA K. 1968. *A Wizard of Earthsea*. Illustrated by Ruth Robbins. Emeryville, CA: Parnassus Press.

LEWIS, C. S. 1988. *The Voyage of the "Dawn Treader."* Illustrated by Pauline Baynes. New York: Macmillan.

LOW, ALICE. 1985. *The Macmillan Book of Greek Gods and Heroes*. Illustrated by Arvis Stewart. New York: Macmillan.

MCCAFFREY, ANNE. 1976. *Dragonsong*. Illustrated by Lynn Lydecker. New York: Macmillan.

MCPHAIL, DAVID. 1978. *The Magical Drawings of Moony B. Finch*. New York: Doubleday.

MAHY, MARGARET. 1992. *The Dragon of an Ordinary Family*. Illustrated by Helen Oxenbury. New York: Dial.

MURPHY, SHIRLEY ROUSSEAU 1985. *Nightpool*. New York: Harper & Row.

PASSES, DAVID. 1993. *Dragons: Truth, Myth, and Legend*. Illustrated by Wayne Anderson. New York: Artists and Writers Guild.

PATTISON, DARCY. 1991. *The River Dragon*. Illustrated by Jean and Mou-sien Tseng. New York: Lothrop, Lee & Shepard.

PRELUTSKY, JACK. 1993. *The Dragons Are Singing Tonight*. Illustrated by Peter Sis. New York: Greenwillow.

SAN SOUCI, ROBERT D. 1990. *Young Merlin*. Illustrated by Daniel Horne. New York: Doubleday.

SHANNON, MARGARET. 1993. *Elvira*. New York: Ticknor & Fields.

SUTCLIFF, ROSEMARY. 1993. *The Minstrel and the Dragon Pup*. Illustrated by Emma Chichester Clark. Cambridge, MA: Candlewick.

———. [1971] 1993. *Tristan & Iseult*. New York: Farrar Sunburst.

TOLKIEN, J. R. R. [1938] 1984. *The Hobbit*. Illustrated by Michael Hague. Boston: Houghton Mifflin.

WANG, ROSALIND C., reteller. 1991. *The Fourth Question: A Chinese Tale*. Illustrated by Ju-Hong Chen. New York: Holiday House.

WILLIAMS, JAY. 1984. *Everyone Knows What a Dragon Looks Like*. Illustrated by Mercer Mayer. New York: Four Winds.

WILLIS, VAL. 1988. *The Secret in the Matchbox*. Illustrated by John Shelley. New York: Farrar Straus & Giroux.

WREDE, C. PATRICIA. 1990. *Dealing with Dragons*. San Diego: Harcourt Brace & Jovanovich.

YEP, LAURENCE. 1982. *Dragon of the Lost Sea*. New York: HarperCollins.

———. 1993. *Dragon's Gate*. HarperCollins.

YOLEN, JANE. 1982. *Dragon's Blood*. New York: Delacorte.

———. 1989. *Dove Isabeau*. Illustrated by Dennis Nolan. San Diego: Harcourt Brace & Jovanovich.

———. 1990. *The Dragon's Boy*. New York: Harper & Row.

———. 1993. *Here There Be Dragons*. Illustrated by David Wilgus. San Diego: Harcourt Brace & Co.

PART FIVE

Living in the Real World
of Children's Books

In the last section we hear from three elementary teachers, a children's bookstore owner, and an elementary school librarian. All five writers live in the world of children's books. I believe the links between trends and issues in children's literature and the world of the people who teach, sell books, and choose books for libraries should be discussed by vital voices. Sharon Scavone and John Milne, two fourth-grade teachers in upstate New York, have evolved a literature-based approach after many years of using basal readers in a frustrated fashion. Their experiences as teachers have been within a school system that is textbook based, like most school systems in the United States, yet Sharon and John became bored and frustrated over time with those materials and felt that children were not developing as lifelong readers. By reading professional materials and attending workshops these two teachers developed a reading-workshop approach to using literature in their classrooms. They do not have the support of a graduate program at a university, nor are they surrounded by literature-based classrooms or a district-wide policy that supports what they are doing. They are simply two teachers who decided that their students were not connecting with the world of reading. I find Sharon and John and teachers like them to be illustrative of what works with the educational system today. Like the Regie Routmans of the world, they are evolving as teachers and learners. Sharon may retire within a year, but says that she may have to hold off until she gets a chance to use some new books that she just bought. Teachers like Sharon and John are always tinkering with what they do, always experimenting with new ways of processing information. There is an excitement in their classrooms about learning.

Sally Oddi has been a bookseller in Columbus, Ohio, for over ten years. The knowledge, the choices, the sensitivity to a wide range of interests and objections are part of her daily world. Does she sell grocery-store books? Does she sell books about same-sex parents? Will you find Nancy Drew in her bookstore? How does she guide her buyers during the selection process? The bottom line is that she has to pay the rent and electricity bill. Are there compromises involved? What is her process of selection and guiding consumers who ask for her direction?

And lastly, Judy Morley, a third-grade teacher, and Sandra Russell, a school librarian, write about the unique links between them. They describe issues of censorship vs. selection in their roles as school librarian and teacher as well as the process of book selection for children in their school. What happens when a parent crosses out offensive passages in a book and demands that it be taken off the library shelves? They describe cases in which books lead to potentially explosive topics or situations. Like Shimmer suggests, books are untamed and once we release them we lose control over them. If this one school is an example of the kind of ongoing censorship that exists in this country, issues related to free speech become even more poignant. Morley and Russell conclude by talking about the impact of technology on the school library. They contend that technology is going to dramatically alter the way in which we connect with print in the not-so-distant future. Chilling words for book lovers.

SEVENTEEN

Let Us Read!
Two Teachers Look Back
at Fifty Years of Teaching

JOHN MILNE AND SHARON SCAVONE

Peareids, questin marks, commas and more
How have I goten into this bundle of bore?
Fantisey, mistry, rides in the sea
Thats more exciting than a spelling bee
rocketships, space shuttles trips to the moon
I hope we dont have to do worksheets soon
Airplaines helicopters things like that
Id love to have Beverly Cleary give me
a pat on the back!

Beth

I'd rather read about Crusoe
beat up on a cannibal or
how Mr. Hyde turned into an animal.
Sequence! Sequence! Sequence!
Verbs and nouns
I'd rather read about funny clowns
Jerry Spinelli and all that jazz! I'd
like to *read* teacher don't have a spazz!
From the *Mixed Up Files* of whatever
her name to people who have lots of fame!
Sinking, sinking in waters of *Treasure Island*
to books about the jungles of Thailand
Respond in writing bah-humbug! As
Ebineiser Scrooge would say, hec!

I'd rather read to my brat brother
who always gets his way! Legends,
magic, ooh I love that stuff!
There's no way I could ever get enough!
I wish I could run like Maniac
Magee to get away from all that work you see!

Jeff

Poems, fiction,
   mystery
These are the books
   for me
Black Beauty, Redwall
   are a ball!
dragons, Knights,
   castles bees
Let me read please
   please please!
War in space, a circus
   clowns
Let me read them or
   I'll frown
If you let me read alot
I'll *promise* I will
   never stop.

Daniel

Three fourth-grade students respond to Kalli Dakos' poem, "I Have No Time To Visit With King Arthur" with a plea for literature and the time to read it. The children's reactions represent two very different experiences to reading and the use of literature in the classroom. Over the years, we have had the opportunity to observe, to participate in, and to evaluate these two different approaches because we are both fourth-grade teachers and are in the process of evolving—as are our students (Weber 1989).

Why Literature?

We are both readers. Literature has always been a priority in our lives both professionally and personally, meeting our needs for information, recreation, and growth. Being life-long readers and realizing the value of literature, we finally asked ourselves several questions: Are we instilling this love for literature in our students? Are we preparing them to become life-long readers? What do *we* do when we share a book or an article with a friend or colleague?

The answers to these important questions have taken us on a journey of ups and downs, of trials and explorations, of failures and successes as we have tried to make literature available and meaningful to our students. Do children read? Yes, but what do they read and why do they choose what they do? Many children arrive in our classrooms on the first day of school with limited literature experience. They are familiar with basal readers and are quite competent "blank fillers." This trend is changing, to a certain degree, since our school district has adopted a "whole language" basal reading series that does not call for as many of these exercises. Exposure to various genres is also limited, and most children are unfamiliar with cooperative learning in groups.

An important ingredient in our reading program today is that the children are free to choose what they want to read. We have observed that given this freedom, our children will initially fall into two categories. Some respond with alacrity; they always have a book at hand, sometimes more than one! Others simply do not know what to do. They pick up a book one day, put it down and grab another. They just cannot connect with a book.

What also concerns us is that while there are many books available in a wide range of genres in our classrooms, many readers choose books from a very narrow range of topics or genres. Our students arrive in our classrooms very gender oriented— dragons, dinosaurs, sports, and adventure seem to be the boys' choices, while girls read series books, like *The Baby Sitters Club, Boxcar Children,* or the *American Girl* series. Favorite authors are also limited to a very few.

Why is this? We feel that the basal readers to which these children have been exposed are partly to blame. Basals are limited in scope and choice and do not provide motivation to read, especially since a large part of the program entails endless worksheets and exercises.

What other factors affect their choices? What do bookstores sell? What do parents and children buy? Go into a local mall to a chain bookstore and observe what is available—precisely the books that our children pull out of their book bags or desks!

How We Use Literature

What do we do to direct and guide our children in their choices of literature? How do we help them see the possibilities that exist in the wide range of genres, authors, and topics? How do we lead them into a meaningful dialogue about what they are reading? Response to literature is developmental; it involves a number of factors beyond a child's experience (Hornsby, Sukarna, and Perry 1988; Routman 1991). Therefore, we strive to create a classroom environment where children can be comfortable "discussing" literature. We do this by providing examples of questions to share with one another, and above all, we model this process.

Who are we? Two fourth-grade teachers who, several years ago, removed half of the movable walls between our classrooms. Teaching and learning has changed over the fourteen years that we have worked together, not only for our students, but also for us. Little by little we discovered that we were frustrated and, yes, bored with the burden of the endless repetitiveness of our lessons and the disjointed manner in which we were teaching, using district mandated textbooks for *every* subject. Armed with this mutual discovery, we began to "digest" as much of the current research and literature that we could find on this topic. We sought, experimented, and discarded lessons and activities that we observed were not meaningful or productive. Thwarted by what we saw, or didn't see, happening in our own school district, we attended a wide variety of workshops and seminars, visited classrooms in neighboring school districts, and finally co-chaired a workshop that attracted teachers from many school districts. This workshop was sponsored by the Greater Capital Region Teacher Center in Castleton, New York, and was designed for teachers to share current trends and issues, to broaden the scope of teaching and learning, and, most importantly, to offer support. As a result, central to our evolution has been how we perceive and use literature in the classrooms.

First, we expose the children to a variety of genres by reading aloud on a daily basis. Through this activity, we challenge and guide our students to see the characteristics of each piece of literature shared and also to connect the piece with other disciplines. Beginning in September, the first book we read aloud is *Indian in the Cupboard* by Lynne Reid Banks (1980). As we read and discuss the elements of fantasy found in Banks' novel, we learn about Little Bear, a fictitious and stereotyped Iroquois brave, who lived during the French and Indian War. The first fruits of reading aloud become evident implicitly when the children begin writing their individual stories. Some of the children's published works include such titles as *The Return of the Hawks, The Magic Leaf*, and *The Magic Teapot*. Out of forty-eight published books by November, eighteen titles are spin-offs from *The Indian in The Cupboard*.

To dovetail with our studies of Native Americans we next read *The Sign of the Beaver* by Elizabeth George Speare (1961). We compare this richly written historical fiction to *The Indian in the Cupboard*. We explore the concept of stereotypes. Many of our students cannot read these two books independently. By reading them aloud we make quality literature accessible to all of our readers. These experiences provide our students with a shared experience of exploring richly developed characters with many layers of meaning. Other genres we introduce include mystery, science fiction, poetry, biography, and informational books.

Teacher as Guide

Even with these varied purposes for literature in our classrooms, we often find it necessary to challenge or invite individuals to vary their reading choices, especially in the beginning of the year. For example, we observed that Tyler had a passion for dinosaurs—it permeated his reading, writing, and speaking. By the end of October he hadn't tried reading books on any other topic.

Oct. 26,1993

The book Jerassic Park was realy good And it was just like the movy. I hope they make a part two of Jurassic park and make a book out of it so I could read it.

Oct. 30,1993

The book *Dinosaur Hunters* told me alot about dinosaurs and dinosaur homes. I realy do want to be a paleontologist when I grow up. As you can see I am a dinosaur nut. I realy enjoyed reading this book.

November 1,1993

I just got done reading The news about Dinosaurs. I lernd a lot about dinosaurs, And the pictors wer so real. I looked like people took real pictors of dinosaurs! But thats inpoiball. It was realy a good book.

A simple suggestion was made in his reading log that he might like to try another type of book. The suggestion was not binding—it was merely an attempt to stretch Tyler as a reader.

November 2, 1993

Dear Tyler,

Thanks for writing. I sure can tell that you *love* dinosaurs and have become a dinosaur *expert*. What a great goal to be a paleontologist! Since you *are* our expert, how about taking a break and choosing a book from a different genre this time. Let me know what you decide.

Love,
Mrs. S

During the resulting oral book conference, Tyler agreed it was time for a change and settled on *Maniac Magee* by Jerry Spinelli (1990). He wrote: "I think I'll read *Maniac Magee* because I liked the sound of it when Scott told us about it during Object Share." We later found out from his mother that Tyler could relate to this book since he, himself, had once run away. By offering Tyler this simple invitation he decided to try another type of book. Several weeks later Tyler's journal entry supported that intervention.

November 19, 1993

Dear Mrs. Scavone,

The book Maniac Magee was the best book I have read this year. Its about this boy named jefry magee. He is an orofin. He meets this girll named amanda and he thinks shes running away too becus she has a soutcase in her hand. So he goes up to her and askes her if she is running away. She started to gigle. Jeffry askes why. She sead shes not running away shes going to school. He bages her to give him a book. Finely she gives him a book. He sead he would reatern it as soon as he could. Jeffry gorded the book with all his life. But this kid caled mars bar sead it was his.

And he tries to rip it out of his handes. Instead he riped a page out of it. A fue days after Mars bar got all his friends together to get the book, but amanda stopes him. Amanda brings Jeff to her house. When Amandas father trise to bring him home Jeff ses this is the plase, but the hous was full of black people. And thats how they find out he was a orofin. So Jeffry got to live with Amanda and her family. If you want to here the rest of the story you will have to read the book. This book mad me feel sad, Hapy, and angry. But still it was a vary goud book.

Tyler

P.S. I'm gonna read a book about whales next.

We were excited with Tyler's written and oral responses to *Maniac Magee* and delighted that his next selection was on the topic of whales. Tyler still has a passion for dinosaurs but has begun to branch out as a reader.

Reading Workshop

As part of our literature program we also provide a framework for children to talk to us and to their peers in both oral and written contexts about the books they have read. We call this framework Reading Workshop (Weber 1989). One of the weekly highlights of this workshop is what is referred to as Object Share. The point of this activity, however, is not to dwell on the object but to use the object to stimulate a point of discussion about the literature children are presently reading. From the moment our students arrive on Object Share day the room is abuzz as the children chatter about where to hide their objects. They don't want anyone to see what they've brought in and consequently, the suspense builds as the day moves forward. We are asked continually, "When are we doing Object Share?" Object Share becomes a pivot to "sell" their books. This activity helps the children make connections between books and authors. They also discover themes and issues that may or may not impact on their lives now but could in the future.

The following dialogue took place among our students as Chris presented his object from *Mossflower* by Brian Jacques (1988):

CHRIS: I am reading *Mossflower* by Brian Jacques, and I brought in a map of Martin's journey because I want to keep track of where he is going.
CLASSMATE: Why did you choose this book?
CHRIS: Because I loved *Redwall* and I wanted to find out what happened before.
CLASSMATE: Where is Martin going?
CHRIS: He has to go to a mountain to get a weapon to beat Tsarmania.
CLASSMATE: Who's Tsarmania?
CHRIS: She's a cat who rules *all* the land around Mossflower and Martin says he's gonna *kill her!*
CLASSMATE: How's he gonna do *that?*
CHRIS: He's trying to get this weapon to help him.

CLASSMATE: Have you found out how Martin and Matthias are related?
CHRIS: I haven't gotten to that part yet.

From this discussion it is obvious that Chris is hooked on this book. The other students are also interested and begin making the connections between the characters and their relationship to each other. These extended conversations often provide the encouragement to investigate a book that they might not have chosen. Certain books, then, become favorites and are passed around throughout the year.

As part of Reading Workshop, students respond to the books they are reading in two ways: by writing letters and by completing teacher-directed responses. When a child finishes a book, he or she writes a letter to us about the story. Points for the students to consider and to write about include setting, main characters, plot or problem, and whatever resolution there may be. These written dialogues vary in quality and quantity and when completed, signify that a conference is necessary. We meet one-on-one with the child to "dig out" the book. This is a time for us to guide, probe, question, and reflect on a book's themes. The children discuss its purpose and try to make connections to other books, authors, disciplines, and so on. Consider the following letters:

Dear Mr. Milne,

I have just finished reading *A String in the Harp* by Nancy Bond. It is a fantasy and takes place in the present which is also the past at times and its weird cause they happen together sometimes. The main charicker is Peter and his family is also in it, his father and 2 sisters Jen and Becky. It takes place in Wales. His father teaches in a college and lives in a village with Peter and Becky. Jen is visiting over Christmas. Her mother died last year in a accident and she is finishing school in the U.S. Anyway Peter hates Wales, hates school, hates his house and just about everything else. On a walk he finds a old harp key. He doesn't know what it is but finds out that it hums sometimes and when he holds it he dreams things from the past. He discovers that what he "sees" is the story of a bard named Taliesin that lived long ago. On a couple of hiking trips he actually sees him several times and learns he has to do something with the harp key. It really gets spooky. I *loved* it! *Please* read it!

Dear Jessica,

I've read this book and I really liked it too! You're right! I loved the spooky ending; it wasn't at all what I expected. Just to get you thinking, in what ways is this book similar to other fantasies you've read? I'll conference with you just as soon as I can.

Mr. Milne

This entry indicates that Jessica read and enjoyed the book and made strong connections to Peter. So, it was decided to steer the conference toward the dynamics of the family and how the relationships change as the story unfolds:

MILNE: Tell me about the situation in the family.

JESSICA: Well, the father spends much of the time in his study working while Becky and Peter are left on their own.

MILNE: How would that make you feel if you were in the same situation?

JESSICA: I'd be scared, sad, and lonely. I already miss my mom and now it seems as if I lost my dad too.

MILNE: When the older daughter arrives . . .

JESSICA: Jen!!

MILNE: Yes, when Jen arrives does this change?

JESSICA: At first it gets worse. Peter finds the key and goes off a lot on his own, and Jen just wants to go back to the U.S. Peter decides to trust her and she refuses to believe him.

MILNE: Then what happens?

JESSICA: The key is the key.

MILNE: What do you mean?

JESSICA: Well, uh, the key tells a story to Peter who gets interested in Wales, I mean he goes to a professor who knows a lot about Wales and who believes him. Peter doesn't tell him what he has but gives him hints. Anyway, he gets in a race with someone from the museum who wants his key and the other part of the race is that he is trying to find out what the story is that the key is telling him. Jen finally believes. The father also supports Peter, and they begin to understand each other. They decide to stay together as a family.

MILNE: Does this family situation seem real to you?

JESSICA: Yeah, my uncle died and his kids had a hard time too.

Jessica got into her book. She was able to empathize with the tightrope that Jen had to walk, realizing that Peter's motivation to leave and her father's reclusive actions were both attempts to "escape." She recognized the fragile nature of the family relationship and the dynamics of several different personalities pulling in different directions. Asking good questions and having real reactions to characters' situations show our students that we value the literature they read. It sends a strong message about the importance of reading.

Not all conferences are as positive, and it would be misleading to insinuate that all are so. Sometimes students choose books that are too difficult for them to read. Contrast Jessica's letter with Bill's.

Dear Mrs. S,

I just got finished reading Treasure Island by Robert Louis Stevenson. It takes place in England on a ship and on a island. The main characters wer gim, Lon gon Sliver, Flint, Dr. Lively and Bengunn. The other characters were gim's mother and Black dog. At the beginning of the story . . . a captain comes into a inn asks for a room and some rum. But before he dies He goes to his trunk and gives His map to gim. As the story progresses, gim shows the map to a guy that says this is

242

a treasure map and gets them a ship to sail to the island. At the story's end they found Ben gunn and Ben gunn show's them were the treasure is, its in a cave.

Your student,
Bill

The resulting conference started like this:

SCAVONE: So Bill, why did you choose to read this book?

BILL: I saw the movie. For my birthday last year my aunt gave me the book.

SCAVONE: One of my favorite characters in literature is in this book. Who would you pick as your favorite character?

BILL: I like Jim.

SCAVONE: Why is that?

BILL: He's a neat kid!

SCAVONE: Why would you say that?

BILL: He was pretty good at getting things done. He met Ben, helped Long John, and stuff like that.

SCAVONE: Could you identify an evil character in the story?

BILL: Some of the sailors were. One shot Jim.

SCAVONE: Anyone else?

BILL: No, not really. Ben was weird.

Bill's responses indicated that he had grasped the sketchy aspects of the story but hadn't processed much in regard to detail involving the characters, setting, or plot. As the conference continued it was evident, and Bill agreed, that the book might be too difficult. Therefore, we checked the card catalog in the library to find more books on pirates, and he settled on an adventure story by Clyde Robert Bulla called *Pirate's Promise* (1958). It was suggested that he go back and reread *Treasure Island* (Stevenson 1961) at a later date. The message to Bill is that it is OK to stop reading a book.

Students also respond to books in their reading logs by writing entries from a character's viewpoint, creating time lines of story events, writing newspaper headlines about particular events or characters, or drawing pictures of characters. We encourage our students to explore books by asking open-ended questions that emphasize divergent thinking. Their dialogues, writings, and artistic responses reflect the richness of that encouragement.

For example, as we read aloud *Redwall* by Brian Jacques (1986), the children respond to this exciting book in a variety of ways. They may eagerly jot down unfamiliar words, which are added to a giant vocabulary "word wall." Sophisticated words such as *buffoon, tapestry, legerdemain* and *consternation* are shared and discussed and often appear in our children's writing: "Mr. Milne looked like a *buffoon* in his Viking costume," and also in their conversation: "Hey, Mrs. S., Mark is in *consternation* over his math grade" or "I saw a *tapestry* on our church wall."

As the characters of the book develop, the children delight in drawing, presenting, and displaying their impressions of Cluny and Matthias. Simple captions often accompany these drawings:

> This is a picture of Cluny the Scourge, the terrible one-eyed rat using his tail as a bullwhip.

> Here is Matthias trying to walk in the abbey with his huge sandals flip-flopping. He trips and falls.

These presentations and the discussions that follow not only entice our children to seek out and devour Jacques' other titles, but also lead them to other fantasy books. The school and public libraries have waiting lists for Jacques' books and the bookstores are reaping a bonanza, as many children don't wait for the library copies to become free and choose instead to buy the paperback versions. Their reading logs overflow with entries about *Mattiemo* (1990), *Mossflower* (1988), *Mariel of Redwall* (1992), *Salamandastron* (1992), and J. R. R. Tolkien's *The Hobbit* (1976).

Controversial Issues

As our children explore a variety of literature, topics inevitably arise that are often difficult to address or to make real; racism, death, war, poverty, hunger, and other social injustices usually have little relevance to our particular fourth graders. Violence, though, is something all children can connect with in some manner. How do children process violence in their reading? In part it will depend upon their real-life experiences. They see it on television, in video games, on the bus, in school, the playground, and increasingly in the home. Violence is also encountered in various literary genres, particularly historical fiction and fantasy.

In a book like *Redwall* (1986), violence occurs as the forces of evil attempt to enslave or kill a nonviolent group of woodland creatures who live in and around Redwall Abbey. It is the good guys versus the bad, light versus darkness as full-scale battle is eagerly anticipated to determine the outcome of conflict. There is no question for whom our students cheer.

One incident in *Redwall* led to a more general discussion of violence and how our students perceive it. During a secret meeting between Constance the badger and Sela the vixen, a third character, a rat named Redtooth, appears and attacks the unarmed badger with a sword. He inflicts several wounds to the badger who, in a rage, takes hold of the naked blade of the sword, breaks it, and then stuns the rat with her huge paw. She then grabs the rat by the tail and whirls him around much like an athlete would do the hammer throw. At a point, she releases him. As Jacques puts it, "Redtooth would have flown a record distance had there not been a stout sycamore tree several yards away" (1986, 172).

Reactions to this incident were varied and somewhat one-dimensional: "It was neat!" "It's really cool." A girl stated: "It was scary but I like how Redtooth died." Almost all of our children liked it. Two children, however, voiced disappointment. One, a girl, was peeved that Redtooth was killed in this manner. She wanted to see *all* the rats die at *once*, not piecemeal. One boy was distressed that a *girl* could do that to a boy! We were somewhat alarmed at their callousness. As the discussion progressed the children compared this act of violence to the violence found at home in their video games. Many of the games mentioned were available at home and were either owned or rented by the children. We discovered that the violence in these games is far ranging and extremely graphic. Included are such things as be-headings and dismemberment, goring and crushing of bodies, and incinerating peo-ple. All are replete with the appropriate noises and splashing blood! A sizable majority of our children, both boys and girls, play these games on a regular basis.

Violence and a certain apathy to it are a part of our students' lives. The daily doses experienced through the media are desensitizing our children. In literature like *Redwall*, however, children come to know the characters; they connect with them and can empathize and sympathize with their problems and lives. They like Matthias, Cornflower, the old Abbot, and Constance. They identify with Silent Sam and do not want to see him or his family hurt by evil rodents. Therefore, the remarks made by the children in our classes represent a certain callousness toward violence and at the same time indicate with whom the children identify.

In contrast to the incident in *Redwall*, when the bully Rubin trips and falls on his axe in *Where the Red Fern Grows* (1961), by Wilson Rawls, and Billy pulls the head of the axe out of Rubin's stomach, the children react with a mixture of sickness and horror. They are not indifferent to the violence described by Rawls. A similar reaction occurs when readers of Elizabeth Laird's *Kiss the Dust* (1991) see a Kurdish boy gunned down in the street through the eyes of Tara. Later they feel Tara's fear as she narrowly escapes death in a bombing attack after she and her family escape the Iraqi secret police and flee to a mountain village. Books like these remind children that acts of violence can have lasting and terrible results.

Children in our classrooms are able to separate the violence depicted in fantasy like that found in *Redwall* from that of the real world as found in books like *Where the Red Fern Grows* and *Kiss the Dust*. Fantasy is a genre that allows children to transport themselves into the roles of characters who have little say in the world but can do the impossible when spurred by a champion or a cause. Often, children and adult lovers of fantasy feel powerless and out of control. However, this genre allows all of us, young and old, to be more optimistic and hopeful as we deal with our everyday lives. Therefore, we see that Jacques uses violence not randomly or for shock value, but as a means to resolve conflict. Other authors, such as Wilson Rawls and Elizabeth Laird, evoke a sympathy and develop depth of their characters, which allows readers to feel and experience violence as it truly relates to someone they feel they know.

Death is another topic that is often encountered in literature. Children close to nine years old understand that death is an end. Some, but not all, have grasped the concept of dying and realize that at some point in time, everyone, including themselves will die. The death of pets, a friend, a grandparent, or an immediate family member immerses a child in this reality. Nikki wrote:

Dear Mr. M.,

The book I read called Beauty touched my heart. It almost made me cry. Even though it was an animal, it was still a friend like my cat.

It made me want to read it again and I would recommend it to anybody who loves horses or any animal.

From,
Nikki

P.S. By Bill Wallis

In view of the fact that death, like other topics, is often difficult to address, literature provides teachers and also parents with the vehicle to do so more easily. The book *Beauty* (Wallis 1988) supplied an outlet for Nikki's grief when she lost her pet cat. Nikki feels for Luke. She imagines herself in the griever's place and experiences the emotions the character must go through. Someday she will have to offer comfort to others or receive it herself. Likewise, Crescent Dragonwagon's poignant *Winter Holding Spring* (1990) was the ideal book to suggest that Molly read after her mother's untimely death. Together, she and her father and brother absorbed the account of Sara and her father as they struggled through the painful year following the loss of a mother and wife. Both Molly and her father expressed their thanks for this book, which helped them through a most difficult stage of bereavement. It allowed them to feel less troubled, to regain energy, to restore ties to others, and to participate in new experiences.

Conclusion

Looking back at over fifty combined years of teaching reading and children's literature, we know that we have changed as teachers. This did not occur overnight, but was a gradual process. One of the most difficult things for us to do was to give up control—that is, to give our children the freedom of choice. We were hesitant to transfer that "responsibility," convinced that they couldn't handle it. Or could they? We took a risk and loosened the reins. We discovered that, indeed, children *can be* and *are* responsible for their own learning. In time, our roles as teachers changed. We became facilitators rather than disseminators of learning and information. We didn't *relinquish* power, but learned to *share* it with our students.

Have our students changed? Most emphatically, yes! One of the most positive changes observed is a change in attitude. We have seen this manifested in a number of ways. First, and most importantly, in our children there is genuine excitement in finding a new book—one by a favorite author, or a title they've been waiting for when their name is tenth on the list! Former students continually stop by to share a book or to ask when we'll be reading a certain title to our classes. They're great advertisements!

Also, parents are an encouragement. Many confide that their children, who have never read before, now have their noses buried in books. One parent said she raised her son's allowance because he spent all he received on books. Another commented that her child's self-esteem had risen immensely simply because he now reads like other children.

In past experience, there was a lack of any kind of communication during reading time. This was a time when we and our children were locked into basals. We didn't know our children!

Today, we all function as a community of readers, learners, and sharers. Where once the children were reticent to discuss anything at all, we now find that we can't contain their enthusiasm and eagerness. We feel that the majority of them are savvier and more discerning in their choice of and their response to literature. A similar change, and a very positive one, has occurred in respect to writing. Written stories are more fully developed, reflecting the elements of good literature. In addition, instead of "delivering" concepts and skills in science and social studies and expecting our children to "throw these back" in the form of written tests, we now take pride as they work cooperatively, with our guidance, to discover these concepts and skills on their own and proudly share real information with their peers.

Reflections

As we sit back and read what we have written in this chapter, it is apparent to us that we are *still* in the process of change and always will be. This process, we now know, is ongoing. As times change, a new variety of issues will occur, and pressures will be exerted to change values as well. Our children come to us with needs, hopes, expectations, and goals that challenge us as teachers from year to year. It is with this knowledge that we are grateful for those authors of children's literature who are willing to address these concerns. We also appreciate the fact that we live in a society where, for the most part, we are free to use those authors' works to assist us in doing what we chose to do, oh, so many years ago: To facilitate our students to become the best that they can be and to take part in their community as valuable, productive citizens no matter what their role, and in turn to teach their children to do the same.

Professional References

HORNSBY, DAVID, DEBORAH SUKARNA, and JO-ANN PARRY. 1988. *Read On: A Conference Approach to Reading.* Portsmouth, NH: Heinemann.

ROUTMAN, REGIE. 1991. *Invitations.* Portsmouth, NH: Heinemann.

WEBER, ROBIN. 1989. *Making a Transition to a Whole Language Classroom.* Workshop at the Greater Capital Region Teacher Center in Castleton, NY.

Children's Literature

BANKS, LYNNE REID. 1980. *Indian in the Cupboard.* New York: Doubleday.

BOND, NANCY. 1976. *A String in the Harp.* New York: Atheneum.

BULLA, CLYDE ROBERT. 1958. *A Pirate's Promise.* New York: Thomas Y. Crowell Co.

DAKOS, KALLI. 1990. *If You're Not Here Please Raise Your Hand.* New York: Macmillan.

DRAGONWAGON, CRESCENT. 1990. *Winter Holding Spring.* New York: Macmillan.

JACQUES, BRIAN. *Redwall.* 1986. New York: Philomel.

————. 1988. *Mossflower.* New York: Philomel.

————. 1990. *Mattimeo.* New York: Philomel.

————. 1992. *Mariel of Redwall.* New York: Philomel.

————. 1992. *Salamandastron.* New York: Philomel.

KONIGSBERG, E. L. 1967. *From the Mixed Up Files of Mrs. Basil E. Frankweiler.* New York: Atheneum.

LAIRD, ELIZABETH. 1991. *Kiss the Dust.* New York: Dutton Children's Books.

RAWLS, WILSON. 1961. *Where the Red Fern Grows.* Garden City, NY: Doubleday.

SEWELL, E. 1980. *Black Beauty.* Mahwah, NJ: Watermill Press.

SPEARE, ELIZABETH GEORGE. 1961. *The Sign of the Beaver.* Boston: Houghton Mifflin.

SPINELLI, JERRY. 1990. *Maniac Magee.* Boston: Little, Brown & Co..

TOLKIEN, J. R. R. 1976. *The Hobbit.* Boston: Houghton Mifflin.

STEVENSON, R. L. 1961. *Treasure Island.* New York: Scholastic.

WALLIS, BILL. 1988. *Beauty.* New York: Holiday House.

EIGHTEEN

But Will They Buy Them?
A Bookseller's Point of View

Sally Oddi

Retailers are not immune to the challenges of society's changing values and mores. Yet it is difficult to imagine a children's bookstore, with its often-presumed aura of innocence and naiveté, being in the midst of just such a foray. As the owner and manager of Cover to Cover Book Store in Columbus, Ohio, I am often made aware of not only the ideas facing the larger society, but also the needs and interests of the families and young readers we serve. A bookseller, by virtue of what she chooses to stock or refuses to carry, reflects her sense of the marketplace as well as her personal values.

Many of the children's booksellers with whom I have contact are strong advocates of free speech, and though they may take issue with the way a given author approaches sensitive issues, they respect the fact that readers, even young readers, have a right to access a variety of ideas. They also recognize their responsibility to be knowledgeable about the books they carry, aware of content that may be controversial in a given book, and aware of how young readers may react to sensitive material. The decision to purchase or forgo a particular title is ultimately the consumer's, but our input and the weight of our recommendation can be significant. An overriding question for me is, is this book well written? Further, are the ideas presented fairly, with various points of view considered? Is there a bias on the author's part? If so, are the ideas presented important enough to share the book with reservation? Finally, will an adult be available to discuss the book with the child after she reads it?

Customers, be they parents, teachers, children, or grandparents are quite willing to share their opinions on the tough issues of the day and their ideas about how they ought to be presented to young readers. When making a sale, I can quickly assess whether the purchaser wants a young reader protected from or challenged by issues and ideas. It is puzzling to me that many adults assume imitation will result if readers are exposed to books that deal with teen pregnancy, the use of drugs, and other social issues. Instead the reader is often quite impressed by the potential difficulties and destructive nature of some of these behaviors. One case in point is a middle school student with whom I worked; he concluded after reading Judy Blume's *Forever* (1975) and after discussing the book with his mother that he was not ready for a sexual relationship. Young readers pull for Jamal Hicks, the young protagonist in Walter Dean Myers' *Scorpions* (1988), as he spurns offers to become a drug runner as his older brother Randy had done. We don't often give young people credit for thinking issues through or even the opportunity to work them through with those of us who truly care for them. Yet a good book that deals realistically with challenges they may face can be an invitation to connect.

Readers of all ages have a curiosity about other people's lives and experiences, and this curiosity leads to sampling of fiction and nonfiction on a variety of subjects. Recent requests have included books dealing with youth violence, drug and alcohol abuse, physical and sexual abuse, alternative families, nontraditional roles for men and women, racism, religions, and the occult. Depending on the age of the reader, there may or may not be titles available dealing with the subject matter requested. Mainstream publishers are often the last to publish books on controversial subjects; however, small presses have been very successful in this arena. In a recent *Publisher's Weekly* article entitled "Gay Books for Young Readers: When Caution Calls the Shots," author Michael Thomas Ford (1994) has summed up very well mainstream publishing's position on that "hot" topic: "Publishers and writers, increasingly worried about the bottom line, hesitate to write or publish books that, while obviously needed, are at best, a financial risk and at worst an invitation for backlash from groups opposed to homosexuality" (24). And so editors and authors censor from within.

While working with teachers and librarians as they build their collections, I encounter issues of appropriateness. When requesting a new read-aloud, teachers often want not only a great action-packed, well-written text, but also one that is squeaky clean, so that no parent or child could criticize language, lifestyle, or values. Although my staff and I read a great percentage of what we sell, that becomes an impossible task, for what offends one reader may not even gain the attention of another. We encourage parents who have read aloud to their children before they became independent readers to continue to do so as they grow older. The shared experience continues to be valuable, and the parent is there to answer questions as they arise.

We encourage teachers and librarians to think through their reasons for the inclusion of a given title in the curricula or library collection. They must be prepared to defend them. Often the challenge can be a positive experience for all involved as in the case of *So Far from the Bamboo Grove* (1986), which was explained to me by author Yoko Kawashima Watkins. She wrote of a Japanese mother, escaping from Korea in the last months of World War II, nursing her infant son on a crowded train. When the baby does not respond to the breast, the mother is told it is dead. Because of their situation as escapees, the dead baby is thrown from the train, and the mother jumps from the train to her death. Some parents in a community near the author's New England home deemed this passage indecent and not appropriate for young readers. After Ms. Watkins answered their objections at a public meeting, read the passage in question aloud to them, and reminded members of the audience they had nursed their own young as an act of love and nurturing, they applauded her and her book.

Many so-called hot topics have emerged as more fundamentalist religious groups have gained membership and influence in school, business, and community organizations. Although I respect the views of all religious groups and their right to raise their families accordingly, I do not believe any one group's values take prominence over any other group. In assisting parents I try to respect their request for material that will not offend but rely on them to make explicit what content might be objectionable. Within the limits of my knowledge of the literature I try to meet that need. In the end, however, it is the parents' responsibility to make the final selection.

As attempts to ban books in schools and public libraries increase, children's booksellers are often called upon to submit statements of support for a particular book or author's work. One aspect of these challenges that is common is the use of a book with readers much younger than the audience the author envisioned. Although I would never condone the banning of a book, I do believe teachers, librarians, and parents have a responsibility to know the reader and the literature in order to make a better match.

Of concern to many booksellers is the expanding availability of multicultural titles and their varying worth. In our store we welcome a selection that reflects the varied nature of our community and the works of authors and illustrators from all backgrounds. Booksellers acknowledge that young readers need to see themselves, their lives, and their experiences reflected in all kinds of stories. For inventory buyers and booksellers the challenge comes in evaluating a given title based on the cultural and racial issues presented, as well as its literary value. Booksellers nationwide have been applauded for titles they have represented and criticized for what some cultural groups feel should or should not be available on bookstore shelves. Booksellers need to be knowledgeable about what they are selling and make an effort to sensitize themselves to issues that are potentially offensive to cultural groups of which they are not a part. Certainly this is essential before promoting titles as representative of a given cultural group.

Often, but not always, our customer is a parent or other interested adult buying for a young reader. Most of what has been said thus far deals with making a sale of potentially sensitive material to that adult. Oftentimes our customer is sixteen years old or younger, and the transaction takes on a different dynamic. An eight-year-old selecting a young adult romance may be asked, "Is this a book for you?" and gently steered to something more age appropriate. We spend time with that reader trying to determine what she is interested in reading. In one instance a thirteen-year-old had ordered a book on guerrilla tactics, including unconventional ways to kill friends. I was extremely concerned, for he had been a regular customer from the age of seven. In this instance I called his mother to see if she was aware of his reading interests. Several months later I learned this young man had attempted suicide, and his interest in this book was one of many indications that he was seriously troubled. For me this was not a privacy or censorship issue, but one of common sense.

As new issues emerge, the challenge becomes one of the bookseller's continued inquiry into the available literature on that topic and her customers' interest. The bottom line for booksellers often is the bottom line. Because their livelihood depends on selling books, booksellers make compromises in order to satisfy a wide range of customers. The inventory on the shelf reflects not only what the bookseller values, but also what customers want to buy regardless of its merit or social conscience. As long as freedom of choice is our right in all areas of our lives, our world will be less than perfect, and our inventories widely varied.

Professional References

FORD, MICHAEL THOMAS. 1994. "Gay Books for Young Readers: When Caution Calls the Shots." *Publisher's Weekly* 241(8): 24–27.

Children's Literature

BLUME, JUDY. 1975. *Forever*. New York: Bradbury Press.

MEYERS, WALTER DEAN. 1988. *Scorpions*. New York: HarperCollins Children's Books.

WATKINS, YOKO KAWASHIMA. 1986. *So Far From the Bamboo Grove*. New York: Lothrop, Lee & Shepard Books.

NINETEEN

Making Literature Meaningful:
A Classroom/Library Partnership

JUDITH A. MORLEY and SANDRA E. RUSSELL

Introduction

Children's books and the way they are used in the classroom have changed since we first became educators. The most striking change is the integration of literature into traditional subject areas, for example, social studies, science, and math, rather than viewing it as distinct and unrelated. Another dramatic change is that topics once the domain of the adult world are now considered acceptable in books written for children and young adults. Twenty years ago the formula for a salable story was "an admirable child who struggles to overcome difficult obstacles to attain a socially worthwhile goal" (Elkind 1981, 84). The difficult obstacles have changed as has society since Elkind wrote *The Hurried Child* in 1981. Contemporary fiction of past decades has been replaced by a new realism covering topics like oppression, home-lessness, divorce, sexuality, abuse, suicide, and prejudice. The traditional book format must now also compete with advancements in technology.

This discourse offers our reflections on contemporary children's literature, the reality of the elementary classroom, and today's challenges and frustrations from our perspectives as a third-grade teacher and an elementary school librarian. We offer our view of reality in a large suburban school system that faces the typical community challenges. We explore the books our students choose to read, how, in the context of budget restraints and parental concerns, the librarian selects good literature and a wide range of other materials and resources for the library, how a thematic unit emerges in the classroom and impacts on library usage, some of the controversial situations we have experienced in our community, and the effects of current technologies in children's literature. Our classroom/library partnership embraces the challenge to integrate literature into curriculum areas in meaningful and authentic ways.

Children's Choices in the Library

Literature-based programs have replaced or at least now supplement basal reading programs in our school as well as in our district. Literature is an integral part of the daily curriculum with content frequently taught through literature. It is critical that our school library holdings reflect this philosophy of learning where the whole child's needs and interests are addressed. According to *Bowker's Annual* (1991), a 16.5 percent increase in the number of juvenile hardcover and paperback books published in this country has occurred over the last two years. In addition to meeting curriculum needs, the library faces outside competition. Book clubs and bookstores provide new products quickly and in such large quantities that school libraries are in competition with these others sources in providing the kind and availability of materials requested by students. As the school librarian, I (Sandy) have to develop a library collection balanced by age, subject, and curriculum, appropriate for a broad range of ability, to support the educational program of our school and students' interest.

Selection is a subjective process colored by individual values. I request and welcome recommendations from parents, teachers, and children. I read through reviews of books and multimedia materials in professional library journals such as *School Library Journal, Booklist, The Horn Book, Emergency Librarian* and educational magazines such as *Science and Children* and *The New Advocate*. I also refer to bibliographies and guides such as *The Elementary School Library Collection*, and *Children's Catalog* when selecting nonfiction materials for a specific subject area. A hands-on examination of new books is done through periodic visits to children's bookstores, and suggestions from the booksellers are taken into account. Wide consultation with reviewers, professionals, and patrons provides a balance to the subjective bias the individual librarian brings to the selection process. Since thousands of books are published annually, choice becomes a complex process. Added to that are the many purchases that must be made to keep resources current and up-to-date. My budget line is finite.

The American Library Association's *Information Power* issues minimum guidelines for the number of books elementary through high school libraries should house, based on the number of students attending the school. I translate those numbers into a meaningful collection reflecting the curriculum, ages, interests, and values of our school population and the community. The connection of nonfiction to the curriculum is more readily apparent than is fiction. It is, therefore, easier to justify nonfiction for purchase in the school library where I work. Fiction is typically used by students for independent reading, but it is now also integrated with the curriculum by some teachers.

With the proliferation of children's books, a systematic process for selecting items is often, I am finding, difficult to establish and justify. I must determine whether the circulation of a particular book will be large enough over a long period of time to justify the cost of a hardcover edition over a paperback. Fiction topics are also difficult to choose because of the wide range of ages suggested by reviewers for a given book (for example, Grades 4–7 or Grades 5–8). At every grade there is a wide range of development, ability, and life experiences. A riveting adventure set in 1832 on the Atlantic Ocean like Avi's *The True Confession of Charlotte Doyle* (1990) might be appropriate for students of middle school age but will also challenge good readers in upper elementary grades. In a given year this book might be read by perhaps three elementary students who enjoy the length and complexity of this historical fiction. My reality is that buying one hardcover fiction book precludes buying three paperbacks. This is without considering the cost of processing and preparation to make it "shelf ready." The same argument could be made for books by other authors, such as Cynthia Voight, Katherine Paterson, and Zilpha Keatley Snyder. Fourth graders in our school are assigned to read Katherine Paterson's *Bridge to Terabithia* (1977). These students will have access to her other books here for only another year since our school ends in fifth grade. All of her books are not equally popular, yet, I must consider adding several of them in the hopes that readers will be inspired to read beyond the assigned classroom title. I cannot foresee how long this title will continue to be assigned and how long she will continue to be recognized by the upcoming fourth graders. These selections in turn occupy space on shelves that already look overwhelming to the reader making the transition to longer fiction. It then becomes a decision whether to keep the collection lean in number and somewhat trendy for easier author recognition or hefty in volumes.

Much of the recommended fiction presents a melange of people, places, and social situations. Making historical and realistic fiction available, appealing, and meaningful to students who choose mysteries, humor, and formula series for their independent reading is the challenge we face as a classroom teacher and librarian, working together to integrate literature with the established curriculum in authentic situations.

Book reviewers who are practicing teachers, librarians, and professors in education and library departments recommend books for purchase that they predict will be enjoyed by a particular age or grade level, but the majority of children do not read them as readily as the reviewers predict. After I purchase new books, I give book talks and prominently display them in the school library. I have found, however, that students do not always choose these for independent reading. Not surprisingly Hickman and Hepler (1982) found that fifth- and sixth-grade students rely primarily on peer recommendations for choosing books.

We have found that what we read aloud to children can be a major influence in the students' selection of books. Multiple copies of Michael Bond's *Paddington* books are available in our library since Paddington is read aloud in at least one grade level. After the stories are read to the children in the classroom, the library staff is flooded with requests for the same title. We have also found that children will request sequels like *The Mystery of the Cupboard* (1993) by Lynne Reid Banks after hearing *Indian in the Cupboard* (1985).

An author or illustrator study that includes an autobiographical sketch, a collection of his or her works, and often personal letters written to students, heightens the children's awareness of that particular author or illustrator and style and results in many requests for his or her books.

The physical arrangement of the library and the elementary school's schedule are other factors affecting selection. For example, long book shelves with book spines showing overwhelm readers who are just beginning to recognize authors and to use the alphabet to locate them. I use stickers with symbols to indicate whether the selection is science fiction, mystery, fantasy, or another genre. Another helpful technique I employ is to offer the students a smaller, more colorful selection of fiction in a paperback format. The tightly scheduled elementary school day does not allow extra time for students to browse in the library. Only my avid readers make time to browse and ask for suggestions.

The connection between my selection of library books and materials and usage by our readers is maximized by the classroom teachers' integration of these resources. In the next section Judy, a third-grade teacher in our school, will describe a thematic unit she introduces in her classroom. It incorporates a wide range of books and genres that we carefully select together. Sometimes Judy needs titles that I do not have or she needs multiple copies of books. It is my job to gather this full range of books from other libraries to help make the classroom studies successful. Thematic units are more effective if the teacher chooses to access a wide variety of appropriate books and other resources to support the classroom studies.

Books in the Classroom

For the past several years I (Judy) have introduced in my classroom a thematic unit that focuses on the study of land and water forms. We explore diverse literature and genres in this particular theme. Many of the titles chosen by Sandy, the librarian, and me are those that my students don't ordinarily choose on their own. I see part of my role as teacher to stretch my readers beyond what they choose to read independently; therefore, our thematic studies and the selections that we read aloud often include historical fiction, poetry, biography, and picture books. I find that reading many of these titles aloud exposes my students to a wealth of vocabulary, historical information, rich character development, and substantive themes that might not be available in *The Plant That Ate Dirty Socks* (McArthur 1988), a popular title with middle grade students. *Dakota Dugout* (Turner 1985), *Island Boy* (Cooney 1988), *The Josefina Story Quilt* (Coerr 1986), *Animals Animals* (Carle 1989), *A House for Hermit Crab* (Carle 1987), and *My Prairie Years* (Harvey 1986) are read in my third-grade classroom along with *Sarah, Plain and Tall* (1985) by Patricia MacLachlan as we study land and water forms. Using *Sarah, Plain and Tall* as the center of a "web," through joint planning with Sandy, a thematic unit evolves. Subject areas are not compartmentalized but instead integrated in authentic ways.

We begin by talking about Sarah's view of the prairie. Many of my students have never seen the prairie, so in a sense they are like Sarah. The children write journal entries as Sarah might have upon her arrival in the plains. The contrast between the Atlantic Ocean, which is Sarah's sea, and the "sea of grass" of the midwestern plains leads to a study of the two biomes, including plant and animal life. After joint planning, we begin a research project on the life in the two biomes. In the classroom we categorize animals and birds from *Sarah, Plain and Tall* into appropriate biomes. The children choose a subject and decide what they know and what they need to learn. I teach note-taking techniques and organization in the classroom. Sandy guides the class in research techniques in the library. Many different kinds of books—fiction and nonfiction—and multimedia resources are utilized as we study these two "seas." The children, discuss, write, and share final reports in the classroom and display them in the library.

We don't just read books either. My growing readers need exposure to all kinds of print. Because the newspaper is such an important part of *Sarah, Plain and Tall*, I spend time exposing students to newspapers in preparation for written responses. Students read them and learn the jargon of the newspaper industry. Various sections of the paper are explored, and the style of language used in each section is noted. Children are asked to explain different sections. For example, I find that a child who likes to laugh or tell jokes often selects the comic section if given the opportunity. The enthusiasm with which my students read and report to the class is supportive of diverse literacy experiences in our classroom. The children then select a feature or column to write to reflect an understanding of the book, and by using a computer desk-top publishing program, we create our own authentic newspaper.

One of the main characters in *Sarah, Plain and Tall*, Jacob Witting, advertised for a wife as was the custom of the 1880s. Students design and write their own advertisements for a wife or husband as Jacob Witting might have written his. A variation includes inviting the students to write an advertisement outlining their own requirements for a friend. Prior to writing the ad, they write to a friend describing themselves as Sarah did to the Witting family. A wedding invitation and an announcement for the Wheaton-Witting marriage are also written.

Sarah Wheaton is an artist; her abilities and use of color introduce a study of chromatography, the separating of colors. The children delight in separating the colors by using filter paper, washable markers, or food coloring and water. They further their understanding of systems, one of our science topics, by observing the interaction of the various components and record their observations. Selecting a scene from the book, the children illustrate it in charcoal pencil available to Sarah in the beginning of the book and then in colored pencils like those she later brought back from town. Empathy for an artist is developed by sharing and discussing two read-aloud books, Lionni's *Frederick* (1967) and *Matthew's Dream* (1991).

The quilt as an art form and as a preserver of memories is also an important part of the time period of MacLachlan's book. *Tar Beach* (Ringgold 1991), *The Keeping Quilt* (Polacco 1988), *The Josefina Story Quilt* (Coerr 1986), and *The Patchwork Quilt* (Flournoy 1985) are rich resources for reading aloud while considering the history of a family as seen through its quilt.

Students are engaged in a wide range of research, writing, conversations, experiments, and artwork. Cookbooks are read for recipes that Sarah and Anna could have prepared; students write their own recipes using ingredients available in the plains region. Clothing styles, communication, and means of transportation during Sarah's time period are explored through the use of carefully selected literature. Comparisons and contrasts between the present and past are made, which reinforces learning about another era. Computer technology allows my students to simulate conditions of wagon travel across America in the mid-1800s with a program such as *Oregon Trail*. Children enjoy the challenge of putting together an itinerary and a list of items needed for travel. They learn quickly that having spare wheels or axles are imperative for survival.

Choice is equally important in this kind of study. Other topics sparked by this book have included a study of herbs in which several children planted a windowsill garden. Some children have pursued an interest in farm animals. Because of the team approach of the classroom teacher and the librarian, the children are engaged in authentic reading, research, technology, critical thinking, cooperative learning, and experimentation.

Popular Literature and Independent Reading

The use of literature in the classroom is not a static event. It is chosen for various reasons and for different purposes. Sometimes our literature selections are based on social studies and science topics. At other times, we choose books for the whole class to read or to read aloud, to provide a common experience. Children choose their own titles for independent reading. We have found that children will read popular literature and find it on their own. It is available both in the classroom and the school library but is not typically assigned. The discussion following indicates what children in our school tend to read on their own during free reading time. It underscores the importance of offering a wide range of topics and genres in the classroom curriculum. Otherwise, as can be seen by the children's choices, popular literature would rule the day.

Natalie Honeycutt's *The All New Jonah Twist* (1986) is a book the whole class reads; we can then share references in our discussions. Many of Jonah's issues are familiar to the students—divorced parents, sibling rivalry, peer relationships, and responsibility. Jonah offers a model for coping strategies and problem solutions, which we explore. I read Aliki's *Feelings* (1984) to them, and we discuss feelings and problem solving, while Sandy introduces the students to the section of the library with books on emotions. We both share poetry on feelings from Shel Silverstein's *The Light in the Attic* (1981) and *Where the Sidewalk Ends* (1974) and Jeff Moss' *The Butterfly Jar* (1989).

Students demonstrate some observable patterns in making their own literature selections. In our building, beginning at the early primary levels, the students' experiences with books have been mostly through those read aloud to them. Among their favorite authors are Dr. Seuss, Jan and Stan Berenstain, H. A. Rey, and Maurice Sendak. The range of reading ability is wide at this age level, and enthusiasm for reading is very high. Emergent readers, using rhyme, repetition, patterns, and illustrations, seek Bill Martin Jr.'s *Brown Bear, Brown Bear* (1983), Nancy W. Carlstrom's *Jesse Bear, What Will You Wear?* (1986), Nancy Shaw's humorous sheep stories, and works by Leo Lionni and Audrey Wood. The colorful books of Lois Ehlert and Ed Young's *Seven Blind Mice* (1992) appeal to them. Kevin Henkes and Marc Brown's books, for example, offer them scenarios with which they can identify. Readers transitioning to "I Can Read" books and beginning chapter books enjoy a wide range including Cynthia Rylant's *Henry and Mudge* series, Jane Yolen's Commander Toad series, Arnold Lobel's Frog and Toad books, Patricia Reilly Giff's *Kids of the Polk Street School* series, Judy Delton's *Pee Wee Scouts* series, as well as books by James Marshall. Illustrations often influence the selection and are as personal as the student's individual tastes. New bilingual books like *Family Pictures/Cuadros de Familia* (Garza 1990) and *Taking a Walk: A Book in Two Languages-Caminando* (Emberley 1990) are gaining in popularity. Children often select nonfiction because of their own interests in certain topics. They are more familiar with topics than with titles or authors. The shelf arrangement of nonfiction by topic makes it easy for them to make their selections. Their choices at the early primary levels typify readers' transition from read alouds with many pictures to easy readers.

Second graders begin to search for longer and more difficult books like Beverly Cleary's *Ramona* and Gertrude Chandler Warner's *Boxcar Children* series. Some children attempt Donald Sobol's *Encyclopedia Brown* series and Matt Christopher's sports books. They are beginning the transition from easy readers to chapter books. Due to an increase in the amount of print and a decrease in illustrations, these books look less like picture books and are at a level where readers perceive themselves to be. The readers at this level also demonstrate an increasing interest in nonfiction without regard to their own reading ability and the complexity of the book. The *Eyewitness* series is very popular with this age group as well as their older peers.

In contrast, middle grade readers who have the ability to read longer books independently revert to picture books, perhaps building fluency with easy and familiar books as Allington (1980) suggests. As they make the transition to longer text and less illustrations, they find comfort in returning to the picture books. Some children find security in the formula books of series like the *Babysitter's Club* (Martin) and Pleasant Company's *American Girl*, the latter offering a combination of the serial formula and historical fiction with a target population of girls in grades three to five. Readers explain simply that the books are "fun to read because they're all about girl stuff." They like the fact that the main characters are all girls and that "the girls are pretty." The characters have "exciting adventures" and "there is just a little bit of sadness." The formula of both series seems to satisfy readers' need for structure, predictability, and ease in reading. These books do not contain heavy plots, rich character development, or substantive themes, which means that readers glide through simple scenarios with few emotional strings attached, knowing that everything will end well.

Among middle grade readers there is a demand for "really scary" books like the ones in R. L. Stine's *Goosebumps* series, which are impossible to keep on the shelves. Bruce Coville's books dealing with the supernatural such as *The Monster's Ring* (1982) and *The Ghost in the Third Row* (1987) are a close second, while his *My Teacher Is an Alien* (1989) and its companions are also very popular. Alvin Schwartz's *Scary Tales to Tell in the Dark* (1981) appeals to both boys and girls at this age. Brian Pinkney, illustrator of *The Dark-Thirty* (McKissack 1992) explains that children need to feel control over things that are frightening. In a book children can exercise that control because they know that the fright will end when they close the book. Bruce Coville introduced the supernatural into some of his books to heighten the mystery and the level of fright that he feels is a natural fascination for children of all ages. He maintains that little "appropriate" literature for young boys was written prior to his books. His observation is that young boys are by nature mischievous and they want to read about male characters who do "naughty" not nasty things. In his own experience, most of the characters in children's literature were girls who usually did everything right—he could not relate to them. Judging from the enthusiastic response of his readers, he is correct.

Upper elementary readers' expanded reading ability enables them to delve into longer and more complex novels; they select among children's, young adult, and adult books. Many will choose the humorous works of authors like Jamie Gilson, Barbara Park, Stephen Manes, and Jerry Spinelli. Mysteries continue to be a favorite of this age level. Students in the same class choose mysteries written in different styles and at different degrees of difficulty, for example, *Alfred Hitchcock and The Three Investigators* series, Eve Bunting's *Someone Is Hiding on Alcatraz Island* (1984), Sir Arthur Conan Doyle's stories, and books by Christopher Pike. Adult writers like Stephen King, John Grisham, and V. C. Andrews are also sought. These choices seem to be dictated by the popularity of the movie version of some of these books or by the influence of their parents or older sibling's reading choices. A small but dedicated group of readers of fantasy look for the classic works of J. R. R. Tolkien and C. S. Lewis; others will choose Susan Cooper's or Brian Jacques' novels. Science-fiction readers enjoy John Christopher's *White Mountains* trilogy, Madeleine L'Engle's *A Wrinkle in Time* (1962), and Robert O'Brien's *Mrs. Frisby and the Rats of NIMH* (1971). The animal genre retains its popularity with the well-known horse stories of Marguerite Henry and Walter Farley; contemporary authors Lyn Hall and Jane Resh Thomas are also read by students at this level. As their maturity level increases, intermediate readers begin to select books dealing with their concerns, their moral issues, and more realistic characters.

The contemporary fiction of a few years ago, now replaced by a gritty new realism or realistic genre, has a large but very individualistic readership. Topics of the new realism include divorce, oppression, homelessness, suicide, sexuality, prejudice, and physical abuse and are no longer reserved for adult literature. Elkind (1981) offers the explanation that literature dealing with such topics is directed toward today's "hurried child" who is pressured to grow up faster intellectually and to deal with topics that are not necessarily emotionally appropriate for him or her at that stage of development. He quotes Charlotte Zolotow, a children's author and editor of Harper Junior Books: "We can't protect our children anymore from what we would like to spare them. We can't protect them from the war and the violent death they see on television every night. . . . All we can do is to help children to see it all, to form their own judgment and defenses and to be honest in the books we write for them about alcohol, drugs, or immorality" (Elkind 1981, 85). Family structures have changed, and the extended family that once referred to grandparent now refers to stepparents and "significant others." The role of nurturing and support once exercised by families alone is now shared by schools. Formal education is directed toward the "whole child," and in addition to traditional school subjects, educators are now responsible for topics once reserved for family discussions. Parents of this generation seek guidance in discussing some of these topics from books. *Fly Away Home* (1991) by Eve Bunting deals with the homeless; *Winter Holding Spring* (1990) by Crescent Dragonwagon relates the story of a child coping with the death of a parent; *How Could You Do It, Diane?* (1989) by Stella Pevsner centers around suicide. Literature of this kind is available beginning at the kindergarten level and gives teachers and librarians the opportunity to use this "honest" literature to integrate social studies and the language arts with critical thinking and even moral development involving judgments and decision-making. The task is often monumental since young people are being asked to deal with adult issues while functioning with the emotions of a youngster who is involved in sorting out his or her identity.

We believe literature in this context is a tool to assist young people in identifying feelings and making decisions in real-life settings that may very well be part of their future. In essence, the main characters in these books become role models who overcome obstacles of unimagined proportion for the young reader.

The cultures explored in certain books may be foreign to our children, but the common bonds of humanity are very evident. The human emotion of empathy and an awareness of diversity are fostered through careful reading and discussion of this literature. *Journey to Jo'burg* (Naidoo 1985), *Chain of Fire* (Naidoo 1989), *Kiss the Dust* (Laird 1991), *Journey to Topaz* (Uchida 1971), *Little Brother* (Baillie 1992), and *Island of the Blue Dolphins* (O'Dell 1960), for example, offer young readers examples of their peers surviving in the harsh realities of their own world, often in different time periods and in settings alien to readers. Some psychologists claim that it is easier for a person to deal with a situation including emotions when one is not immediately involved. Our goal is to provide our children with models for dealing with difficult situations within the safety of the classroom. Once established, these models can be drawn upon when and if needed.

A Shift in the Meaning of Censorship

The decision to use literature in a school creates a dilemma for the librarian and the teacher. The world in which the students are growing up is not necessarily the world of the author or the teacher. Censorship, which refers to eliminating anything that is "unsuitable" or "inappropriate," takes on a new dimension. In our society, children not only are aware of "adult" topics, but some have also personally experienced them. Censorship in our context becomes a question of sensitivity to or awareness of the reality in which our students exist. Although parents, teachers, students, and the librarian play a part in the selection process of materials purchased for our school library, I (Sandy) realized the effects of censorship first hand.

A copy of *Best Wishes Amen* (Morrison 1974), a book of traditional jump-rope verses, was borrowed from our library by a student. This book, printed in 1974, was still included in the *Children's Catalog* and considered appropriate for the elementary school library. The book, with verses boldly crossed out by the parent, was returned to the library by the child, and a hostile letter to the principal and superintendent questioning its place on the shelves followed. The parent wrote that some of the verses promoted suicide and sexuality. After the shock of the book's defacement and threats of going to the news media abated, I began the process established by our district for handling complaints of selected materials. The superintendent's office awaited recommendation "by a committee consisting of the principal, the librarian and the department head of the subject field involved," which I formed following the American Library Association's guidelines.

After the committee discussed the book and the objections, it sent a letter to the parent stating that the book was deemed appropriate and would be retained. This challenge raised the issue of our society's changing social mores in a short period of ten to twenty years and the importance of funding for up-to-date resources. It also reinforced the necessity to constantly "weed" or reevaluate resources that do not reflect current attitudes or beliefs. Balancing current beliefs and attitudes with the fundamental value of freedom of speech is a juggling act we will continue to perform if we are to truly educate our students. This experience made me respect the importance of a process being in place when challenges occur. A process provides an opportunity for discussion where misinformation or misinterpretation can be further addressed. Thus, it allows all parties, including parents, a forum for objective discussion and provides an outlet for blind or personal emotion. This procedure also should be revisited frequently to evaluate its relevancy in today's society. In New York State parents are expected to assume active roles on school committees as shareholders in their children's education. Parents, I believe, have the right to choose what their children are exposed to but not to demand that all conform to their beliefs.

Small but very vocal religious groups that refuse to allow their children to have any dealing with any references to Satan, trolls, witches, or Halloween have formed in many communities. Some of their children censor books by refusing to read those that refer to the underworld while others secretly read them. Books that use the words *hell* or *damn* or refer to the occult are frequent targets. A student in a class I had introduced to Zilpha K. Snyder's *The Headless Cupid* (1975) through a filmstrip, later sought to finish the book on her own. After obtaining the book from the public library because our copies were signed out, she was forbidden to read the book by her parent. When I attempted to finish showing the conclusion of the filmstrip, this student asked to be excused because of her parent's concern with references to the occult in this mystery. It was interesting to observe the student later querying a friend in the class on the final outcome of the story. In the classroom if an assigned book is objected to, we have available a book on the same topic without the objection-able references or vocabulary. The child is excused from the class discussions, and the teacher makes arrangements for discussion of the alternate title. Such a situation causes a degree of discomfort for all parties, but it can also be used as an opportunity to teach empathy. The attitude of the teacher and librarian sets the tone.

Our children are growing up in a world in which they have been inundated by visual imagery. The media has helped to heighten their awareness of social issues. Acts of violence, including child abuse, are experienced by some of our children; others are very much aware of their existence because of the media. Reactions to some pieces of literature, including fairy tales, can be unpredictable. We support Bruno Bettelheim (1976), a noted child psychologist, who proclaims the importance of fairy tales in a young child's life. He maintains that this fantasy is remote from the child's experience and provides children with the opportunity to make sense of their world. As one of our first-grade teachers looks forward to her unit on the Brothers Grimm, she notes, however, that her awareness of situations in the lives of some of her students and their increased exposure to violence through television and video has led her to paraphrase and ad lib some of the stories in an attempt to "soften them" as she reads them aloud. She is sensitive to the fact that "a scary story told or read aloud in the safe and loving environment of a bedtime story takes on a different dimension when written down and shared with a group of children." She reflected that we might be using these books in a way in which they were never intended—reading them aloud with the children "getting the full-blown scary version on a first reading." She feels that these stories are part of the oral tradition in which stories were passed down from generation to generation with the story adapted for the audience. They could be told gently to the four-year-old and embellished and made scarier for the eight-year-old, at the child's request. We agree with these adaptations made by an educator sensitive to the comfort level and needs of her children.

Societal changes can influence the ability of children to enjoy these tales. For some children these fairy tales are not at all remote from their own experiences. A stepmother is a real part of some of these children's lives; in traditional literature she is evil and has the same bad name the wolf has had. First graders in a new relationship with a stepparent, especially a stepmother, can find little comfort in "Hansel and Gretel." Frustrated parents tell their children they are "bad," and the consequences "bad" children in the folk tales endure can be frightening and, unfortunately, real to our children. Many have been relegated to similar neglect and abuse as the child in "Baba Yaga." Society's concentration on the "thin" image brings a different perspective to today's child who listens as the witch in "Hansel and Gretel" and other tales where children are to be eaten concentrates on fattening them up. In the library setting, I choose to read the less violent fairy tales to some classes since I do not have the benefit of knowing all of my students closely. This reinforces the importance of the library/classroom partnership in meeting our students' needs through literature.

While reading *Molly Whuppie* (DelaMare 1983) to third graders recently, Judy came to a new realization when she reached the part where the giant places necklaces of gold around his own daughters' neck so that he can readily distinguish them from the other girls asleep at night. For the past eight years she had shared this story with her children. Up until then, this teacher was unaware of the connotations of sexual abuse alluded to in the story. Along with the school's counselor, Judy had just finished a unit on child-abuse protection with her children. Since the giant's wife continues in her long-suffering role and even succumbs to a beating by the giant, a somewhat painful silence followed the reading of this story, and the children readily shared their distaste for the giant's violence and his treatment of his wife. For a few of these children, the scene was one in which the fantasy was not removed from their personal experience.

Judy's classroom environment is one that encourages active listening where class members listen to each other and restate what they hear. Speakers are either affirmed or have the opportunity to clarify their statements. Members establish a level of trust within the group. In such a setting, the literature becomes an affective vehicle for the exploration of problems and, more importantly, solutions. Sensitivity in the use of a particular story is the awareness of the personal experiences of the children with whom the book is shared and requires a secure environment. This sensitivity is a form of censorship.

In the same classroom a discussion followed the retelling of "Jack and the Beanstalk." Third graders were adamant that Jack should be punished and forced to return the stolen goods on two counts: they were after all, stolen from the giant and, secondly, Jack had broken into the giant's house. They assumed the roles of the judge and the lawyers on the TV court programs. Jail, they felt, was probably most appropriate for such crimes. The teacher was relieved that no one felt the need to bring Jack up on murder charges for his part in the death of the giant!

When literature is used as part of the curriculum it can be a catalyst for intense reactions. Children can relate so strongly to a character that it affects their conversations and decisions at home. After reading Clyde Robert Bulla's *Chalk Box Kid* (1987) children in Judy's class discussed and identified Gregory's main problem and proposed a peaceful solution. One third-grade girl discussed her frustrations at having her younger brothers invade her privacy. After reading this book she proposed to her parents that she be allowed to create her own secret place in the basement and requested that a lock be placed on the door so her brothers could not gain entry. She and her father built a private playhouse in which she frequently sought refuge. Another boy found the book an extremely painful reminder of some situation in his own life. He chose not to share and instead threw a violent temper tantrum and refused to participate in any of the extensions or discussions. Judy honored his decision. Literature is often unpredictable and so are the responses of children.

Literature can be a tool to foster emotional and social development, and it can be an uncomfortable and painful reminder of situations over which one has no control. The educator's awareness of situations that the students encounter in their everyday lives and her comfort level in dealing with unpredictable reactions, active listening, and problem solving are important factors in choosing and using literature that is "appropriate" for the readers under her care. A teacher has a professional responsibility to herself and to her students to educate herself in these areas and to share challenging literature with her students.

Technology and Children's Literature

Just as the printing press had a significant impact upon the oral tradition, present technology is challenging the role of books, magazines, and newspapers for our students. Meaningful integration of technology into our children's world is appropriate considering the environment in which these children have developed. From infancy, they have been exposed to television, video games and computers. The computer and all its peripherals, including CD-ROMs, laser discs, and modems, are information sources that are rapidly transforming the resources and services of libraries. In response to the introduction of the multimedia of filmstrips, transparencies, study prints, film loops, cassettes, and videos, in the 1970s and 1980s libraries became known as media centers. Today our elementary school library has already replaced many of these mediums with the new format of computer software in varied sizes and titles, including CD-ROMs and laser disks. Together with traditional books, they form the library's collection. With the rapid changes we see each year, these resources will quickly become outmoded and necessitate the same "weeding" required of books.

Teachers are at varying stages of comfort and expertise in using technology, including computers, and integrating it into their curriculum. Some classrooms function with stand-alone computers while others are networked with each other inside the building and connected with other buildings around the world. The role of the computer in the instructional program remains under debate as its capabilities evolve, the prices decrease, and districts commit financially to its implementation.

Children's literature has been affected by the new technology of computers.

Whether or not you agree with Walt Disney's gender characterizations or his preservation of the integrity of the original fairy tales, it is undeniable that through animation he has made these tales appealing and accessible to all kinds of audiences. What Disney did for movies, CD-ROMs are doing for children's books. Modern computer technology offers us new opportunities to engage with literature through sound and animation.

Two of the more innovative pieces of software presently in use in our elementary school are the "Discis Books" and "Living Books" offered on CD-ROMs. The former has ten titles in the series, ranging from *The Paper Bag Princess* to *The Tale of Peter Rabbit*. As the program appears on the screen, graphics portray an open book with text on the left side and an illustration on the right. The child reads the book, or he or she can customize it to be read aloud by the computer. Options include reading by phrases, word by word, in a foreign language or English, and at varying speeds. The viewer interacts with the computer and the story by clicking the mouse to "turn the pages," activate the identification of an object, or get the pronunciation of a word. These books are appealing to children and require interaction in ways that true books cannot. They also provide new ways of exposing children to literature and can be used for skill reinforcement.

The "Living Books" by Broderbund, including titles such as *Arthur's Teacher Trouble, Grandma and Me,* and *The Tortoise and the Hare*, have improved upon the technology described above. Instead of a screen with an open book, the student opens to a full color illustration from the book. Printed text is relegated to a few lines at the top. By clicking on various parts of the screen, the student interacts with selected objects that move or make sounds. The story becomes an exciting adventure capturing the viewer's imagination. This becomes an opportunity for the teacher to read the actual story to the whole class or to embark on a writing activity based on the book.

The bilingual features of these CD-ROM books extend children's literature to students formerly inhibited by a language barrier. With the influx of ESL students into our schools, this technology becomes an important asset in making adaptations rapidly.

Other computer programs attempt to extend literature in different ways varying from cloze passages to comprehension questions based on the literature passage read. The formats of such programs as *Success With Reading* are based on drill and practice, but the selections to be read are, at a minimum, excerpts from acknowledged literature. Word-processing programs such as *The Writing Center* and *Magic Slate* provide children with creative opportunities to use word processing and graphics to extend literature and to use writing in authentic ways. Educators in our school, using different methods to achieve outcomes, find these programs appropriate and useful.

Computer simulations, databases, and teleconferencing are other ways of extending children's literature in our elementary school. Databases like *Mac USA* help to expand our students' knowledge of geography, since children can access information about each of the states, including capitals, cities, population, topography, and natural resources. Geographical boundaries are extended through teleconferencing when our students share their literature responses via modem with peers as far away as Saskatchewan and Alaska. This is easily accomplished individually from school to school through modems and by subscribing to national electronic bulletin boards. AT & T's Learning Network is specifically geared to language arts activities. Students are invited to design their own projects involving reading, writing, and communicating. The more comprehensive Scholastic Network—a "full-service online network"—offers our students opportunities to share literature experiences with other classrooms and with well-known authors on a regular basis. In addition, teachers have access to other teachers and to educator forums like our state university's literature network for exchange of ideas and easy access to research underway in curriculum areas throughout the nation.

By the time this chapter is published many of the software programs discussed here will already be obsolete or upgraded. I attempt to keep our holdings current by consulting education software guides like *Only the Best*, which narrow the large field of available educational software by offering the "highest rated" in a given year. The rapid development of new software necessitates that it be evaluated before purchase, in light of meeting the educational goals of the curriculum and the realization that it will be quickly outdated. The computer and all its peripherals are tools meant to be utilized to gather, manage, synthesize, and communicate information. Today, teachers in our school use CD-ROM technology projected on a large screen or monitor to share a piece of literature in much the same way as they share Big Books. The added dimensions of sound, animation, and individualization offered by the computer assist the learner in the reading and writing processes and in enjoying the literature's added dimensions.

Change can be perceived as threatening but technology offers educators opportunities unknown before in the history of mankind. The debate should not become whether the computer will replace the book as the advent of television was compared to the demise of the radio. The focus should be on the strong points of each medium. Our ambition to keep students reading and appreciating meaningful literature demands that we use every appropriate extension. As educators, we believe this includes multidimensional resources. Reading for information and pleasure is our goal. Whether it is between two covers or on a screen, reading will become a matter of choice in the same way we choose television, radio, newspaper, or our neighbor to give us the news. Its format will vary according to our individual preferences thus guaranteeing a place for books as we know them.

Conclusion

Changes in pedagogy and in society have directly influenced the kinds of literature offered to children today and how it is used in the classroom and school library. The decision to use literature in the elementary school involves much more than bringing books into the classroom and library. A successful program that uses literature to develop the "whole child" benefits from the cooperative efforts of the classroom teacher and the school librarian. Students are actively engaged in intellectual, emotional, social, and moral development while using literature in the classroom. The effective use of a book goes beyond selecting a title; it requires accruing many resources in a variety of formats to place a book in context and to extend it in authentic ways.

The partnership and expertise of the classroom teacher and the school librarian is the basis for the effective selection and utilization of these materials. The selection process includes an awareness of the interests and needs of the intended audience, a sensitivity to societal change, and a consciousness of multimedia resources, including computer technology, to address different learning modalities. Educators have the opportunity to use fiction genres to model responses to difficult situations and to broaden students' cultural, historical, and geographical knowledge. The combination of self-selection and guided selection both in the classroom and in the library, develops well-balanced readers by exposing them to a variety of literature. Technology affords enrichment opportunities by providing new formats for literature and possibilities for literature extensions both within the classroom and globally. The cultivation of the "whole child" into a lifelong learner and a well-rounded reader is enriched through a working partnership of the classroom teacher and the school librarian in the elementary school.

Professional References

ALLINGTON, R. 1980. "Fluency: The Neglected Reading Goal." *The Reading Teacher* (February).

BETTELHEIM, BRUNO. 1976. *The Uses of Enchantment*. New York: Knopf.

Booklist. Chicago: American Library Association.

Bowker's Annual of Library and Book Trade Information. 1991. New York: Bowker.

Children's Catalog. 1991. New York: H. W. Wilson Co.

The Elementary School Library Collection. 1990. Williamsport: Bro-Dart Foundation.

ELKIND, DAVID. 1981. *The Hurried Child*. Reading, PA: Addison-Wesley Publishing Co.

Emergency Librarian. Vancouver: Rockland Press.

HEPLER, SUSAN I., and JANET HICKMAN. 1982. "'The Book Was Okay, I Love You'—Social Aspects of Response to Literature." *Theory into Practice* 21: 279.

The Horn Book. Boston: Horn Book, Inc.

Information Power. 1988. Chicago: American Library Association and Association for Educational Communications and Technology.

NEILL, SHIRLEY B., and GEORGE W. NEILL. 1992. *Only the Best*. New York: R. R. Bowker.

The New Advocate. Norwood, MA: Christopher-Gordon Publishers.

School Library Journal. Philadelphia: R. R. Bowker and Co.

Science & Children. Arlington: National Science Teachers Association.

Children's Literature

Alfred Hitchcock and the Three Investigators series. New York: Random House.

ALIKI. 1984. *Feelings.* New York: Greewillow Books.

American Girl series. Madison: Pleasant Co.

AVI. 1990. *The True Confessions of Charlotte Doyle.* New York: Orchard Books.

BAILLIE, ALLAN. 1992. *Little Brother.* New York: Viking.

BANKS, LYNNE REID. 1985. *The Indian in the Cupboard.* New York: Doubleday.

———. 1993. *Mystery of the Cupboard.* New York: Morrow Junior Books.

BOND, MICHAEL. *Paddington* series. Boston: Houghton Mifflin.

BULLA, CLYDE ROBERT. 1984. *Someone Is Hiding on Alcatraz Island.* New York: Clarion Books.

———. 1987. *Chalk Box Kid.* New York: Random House.

BUNTING, EVE. 1987. *A House for Hermit Crab.* Saxonville: Picture Book Studio.

———. 1991. *Fly Away Home.* New York: Clarion Books.

CARLE, ERIC. 1989. *Animals, Animals.* New York: Harper & Row.

CARLSTROM, NANCY W. 1986. *Jesse Bear, What Will You Wear?* New York: Macmillan.

CHRISTOPHER, JOHN. 1967a. *The City of Gold and Lead.* New York: Macmillan.

———. 1967b. *The White Mountains.* New York: Macmillan.

———. 1968. *The Pool of Fire.* New York: Macmillan.

CLEARY, BEVERLY. *Ramona* series. New York: Morrow.

COERR, ELEANOR. 1986. *The Josefina Story Quilt.* New York: Harper.

COONEY, BARBARA. 1988. *Island Boy.* New York: Viking.

COVILLE, BRUCE. 1982. *The Monster's Ring.* New York: Pantheon.

———. 1987. *The Ghost in the Third Row.* New York: Bantam.

———. 1989. *My Teacher Is an Alien.* New York: Pocket Books.

DE LA MARE, WALTER. 1983. *Molly Whuppie.* New York: Farrar, Straus & Giroux.

DELTON, JUDY. *Pee Wee Scouts* series. New York: Dell.

DRAGONWAGON, CRESCENT. 1990. *Winter Holding Spring.* New York: Macmillan.

EMBERLEY, REBECCA. 1990. *Taking a Walk: a Book in Two Languages-Caminando.* Boston: Little, Brown.

Eyewitness Books series. New York: Knopf.

FLOURNOY, VALERIE. 1985. *The Patchwork Quilt.* New York: Dial Books for Young Readers.

Garza, Carmen L. 1990. *Family Pictures/Cuadros de Familia*. San Francisco: Children's Book Press.

Giff, Patricia Reilly. *Kids of the Polk Street School* series. New York: Delacorte Press.

Grimm, Jacob. 1975. *Hansel and Gretel*. New York: Scribner.

Harvey, Brett. 1986. *My Prairie Years*. New York: Holiday House.

Honeycutt, Natalie. 1986. *The All New Jonah Twist*. New York: Bradbury.

Laird, Elizabeth. 1991. *Kiss the Dust*. New York: Dutton Children's Books.

L'Engle, Madeleine. 1962. *A Wrinkle in Time*. New York: Farrar.

Lionni, Leo. 1967. *Frederick*. New York: Pantheon.

———. 1991. *Matthew's Dream*. New York: Knopf.

Lobel, Arnold. *Frog and Toad* series. New York: Harper & Row.

McArthur, Nancy. 1988. *The Plant That Ate Dirty Socks*. New York: Avon.

McKissack, Patricia. 1992. *The Dark-Thirty*. New York: Knopf.

MacLachlan, Patricia. 1985. *Sarah, Plain and Tall*. New York: Harper & Row.

Martin, Ann M. *Babysitters Club* series. New York: Scholastic.

Martin, Bill, Jr. 1983. *Brown Bear, Brown Bear, What Do You See?* New York: Henry Holt.

Morrison, Lillian, ed. 1974. *Best Wishes, Amen*. New York: Crowell.

Moss, Jeff. 1989. *The Butterfly Jar*. New York: Bantam Books.

Naidoo, Beverley. 1985. *Journey to Jo'burg*. New York: Lippincott.

———. 1989. *Chain of Fire*. New York: Lippincott.

O'Brien, Robert C. 1971. *Mrs. Frisby and the Rats of NIMH*. New York: Atheneum.

O'Dell, Scott. 1960. *Island of the Blue Dolphins*. Boston: Houghton Mifflin.

Paterson, Katherine. 1977. *Bridge to Terabithia*. New York: Crowell.

Pevsner, Stella. 1989. *How Could You Do It, Diane?* New York: Clarion.

Polacco, Patricia. 1988. *The Keeping Quilt*. New York: Simon & Schuster.

Ringgold, Faith. 1991. *Tar Beach*. New York: Crown Publishers.

Rylant, Cynthia. *Henry and Mudge* series. New York: Bradbury Press.

Schwartz, Alvin. 1981. *Scary Stories to Tell in the Dark*. New York: Lippincott.

Silverstein, Shel. 1974. *Where the Sidewalk Ends*. New York: Harper & Row.

———. 1981. *The Light in the Attic*. New York: Harper & Row.

Snyder, Zilpha K. 1975. *The Headless Cupid*. New York: Atheneum.

Sobol, Donald J. *Encyclopedia Brown* series. Nashville: Nelson.

Stine, R. L. *Goosebumps* series. New York: Scholastic.

Turner, Ann. 1985. *Dakota Dugout*. New York: Macmillan.

Uchida, Yoshiko. 1971. *Journey to Topaz*. New York: Scribner.

Warner, Gertrude Chandler. 1950. *The Boxcar Children*. Chicago: Albert Whitman.

YOLEN, JANE. 1980. *Commander Toad in Space.* New York: Coward, McCann & Geoghegan.

YOUNG, ED. 1991. *Seven Blind Mice.* New York: Philomel.

Multimedia

AT & T Learning Network. Mac. Bridgewater: AT & T Easy Link Services: Bridgewater.

Discis Books. Mac. Buffalo: Discis Knowledge Research Inc..

Everybody's Reading! 1993. Video recording. New York: Scholastic Inc.

Living Books. Mac. Novato: Broderbund.

Mac Usa. Mac. Novato: Broderbund.

Magic Slate. Apple. Pleasantville: Sunburst Communications.

Oregon Trail. Mac. St. Paul: Minnesota Educational Computing Consortium.

Scholastic Network. New York: Scholastic Inc.

Success with Reading. Apple. Jefferson City: Scholastic.

The Writing Center. Mac. Fremont: Learning Company.

Afterword

When I invited Violet Harris to write a response to *Battling Dragons*, I challenged her to raise issues and questions in response to the many voices and perspectives in this volume. I value her voice as an educator, as a female, as an African American, as a historian, as a lover of good literature. Her book on multicultural literature calls on us to teach with books that are inclusive and that support diversity across society.

In this chapter, Harris takes a critical look at some of the issues raised in *Battling Dragons* through the lens of a multicultural perspective. Although the dialogue in this book has been much broader, Harris provides insight about continued invisibility for certain minorities in this country. She challenges us to deal with prejudice, racism, and stereotyping in children's literature.

When one passionately holds a particular set of beliefs, one also can become blinded to other issues that may be no less powerful or significant to other groups of people. Harris' plea for balanced multicultural literature collections is so passionate that at times she dismisses the passionate beliefs of others. I don't believe that one can quantify or rank passionate beliefs.

Harris' questioning of whether female authors need to challenge the dominant male institution seems inconsistent with her pleas for inclusive, multicultural literature. She cautions, for example, that fantasy books might propagandize images of girls and compromise on sharing the truth with girls. But don't we applaud the authors who successfully challenge stereotypes and offer fresh visions of what one can become? Isn't that the message in *Amazing Grace* and in *The Woman Who Rides Like a Man*? Both books challenge what is and suggest what can be. Are we only to share realistic visions of what exists today? Can't we also explore futures in which characters struggle for freedom and equality and are successful? I believe we can, although I would never suggest that all authors write from only this perspective.

In addressing censorship, Harris urges us to engage in dialogue. I agree that dialogue is essential, but her example of opponents in California who unsuccessfully tried to remove passages by Alice Walker from a state test brings up the question of what constitutes true dialogue. The censors in California were overwhelmed and outvoted. Cynically, I would imagine that the censors still hold passionately to

273

their marriage-and-meat-eating perspectives, and I question whether real dialogue occurred.

Harris also talks about being tempted to restrict access to certain kinds of books and gives *The Story of Little Black Sambo* (a picture book from 1899 about a child in India) as an example. I don't believe censorship is the answer in either case. Should we lock up all the bad books? I really don't think so, because then you are forced to decide which books should go to jail.

A basic question emerges. Is enough good literature getting into the hands of children? I agree with Harris. I see teachers across the country who do not know or use literature extensively with children. I would suggest that we continue to explore ways to increase the knowledge base of teachers, that we explore ways to reduce costly textbook and disposable workbook expenditures, that we reallocate the monies into better school and classroom libraries (as Charlotte Huck has been suggesting for thirty-five years), and that we ensure that preservice programs at the colleges and universities in which we work are graduating teachers who know and are able to use children's literature effectively with children. We need to focus on exploring the possibilities for response with readers. We need good books and grand conversations, as Peterson and Eeds have said.

And lastly, in reference to Harris' conclusion, if we dismiss the voices of the three teachers and one school librarian because they read *The Indian in the Cupboard* to their students, have we really dialogued about the issues? If these four educators are unaware of the controversy swirling around *The Indian in the Cupboard* or the broader implications with regard to their own personal values, does ignoring the broader issues of what they have to say improve the situation? Dismissing them will not challenge them to challenge their own assumptions. Do we even know what their assumptions are?

We all sift information through our own personal value systems. What offends me might not offend you. What perplexes or alarms me may be of little consequence to you. Dialogue is the key. Challenging each other's assumptions is critical. Will Violet and I walk from this discussion passionately challenging and accepting each other's criticism? I hope so.

"May I Read This Book?"
Controversies, Dilemmas, and Delights in Children's Literature

VIOLET J. HARRIS

Somewhere between the endpoints of commodity and treasured cultural artifact lies an adult perception of children's books as magic, whimsy, and innocence. The following vignettes capture the intricate conceptions of children's books that many of us possess.

W. E. B. Du Bois, the editor of the National Association for the Advancement of Colored People's (NAACP) *Crisis Magazine*, posed a question to an assortment of writers, publishers, and cultural activists (1926). Each person responded to a query about the portrayal of the "Negro" in art. The responses from individuals such as poet Countee Cullen, novelist Jessie Fauset, and publisher Alfred A. Knopf mirror contemporary views about children's literature generally and multiethnic and multicultural literature in particular. A few of the respondents wrote of the artistic freedom the artist required in order to remain true to her vision. Others wrote about the conflicts that arise when a group is dissatisfied with its image in popular culture, particularly when those outside the group are responsible for that image. Still others, notably Alfred A. Knopf, reminded readers that publishing is a business not a philanthropy. Inherent in Knopf's response is the assumption that business goals rather than socio-cultural concerns would reign supreme. The tensions highlighted within the pages of the *Crisis Magazine* in 1926 capture the contradictions, still apparent today, that arise when art meets commerce, especially art created for children.

Columnist Barbara Brotman (1994) dissected a newly emerging trend that illustrates the continued conflicts and complexities in children's literature. She suggested that scholarly articles and dissertations that remove the "magic" from children's books are on the horizon. Brotman cites the example of an upcoming article in the *Journal of Children's Literature* in which Dr. Seuss' *Green Eggs and Ham* is characterized as a symbol of "parental rejection of an anarchic and inventive child figure" as well as a "child's attempts to win a parent's affection, and to ease adult gloom with the gift of childlike imagination" (1994, 1). Brotman quotes Professors Tim Wolf (Middle Tennessee State University) and Mary Harris Veeder (Indiana University Northwest in Gary), who argue that children's books are complex and symbolic of many cultural referents. Wolf contends that children's books provide opportunities for analyses based on feminist and Marxist theories. Brotman concludes her column about the alleged new insights that feminist or Marxist critiques can yield in this manner: "However, I am not sure I wanted to know it" (1994, 1).

Children's literature embodies a multitude of images and realities that collide and compete for authority. Mercifully, many children do not understand or care about the ways in which we deconstruct *Where the Wild Things Are* (Sendak 1963) or sift through the symbolism in a book. Children, at least some, continue to read books that appeal to them and reject those that do not.

Many of the adults who enjoy and work with children's literature do not have the luxury of simply reading a book. We must play the "heavy." Our tasks are to read and judge the books on the basis of literary value, perpetuation of stereotypes, cost, educational utility, children's interests, and other issues. These are difficult tasks because, unfortunately, children are not our primary constituencies. Librarians, teachers, parents, critics, and publishers are central parts, too.

Books are powerful. They can serve as catalysts for the greater good or they bolster the tyranny of a few. Consider, for example, the controversies that continue to swirl around children's literature "classics," traditional and contemporary, such as *The Five Chinese Brothers* (Bishop and Wiese 1938) and *The Indian in the Cupboard* (Banks 1980). When one despairs that these two books are perennial best-sellers, authors such as Laurence Yep, Virginia Hamilton, and Michael Dorris remind us that one can create "culturally conscious" (Sims 1982) literature that entertains and enlightens. Nevertheless, the aforementioned authors and their books cannot challenge the popularity of the controversial books if teachers, librarians, children, and parents choose not to read them.

The authors of chapters in this volume address these and other issues. They all care about children and the books made available to them. They express a range of viewpoints about children's literature that are not usually combined in one volume. Many of the authors share my views; a few do not. I hope that the following comments engender additional discussion.

Books Suitable for the Pyre?

One comment heard in children's literature circles is that we fight so hard about the books children read because fewer and fewer children select reading as a leisure activity. Other activities fascinate them equally or more so. Unquestionably, some individuals wish to censor the books children read as articulated by the authors in

Part 1. We should not dismiss that concern or only characterize the individuals as left- or right-wing fanatics. Their complaints about books merit discussion and not dismissal. Increasingly, adults who censor are elected to school boards and textbook committees. Those on the "right" are better organized and more successful than those on the "left." For example, opponents in California managed to force the removal of two short stories written by Alice Walker from a state test. The selections were removed because one was alleged to have presented a negative perspective on marriage and the other, a negative portrayal of meat-eating. The resulting local, state, and national outcry caused state educators to retain the passages. If one were to follow the logic of the protestors, then "classics" such as *Treasure Island*, which contains murder and deception, rate banishment, too. Few classics would pass the "purity" tests.

Honest discussion about book selection is limited. The limitations do not emanate from so-called PC proponents monopolizing print and electronic media or creating a climate of intimidation (Joel Taxel's chapter presents an exceptional overview of the issue). Rather, candor is not evident in many discussions because many individuals engage in what author Toni Morrison characterizes as "willful critical blindness" (1992, 18). That is, authors and critics, wittingly and unwittingly, envision the typical reader as "white," possessing a particular unacknowledged ideological stance. Whiteness is privileged even in those instances when an alternative interpretation is warranted or valid. One need not entertain requests for reexaminations of books or grant limited access if one assumes this stance of willful critical blindness. Further, those putting forth new interpretations or oppositional texts, especially the so-called left, typically lack the power to remove books or make their alternative interpretations widely available.

Amy McClure aptly delineates instances in which censorship activities prevent access to books. She presents instances of attempted censorship on the part of individuals associated with the "right" and the "left." I caution against presenting issues as polar opposites and associating them only with extremes. What about the "center"? The center engages in censoring actions, too. A continuum of opposition is probably warranted. For instance, the coalition of groups organized against the Rainbow Curriculum of the New York City public schools represented the extremes and the middle of the political spectrum and demonstrates the limitations of vague terminology such as the left and right. In this instance, groups that normally oppose each other or rarely join together, such as ethnic whites, African Americans, and Latinos, coalesced in opposition to the inclusion of children's books about gays and lesbians. This coalition did not characterize itself as comprised of politically correct zealots (another vague term appropriated to stifle honest discussion); rather, they identified themselves as defenders of family values (another term with dubious contemporary usage).

I disagree with what I perceive of as an underlying assumption in McClure's chapter. That assumption is that children have access to a wide range of children's literature. My interactions with teachers across the country indicate that many are unaware of trends, issues, authors, and books. Teachers tend to know the least about literature labeled multicultural. Further, many lack knowledge about sources that provide this type of information, such as the *The Horn Book Magazine*.

This lack of diversity is why I am sometimes tempted to argue for limited access. Intellectually, I would like to argue that we should never waver in our commitment to free access to all children's books. I am occasionally tempted to support restrictions on some books, however. Most of these are books about people of color that are regarded as stereotypic, derogatory, or inaccurate. More than likely, I will not entertain thoughts of censorship when the number of culturally accurate books about people of color equals or surpasses the number of books about animals and inanimate objects. Let me share the book that tempts any censorship inclinations I might have.

My personal candidate for the pyre is *The Story of Little Black Sambo* (SLBS) (Bannerman 1899; 1943). It is a prime example how willful critical blindness manifests itself. This book remains a favorite of a number of individuals who pass it on generation after generation. Additionally, the Sambo image has been exported around the world. Recently, a friend gave me a copy of the wrapping for origami paper—currently sold in Japan—that contains one of the pernicious images. Amazingly, Harper Collins sells fourteen thousand copies of the book each year (Briley 1993). I would argue that it will remain in publication indefinitely because it is deemed a classic. Many whites have told me they enjoyed the book because of the humor, the action, the suspense, and the pancakes. Rarely have they noted the horrible illustrations of African Americans and the perpetuation of the stereotypes in all cultural institutions. The invisibility described by Ralph Ellison continues.

I recognize *The Story of Little Black Sambo* as an example of differential power and the ability of one group to control another group's image. Helen Bannerman's works were not aberrations. One need only examine the copycat books, salt and pepper shakers, cookie jars, sheet music, postcards, and other artifacts of culture to recognize the pervasiveness of the Sambo image. Books published by African Americans and non-African Americans, with culturally accurate images, offered an alternative but were unable to supplant the popularity of the *SLBS*. I wonder what the reaction would be to books titled *The Story of Little White Honky*, *The Anglo in the Pantry*, or *The Eight Sicilians on the Lower East Side*?

Perhaps I am being hypersensitive, but I do not believe that *SLBS*, *The Indian in the Cupboard*, or *The Five Chinese Brothers*, and others are the first books that children should read about people of color or others depicted in stereotypic fashion. Nor do I believe that opposition to these books is the same as opposition to books that depict *Little Red Riding Hood* carrying a wine jug. I do not in any way deny the importance of issues such as drug and alcohol abuse; however, degrees of oppression exist.

Beverley Naidoo eloquently writes from the perspective of one who has undergone profound intellectual changes and who understands the privileged position she held as a white in a system of apartheid and, conversely, the limited one of a writer within that system. She reminds us of an obligation to inform children of injustices and the folly of our attempts to shield them from such realities. I especially take to heart her notions of racism as a form of gratuitous violence and her suggestion that we deconstruct racist imagery. Her novels, *Journey to Jo'burg* (1986) and *Chain of Fire* (1990), are examples of an author who transcends the limitations of an "outsider" perspective and creates credible and riveting fiction. Naidoo should apply her talent, honesty, and sensitivity to writing stories about white children in South Africa. Tell us about the process that trains children to become racists. Describe how it feels to hold life-and-death power over individuals. Until these stories are available, the story remains incomplete.

The violence Naidoo writes about becomes even more palpable as described in the chapters written by Barbara Kiefer and Carl Tomlinson. Tomlinson states that violence is a part of the human condition. If that is so, can we ever hope to teach pacifism? Can books bear the burden of imbuing readers with an abhorrence of violence? Perhaps the stark imagery and blunt language of the books may provide children with opportunities to empathize with the pain and suffering of book characters and, ultimately, real humans. Gratuitous violence requires rejection in much the same manner as racist behavior. We now should determine how visual images evoke the intellectual and emotional responses that result in an aversion to violence.

I thought of Brotman's comments as I read the chapters. How do authors feel about the various deep meanings that critics unveil in their works? Certainly, it is important to take note of and evaluate various "isms," but literary merit should remain in the forefront as well. I, too, must remind myself that the lack of "isms" does not equate with literary merit. These thoughts and hesitations color my readings of the chapters in Part 2.

When Women Share in Power . . .

One of the tenets of feminism is that women will humanize institutions and cultural products when they gain a modicum of power. Sometimes this occurs as with Charlotte Huck's recounting of the writing of *Princess Furball* (1989). Her chapter answers one of my questions about the manner in which authors respond to opposition. I know that she is acutely concerned about the images that she presents to readers as well as matters of aesthetics. The manner in which she solved the issues of violence, sexism, and abuse is a model for other authors. She includes in her retelling that which is true to the literary heritage of the tale but tempers the presentation with consideration for the sensibilities of children.

Deborah Thompson's chapter parallels Huck in some ways. She balances the need to assess the depiction of African Americans with the responsibility of the critic to assess the merit of the books. Once again, the categories developed by Sims (1982) retain their value. However, Thompson does inform us that a reconsideration of the melting-pot category is necessary. Any revision of that category should include a recognition that African Americans share in and contribute to "American" culture.

Judith Gilliland presents a convincing case for using literature to create an understanding of oneself and others. Often, multicultural literature is perceived as lacking in universality. Gilliland argues that books labeled multicultural have the ability to convey universal truths through the prism of a specific culture. Equally important, she recognizes that multicultural books can engender a sense of hopefulness in the reader.

Women's roles in children's book publishing remain complex and contradictory. Shirley Ernst addresses some of the issues related to gender and children's book publishing in an informative manner. She delineates some of the changes apparent in the portrayal of girls, primarily European American, and the exclusion of gender issues in book selection, sharing, and discussions. Ernst does not explain how a profession with a significant number of women, mainly European American, in influential editorial, sales, and marketing positions, continues to create works in which girls and women are stereotyped. This reality contradicts the folk wisdom that women will alter cultural institutions in fundamental, humanistic ways. Given the large number of female authors, one might expect at least a wider range of books featuring girls and women in both traditional and progressive roles. Instead, Ernst suggests that progress has been limited. Why? Some possible answers are that the women in publishing believe and accept a worldview of girls and women that is conservative. Or, publishers are in tune with their customers and publish books that reflect their ideological stances and book preferences. The gendered nature of children's book publishing suggests a need for in-depth interviews with some of the pioneering women and current workers in order to determine the socio-cultural and economic factors that influence the contents of books. The information acquired about the role of women will, more than likely, provide insights about depiction of other under-represented groups.

Part 3 places the reader directly in the center of topics that many deem inappropriate for children. True experiences from those on the front lines in libraries, classrooms, and authors' writing niches help us to understand that children are not as fragile as we might think they are.

True Grit in Children's Fiction

The inclusion of one reader-response study in the volume is crucial. Children are at the center of the issues debated within these pages, and it is important to include their voices. A central point made by Susan Lehr is the futility of adults prescribing the type of personal transaction that should occur when children read. We sometimes forget this as we share books that dramatize historical and realistic grit. Humanitarian concern is expected, and we are shocked when it does not appear. Lehr displays some of this shock in her response to the statements made about *Kiss the Dust* (Laird 1991). To her credit, she pulls back, reasserts the validity of children's responses, and posits reasons for the responses. Again, her chapter demonstrates that children are capable of engaging with true grit and exiting unscathed and, we hope, enlightened.

Minfong Ho and Allan Baillie are eloquent as they describe the impulses that compel an author to write about silent screams and longings. Their writings are the types that I want to share with children as they read these novels. Ho's lyrical statements such as "It was a terrible thing, this silence, like some thick web which had descended and choked everyone underneath" and "I understood then that between the silence and the scream, there could be a song" convey the terror and hope in those fleeting moments when an individual's life is irrevocably altered. Baillie also reminds us that the potential for horrific acts exists within us all and chance or grace prevents us from perpetuating violence against others.

Joel Taxel's chapter should be sent to media pundits such as Rush Limbaugh and George Wills, critics, and publishers who whip up hysteria about the marauding political-correctness barbarians. The historical overview clearly traces the development of opposition to multiculturalism and the attempts of opponents to stifle discussion. Taxel identifies the real threats to children's literature—crass commercialism, the expansion of multinational corporations into publishing, and the significant costs of books. I would add to these threats the reluctance of some to share literature with all children especially given the increasing use of literature in literacy curricula.

As I read Part 4, I wondered why Lehr selected heroes who battle good and evil as a thematic issue. Some cynicism crept in as I thought about all of the fallen heroes of today and the cries for role models. Are children searching for role models in literary texts or do rock musicians, athletes, and actors hold a monopoly? Grace Chetwin, Susan Lehr, Brian Jacques, and Susan Hepler convince us that literature can lead children to worthy heroes.

Searching for Heroes and Sheroes

Grace Chetwin's metaphor of the primal pot is thought-provoking. What combination of spices, herbs, vegetables, meat, fish, or fowl create the hero, the anti-hero, and the villain? Chetwin tells us that the answers reside in all of the elements that make us human. It is refreshing to read an author's assertions about responsibility to readers. A few comments continue to stir my imagination: all children possess giftedness; fantasy nourishes the mind, and dare I say, the soul; and one essential function of fantasy is the conquest of the self.

Susan Lehr's chapter on the gender differences in fantasy relates to the issues raised by Ernst. I question why we expect women to accept and write from ideological stances that result in conflict with dominant institutions. Creating oppositional images requires a great deal of stamina and a keen critical eye so that the resulting story does not become propaganda. This hoped-for emancipating fantasy literature must inspire, but it cannot compromise on sharing the truth with girls. It is difficult being the pioneer or bearing the weight of one's gender. How do we tell girls the truth without crushing their exuberance. I also caution against assuming that men do not understand women's power. Do we as women really understand male power and its unequal distribution among men?

I relished the lively and hearty manner in which Brian Jacques shared his odyssey as a writer. His journey underscores the need to provide all children with literature and the need to eliminate some of the pretentious notions we associate with "Literature." I shudder to think of children like the young Jacques in many places around the world who do not have access to literature, do not see themselves depicted or depicted positively in children's books, or have not found that special book or author that opens the world to them. Some of Jacques' comments echo those of Brotman as he contemplates the scholarly community's discovery of children's books. Perhaps we should heed these warnings. I also applaud Jacques' assertion of moral responsibility. His questioning of cycles in fantasy literature that leave children hanging and force them to purchase several books in order to complete a story is intriguing.

Taken together, these chapters offer strong rationales for sharing fantasy literature with children. Are the rationales offered in this section strong enough to convince critics that realism is necessary for the modern technological world in which we live? I am not certain given the caution with which many approach fantasy literature.

I applaud the expansion of children's literature as evidenced by the tremendous number of books published, the growth in children's bookstores, and the advancement of pedagogical movements such as whole language and literature-based curricula that bring a new sense of respectability to children's literature. I am still not convinced that enough children have opportunities to read a variety of literature. I am afraid that some children will only have access to literature if a teacher or librarian shares it or distributes order forms from school book clubs. Part 5 places us squarely in the "authentic" worlds of the bookstore, classroom, and library.

Entering the Real World

Children's bookstores bring economic issues to the forefront. Sally Oddi offers an enlightened perspective. Booksellers do not simply sell books, although that is a primary role. They exert tremendous influence in terms of the kinds of books they select and the recommendations that they offer. Feminist and ethnic bookstores come to mind as two types that advance a specific ideology as one reason for their existence. Some of Oddi's comments cause me to question whether a function of booksellers is to lead customers to more progressive perspectives or simply cater to their existing tastes. Oddi's chapter is quite helpful for those who waver between censorship and selection.

In contrast to my favorable response to Oddi's chapter, I was somewhat alarmed as I read the chapters written by Scavone and Milne and Morley and Russell. The author teams identify the obligations of librarians and teachers. Undoubtedly they are sincere and dedicated to sharing literature with children. They are probably quite successful. However, I cringed when reading that both teams shared *The Indian in the Cupboard* with students as a way of motivating them and sharing information about Native Americans. These writing teams face a dilemma that they may not perceive. Are they under any obligations to present works written by Native Americans so that children do not leave their classroom with visions of marauding Indians? My answer is a resounding yes, and it is not a matter of political correctness. Again, we have so few opportunities to share literature with children that each issue becomes magnified; however, we still have a responsibility to share all kinds of literature with children.

I enjoyed reading the chapters in this volume. Some of my opinions and perceptions have changed. Others remain steadfast. I came away with the feeling that each author cared tremendously about children, their books, and their engagement with books.

Professional References

BRILEY, DOROTHY. 1993. "The Impact of Reviewing on Children's Book Publishing." In *Evaluating Children's Books: A Critical Look*, edited by Betsy Hearne and Roger Sutton, 105–117. Urbana, IL: The Graduate School of Library and Information, University of Illinois at Urbana-Champaign.

BROTMAN, BARBARA. 1994. "*Green Eggs and Ham* Serves Up Food for Thought." *Chicago Tribune*, 12 June, Section 6, 1.

DU BOIS, W. E. B. 1926. "How Should the Negro Be Portrayed in Art?" *Crisis Magazine* 31: 219–20.

MORRISON, TONI. 1992. *Playing in the Dark*. Cambridge: Harvard University Press.

SIMS, RUDINE. 1982. *Shadow and Substance*. Urbana, IL: National Council of Teachers of English.

Children's Literature

BANKS, LYNNE R. 1980. *The Indian in the Cupboard*. Garden City, NY: Doubleday.

BANNERMAN, HELEN. [1899] 1943. *The Story of Little Black Sambo*. New York: HarperCollins.

BISHOP, CLAIRE H., and K. WIESE. 1938. *The Five Chinese Brothers*. New York: Coward, McCann.

HUCK, CHARLOTTE. 1989. *Princess Furball*. Illustrated by Anita Lobel. New York: Greenwillow.

NAIDOO, BEVERLEY. 1986. *Journey to Jo'burg*. New York: J. B. Lippincott.

———. 1990. *Chain of Fire*. New York: J. B. Lippincott.

SENDAK, MAURICE. 1963. *Where the Wild Things Are*. New York: Harper.

Contributors

Allan Baillie is an author of children's books from Newport, NSW, Australia. His books include *Little Brother* and *Adrift*.

Grace Chetwin, a native of England now residing on Long Island, New York, is an author of children's books. Her books include *Gom on Windy Mountain*, *The Riddle and the Rune*, *The Starstone*, *Jason's Seven Magical Night Rides*, and *Collidescope*.

Shirley B. Ernst, Ph.D., is a professor at Eastern Connecticut State University in Willamantic. Ernst is an active member of the Children's Literature Assembly and has served as the editor of *The CLA Bulletin* for six years.

Judith Heide Gilliland is an author of children's books living in New Hampshire. Her books include *The Day of Ahmed's Secret* and *Sami and the Time of the Troubles*, both of which are illustrated by Ted Lewin and co-authored with Florence Parry Heide.

Violet J. Harris is an associate professor at the University of Illinois, Champagne, Illinois. Her text *Teaching Multicultural Literature* has just been revised by Christopher-Gordon Publishers.

Susan Hepler, Ph.D., is an educational consultant in Alexandria, Virginia. She co-authored the fifth edition of *Children's Literature in the Elementary School* with Charlotte Huck and Janet Hickman.

Minfong Ho, a Singaporean Chinese born in Burma and raised in Thailand, is an author of children's books currently residing in Ithaca, New York. Her books include *The Clay Marble* and *Rice Without Rain* and are set in Southeast Asia.

Charlotte S. Huck, Ph.D., of Redlands, CA, is a professor emeritus of children's literature from The Ohio State University and wrote *Children's Literature in the Elementary School* in 1961. This text is now in its fifth edition.

Brian Jacques, from Liverpool, England, is an author of children's books. His titles about Matthias and Martin the Warrior include *Redwall*, *Mossflower*, *Mattimeo*, *Mariel of Redwall* and *Salamandastron*.

Barbara Kiefer, Ph.D., is an associate professor at Teachers College, Columbia University in New York. Her language arts text, co-authored with Christine Pappas and Linda Levstik is entitled *An Integrated Language Perspective in the Elementary School*.

Susan Lehr, Ph.D., is an associate professor and department chair at Skidmore College, Saratoga Springs, New York. Her book *The Child's Developing Sense of Theme* explores the child's response to literature. Lehr is also president of the Children's Literature Assembly.

Amy McClure, Ph.D., is a professor of Education at Ohio Wesleyan University, Delaware, Ohio. Her book *Sunrise and Sunsongs* takes a look at children's responses to poetry. She is also editor of *Inviting Children's Responses to Literature* and *Booktalks*.

John Milne is a fourth-grade teacher at Geyser Elementary School, Saratoga Springs, New York. He is an active member of the New York State Reading Association's Charlotte Book Award Committee.

Judith A. Morley is a third-grade teacher at Chango Elementary School in Ballston Lake, New York.

Beverley Naidoo, Ph.D., a native of South Africa, is an author of children's books, advisory teacher, and visiting fellow at the University of Southhampton, England. Her book *Through Whose Eyes? Exploring Racism: Reader, Text and Context* takes a powerful look at students' responses.

Sally Oddi is the proprieter of Cover to Cover Books in Columbus, Ohio.

Sandra E. Russell is a librarian at Chango Elementary School in Ballston Lake, New York.

Sharon Scavone is a fourth-grade teacher at Geyser Elementary School, Saratoga Springs, New York.

Joel Taxel is a professor at the University of Georgia, Athens, Georgia. Taxel is the founding editor of *The New Advocate*.

Deborah Thompson, Ph.D., is an assistant professor at American University, Washington, D.C. She writes and speaks on multicultural literature. She has also chaired the Notable Children's Books in the Language Arts Committee.

Carl Tomlinson is an associate professor at Northern Illinois University, DeKalb, Illinois. He is the co-author of *Essentials of Children's Literature*, a survey text for undergraduate courses.